Strategies in Prose

BRIEFER EDITION

Strategies in Prose

WILFRED A. FERRELL
NICHOLAS A. SALERNO
Arizona State University

HOLT, RINEHART AND WINSTON, INC.
New York   Chicago   San Francisco   Atlanta   Dallas

PREFACE

THIS BRIEFER EDITION OF *Strategies in Prose* is designed for those students and their teachers who prefer a reader with fewer selections than are included in the Second Edition of *Strategies in Prose*. In our Briefer Edition we have followed the design and purpose of the longer edition. And we also followed our committment to recognized principles and practices that justify the reader as a text for the composition course. These derive from the long-established fact that people best learn to write by writing.

But the writing experience serves this purpose only when the student writer has something to say and has a reason for saying it. The student in the freshman composition course may discover the substance for his writing by reading and discussing those writings that lie within the range of his interests and experiences, that engage his intellectual capabilities, and that cause him to make a response. And by analyzing and studying *how* the authors present their ideas, he may develop a sense for stylistics and rhetorical strategy.

The selections in the Briefer Edition of *Strategies in Prose* reflect the range of interest and experience of freshman composition students. It further reflects what we believe should be the province of their awareness and concerns.

To obtain a desirable range of subjects and viewpoints we have forty-seven selections organized into six sections: the individual, modern social problems, science, language, education, and popular culture. Our purpose in each section is to offer a variety of writings about the general area, as well as a number of different styles and rhetorical methods.

As a special feature in three of the sections we have included a selection by a controversial writer or a chapter from a controversial book. Immediately following each of these we have a *pro* review and a *con* review of the book from which the selection was taken. The reviews lend another dimension to the variety of viewpoints in the sections, as well as giving the students an opportunity to analyze critical writing and to examine several forms of the review, a type of essay they may be required to produce many times during their college years.

The authors of the selections are, for the most part, all recognized authorities, either as writers or as experts in their field of specialization. We give a brief biographical sketch of the author on the first page of each selection and indicate when and where the selection originally appeared. Although most of our selections come from twentieth-century writers, we do include a few from writers of earlier periods. Most of these latter selections have gained acceptance as classics of their type, and they provide a means for the students to compare and contrast the styles and rhetorical methods of different periods.

In the table of contents we have indicated the rhetorical type of each selection. These labels are not to be considered exclusive, since any given essay may incorporate forms of several different rhetorical methods and modes. Our designations are intended to serve as a ready reference for those who wish to examine a particular rhetorical type.

We are deeply grateful to friends and colleagues who kindly offered suggestions and recommendations for the Briefer Edition of *Strategies in Prose*. In particular we wish to acknowledge the generous assistance of Richard Beal, David Donaldson, Luayn Fleming, Kay Fuller, Del Kehl, Wanda McPherson, James Merrill, Carleton Moore, Paul O'Connell, Dixie Lee Powell, Daniel Quirk, Betty B. Renshaw, Robert V. Wilson, and Terry Withers.

W.A.F.
N.A.S.

Tempe, Arizona
November 1969

CONTENTS

Contents   ix

Strategies in Prose

Section One

The Individual

"This Above All"

Benjamin Franklin

A BOLD AND ARDUOUS PROJECT

Benjamin Franklin (1706–1790) was born in Boston, Massachusetts. Perhaps the best representative of the American Enlightenment, he has been called the founder of America's first circulating library, first colonial hospital, and first learned society. He studied earthquakes, the Gulf Stream, and electricity and lightning, becoming famous as a scientist with the publication of *Experiments and Observations on Electricity* (1751–1753). His political career was equally distinguished—clerk to the Pennsylvania assembly; member of the Second Continental Congress, the committee which drafted the Declaration of Independence, and the Constitutional Convention; and ambassador to France. Jefferson, who followed Franklin as ambassador to France, said: "No one can replace him, Sir; I am only his successor." Franklin's *Poor Richard's Almanack* and his *Autobiography* have earned him a place in American literary history.

IT WAS about this time I conceived the bold and arduous project of arriving at *moral perfection;* I wished to live without committing any fault at any time, and to conquer all that either natural inclination, custom or company, might lead me into. As I knew, or thought I knew what was right and wrong, I did not see why I might not *always* do the one and avoid the other. But I soon found I had undertaken a task of more difficulty than I had imagined: while my attention was taken up, and care employed in guarding against one fault, I was often surprised by another: habit took the advantage of inattention; inclination was sometimes too strong for reason. I concluded at length that the mere speculative conviction, that it was our interest to be completely virtuous, was not sufficient to prevent our slipping; and that the contrary habits must be broken, and good ones acquired and established, before we can have any dependence on a steady uniform rectitude of conduct. For this purpose I therefore tried the following method.

In the various enumerations of the *moral virtues* I had met with in my reading, I found the catalogue more or less numerous, as different writers included more or fewer ideas under the same name. *Temperance* for exam-

First published 1868.

ple, was by some confined to eating and drinking; while by others it was extended to mean the moderating every other pleasure, appetite, inclination or passion, bodily or mental, even to our avarice and ambition. I proposed to myself, for the sake of clearness, to use rather more names, with fewer ideas annexed to each, than a few names with more ideas; and I included under thirteen names of virtues, all that at that time occurred to me as necessary or desirable; and annexed to each a short precept, which fully expressed the extent I gave to its meaning.

These names of *virtues,* with their precepts, were;

1. TEMPERANCE.—Eat not to dulness: drink not to elevation.
2. SILENCE.—Speak not but what may benefit others or yourself: avoid trifling conversation.
3. ORDER.—Let all your things have their places: let each part of your business have its time.
4. RESOLUTION.—Resolve to perform what you ought; perform without fail what you resolve.
5. FRUGALITY.—Make no expence but to do good to others or yourself; i. e. Waste nothing.
6. INDUSTRY.—Lose no time; be always employed in something useful; cut off all unnecessary actions.
7. SINCERITY.—Use no hurtful deceit; think innocently and justly; and if you speak, speak accordingly.
8. JUSTICE.—Wrong none by doing injuries, or omitting the benefits that are your duty.
9. MODERATION.—Avoid extremes: forbear resenting injuries so much as you think they deserve.
10. CLEANLINESS.—Tolerate no uncleanliness in body, clothes, or habitation.
11. TRANQUILLITY.—Be not disturbed at trifles, or at accidents common or unavoidable.
12. CHASTITY.—Rarely use venery, but for health or offspring; never to dulness or weakness, or the injury of your own or another's peace or reputation.
13. HUMILITY.—Imitate *Jesus* and *Socrates.*

My intention being to acquire the *habitude* of all these virtues, I judged it would be well not to distract my attention by attempting the whole at once, but to fix it on *one* of them at a time; and when I should be master of that, then to proceed to another; and so on till I should have gone through the thirteen. And as the previous acquisition of some, might facilitate the acquisition of certain others, I arranged them with that view as they stand above. *Temperance* first, as it tends to procure that coolness and clearness of head, which is so necessary where constant vigilance was to be kept up, and a guard maintained against the unremitting attraction of ancient habits and the force of perpetual temptations. This being acquired and established, *Silence* would be more easy; and my desire being to gain knowledge at the same time that I improved in virtue; and considering that in conversation it was obtained rather by the use of the ear than of the tongue, and therefore wishing to break a habit I was getting into of prattling, punning and jesting, (which only made me acceptable to trifling company) I gave *Silence* the second place. This and the next, *Order,* I expected would allow me more time for attending to my project and my studies. *Resolution* once become habitual, would keep me firm in my endeavours to obtain all the subsequent virtues; *Frugality* and *Industry* relieving me from my remaining debt and producing affluence and independence, would make more easy the practice of *Sincerity* and *Justice,* &c. &c. Conceiving then, that agreeably to the advice of Pythagoras in his Golden Verses, daily examination would be necessary; I contrived the following method for conducting that examination.

I made a little book in which I allotted a page for each of the virtues. I ruled each page with red ink, so as to have seven columns, one for each day of the week, marking each column with a letter for the day. I crossed these columns with thirteen red lines, marking the beginning of each line with the first letter of one of the virtues; on which line, and in its proper column, I might mark by a little black spot, every fault I found upon examination to have been committed respecting that virtue, upon that day.

FORM OF THE PAGES.

TEMPERANCE.

Eat not to dulness : drink not to elevation.

	Sun.	M.	T.	W.	Th.	F.	S.
Tem.							
Sil.	•	•		•		•	
Ord.	•	•	•		•	•	•
Res.		•				•	
Fru.		•				•	
Ind.			•				
Sinc.							
Jus.							
Mod.							
Clea.							
Tran.							
Chas.							
Hum.							

I determined to give a week's strict attention to each of the virtues successively. Thus in the first week, my great guard was to avoid every the least
offence against *Temperance;* leaving the other virtues to their ordinary
chance, only marking every evening the faults of the day. Thus, if in the first
week I could keep my first line marked T. clear of spots, I supposed the habit
of that virtue so much strengthened, and its opposite weakened, that I might
venture extending my attention to include the next; and for the following
week keep both lines clear of spots. Proceeding thus to the last, I could get
through a course complete in thirteen weeks, and four courses in a year. And
like him who having a garden to weed, does not attempt to eradicate all the
bad herbs at once, (which would exceed his reach and his strength,) but
works on one of the beds at a time, and having accomplished the first, pro-
ceeds to a second; so I should have (I hoped) the encouraging pleasure, of
seeing on my pages the progress made in virtue, by clearing successively my
lines of their spots; 'till in the end by a number of courses, I should be happy
in viewing a clean book, after a thirteen weeks' daily examination.

This my little book had for its motto, these lines from Addison's Cato:

> *"Here will I hold: If there's a Power above us,*
> *(And that there is, all Nature cries aloud*
> *Through all her works,) He must delight in Virtue;*
> *And that which he delights in must be happy."*

Another from Cicero,

*"O Vitæ Philosophia Dux! O Virtutum indagatrix expultrixque viti-
orum! Unus Dies bene, et ex præceptis tuis actus, peccanti immortalitati est
anteponendus."*

Another from the Proverbs of Solomon, speaking of wisdom or virtue:

*"Length of days is in her right hand, and in her left hand riches and
honor. Her ways are ways of pleasantness, and all her paths are peace."*

And conceiving God to be the fountain of wisdom, I thought it right and
necessary to solicit his assistance for obtaining it; to this end I formed the
following little prayer, which was prefixed to my tables of examination, for
daily use.

*"O powerful goodness! bountiful father! merciful guide! Increase in me
that wisdom which discovers my truest interest. Strengthen my resolution to
perform what that wisdom dictates. Accept my kind offices to thy other children, as the only return in my power for thy continual favors to me."*

I used also sometimes a little prayer which I took from Thomson's Poems, viz.

"Father of light and life, thou God supreme!
O teach me what is good; teach me thyself!
Save me from folly, vanity, and vice,
From every low pursuit; and fill my soul
With knowledge, conscious peace and virtue pure;
Sacred, substantial, never-fading bliss!"

The precept of Order, requiring that *every part of my business should have its allotted time,* one page in my little book contained the following scheme of employment for the twenty-four hours of a natural day.

SCHEME.

Hours.

MORNING. The *Question.* What good shall I do this day?	5 6 7	Rise, wash, and address *Powerful Good-ness!* contrive day's business and take the resolution of the day; prosecute the present study and breakfast.
	8 9 10 11	Work.
NOON.	12 1	Read, or look over my accounts and dine.
AFTERNOON.	2 3 4 5	Work.
EVENING. The *Question.* What good have I done today?	6 7 8 9	Put things in their places. Supper. Music or diversion, or conversation. Examination of the day.
NIGHT.	10 11 12 1 2 3 4	Sleep.

I entered upon the execution of this plan for self-examination, and continued it with occasional intermissions for some time. I was surprised to find myself so much fuller of faults than I had imagined; but I had the satisfaction of seeing them diminish. To avoid the trouble of renewing now and then my little book, which, by scraping out the marks on the paper of old faults to make room for new ones in a new course, became full of holes, I transformed my tables and precepts to the ivory leaves of a memorandum book, on which the lines were drawn with red ink, that made a durable stain; and on those lines I marked my faults with a black-lead pencil; which marks I could easily wipe out with a wet spunge. After a while I went through one course only in a year; and afterwards only one in several years; till at length I omitted them entirely, being employed in voyages and business abroad, with a multiplicity of affairs, that interfered; but I always carried my little book with me. My scheme of *Order* gave me the most trouble; and I found that though it might be practicable where a man's business was such as to leave him the disposition of his time, that of a journeyman printer for instance, it was not possible to be exactly observed by a master, who must mix with the world, and often receive people of business at their own hours. Order too, with regard to places for things, papers, &c. I found extremely difficult to acquire. I had not been early accustomed to *method,* and having an exceeding good memory, I was not so sensible of the inconvenience attending want of method. This article therefore cost me much painful attention, and my faults in it vexed me so much, and I made so little progress in amendment, and had such frequent relapses, that I was almost ready to give up the attempt, and content myself with a faulty character in that respect. Like the man who in buying an axe of a smith my neighbour, desired to have the whole of its surface as bright as the edge: the smith consented to grind it bright for him if he would turn the wheel: he turned while the smith pressed the broad face of the axe hard and heavily on the stone, which made the turning of it very fatiguing. The man came every now and then from the wheel to see how the work went on; and at length would take his axe as it was, without further grinding. No, said the smith, turn on, turn on, we shall have it bright by and by; as yet 'tis only speckled. Yes, said the man, but *"I think I like a speckled axe best."* And I believe this may have been the case with many, who having for want of some such means as I employed, found the difficulty of obtaining good and breaking bad habits in other points of vice and virtue, have given up the struggle, and concluded that *"a speckled axe was best."* For something, that pretended to be reason, was every now and then suggesting to me, that such extreme nicety as I exacted of myself might be a kind of foppery in morals, which if it were known, would make me ridiculous; that a perfect character might be attended with the inconvenience of being envied and hated; and that a benevolent man should allow a few faults in himself, to keep his friends in countenance. In truth I found myself incorrigible with respect to *Order;* and now I am grown old, and my memory bad, I feel very sensibly the want of it. But on the whole, though I never arrived at the perfection I had been so ambitious of obtaining, but fell far short of it, yet I was by the endeavour, a better and a happier man than I otherwise should have been, if I had not attempted it; as those who aim at perfect writing by imitating the engraved copies, though they never reach the wished for excellence of those copies, their hand is mended by the endeavour, and is tolerable while it continues fair and legible.

It may be well my posterity should be informed, that to this little artifice, with the blessing of God, their ancestor owed the constant felicity of his life down to his 79th year, in which this is written. What reverses may attend the remainder is in the hand of Providence: but if they arrive, the reflection on past happiness enjoyed, ought to help his bearing them with more resignation. To *Temperance* he ascribes his long continued health, and what is still left to him of a good constitution. To *Industry* and *Frugality,* the early easiness of his circumstances, and acquisition of his fortune, with all that knowledge that enabled him to be an useful citizen and obtained for him some degree of reputation among the learned. To *Sincerity* and *Justice,* the confidence of his country, and the honorable employs it conferred upon him: and to the joint influence of the whole mass of the virtues, even in the imperfect state he was able to acquire them, all that evenness of temper and that cheerfulness in conversation which makes his company still sought for, and agreeable even to his young acquaintance. I hope therefore that some of my descendants may follow the example and reap the benefit.

It will be remarked that, though my scheme was not wholly without religion, there was in it no mark of any of the distinguishing tenets of any particular sect; I had purposely avoided them; for being fully persuaded of the utility and excellency of my method, and that it might be serviceable to people in all religions, and intending some time or other to publish it, I would not have any thing in it, that should prejudice any one, of any sect, against it. I proposed writing a little comment on each virtue, in which I would have shewn the advantages of possessing it, and the mischiefs attending its opposite vice; I should have called my book THE ART OF VIRTUE, because it would have shewn the means and manner of obtaining virtue, which would have distinguished it from the mere exhortation to be good, that does not instruct and indicate the means; but is like the apostle's man of verbal charity, who without shewing to the naked and hungry, how or where they might get clothes or victuals, only exhorted them to be fed and clothed. *James* II. 15, 16.

But it so happened that my intention of writing and publishing this comment was never fulfilled. I had indeed from time to time put down short hints of the sentiments, reasonings &c. to be made use of in it; some of which I have still by me: but the necessary close attention to private business, in

the earlier part of life; and public business since, have occasioned my post-
poning it. For it being connected in my mind with *a great and extensive
project,* that required the whole man to execute, and which an unforeseen
succession of employs prevented my attending to, it has hitherto remained
unfinished.

In this piece it was my design to explain and enforce this doctrine, *that
vicious actions are not hurtful because they are forbidden, but forbidden
because they are hurtful;* the nature of man alone considered: that it was
therefore every one's interest to be virtuous, who wished to be happy even in
this world: and I should from this circumstance, (there being always in the
world a number of rich merchants, nobility, states and princes who have
need of honest instruments for the management of their affairs, and such
being so rare) have endeavoured to convince young persons, that no qualities are so likely to make a poor man's fortune, as those of *probity* and *integrity.*

My list of virtues contained at first but twelve: but a quaker friend having
kindly informed me that I was generally thought proud; that my pride
shewed itself frequently in conversation; that I was not content with being in
the right when discussing any point, but was overbearing, and rather inso-
lent; (of which he convinced me by mentioning several instances) I determined to endeavour to cure myself if I could of this vice or folly among the
rest; and I added *Humility* to my list, giving an extensive meaning to the
word. I cannot boast of much success in acquiring the *reality* of this virtue,
but I had a good deal with regard to the appearance of it. I made it a rule to
forbear all direct contradiction to the sentiments of others, and all positive
assertion of mine own. I even forbid myself, agreeably to the old laws of our
Junto, the use of every word or expression in the language that imported a
fixed opinion; such as *certainly, undoubtedly* &c. and I adopted instead of
them, *I conceive, I apprehend,* or *I imagine,* a thing to be so, or so; or it so
appears to me at present. When another asserted something that I thought
an error, I denied myself the pleasure of contradicting him abruptly, and of
shewing immediately some absurdity in his proposition; and in answering I
began by observing, that in certain cases or circumstances, his opinion
would be right, but in the present case there *appeared* or *seemed to me* some
difference &c. I soon found the advantage of this change in my manners; the
conversations I engaged in went on more pleasantly. The modest way in
which I proposed my opinions, procured them a readier reception and less
contradiction; I had less mortification when I was found to be in the wrong,
and I more easily prevailed with others to give up their mistakes and join
with me when I happened to be in the right. And this mode, which I at first
put on with some violence to natural inclination, became at length easy, and
so habitual to me, that perhaps for the fifty years past no one has ever heard
a dogmatical expression escape me. And to this habit (after my character of
integrity) I think it principally owing that I had early so much weight with

my fellow-citizens, when I proposed new institutions, or alterations in the old; and so much influence in public councils, when I became a member: for I was but a bad speaker, never eloquent, subject to much hesitation in my choice of words, hardly correct in language, and yet I generally carried my point.

In reality there is perhaps no one of our natural passions so hard to subdue, as *Pride;* disguise it, struggle with it, stifle it, mortify it as much as one pleases, it is still alive, and will every now and then peep out and show itself; you will see it perhaps often in this history. For even if I could conceive that I had completely overcome it, I should probably be *proud* of my *humility.*

STUDY QUESTIONS

1. At times, Franklin wondered if his project of arriving at moral perfection "might be a kind of foppery in morals." Do you think the project was a "ridiculous" one? To what extent?

2. Why was Virtue #3 the most difficult to acquire?

3. How effective are Franklin's similes about weeding a garden and the man with a new ax?

4. Why did Franklin deliberately avoid mentioning religion in his project?

5. Franklin felt he had more success in attaining the "appearance" of Humility than the "reality" of it. Was he, then, a hypocrite?

D. H. Lawrence

BENJAMIN FRANKLIN

D. H. Lawrence (1885–1930) was born in Eastwood, near Nottingham, England, and educated at Nottingham University College. He ranks among the most important contemporary novelists for books which include *White Peacock* (1911), *Sons and Lovers* (1913), *The Rainbow* (1915), *Women in*

Love (1920), *Aaron's Rod* (1922), *The Plumed Serpent* (1926), and *Lady Chatterley's Lover* (1928). Lawrence made history when, in 1928, he was prosecuted for the obscenity of *Lady Chatterley's Lover* and his paintings, exhibited that year in London. As a writer, he is equally famous for his short stories, such as *The Prussian Officer* (1914); travel books, including *Sea and Sardinia* (1921); his literary criticism, which includes the controversial *Studies in Classical American Literature* (1923); and his volumes of poetry, such as *Pansies* (1929).

THE PERFECTIBILITY of Man! Ah heaven, what a dreary theme! The perfectibility of the Ford car! The perfectibility of which man? I am many men. Which of them are you going to perfect? I am not a mechanical contrivance.

Education! Which of the various me's do you propose to educate, and which do you propose to suppress?

Anyhow I defy you. I defy you, oh society, to educate me or to suppress me, according to your dummy standards.

The ideal man! And which is he, if you please? Benjamin Franklin or Abraham Lincoln? The ideal man! Roosevelt or Porfirio Diaz?

There are other men in me, besides this patient ass who sits here in a tweed jacket. What am I doing, playing the patient ass in a tweed jacket? Who am I talking to? Who are you, at the other end of this patience?

Who are you? How many selves have you? And which of these selves do you want to be?

Is Yale College going to educate the self that is in the dark of you, or Harvard College?

The ideal self! Oh, but I have a strange and fugitive self shut out and howling like a wolf or a coyote under the ideal windows. See his red eyes in the dark? This is the self who is coming into his own.

The perfectibility of man, dear God! When every man as long as he remains alive is in himself a multitude of conflicting men. Which of these do you choose to perfect, at the expense of every other?

Old Daddy Franklin will tell you. He'll rig him up for you, the pattern American. Oh, Franklin was the first downright American. He knew what he was about, the sharp little man. He set up the first dummy American.

At the beginning of his career this cunning little Benjamin drew up for himself a creed that should "satisfy the professors of every religion, but shock none."

Now wasn't that a real American thing to do?

"That there is One God, who made all things."

(But Benjamin made Him.)

"That He governs the world by His Providence."

(Benjamin knowing all about Providence.)

"That He ought to be worshipped with adoration, prayer, and thanksgiving."

(Which cost nothing.)

"But—" But me no buts, Benjamin, saith the Lord.

"But that the most acceptable service of God is doing good to men."

(God having no choice in the matter.)

"That the soul is immortal."

(You'll see why, in the next clause.)

"And that God will certainly reward virtue and punish vice, either here or hereafter."

Now if Mr. Andrew Carnegie, or any other millionaire, had wished to invent a God to suit his ends, he could not have done better. Benjamin did it for him in the eighteenth century. God is the supreme servant of men who want to get on, to *produce*. Providence. The provider. The heavenly storekeeper. The everlasting Wanamaker.

And this is all the God the grandsons of the Pilgrim Fathers had left. Aloft on a pillar of dollars.

"That the soul is immortal."

The trite way Benjamin says it!

But man has a soul, though you can't locate it either in his purse or his pocket-book or his heart or his stomach or his head. The *wholeness* of a man is his soul. Not merely that nice little comfortable bit which Benjamin marks out.

It's a queer thing, is a man's soul. It is the whole of him. Which means it is the unknown him, as well as the known. It seems to me just funny, professors and Benjamins fixing the functions of the soul. Why the soul of man is a vast forest, and all Benjamin intended was a neat back garden. And we've all got to fit into his kitchen garden scheme of things. Hail Columbia!

The soul of man is a dark forest. The Hercynian Wood that scared the Romans so, and out of which came the white-skinned hordes of the next civilization.

Who knows what will come out of the soul of man? The soul of man is a dark vast forest, with wild life in it. Think of Benjamin fencing it off!

Oh, but Benjamin fenced a little tract that he called the soul of man, and proceeded to get it into cultivation. Providence, forsooth! And they think that bit of barbed wire is going to keep us in pound forever? More fools them.

This is Benjamin's barbed wire fence. He made himself a list of virtues, which he trotted inside like a grey nag in a paddock.

1.   TEMPERANCE   Eat not to dulness; drink not to elevation.
2.   SILENCE   Speak not but what may benefit others or yourself; avoid trifling conversation.

3. ORDER Let all your things have their places; let each part of your business have its time.
4. RESOLUTION Resolve to perform what you ought; perform without fail what you resolve.
5. FRUGALITY Make no expence but to do good to others or yourself—i.e., waste nothing.
6. INDUSTRY Lose no time, be always employed in something useful; cut off all unnecessary actions.
7. SINCERITY Use no hurtful deceit; think innocently and justly, and, if you speak, speak accordingly.
8. JUSTICE Wrong none by doing injuries, or omitting the benefits that are your duty.
9. MODERATION Avoid extremes, forbear resenting injuries as much as you think they deserve.
10. CLEANLINESS Tolerate no uncleanliness in body, clothes, or habitation.
11. TRANQUILLITY Be not disturbed at trifles, or at accidents common or unavoidable.
12. CHASTITY Rarely use venery but for health and offspring, never to dulness, weakness, or the injury of your own or another's peace or reputation.
13. HUMILITY Imitate Jesus and Socrates.

A Quaker friend told Franklin that he, Benjamin, was generally considered proud, so Benjamin put in the Humility touch as an afterthought. The amusing part is the sort of humility it displays. "Imitate Jesus and Socrates," and mind you don't outshine either of these two. One can just imagine Socrates and Alcibiades roaring in their cups over Philadelphian Benjamin, and Jesus looking at him a little puzzled, and murmuring: "Aren't you wise in your own conceit, Ben?"

"Henceforth be masterless," retorts Ben. "Be ye each one his own master unto himself, and don't let even the Lord put his spoke in." "Each man his own master" is but a puffing up of masterlessness.

Well, the first of Americans practised this enticing list with assiduity, setting a national example. He had the virtues in columns, and gave himself good and bad marks according as he thought his behaviour deserved. Pity these conduct charts are lost to us. He only remarks that Order was his stumbling block. He could not learn to be neat and tidy.

Isn't it nice to have nothing worse to confess?

He was a little model, was Benjamin. Doctor Franklin. Snuff-coloured little man! Immortal soul and all!

The immortal soul part was a sort of cheap insurance policy.

Benjamin had no concern, really, with the immortal soul. He was too busy with social man.

1. He swept and lighted the streets of young Philadelphia.
2. He invented electrical appliances.
3. He was the centre of a moralizing club in Philadelphia, and he wrote the moral humorisms of Poor Richard.
4. He was a member of all the important councils of Philadelphia, and then of the American colonies.
5. He won the cause of American Independence at the French Court, and was the economic father of the United States.

Now what more can you want of a man? And yet he is *infra dig,* even in Philadelphia.

I admire him. I admire his sturdy courage first of all, then his sagacity, then his glimpsing into the thunders of electricity, then his common-sense humour. All the qualities of a great man, and never more than a great citizen. Middle-sized, sturdy, snuff-coloured Doctor Franklin, one of the soundest citizens that ever trod or "used venery."

I do not like him.

And, by the way, I always thought books of venery were about hunting deer.

There is a certain earnest naïveté about him. Like a child. And like a little old man. He has again become as a little child, always as wise as his grandfather, or wiser.

Perhaps, as I say, the most complete citizen that ever "used venery."

Printer, philosopher, scientist, author and patriot, impeccable husband and citizen, why isn't he an archetype?

Pioneer, Oh Pioneers! Benjamin was one of the greatest pioneers of the United States. Yet we just can't do with him.

What's wrong with him then? Or what's wrong with us?

I can remember, when I was a little boy, my father used to buy a scrubby yearly almanack with the sun and moon and stars on the cover. And it used to prophesy bloodshed and famine. But also crammed in corners it had little anecdotes and humorisms, with a moral tag. And I used to have my little priggish laugh at the woman who counted her chickens before they were hatched, and so forth, and I was convinced that honesty was the best policy, also a little priggishly. The author of these bits was Poor Richard, and Poor Richard was Benjamin Franklin, writing in Philadelphia well over a hundred years before.

And probably I haven't got over those Poor Richard tags yet. I rankle still with them. They are thorns in young flesh.

Because although I still believe that honesty is the best policy, I dislike policy altogether; though it is just as well not to count your chickens before they are hatched, it's still more hateful to count them with gloating when they *are* hatched. It has taken me many years and countless smarts to get out of that barbed wire moral enclosure that Poor Richard rigged up. Here am I now in tatters and scratched to ribbons, sitting in the middle of Benjamin's America looking at the barbed wire, and the fat sheep crawling under the fence to get fat outside and the watchdogs yelling at the gate lest by chance anyone should get out by the proper exit. Oh America! Oh Benjamin! And I just utter a long loud curse against Benjamin and the American corral.

Moral America! Most moral Benjamin. Sound, satisfied Ben!

He had to go to the frontiers of his State to settle some disturbance among the Indians. On this occasion he writes:

We found that they had made a great bonfire in the middle of the square; they were all drunk, men and women quarrelling and fighting. Their dark-coloured bodies, half naked, seen only by the gloomy light of the bonfire, running after and beating one another with fire-brands, accompanied by their horrid yellings, formed a scene the most resembling our ideas of hell that could well be imagined. There was no appeasing the tumult, and we retired to our lodging. At midnight a number of them came thundering at our door, demanding more rum, of which we took no notice.

The next day, sensible they had misbehaved in giving us that disturbance, they sent three of their counsellors to make their apology. The orator acknowledged the fault, but laid it upon the rum, and then endeavoured to excuse the rum by saying: "The Great Spirit, who made all things, made everything for some use; and whatever he designed anything for, that use it should always be put to. Now, when he had made rum, he said: 'Let this be for the Indians to get drunk with.' And it must be so."

And, indeed, if it be the design of Providence to extirpate these savages in order to make room for the cultivators of the earth, it seems not improbable that rum may be the appointed means. It has already annihilated all the tribes who formerly inhabited all the seacoast. . . .

This, from the good doctor, with such suave complacency is a little disenchanting. Almost too good to be true.

But there you are! The barbed wire fence. "Extirpate these savages in order to make room for the cultivators of the earth." Oh, Benjamin Franklin! He even "used venery" as a cultivator of seed.

Cultivate the earth, ye gods! The Indians did that, as much as they needed. And they left off there. Who built Chicago? Who cultivated the earth until it spawned Pittsburgh, Pa.?

The moral issue! Just look at it! Cultivation included. If it's a mere choice of Kultur or cultivation, I give up.

Which brings us right back to our question, what's wrong with Benjamin, that we can't stand him? Or else, what's wrong with us, that we find fault with such a paragon?

Man is a moral animal. All right. I am a moral animal. And I'm going to remain such. I'm not going to be turned into a virtuous little automaton as

Benjamin would have me. "This is good, that is bad. Turn the little handle and let the good tap flow," saith Benjamin and all America with him. "But first of all extirpate those savages who are always turning on the bad tap."

I am a moral animal. But I am not a moral machine. I don't work with a little set of handles or levers. The Temperance-silence-order-resolution-frugality-industry-sincerity-justice-moderation-cleanliness-tranquillity-chastity-humility keyboard is not going to get me going. I'm really not just an automatic piano with a moral Benjamin getting tunes out of me.

Here's my creed, against Benjamin's. This is what I believe:

"That I am I."

"That my soul is a dark forest."

"That my known self will never be more than a little clearing in the forest."

"That gods, strange gods, come forth from the forest into the clearing of my known self, and then go back."

"That I must have the courage to let them come and go."

"That I will never let mankind put anything over me, but that I will try always to recognize and submit to the gods in me and the gods in other men and women."

There is my creed. He who runs may read. He who prefers to crawl, or to go by gasoline, can call it rot.

Then for a "list." It is rather fun to play at Benjamin.

1. TEMPERANCE Eat and carouse with Bacchus, or munch dry bread with Jesus, but don't sit down without one of the gods.

2. SILENCE Be still when you have nothing to say; when genuine passion moves you, say what you've got to say, and say it hot.

3. ORDER Know that you are responsible to the gods inside you and to the men in whom the gods are manifest. Recognize your superiors and your inferiors, according to the gods. This is the root of all order.

4. RESOLUTION Resolve to abide by your own deepest promptings, and to sacrifice the smaller thing to the greater. Kill when you must, and be killed the same: the *must* coming from the gods inside you, or from the men in whom you recognize the Holy Ghost.

5. FRUGALITY Demand nothing; accept what you see fit. Don't waste your pride or squander your emotion.

6. INDUSTRY Lose no time with ideals; serve the Holy Ghost; never serve mankind.

7. SINCERITY   To be sincere is to remember that I am I, and that the other man is not me.
8. JUSTICE   The only justice is to follow the sincere intuition of the soul, angry or gentle. Anger is just, and pity is just, but judgment is never just.
9. MODERATION   Beware of absolutes. There are many gods.
10. CLEANLINESS   Don't be too clean. It impoverishes the blood.
11. TRANQUILLITY   The soul has many emotions, many gods come and go. Try and find your deepest issue, in every confusion, and abide by that. Obey the man in whom you recognize the Holy Ghost; command when your honour comes to command.
12. CHASTITY   Never "use" venery at all. Follow your passional impulse, if it be answered in the other being; but never have any motive in mind, neither off-spring nor health nor even pleasure, nor even service. Only know that "venery" is of the great gods. An offering-up of yourself to the very great gods, the dark ones, and nothing else.
13. HUMILITY   See all men and women according to the Holy Ghost that is within them. Never yield before the barren.

There's my list. I have been trying dimly to realize it for a long time, and only America and old Benjamin have at last goaded me into trying to formulate it.

And now I, at least, know why I can't stand Benjamin. He tries to take away my wholeness and my dark forest, my freedom. For how can any man be free, without an illimitable background? And Benjamin tries to shove me into a barbed-wire paddock and make me grow potatoes or Chicagoes.

And how can I be free, without gods that come and go? But Benjamin won't let anything exist except my useful fellow-men, and I'm sick of them; as for his Godhead, his Providence, He is Head of nothing except a vast heavenly store that keeps every imaginable line of goods, from victrolas to cat-o-nine tails.

And how can any man be free without a soul of his own, that he believes in and won't sell at any price? But Benjamin doesn't let me have a soul of my own. He says I am nothing but a servant of mankind—galley-slave I call it—and if I don't get my wages here below—that is, if Mr. Pierpont Morgan or Mr. Nosey Hebrew or the grand United States Government, the great US, US or SOMEOFUS, manages to scoop in my bit along with their lump— why, never mind, I shall get my wages HEREAFTER.

Oh Benjamin! Oh Binjum! You do NOT suck me in any longer.

And why oh why should the snuff-coloured little trap have wanted to take us all in? Why did he do it?

Out of sheer human cussedness, in the first place. We do all like to get things inside a barbed-wire corral. Especially our fellow-men. We love to round them up inside the barbed-wire enclosure of FREEDOM, and make 'em work. *"Work, you free jewel,* WORK!" shouts the liberator, cracking his whip. Benjamin, I will not work. I do not choose to be a free democrat. I am absolutely a servant of my own Holy Ghost.

Sheer cussedness! But there was as well the salt of a subtler purpose. Benjamin was just in his eyeholes—to use an English vulgarism meaning he was just delighted—when he was at Paris judiciously milking money out of the French monarchy for the overthrow of all monarchy. If you want to ride your horse to somewhere you must put a bit in his mouth. And Benjamin wanted to ride his horse so that it would upset the whole apple-cart of the old masters. He wanted the whole European apple-cart upset. So he had to put a strong bit in the mouth of his ass.

"Henceforth be masterless."

That is, he had to break-in the human ass completely, so that much more might be broken, in the long run. For the moment it was the British Government that had to have a hole knocked in it. The first real hole it ever had: the breach of the American rebellion.

Benjamin, in his sagacity, knew that the breaking of the old world was a long process. In the depths of his own under-consciousness he hated England, he hated Europe, he hated the whole corpus of the European being. He wanted to be American. But you can't change your nature and mode of consciousness like changing your shoes. It is a gradual shedding. Years must go by, and centuries must elapse before you have finished. Like a son escaping from the domination of his parents. The escape is not just one rupture. It is a long and half-secret process.

So with the American. He was a European when he first went over the Atlantic. He is in the main a recreant European still. From Benjamin Franklin to Woodrow Wilson may be a long stride, but it is a stride along the same road. There is no new road. The same old road, become dreary and futile. Theoretic and materialistic.

Why then did Benjamin set up this dummy of a perfect citizen as a pattern to America? Of course he did it in perfect good faith, as far as he knew. He thought it simply was the true ideal. But what we *think* we do is not very important. We never really know what we are doing. Either we are materialistic instruments, like Benjamin or we move in the gesture of creation, from our deepest self, usually unconscious. We are only the actors, we are never wholly the authors of our own deeds or works. It is the author, the unknown inside us or outside us. The best we can do is to try to hold ourselves in unison with the deeps which are inside us. And the worst we can do is to try to have things our own way, when we run counter to IT, and in the long run get our knuckles rapped for our presumption.

So Benjamin contriving money out of the Court of France. He was contriving the first steps of the overthrow of all Europe, France included. You can never have a new thing without breaking an old. Europe happens to be the old thing. America, unless the people in America assert themselves too much in opposition to the inner gods, should be the new thing. The new thing is the death of the old. But you can't cut the throat of an epoch. You've got to steal the life from it through several centuries.

And Benjamin worked for this both directly and indirectly. Directly, at the Court of France, making a small but very dangerous hole in the side of England, through which hole Europe has by now almost bled to death. And indirectly in Philadelphia, setting up this unlovely, snuff-coloured little ideal, or automaton, of a pattern American. The pattern American, this dry, moral, utilitarian little democrat, has done more to ruin the old Europe than any Russian nihilist. He has done it by slow attrition, like a son who has stayed at home and obeyed his parents, all the while silently hating their authority, and silently, in his soul, destroying not only their authority but their whole existence. For the American spiritually stayed at home in Europe. The spiritual home of America was and still is Europe. This is the galling bondage, in spite of several billions of heaped-up gold. Your heaps of gold are only so many muck-heaps, America, and will remain so till you become a reality to yourselves.

All this Americanizing and mechanizing has been for the purpose of overthrowing the past. And now look at America, tangled in her own barbed wire, and mastered by her own machines. Absolutely got down by her own barbed wire of shalt-nots, and shut up fast in her own "productive" machines like millions of squirrels running in millions of cages. It is just a farce.

Now is your chance, Europe. Now let Hell loose and get your own back, and paddle your own canoe on a new sea, while clever America lies on her muck-heaps of gold, strangled in her own barbed-wire of shalt-not ideals and shalt-not moralisms. While she goes out to work like millions of squirrels in millions of cages. Production!

Let Hell loose, and get your own back, Europe!

STUDY QUESTIONS

1. Clearly, Franklin and Lawrence do not think alike. Nor do they write alike. What are the most obvious differences in their styles? Does the century in which each man lived, by itself, account for the man and his style?

2. Franklin used figurative language infrequently. Lawrence used it often. Is the

effectiveness of Lawrence's similes and metaphors diminished by the frequency of their occurrence?

3. For what reasons and in what ways does Lawrence play with the word *venery?*

4. How different are the interpretations which Franklin and Lawrence place on the virtues of Silence, Moderation, and Tranquillity?

5. According to Lawrence, what motivated Franklin to spring his "snuff-coloured little trap" on us?

Joseph Wood Krutch

STRAIGHT MEN IN A CROOKED WORLD

Joseph Wood Krutch (1893–   ) was born in Knoxville, Tennessee. He received his B.A. (1915) from the University of Tennessee and his M.A. (1916) and Ph.D. (1932) from Columbia University. He has taught English, journalism, and drama at Columbia; lectured at the New School for Social Research; served as drama critic for the *Nation;* and acted as president of the New York Drama Critics Circle. Krutch now lives in Tucson, Arizona, and is a trustee of the Arizona–Sonora Desert Museum. He has edited the works of William Congreve, Eugene O'Neill, Marcel Proust, and Thomas Gray, and written critical studies of Restoration comedy, and of Samuel Johnson, Edgar Allan Poe, and Henry David Thoreau. Other books include *The Modern Temper* (1929), *The Desert Year* (1952), *The Measure of Man* (1954), *Grand Canyon* (1958), and the revised *Baja California, and the Geography of Hope* (1969).

SOME YEARS ago a distinguished playwright told me how he had taken his East Side mother-in-law to see Maurice Evans in *Richard III.* The old lady—whose experience

From *If You Don't Mind My Saying So* by Joseph Wood Krutch. First published in *The American Scholar.* Published by William Sloane Associates. Reprinted by permission of William Morrow and Company, Inc. Copyright © 1960 by Joseph Wood Krutch.

with both literature and the theatre was extremely limited—listened intently in silence for half an hour, then waved a derisive thumb in the direction of the mellifluously complaining Richard and announced firmly: "I don't sympathize."

Now this was, of course, a fine tribute to the purely dramatic skill of Shakespeare. He had provoked the reaction he aimed at without any direct indication of what his own attitude was. I remember the anecdote at the moment for a simple reason. "I don't sympathize" vigorously sums up my own response to certain modern Richards, namely those who enlarge with too much self-pity upon their "alienation" from modern society, modern man and, indeed, from the universe as a whole. On the one hand I find myself ready to agree with a good deal of their criticism; on the other I am irritated by their chronic reaction to the things we both abhor.

To take the most obvious and least significant case, consider the beatniks. I dislike—almost if not quite as much as they do—the dominant middleclass and organization-man concept of the Good Life. Although we can't all be philosophers, scholars, artists or monks, I agree that too many moderns aspire to nothing more than the "status symbols" that money can buy, and far too few to what George N. Shuster recently defined as the ultimate aim of education: "sharing the life of the scholar, poet and saint." But to respond to this situation by taking a shot of heroin and driving a car at ninety miles an hour seems unlikely either to improve society or, what is more relevant, lead to a Good Life.

Sympathetic interpreters of the beatniks have described them as "taking a revenge on society." For example, the hero of a recent novel is described by a reviewer thus: "Seeing too well in a world dazed by the bomb, Renaud undertakes an alcoholic strike against humanity." But the phrase "an alcoholic strike," like "a revenge on society," seems to me merely comic. It suggests the popular saying about "biting off your nose to spite your face," that being precisely what some intellectuals (including many somewhat above the beatnik level) are doing—as though turning into a dope addict does not hurt oneself even more than it hurts anyone else. It seems only slightly less obvious that the more respectable intellectuals who devote themselves exclusively to exploring and exploiting their "alienation" are doing much the same thing. Surely it is more productive of personal happiness and even "more useful to society" to be a candle throwing its beams into a naughty world than a beatnik crying "revenge, revenge" from the gutter. We hear a great deal about the responsibility of society toward the individual. The individual also has a responsibility toward society. And if things are as bad as the alienated say, the only way one can discharge that responsibility is by being an honorable man.

I presume that this thesis hardly needs elaboration and is not likely to be contested outside beatnik circles. But a considerable number of the most talented novelists, poets, painters and composers of the present day reveal, even if they do not proclaim, their alienation; and it seems to me that their most frequent response is only less grotesque, not more fruitful, than that of the beatniks. Even granted, as most of them proclaim in some version of Yeats's often quoted words that "Things fall apart; the center cannot hold," is there still nothing for a wise man to do except take heroin with the beatniks or, as is usual among the alienated squares, elaborate in more and more complicated phrases their dark convictions?

To this question the hearty do-gooder will of course reply: "Why obviously the thing to do is to work for social improvement. Join the party of your choice and the church of your choice; be sure to register for all elections and attend the meetings of your local P.T.A." Without entering into any question concerning the ultimate effectiveness of such a method of employing one's time, it must be admitted that your alienated artist or philosopher is no more likely than a beatnik to undertake it. Let us suppose, therefore, that he has, like Thoreau, both "signed off" from the church and wished that he could as easily sign off from society as a whole. Of course he will be thoroughly disapproved of almost everywhere outside the circle of the completely alienated; but he might, like a few others besides Thoreau, find in this determination to stand alone the possibility of making for himself a private world from which he was *not* alienated, instead of devoting himself exclusively to the task of saying just how alienated he is. He could even find a few justifications formulated in the past for doing just what he has done.

I seem to remember somewhere in Plato the opinion that when times are thoroughly bad a wise man will merely stand by the wall. Similarly, it would appear from the *Meditations* of Marcus Aurelius that although the Emperor was no less aware than Yeats of a world in which "things fall apart," he spent relatively little time in either elaborating or bemoaning the lack of wisdom or virtue in society. He determined instead to cultivate them in himself. Then there is even a wholehearted defense of the mere slacker, which is quoted by Montaigne from one Theodorus who held that "It is not just that a wise man should risk his life for the good of his country and imperil wisdom for fools."

As I see it, the question is not so much whether the alienated would do better to imitate Marcus Aurelius rather than Baudelaire and Apollinaire, for it is a larger and, so many will think, an outrageous question. Is it possible that present-day civilization would be in some important respects better than it is if more people had thought less about how to improve society and more about how to improve themselves?

No doubt the medieval monk was too exclusively concerned with his private salvation. But we have gone to the other extreme and are so obsessed with the idea of society as a whole that it no longer seems quite respectable to seek even intellectual or spiritual self-improvement. I am not saying that we are, in actual fact, excessively unselfish. But the cant of the time requires that we should always be asking of any proposed good, "Can everybody have it?" or "Is it an answer to the general problem?" With astonishing regularity I get letters from people who comment on something I have written with a "Well that's the answer so far as you are concerned; I guess it could be the answer so far as I am concerned. But only the privileged, or the lucky, or the well educated, or the intelligent, or the whatnot, can do what you and I can. So what is the answer for society as a whole?"

No doubt it would be fine if we could find a universal formula for salvation. I would welcome a convincing one if I ever heard it. But I never have, and I see no reason why, this being true, the individual should not save himself so long as he is not doing so at somebody else's expense. After all, society is composed of individuals. It cannot be "saved" except insofar as the individuals who compose it are.

I am not preaching universal indifference to society and social action as the highest wisdom. I am saying simply that if and when one individual feels (as so many articulate people do seem to feel) that the world is hopeless, then it is wiser to see what one can do about oneself than to give up all hope of that also. "I came into this world," said Thoreau, "not primarily to make it better but to live in it be it good or bad." If you insist, you may soften that a little by substituting "exclusively" for "primarily," but the meaning will still point in the same direction. Or as the same argument was recently discussed in that excellent "little magazine" called *Manas:* "If an artist can find nothing but bad brushes to paint with, he will not dissipate all his energies leading a revolution against bad brushes—but will develop techniques which make it possible for him to paint with bad brushes. He may even discover things that bad brushes do better than good brushes. It is one thing to fight the good fight for good brushes, and another to start to paint."

During the thirties, when most intellectuals moved leftward, quite a number of those who confessed (at least to their friends) that they had embraced communism were nevertheless engaged in writing movies for Hollywood or advertisements for Madison Avenue, while at the same time professing to regard both the movies and advertising as poisonous exhalations from a deliquescent society. Often (and I report from my own experience) they justified themselves by saying that there was no use trying to be anything but rotten in a rotten society. Comes the revolution and we will all be decent. Meanwhile, since we live in an evil society, we submit to it without any bourgeois nonsense about merely personal decency.

Such an attitude is only a logical extreme of the one taken by those who may not completely renounce either personal integrity or personal happiness, but insist upon our duty to think primarily in terms of what can be done for "society," and who sink into despair if we do not know an answer. I will even go so far as to suggest the possibility that society may be in a bad way partly because we have laid so much stress on public education—to take one example—and so little upon self-education. (Perhaps it also has something to do with the fact that I have met "educators" who were not and made no effort to be educated themselves.)

"Philanthropy," so Thoreau wrote, "is almost the only virtue which is sufficiently appreciated by mankind. . . . The kind uncles and aunts of the race are more esteemed than its true spiritual fathers and mothers. I once heard a reverend lecturer on England, a man of learning and intelligence, after enumerating her scientific, literary and political worthies, Shakespeare, Bacon, Cromwell, Milton, Newton and others, speak next of her Christian heroes, whom, as if his profession required it of him, he elevated to a place far above all the rest, as the greatest of the great. They were Penn, Howard and Mrs. Fry. Everyone must feel the falsehood and cant of this. The last were not England's best men and women; only, perhaps, her best philanthropists." This is a tough-minded opinion. It is stated with characteristic exaggeration. But at least there is something to be said for those who do their best even though they do not see at the moment just what practical good it is going to do "for the common man."

After all the medieval monk did perform a service. Neither the God he served nor the learning he preserved counted for much in the world from which he had retired. But he did exemplify in himself virtues that might otherwise have ceased to exist entirely, and he did preserve learning that without him would have been lost.

What it all comes down to in practice is simply this: if you despair of the world, don't despair of yourself. And it is because so many of the alienated critics of our society with whose criticisms I agree seem unable to do anything of the sort that I find myself alienated from them also.

Thirty years ago when I published a book much more pessimistic than I could possibly write now, I received a good many letters that might have been boiled down to a sentence in one of them: "If these are your convictions why don't you go hang yourself?" The answer was, and has continued to be through all such changes of opinion as I have undergone, that there is a private world of thought and endeavor which society has never been able to take away from me.

Perhaps the most curious and shocking result of the exclusive stress upon social rather than upon private ethics is the disappearance of the concept of honor as distinct from that of morality. One of the differences between the two is simply that honor is relevant to the individual only. True, society may be more affected than some social scientists seem to think by the prevalence or scarcity of honor in the code of the individuals who make it up. But the man of honor always asks first whether or not an action would dishonor him personally, and he is not influenced by an argument that his dishonorable act would have no bad (perhaps even some good) effect upon society and is therefore "moral" even if dishonorable.

The world would not now be as profoundly shocked as it was a generation ago by the phrase "a scrap of paper." We are used to having promises so treated. But the Junkers were merely a little ahead of us in their willingness to believe that since the triumph of Germany would promote the advent of the superman, there was nothing immoral in a broken oath.

Many college students, so the pollsters tell us, see nothing wrong about cheating on examinations. "Everybody does it and it doesn't really *hurt* anyone."

In such statements it is easy to see a reasonable application of the two leading principles of ethics-without-absolutes-and-without-honor, which is sometimes called "socialized morality." These two leading principles are: (1) What everybody does must be permissible since the *mores* determine morality; and (2) "Wrong" can mean only "socially harmful."

If you believe all this and also that the only difference between, let us say, an honest man and a thief is the difference between a man who has been "conditioned" to act honestly and one who has not, then there isn't much basis for argument with the student opinion.

When some scandal breaks in government or journalism or business or broadcasting, the usual reaction of even that part of the public which is shocked by it is to say that it could not have happened if there had been adequate laws supervising this or that activity. But, usually, is it not equally true that it could not have happened if a whole group of men, often including the supposed guardians of public morality, had not been devoid of any sense of the meaning and importance of individual integrity? May one not go further and ask whether any amount of "social consciousness" and government control can make decent a society composed of people who have no conception of personal dignity and honor? It was a favorite and no doubt sound argument among early twentieth-century reformers that "playing the game" as the gentleman was supposed to play it was not enough. But has the time not come to add that it is, nevertheless, indispensable?

If the relevance of all this to the first part of the present discussion is not obvious, please allow me to dot the *i*'s. To those who believe that society is corrupt beyond redemption I propose the ancient but neglected concept of personal integrity, virtue and honor accompanied, if they feel it necessary, with the contempt and scorn recently advocated in a telling article in the [*American*] *Scholar* itself.

Those who hold that "social morality" is the only kind worth considering tend to assume that the end justifies the means. If a broken promise or a cynical invasion of a private right promotes "the greatest good of the greatest number" then it is an act of "higher morality." That seems to me a curiously inverted, soft-hearted and soft-headed Machiavellianism. The man of honor is reluctant to use dishonorable means no matter what ends seem to justify them. And he seems to me to be a safer member of society.

STUDY QUESTIONS

1. Explain George N. Shuster's definition of the ultimate aim of education. Is that indeed the ultimate aim of education?

2. What responsibility *does* society have toward the individual? The individual toward society?

3. In recent years, what groups have been notably and noticeably alienated from society? The beats? The angry young men? The hippies? The yippies? Hell's Angels? SDS? Black Muslims? How has the behavior of these groups revealed their alienation?

4. Krutch feels that we are in a bad way partly because we have placed too much emphasis on public education and too little on self-education. Has public education contributed to the alienation of contemporary youth? How?

5. Is there anything wrong about cheating on examinations? If there is, who is wronged? If there isn't, what justifications for cheating can you suggest? How does your instructor feel about the matter? Should examinations be proctored?

Time

ON BEING A CONTEMPORARY CHRISTIAN

"WHAT is bothering me is the question what Christianity really is, or indeed who Christ really is, for us today." So wrote the young Lutheran Theologian Dietrich Bon-

Reprinted by permission from TIME, The Weekly Newsmagazine; Copyright Time Inc. 1968.

hoeffer from his Berlin prison cell in April 1944, one year before he was executed by the SS for complicity in the plots against Hitler's life. It is a question that today—for more complicated reasons—concerns countless thousands of U.S. churchgoers, who see about them a Christianity in the midst of change, confusion and disarray.

For Roman Catholics, the religious revolution set loose by the Second Vatican Council has changed many traditional patterns of worship and thought, and seemingly unleashed a legion of priests, nuns and laymen who feel free to cast doubt on every article of defined dogma. Protestants too have been stunned by the spectacle of an Episcopal bishop openly denying the Trinity and the Virgin Birth, and ordained ministers teaching in seminaries proclaiming the news that God is dead. On the theological right, evangelical preachers summon believers back to a strict Biblical orthodoxy; on the left, angry young activists insist that to be a Christian is to be a revolutionary, and propose to substitute picket lines for prayer.

It is not really surprising that the churches should be sounding uncertain trumpets, or that Christians should be insecure as to the meaning and direction of their spiritual commitment. Undeniably, one of the most telling events of modern history has been a revolution in the relationship of religion to Western civilization. The churchgoer could once take comfort in the fact that he belonged to what was essentially a Christian society, in which the existence of an omnipotent God was the focus of ultimate meaning. No such security exists today, in a secular-minded culture that suggests the eclipse rather than the presence of God.

Science and technology have long since made it unnecessary to posit a creative Deity as a hypothesis to explain anything in the universe. From Marxists, existentialists and assorted humanists has come the persistent message that the idea of God is an intellectual bogy that prevents man from claiming his mature heritage of freedom. In the U.S., which probably has a higher percentage of regular Sunday churchgoers than any other nation on earth, the impact of organized Christianity appears to be on the wane. One problem for the future of the churches is the indifference and even hostility toward them on the part of the young. Even those drawn to the person of Christ chafe against outmoded rules, irrelevant sermons, dogmas that apparently have no personal meaning to a generation struggling to understand themselves, to grapple with such concrete issues as sex and social injustice.

Also a Man

Undeniably, one major task of theology today is to define what it means to be a Christian in a secular society. For millions, of course, there is no real problem. Baptism and church membership are the external criteria of faith, and a true follower of Jesus is one who keeps his beliefs free from heresy and tries to live a decent, upright, moral life. Yet to the most thoughtful spokesmen of modern Christianity, these criteria are not only minimal, they are secondary and even somewhat irrelevant. Instead, they argue that faith is not an intellectual assent to a series of dogmatic propositions but a commitment of one's entire being; ethical concern is directed not primarily toward one's own life but toward one's neighbor and the world. The mortal sins, in this new morality, are not those of the flesh but those of society; more important than the evil man does to himself is the evil he does to his fellow man. "The Christian's role is to bear witness to God in man," says Jesuit Clinical Psychologist Carlo Weber. "Jesus Christ is the wedding of the divine and the human. Being a Christian for me means bearing witness to the wedding of divinity and humanity, to love God and man—to be involved, therefore, in human affairs."

Although the churches have always taught that Christ was both God and man, Christians have hardly ever seemed to accept his humanity. Historically, preaching has emphasized the Risen Christ, who sits at the right hand of God, and will come in glory to the Last Judgment. This is a basic premise of faith, but it is equally true that Jesus was emphatically a man—a lowly carpenter who walked the earth of Palestine at a specific moment in human history, and whose death fulfilled Isaiah's prophesy of the Suffering Servant. Jesus, as Bonhoeffer memorably put it, was "the man for others."

Summing up his message to man, Jesus asked his followers to love God, and "thy neighbor as thyself." For centuries, Christians have seemed to emphasize the first of those commands—and all too frequently, when there was a conflict between the two, it was love of man that went by the boards. But Biblical scholars point out that the New Testament is a very secular book, and there is an unmistakable social concern in Jesus' moral teachings. In *Matthew 23,* for example, Jesus condemns as hypocrites the scribes and Pharisees who ostentatiously tithe their possessions but neglect "the weightier matters of the law, justice and mercy and faith."

Christian & Atheist

There is nothing fundamentally new about the insight that Christian ethics are corporate rather than individualistic. The medieval monasteries, for example, were dedicated to serving their communities as well as to praising God in communal prayer; the Mennonites and Quakers have always emphasized brotherly love and peace rather than dogma. The difference is that theologians now take it for granted that Christian love is something that cannot be confined to the church but is directed toward all the world. The commitment of a man who follows Jesus is not to an institution, but to life itself.

Within the churches, there is considerably less agreement on how this commitment should be exercised. Christian radicals—such as the young firebrands who dominated the National Council of Churches' Conference on Church and Society in Detroit last fall—argue that the true follower of Jesus is the revolutionary, siding with forces and events that seek to over-throw established disorder. On the other hand, Protestant Theologian Hans-Joachim Margull of Hamburg University points out that it is not always so easy to identify the secular causes that Christians have a clear moral duty to support.

It is easy enough to argue that Christians have a God-given duty to work for racial equality, or for the eradication of hunger and disease in the world. The strategies to be followed in achieving these goals do not so easily acquire universal assent. For that reason, Dean Jerald Brauer of the University of Chicago Divinity School argues that churches should not necessarily be en-gaged in trying to hand down specific solutions to social and political prob-lems from the pulpit. Christian creativity in trying to solve these questions, he says, "won't be a case of the churches poking their noses into areas where they have no right to be. Churches may have so special answers, al-though they certainly have a responsibility to sensitize their people to the questions. But the answers will have to be worked out by the body politic."

What this means, in essence, is that a commitment to love in worldly life cannot be separated from faith in Christ, who demanded that commitment. One argument against trying to build Christianity on moral action alone is that Jesus' teachings, unlike those of, say, Confucius, make sense only when understood as counsels of perfection in obedience to God rather than as workable guidelines of behavior. The Rev. David H. C. Read, pastor of Manhattan's Madison Avenue Presbyterian Church, points out that in fac-ing many problems of life the behavior of the Christian and the humanist might well be identical. Bertrand Russell and the Archbishop of Canter-bury, for example, could equably serve on the same committee to improve housing. "The distinction is not in their action," Read argues. "It is in their motivation and ultimate conviction on the meaning of life." This suggests that the committed Christian who is immersed in the secular world will also be to some extent an anonymous Christian; his light will still shine before the world, but it will not be so easily identified.

Since faith is the reason for commitment, most churchmen regard the idea of a "Christian atheist" or a "Christian agnostic" as something of a contra-diction in terms. "I can't see how it is possible to be a Christian atheist," says Episcopal Bishop James A. Pike, who has been accused of being just that by some of his fellow clerics. "You cannot attack the idea of an ultimate and at the same time accept Jesus as an ultimate." Swiss Catholic Theologian Hans Küng points out that "Jesus had no sense of himself without God. He made it clear that his radical commitment to men presupposed a radical commit-ment to God."

Nonetheless, theologians also acknowledge that only God is the final judge of who can rightly be considered a Christian. Austrian Jesuit Theologian Karl Rahner, for example, suggests that there is today "an invisible Christianity which does indeed possess the justification of sanctifying grace from God. A man belonging to this invisible Christianity may deny his Christianity or maintain that he does not know whether he is a Christian or not. Yet God may have chosen him in grace." Similarly, the late Protestant theologian Paul Tillich contrasted the "manifest church" of confessed believers with what he called the "latent church," whose membership included all men engaged with the ultimate realities of life.

The Decline of Dogma

Since faith is primarily a way of life rather than a creed to be so proclaimed, it is not something that can be reduced to an articulated set of principles. In an age of ecumenical breakthrough and doctrinal pluralism, sectarian particularities of belief seem largely irrelevant and even a little quaint. What is important is not the doctrine of predestination, for example, but the mystery of man's relationship to God that lies behind it. A Christian must accept the Incarnation—but there is room for differing interpretations of Jesus' unique relationship to God. The Resurrection is, as St. Paul insisted, the cornerstone of faith; but how one defines this unique defiance of death is of less moment.

Even in the Roman Catholic Church, which has traditionally upheld the immutability of dogma, there is widespread recognition by theologians that all formulas of faith are man's frail and imperfect vessels for carrying God's truth, and are forever in need of reformulation. In the light of Christianity's need to respond to the human needs of the earth, many of these ancient formulas hardly seem worth rethinking. "The central axis of religious concern," notes Langdon Gilkey of the University of Chicago Divinity School, "has shifted from matters of ultimate 'salvation,' and of heaven or hell, to questions of the meaning, necessity, or usefulness of religion for this life." In other words, the theological task is to justify Christianity in this world— and let God take care of the next.

The faith commitment of the Christian also implies the need for allegiance to a church—or at least to some kind of community of faith. Theoretically, it may be possible for a Christian to survive without any institutional identity—but the majority of modern theologians would agree that to be "a man for others" there must be others to be with, and that faith is sustained by communal structure. Churchmen would also argue that there is nothing obsolete about the basic necessity for worship and prayer. "Liturgy must be an expression of something that is happening in the community," says the Rev. David Kirk, a Melchite Catholic priest who is founder of a unique interfaith center in Manhattan called Emmaus House. "Without worship, the community is a piece of rubbish." On the other hand, there is little doubt that the churches are in desperate need of new, this-worldly liturgies that reflect present needs rather than past glories.

A Band of Soul Brothers

While a church—in the sense of a community—may be necessary for a viable Christian life, institutional or denominational churches are not. Today it would be hard to find an atheist whose criticism of religion is any more vociferous than the attack on the irrelevance, stagnation and nonutility of organized Christendom offered by its adherents. "Christianity is like a trip," muses Episcopal Bishop Edward Crowther, a Fellow of the Center for the Study of Democratic Institutions at Santa Barbara, Calif. "The church is like a travel agent with a lot of pictures in her office describing what it's like. But either she's never been there, or was there so long ago that she doesn't remember what it was all about."

Methodist Theologian Van Harvey suggests that the church should not be "a place where men come to be more pious. The church is a place of edification, where one comes to learn to be an honest-to-God person living in dialogue with others." Despite all the yearning for spirituality that may exist in the average American church, it is questionable how many churchgoers can and do live up to this ideal. The stratified irrelevance of the established parish, whether Catholic or Protestant, is a major reason for the growth of what Episcopal Chaplain Malcolm Boyd has dubbed "the underground church" —informal, *ad hoc* gatherings of Christians who cross over and above denominational lines to celebrate improvised Eucharists in each other's homes, and study Scripture or theology together.

To some theologians, the emergence of this underground church is a sign of spiritual health, a harbinger of renewal. To be sure, there is the possibility that these unstructured groups might coalesce into a new kind of gnostic sect—an elect that considers itself set apart from the erring mass of nominal believers. On the other hand, there is the far greater danger that institutional Christianity, without an extraordinary amount of reform, will end up as a monumental irrelevancy. Faced with a choice between the church in its present form and the underground cell, it is likely that a majority of Christian thinkers would opt for the small, unstructured community as a likely model for the future. Jesus never explicitly said that all men would be converted to believe in his word. Far more meaningful is his image of his followers as the "salt of the earth" and "the light of the world"—similes suggesting that the status of Christianity, until God's final reckoning, is properly that of a band of soul brothers rather than a numberless army.

Despite the visible health and prosperity of existing denominations, there is a considerable number of future-oriented theologians who feel that the church, in large parts of the world, is entering a stage of Diaspora—when, like Judaism, it will survive in the form of a scattered few, the hidden remnant. Strangely enough, there are any number of Christians who rejoice at this prospect rather than fear it. This is not because they want to see the fainthearted and the half convinced drift away into unbelief. Rather, they prefer that the choice of being Christian once again become openly, as Kierkegaard puts it, a leap of faith, an adult decision to serve as one of God's pilgrims on the road of life.

It is conceivable that Christianity is heading toward an era in which its status will be akin to that of the despised minority who proclaimed faith in the one God against the idolatry of the Roman Empire. To be sure, the Christian burden in the future will be different from that of the past: less to proclaim Jesus by word than to follow him in deed and loving service. It may prove a perilous course, but the opportunity is great: the courage and zeal of that first despised minority changed the history of the world.

STUDY QUESTIONS

1. Does the *TIME* essay answer the question raised in the introductory paragraph?

2. What evidence does *TIME* provide for its statements that Christians have "hardly ever seemed to accept" the humanity of Christ, and that Christians have failed to love their neighbors as themselves?

3. What are the implications of the words *to the most thoughtful* in the fifth paragraph?

4. What is accomplished by the frequent quotations from scholars and theologians?

5. What rhetorical devices are used to unify paragraphs? What transitional devices are used between paragraphs?

Jonathan Swift

AN ARGUMENT AGAINST
ABOLISHING CHRISTIANITY

Jonathan Swift (1667–1745) is one of England's greatest prose writers. He
was born in Dublin, Ireland, and was educated there at Trinity College. The
fact that he took orders in the Church of England did not prevent him from
becoming one of the Tory propagandists. However, Queen Anne disapproved of *A Tale of a Tub* (1704), and Swift was given the deanery of St.
Patrick's, Dublin, instead of the English preferment he wanted. Among his
now-classic works are *The Battle of the Books* (1704), *Gulliver's Travels*
(1726), *A Modest Proposal* (1729), and *The Journal to Stella* (1766).

I AM very sensible what a weakness and presumption it is,
to reason against the general humor and disposition of
the world. I remember it was with great justice, and a
due regard to the freedom both of the public and the press, forbidden upon
severe penalties to write or discourse, or lay wagers against the Union, even
before it was confirmed by parliament; because that was looked upon as a
design, to oppose the current of the people, which, besides the folly of it, is a
manifest breach of the fundamental law that makes this majority of opinion
the voice of God. In like manner, and for the very same reasons, it may perhaps be neither safe nor prudent to argue against the abolishing of Christianity, at a juncture when all parties appear so unanimously determined
upon the point, as we cannot but allow from their actions, their discourses,
and their writings. However, I know not how, whether from the affectation
of singularity, or the perverseness of human nature, but so it unhappily falls
out, that I cannot be entirely of this opinion. Nay, although I were sure an
order were issued for my immediate prosecution by the Attorney General, I
should still confess that in the present posture of our affairs at home or
abroad, I do not yet see the absolute necessity of extirpating the Christian
religion from among us.

First published 1711.

This perhaps may appear too great a paradox even for our wise and paradoxical age to endure; therefore I shall handle it with all tenderness, and with the utmost deference to that great and profound majority which is of another sentiment.

And yet the curious may please to observe, how much the genius of a nation is liable to alter in half an age. I have heard it affirmed for certain by some very old people, that the contrary opinion was even in their memories as much in vogue as the other is now; and, that a project for the abolishing of Christianity would then have appeared as singular, and been thought as absurd, as it would be at this time to write or discourse in its defense.

Therefore I freely own that all appearances are against me. The system of the Gospel, after the fate of other systems, is generally antiquated and exploded; and the mass or body of the common people, among whom it seems to have had its latest credit, are now grown as much ashamed of it as their betters; opinions, like fashions, always descending from those of quality to the middle sort, and thence to the vulgar, where at length they are dropped and vanish.

But here I would not be mistaken, and must therefore be so bold as to borrow a distinction from the writers on the other side, when they make a difference between nominal and real Trinitarians. I hope no reader imagines me so weak to stand up in the defense of *real* Christianity, such as used in primitive times (if we may believe the authors of those ages) to have an influence upon men's belief and actions. To offer at the restoring of that would indeed be a wild project; it would be to dig up foundations; to destroy at one blow *all* the wit, and *half* the learning of the kingdom; to break the entire frame and constitution of things; to ruin trade, extinguish arts and sciences with the professors of them; in short, to turn our courts, exchanges, and shops into deserts; and would be full as absurd as the proposal of Horace, where he advises the Romans all in a body to leave their city, and seek a new seat in some remote part of the world, by way of cure for the corruption of their manners.

Therefore I think this caution was in itself altogether unnecessary (which I have inserted only to prevent all possibility of caviling), since every candid reader will easily understand my discourse to be intended only in defense of *nominal* Christianity; the other having been for some time wholly laid aside by general consent, as utterly inconsistent with our present schemes of wealth and power.

But why we should therefore cast off the name and title of Christians, although the general opinion and resolution be so violent for it, I confess I cannot (with submission) apprehend the consequence necessary. However, since the undertakers propose such wonderful advantages to the nation by this project, and advance many plausible objections against the system of Christianity, I shall briefly consider the strength of both, fairly allow them their greatest weight, and offer such answers as I think most reasonable. After which I will beg leave to show what inconveniences may possibly happen by such an innovation, in the present posture of our affairs.

First, One great advantage proposed by the abolishing of Christianity is, that it would very much enlarge and establish liberty of conscience, that great bulwark of our nation, and of the Protestant religion, which is still too much limited by priestcraft, notwithstanding all the good intentions of the legislature, as we have lately found by a severe instance. For it is confidently reported, that two young gentlemen of real hopes, bright wit, and profound judgment, who upon a thorough examination of causes and effects, and by the mere force of natural abilities, without the least tincture of learning, having made a discovery, that there was no God, and generously communicating their thoughs for the good of the public, were some time ago, by an unparalleled severity, and upon I know not what *obsolete* law, broke *only* for *blasphemy*. And as it hath been wisely observed, if persecution once begins, no man alive knows how far it may reach, or where it will end.

In answer to all which, with deference to wiser judgments, I think this rather shows the necessity of a *nominal* religion among us. Great wits love to be free with the highest objects; and if they cannot be allowed a *God* to revile or renounce, they will *speak evil of dignitites,* abuse the government, and reflect upon the ministry; which I am sure few will deny to be of much more pernicious consequence, according to the saying of Tiberius, *Deorum offensa diis curae.*

As to the particular fact related, I think it is not fair to argue from one instance, perhaps another cannot be produced; yet (to the comfort of all those who may be apprehensive of persecution) blasphemy we know is freely spoken a million of times in every coffeehouse and tavern, or wherever else *good company* meet. It must be allowed indeed, that to break an *English freeborn* officer only for blasphemy, was, to speak the gentlest of such an action, a very high strain of absolute power. Little can be said in excuse for the general; perhaps he was afraid it might give offense to the allies, among whom, for aught I know, it may be the custom of the country to believe a God. But if he argued, as some have done, upon a mistaken principle, that an officer who is guilty of speaking blasphemy, may some time or other proceed so far as to raise a mutiny, the consequence is by no means to be admitted; for, surely the commander of an *English* army is likely to be but ill obeyed, whose soldiers fear and reverence him as little as they do a deity.

It is further objected against the Gospel system that it obliges men to the belief of things too difficult for freethinkers, and such who have shaken off the prejudices that usually cling to a confined education. To which I answer, that men should be cautious how they raise objections which reflect upon the wisdom of the nation. Is not everybody freely allowed to believe whatever he pleases, and to publish his belief to the world whenever he thinks fit, especially if it serves to strengthen the party which is in the right? Would any indifferent foreigner, who should read the trumpery lately written by Asgil, Tindal, Toland, Coward, and forty more, imagine the Gospel to be our rule of faith, and confirmed by parliaments? Does any man either believe, or say he believes, or desire to have it thought that he says he believes one syllable of the matter? And is any man worse received upon that score, or does he find his want of *nominal* faith a disadvantage to him in the pursuit of any civil or military employment? What if there be an old dormant statute or two against him, are they not now obsolete, to a degree, that Empson and Dudley themselves if they were now alive, would find it impossible to put them in execution?

It is likewise urged, that there are, by computation, in this kingdom, above ten thousand parsons, whose revenues added to those of my lords the bishops, would suffice to maintain at least two hundred young gentlemen of wit and pleasure, and freethinking, enemies to priestcraft, narrow principles, pedantry, and prejudices; who might be an ornament to the court and town. And then, again, so great a number of able (bodied) divines might be a recruit to our fleet and armies. This indeed appears to be a consideration of some weight. But then, on the other side, several things deserve to be considered likewise: As, first, whether it may not be thought necessary that in certain tracts of country, like what we call parishes, there should be *one* man at least of abilities to read and write. Then it seems a wrong computation, that the revenues of the Church throughout this island would be large enough to maintain two hundred young gentlemen, or even half that number, after the present refined way of living; that is, to allow each of them such a rent, as in the modern form of speech, would make them *easy*. But still there is in this project a greater mischief behind; and we ought to beware of the woman's folly, who killed the hen that every morning laid her a golden egg. For, pray what would become of the race of men in the next age, if we had nothing to trust to beside the scrofulous, consumptive productions, furnished by our men of wit and pleasure, when, having squandered away their vigor, health, and estates, they are forced by some disagreeable marriage to piece up their broken fortunes and entail rottenness and politeness on their posterity? Now, here are ten thousand persons reduced by the wise regulations of Henry the Eighth, to the necessity of a low diet, and moderate exercise, who are the only great restorers of our breed, without which the nation would in an age or two become but one great hospital.

Another advantage proposed by the abolishing of Christianity, is the clear gain of one day in seven, which is now entirely lost, and consequently the kingdom one-seventh less considerable in trade, business, and pleasure; beside the loss to the public of so many stately structures now in the hands of the clergy, which might be converted into theaters, exchanges, market houses, common dormitories, and other public edifices.

I hope I shall be forgiven a hard word, if I call this a perfect cavil. I readily own there has been an old custom time out of mind, for people to assemble in the churches every Sunday, and that shops are still frequently shut, in order as it is conceived, to preserve the memory of that ancient practice; but how this can prove a hindrance to business or pleasure, is hard to imagine. What if the men of pleasure are forced one day in the week, to game at home instead of the chocolate house? Are not the taverns and coffeehouses open? Can there be a more convenient season for taking a dose of physic? Are fewer claps got upon Sundays than other days? Is not that the chief day for traders to sum up the accounts of the week, and for lawyers to prepare their briefs? But I would fain know how it can be pretended that the churches are misapplied? Where are more appointments and rendezvous of gallantry? Where more care to appear in the foremost box with greater advantage of dress? Where more meetings for business? Where more bargains driven of all sorts? And where so many conveniences or incitements to sleep?

There is one advantage greater than any of the foregoing, proposed by the abolishing of Christianity: that it will utterly extinguish parties among us, by removing those factious distinctions of High and Low Church, of Whig and Tory, Presbyterian and Church of England, which are now so many grievous clogs upon public proceedings, and dispose men to prefer the gratifying themselves, or depressing their adversaries, before the most important interest of the state.

I confess, if it were certain that so great an advantage would redound to the nation by this expedient, I would submit and be silent. But will any man say, that if the words *whoring, drinking, cheating, lying, stealing,* were by act of parliament ejected out of the English tongue and dictionaries, we should all awake next morning chaste and temperate, honest and just, and lovers of truth? Is this a fair consequence? Or, if the physicians would forbid us to pronounce the words *pox, gout, rheumatism,* and *stone,* would that expedient serve like so many talismans to destroy the diseases themselves? Are party and faction rooted in men's hearts no deeper than phrases borrowed from religion, or founded upon no firmer principles? And is our language so poor that we cannot find other terms to express them? Are envy, pride, avarice, and ambition such ill nomenclators, that they cannot furnish appellations for their owners? Will not *heydukes* and *mamalukes, mandarins* and *potshaws,* or any other words formed at pleasure, serve to distinguish those who are in the ministry from others who *would be in it if they could?* What, for instance, is easier than to vary the form of speech, and instead of the word *Church,* make it a question in politics, whether the *Monument* be in danger? Because religion was nearest at hand to furnish a few convenient phrases, is our invention so barren, we can find no others? Suppose, for argument sake, that the Tories favored Margarita, the Whigs Mrs. Tofts, and the Trimmers Valentini, would not *Margaritians, Toftians,* and *Balentinians* be very tolerable marks of distinction? The *Prasini* and *Veneti,* two most virulent factions in Italy, began (if I remember right) by a distinction of colors in ribbons, which we might do, with as good a grace, about the dignity of the *Blue* and the *Green;* and would serve as properly to divide the court, the parliament, and the kingdom between them, as any terms of art whatsoever, borrowed from religion. Therefore, I think there is little force in this objection against Christianity, or prospect of so great an advantage as is proposed in the abolishing of it.

It is again objected, as a very absurd, ridiculous custom, that a set of men should be suffered, much less employed and hired, to bawl one day in seven against the lawfulness of those methods most in use toward the pursuit of greatness, riches, and pleasure, which are the constant practice of all men alive on the other six. But this objection is, I think, a little unworthy in so refined an age as ours. Let us argue this matter calmly. I appeal to the breast of any polite freethinker, whether in the pursuit of gratifying a predominant passion, he hath not always felt a wonderful incitement, by reflecting it was a thing forbidden; and therefore we see, in order to cultivate this taste, the wisdom of the nation hath taken special care, that the ladies should be furnished with prohibited silks, and the men with prohibited wine. And indeed it were to be wished, that some other prohibitions were promoted, in order to improve the pleasures of the town; which, for want of such expedients, begin already, as I am told, to flag and grow languid, giving way daily to cruel inroads from the spleen.

It is likewise proposed as a great advantage to the public, that if we once discard the system of the Gospel, all religion will of course be banished forever; and consequently, along with it, those grievous prejudices of education, which under the names of virtue, conscience, honor, justice, and the like, are so apt to disturb the peace of human minds; and the notions whereof are so hard to be eradicated by right reason or freethinking, sometimes during the whole course of our lives.

Here first, I observe how difficult it is to get rid of a phrase, which the world is once grown fond of, although the occasion that first produced it, be entirely taken away. For several years past, if a man had but an ill-favored nose, the deep thinkers of the age would some way or other contrive to impute the cause to the prejudice of his education. From this fountain are said to be derived all our foolish notions of justice, piety, love of our country; all our opinions of God, or a future state, Heaven, hell, and the like. And there might formerly perhaps have been some pretense for this charge. But so effectual care has been taken to remove those prejudices, by an entire change in the methods of education, that (with honor I mention it to our polite innovators) the young gentlemen who are now on the scene, seem to have not the

least tincture left of those infusions, or string of those weeds; and, by consequence, the reason for abolishing *nominal* Christianity upon that pretext, is
wholly ceased.

For the rest, it may perhaps admit a controversy, whether the banishing
all notions of religion whatsoever, would be convenient for the vulgar. Not
that I am in the least of opinion with those who hold religion to have been
the invention of politicians, to keep the lower part of the world in awe by the
fear of invisible powers; unless mankind were then very different from what
it is now. For I look upon the mass or body of our people here in England, to
be as freethinkers, that is to say, as staunch unbelievers, as any of the highest rank. But I conceive some scattered notions about a superior power to be
of singular use for the common people, as furnishing excellent materials to
keep children quiet when they grow peevish and providing topics of amuse-
ment in a tedious winter night.

Lastly, it is proposed as a singular advantage, that the abolishing of
Christianity will very much contribute to the uniting of Protestants, by en-
larging the terms of communion so as to take in all sorts of dissenters, who
are now shut out of the pale upon account of a few ceremonies which all
sides confess to be things indifferent: That this alone will effectually answer
the great ends of a scheme for comprehension, by opening a large noble
gate, at which all bodies may enter; whereas the chaffering with dissenter,
and dodging about this or the other ceremony, is but like opening a few
wickets, and leaving them ajar, by which no more than one can get in at a
time, and that, not without stooping, and sidling, and squeezing his body.

To all this I answer; that there is one darling inclination of mankind,
which usually affects to be a retainer to religion, though she be neither its
parent, its godmother, or its friend; I mean the spirit of opposition, that
lived long before Christianity, and can easily subsist without it. Let us, for
instance, examine wherein the opposition of sectaries among us consists, we
shall find Christianity to have no share in it at all. Does the Gospel anywhere
prescribe a starched, squeezed countenance, a stiff, formal gait, a singularity of manners and habit, or any affected modes of speech different from the
reasonable part of mankind? Yet, if Christianity did not lend its name to
stand in the gap, and to employ or divert these humors, they must of necessity be spent in contraventions to the laws of the land, and disturbance of the
public peace. There is a portion of enthusiasm assigned to every nation,
which, if it hath not proper objects to work on, will burst out, and set all in a
flame. If the quiet of a state can be bought by only flinging men a few ceremonies to devour, it is a purchase no wise man would refuse. Let the mastiffs
amuse themselves about a sheepskin stuffed with hay, provided it will keep
them from worrying the flock. The institution of convents abroad, seems in
one point a strain of great wisdom, there being few irregularities in human
passions, which may not have recourse to vent themselves in some of those

orders, which are so many retreats for the speculative, the melancholy, the proud, the silent, the politic, and the morose, to spend themselves, and evaporate the noxious particles; for each of whom we in this island are forced to provide a several sect of religion, to keep them quiet: And whenever Christianity shall be abolished, the legislature must find some other expedient to employ and entertain them. For what imports it how large a gate you open, if there will be always left a number who place a pride and a merit in refusing to enter?

Having thus considered the most important objections against Christianity, and the chief advantages proposed by the abolishing thereof, I shall now with equal deference and submission to wiser judgments as before, proceed to mention a few inconveniences that may happen, if the Gospel should be repealed; which perhaps the projectors may not have sufficiently considered.

And first, I am very sensible how much the gentlemen of wit and pleasure are apt to murmur, and be shocked at the sight of so many draggled-tail parsons, who happen to fall in their way, and offend their eyes; but at the same time, these wise reformers do not consider what an advantage and felicity it is, for great wits to be always provided with objects of scorn and contempt, in order to exercise and improve their talents, and divert their spleen from falling on each other or on themselves; especially when all this may be done without the least imaginable *danger to their persons.*

And to urge another argument of a parallel nature: If Christianity were once abolished, how would the freethinkers, the strong reasoners, and the men of profound learning, be able to find another subject so calculated in all points whereon to display their abilities? What wonderful productions of wit should we be deprived of, from those whose genius by continual practice hath been wholly turned upon raillery and invectives against religion, and would therefore never be able to shine or distinguish themselves upon any other subject! We are daily complaining of the great decline of wit among us, and would we take away the greatest, perhaps the only topic we have left? Who would ever have suspected Asgil for a wit, or Toland for a philosopher, if the inexhaustible stock of Christianity had not been at hand to provide them with materials? What other subject, through all art or nature, could have produced Tindal for a profound author, or furnished him with readers? It is the wise choice of the subject that alone adorns and distinguishes the writer. For, had a hundred such pens as these been employed on the side of religion, they would have immediately sunk into silence and oblivion.

Nor do I think it wholly groundless, or my fears altogether imaginary, that the abolishing of Christianity may perhaps bring the Church into danger, or at least put the senate to the trouble of another securing vote. I desire I may not be mistaken; I am far from presuming to affirm or think that the

Church is in danger at present, or as things now stand; but we know not how soon it may be so when the Christian religion is repealed. As plausible as this project seems, there may a dangerous design lurk under it. Nothing can be more notorious, than that the atheists, deists, Socinians, anti-Trinitarians, and other subdivisions of free-thinkers, are persons of little zeal for the present ecclesiastical establishment: Their declared opinion is for repealing the Sacramental Test; they are very indifferent with regard to ceremonies; nor do they hold the *jus divinum* of Episcopacy. Therefore this may be intended as one politic step toward altering the constitution of the Church established, and setting up Presbytery in the stead, which I leave to be further considered by those at the helm.

In the last place, I think nothing can be more plain, than that by this expedient, we shall run into the evil we chiefly pretend to avoid; and that the abolishment of the Christian religion will be the readiest course we can take to introduce popery. And I am more inclined to this opinion, because we know it has been the constant practice of the Jesuits to send over emissaries, with instructions to personate themselves members of the several prevailing sects among us. So it is recorded, that they have at sundry times appeared in the guise of Presbyterians, Anabaptists, Independents, and Quakers, according as any of these were most in credit; so, since the fashion hath been taken up of exploding religion, the popish missionaries have not been wanting to mix with the freethinkers; among whom, Toland the great oracle of the anti-Christians is an Irish priest, the son of an Irish priest; and the most learned and ingenious author of a book called *The Rights of the Christian Church* was in a proper juncture reconciled to the Romish faith, whose true son, as appears by a hundred passages in his treatise, he still continues. Perhaps I could add some others to the number; but the fact is beyond dispute, and the reasoning they proceed by is right; for, supposing Christianity to be extinguished, the people will never be at ease until they find out some other method of worship; which will as infallibly produce superstition, as this will end in popery.

And therefore, if notwithstanding all I have said, it shall still be thought necessary to have a bill brought in for repealing Christianity, I would humbly offer an amendment; that instead of the word *Christianity,* may be put *Religion* in general; which I conceive will much better answer all the good ends proposed by the projectors of it. For, as long as we leave in being a God and his providence, with all the necessary consequences which curious and inquisitive men will be apt to draw from such premises, we do not strike at the root of the evil, although we should ever so effectually annihilate the present scheme of the Gospel. For, of what use is freedom of thought, if it will not produce freedom of action, which is the sole end, how remote soever in appearance, of all objections against Christianity? And therefore, the freethinkers consider it as a sort of edifice, wherein all the parts have such a mutual dependence on each other, that if you happen to pull out one single nail, the whole fabric must fall to the ground. This was happily expressed by him who had heard of a text brought for proof of the Trinity, which in an ancient manuscript was differently read; he thereupon immediately took the hint, and by a sudden deduction of a long sorites, most logically concluded: "Why, if it be as you say, I may safely whore and drink on, and defy the parson." From which, and many the like instances easy to be produced, I think nothing can be more manifest, than that the quarrel is not against any particular points of hard digestion in the Christian system, but against religion in general; which, by laying restraints on human nature, is supposed the great enemy to the freedom of thought and action.

Upon the whole, if it shall still be thought for the benefit of Church and state, that Christianity be abolished; I conceive however, it may be more convenient to defer the execution to a time of peace, and not venture in this conjuncture to disoblige our allies, who, as it falls out, are all Christians, and many of them, by the prejudices of their education, so bigoted, as to place a sort of pride in the appellation. If upon being rejected by them, we are to trust to an alliance with the Turk, we shall find ourselves much deceived: For, as he is too remote, and generally engaged in war with the Persian emperor, so his people would be more scandalized at our infidelity, than our Christian neighbors. Because the Turks are not only strict observers of religious worship, but, what is worse, believe a God; which is more than is required of us, even while we preserve the name of Christians.

To conclude: Whatever some may think of the great advantages to trade by this favorite scheme, I do very much apprehend, that in six months' time after the act is passed for the extirpation of the Gospel, the Bank and East India stock may fall, at least, one *per cent*. And, since that is fifty times more than ever the wisdom of our age thought fit to venture for the *preservation* of Christianity, there is no reason we should be at so great a loss, merely for the sake of *destroying* it.

STUDY QUESTIONS

1. By what means does Swift try to convince his readers of his obvious sincerity?

2. What distinction does he make between *real* Christianity and *nominal* Christianity?

3. How does Swift turn to his advantage the argument that the Gospel obliges men to believe things too difficult for freethinkers?

4. What use does Swift make of the seemingly incontrovertible evidence of
   statistics?

5. How does he appeal to the economic interests of his audience? What is
   his concluding and most important argument against abolishing Christianity?

Martin Buber

BOOKS AND MEN

Martin Buber (1878–1965) was born in Vienna. He studied at the Universities of Vienna, Berlin, and Zurich. Although he is now considered the
most important contemporary Jewish theologian and philosopher, he did
not become publicly committed to the Zionist movement and Judaism until
1923, at the University of Leipzig. In Germany he edited *Die Welt, Der
Jude,* and *Die Kreatur.* His first teaching position, in 1923, was at the University of Frankfurt. Buber left Germany in 1938 for Palestine, where he
lived, teaching until his retirement in 1951 at the University of Jerusalem.
Among his honorary degrees is one from the University of Aberdeen, Scot-
land. His books include *I and Thou* (1937), *Between Man and Man* (1947),
Hasidism (1948), *Images of Good and Evil, The Eclipse of God, Israel and
Palestine,* and *Right and Wrong* (1952).

I F I HAD been asked in my early youth whether I preferred
to have dealings only with men or only with books, my
answer would certainly have been in favour of books. In
later years this has become less and less the case. Not that I have had so
much better experiences with men than with books; on the contrary, purely
delightful books even now come my way more often than purely delightful
men. But the many bad experiences with men have nourished the meadow of
my life as the noblest book could not do, and the good experiences have
made the earth into a garden for me. On the other hand, no book does more
than remove me into a paradise of great spirits, where my innermost heart
never forgets I cannot dwell long, nor even wish that I could do so. For (I

must say this straight out in order to be understood) my innermost heart loves the world more than it loves the spirit. I have not, indeed, cleaved to life in the world as I might have; in my relations with it I fail it again and again; again and again I remain guilty towards it for falling short of what it expects of me, and this is partly, to be sure, because I am so indebted to the spirit. I am indebted to the spirit as I am to myself, but I do not, strictly speaking, love it, even as I do not, strictly speaking, love myself. I do not in reality love him who has seized me with his heavenly clutch and holds me fast; rather I love her, the "world," who comes again and again to meet me and extends to me a pair of fingers.

Both have gifts to share. The former showers on me his manna of books; the latter extends to me the brown bread on whose crust I break my teeth, a bread of which I can never have enough: men. Aye, these tousle-heads and good-for-nothings, how I love them! I revere books—those that I really read—too much to be able to love them. But in the most venerable of living men I always find more to love than to revere: I find in him something of this world, that is simply there as the spirit never can be there. The spirit hovers above me powerfully and pours out his exalted gift of speech, books; how glorious, how weird! But she, the human world, needs only to cast a word- less smile, and I cannot live without her. She is mute; all the prattle of men yields no word such as sounds forth constantly out of books. And I listen to it all in order to receive the silence that penetrates to me through it, the silence of the creature. But just the human creature! That creature means a mixture. Books are pure, men are mixed; books are spirit and word, pure spirit and purified word; men are made up of prattle and silence, and their silence is not that of animals but of men. Out of the human silence behind the prattle the spirit whispers to you, the spirit *as soul*. She, she is the beloved.

Here is an infallible test. Imagine yourself in a situation where you are alone, wholly alone on earth, and you are offered one of the two, books or men. I often hear men prizing their solitude, but that is only because there are still men somewhere on earth, even though in the far distance. I knew nothing of books when I came forth from the womb of my mother, and I shall die without books, with another human hand in my own. I do, indeed, close my door at times and surrender myself to a book, but only because I can open the door again and see a human being looking at me.

STUDY QUESTIONS

1. How and why did Buber's love of men and books change as he matured?

2. What does Buber mean by "him who has seized me with his heavenly clutch and holds me fast"?

3. How "infallible" is the test posited in the last paragraph?

4. Buber contrasts books and men; although his essay is titled "Books and Men," most of it is really a discussion of books *or* men. Do Buber's sentence patterns reinforce the contrasts?

Harry Golden

FOR TWO CENTS PLAIN

Harry Golden (1902–   ) was born in New York City. He attended The City College of New York from 1919 to 1922, and was named Doctor of Letters by Belmont Abbey College in 1962. He lives in Charlotte, North Carolina, where he has edited the *Carolina Israelite* since 1942. His books include *Only in America* (1958), *For 2¢ Plain* (1959), *Enjoy! Enjoy!* and *Carl Sandburg* (1961), *You're Entitle* (1962), *Forgotten Pioneer* (1963), *Mr. Kennedy and the Negroes* (1964), *So What Else Is New?* and *A Little Girl Is Dead* (1965), *Ess, Ess, Mein Kindt* (1966), *The Best of Harry Golden* (1967), and *Right Time* (1969).

THE RABBINICAL students in Europe and in America had a regular schedule of "eating days." Mondays he ate with family A; Tuesdays with B; and so forth. On the Lower East Side this system still lingered to some extent, but it usually involved a young boy who had immigrated without a family. His fellow-townsmen set up his seven eating days. Usually this was a very religious boy who would not take a chance to eat "out" or could not yet afford to buy his meals. Some of the hosts on these eating days used the fellow to check up on the melamed (Hebrew teacher). The melamed came at half past three and taught the children for a half-hour—for a twenty-five-cent fee. Learning the prayers was entirely by rote. There was no explanation or translation of the Hebrew into

English or Yiddish. Once in a while the mother would ask the eating-days fellow to come a half-hour earlier. The boy came with his usual appetite, but soon learned the reason for the early appointment. The mother wanted him to test the children to see if the melamed was doing all right. The boy always gave the melamed a clean bill of health.

Sometimes the eating-days boy ate too much and in poor households this was quite a problem. But in most homes the mother saw to it that he kept packing it away, and in addition always had something wrapped up for him to take back to his room—for later. Many households had these strangers at their tables, but only the very religious boys remained, those who expected to continue their religious studies.

The others were soon gone. America was too great and too wonderful; there were too many things to see and do, and even a hot dog at a pushcart was an adventure, to say nothing of the wonderful Max's Busy Bee.

The streets were crowded with vendors with all sorts of delightful and exotic tidbits and nasherei (delicacies).

Across the border (the Bowery) was the Italian hot-dog man. The hot plate (a coal fire) was mounted on his pushcart, and behind the stove was a barrel of lemonade to which he added chunks of ice every few hours. The hot dog, roll, mustard, and relish was three cents; the drink, two cents; and it was all a memorable experience.

A few years ago I saw a fellow with a similar cart near the Battery on Lower Broadway and I made a mad dash for him. The whole operation was now fifteen cents, but it wasn't anywhere near as wonderful as it was when I was twelve years old.

In the late fall and winter came the fellow with the haiseh arbus (hot chick-peas). He started to make his rounds a few minutes before noon as the children were leaving the schools for lunch. You sat in the classroom and everything was quiet and dignified, and all of a sudden you heard those loud blasts—"Haiseh arbus," "Haiseh, haiseh" (hot, hot)—and you knew it was time to go. Sometimes he was a little early and the teacher had to close the window. The price was one penny for a portion which the man served in a rolled-up piece of newspaper, like the English working people buy their fish and chips. There were also fellows with roasted sweet potatoes; two cents each, and three cents for an extra large one. These people used a galvanized tin contraption on wheels which looked exactly like a bedroom dresser with three drawers. In the bottom drawer were the potatoes he was roasting, while in the upper drawers were the two different sizes ready to serve. On the bottom of everything, of course, was the coal-burning fire. He had a small bag of coal attached to the front of the stove and every once in a while he shook up the fire.

My uncle Berger once operated one of those sweet-potato pushcarts with the stove on the bottom, and years later he always said that he began life in

America as an engineer. He boasted of this after he had made a million dollars operating the Hotel Normandie on Broadway and 38th Street during World War I.

An interesting fellow was the peddler with a red fez, a "Turk," who sold an exotic sweet drink. He carried a huge bronze water container strapped to his back. This beautiful container had a long curved spout which came over his left shoulder. Attached to his belt, in front, was a small pail of warm water to rinse his two glasses. The drink was one penny. You held the glass, and he leaned toward you as the liquid came forth.

Nuts were very popular. There were pushcarts loaded down with "polly seeds." I have forgotten the authentic name for this nut but the East Side literally bathed in the stuff. "Polly seed" because it was the favorite food of parrots—"Polly want a cracker?"

Indian nuts, little round brown nuts. The father of one of the kids on the block sold Indian nuts, of all things. On his pushcart he had a huge glass bowl the size of an army soup vat, and it was filled with Indian nuts. I had daydreams of taking my shoes off and jumping up and down in that vat of Indian nuts, like the French girls make champagne.

This was the era when people walked a great deal. Shoeshine parlors were all over the place. On Sunday mornings you went out to get a shine and did not mind waiting in line for it either. "We are going for a walk next Saturday night." Sounds silly today, but it was an event, and make no mistake. And on every corner there were pushcarts selling fruit in season. Apples, pears, peaches, and above all, grapes. A common sight was a boy and girl eating grapes. The boy held the stem aloft as each of them pulled at the bunch and walked along the street. The grapes were sold by weight per bunch; the other fruits were sold individually, of course. And "in season" there was the man or the woman with "hot corn." I did not hear the term "corn-on-the-cob" till quite a few years later. We knew it only as "hot corn." The vendor had boiled the ears at home and usually carried the large vat to a convenient street corner, or he put the vat on a baby carriage and wheeled it around the neighborhood. A lot of women were in this hot-corn business. The hot corn was a nickel, and there was plenty of bargaining. "Throw it back, give me that one, the one over there." We kids waited around until the lady was all sold out, except the ones which had been thrown back, and often we paid no more than a penny. There are two moments when it is best to buy from a peddler, a "first" and the "close-out."

Confections of all sorts were sold, many of them famous in the Orient and eastern Europe. Fellows sold candy known as "rah-hott," which sounds Turkish or Arabic. It was beautiful to look at and there were two or three different tastes with each bite. Halvah, of course, was the real big seller, and the memory of this has lingered to this day. No delicatessen store today is without halvah, although I shall not do them the injustice of comparing the

East Side halvah and the stuff they sell today. But at least you are getting a whiff of it, which is worth anything you pay. I had a Gentile friend here who had been courting a widow for years without any success and I gave him a box of chocolate-covered halvah to take to her, and the next time I saw the guy he was dancing in the streets of Charlotte. We used to eat it between slices of rye bread, "a halvah sonavich," and it was out of this world. There was another candy called "buckser" (St. John's bread), imported from Palestine. It had a long, hard, curved shell and inside a very black seed with an interesting taste which is hard to describe.

There were pushcarts loaded down with barrels of dill pickles and pickled tomatoes, which we called "sour tomatoes." Working people, men and women on the way home from the needle factories, stopped off to buy a sour tomato as a sort of appetizer for their evening meal, or perhaps to take the edge off the appetite. These tidbits sold for two and three cents each, and you served yourself. You put your hand into the vinegar barrel and pulled one out. Years later a relative of mine asked me to accompany him to a lawyer's office to "talk for him." I met him on the old East Side and we decided to walk out of the district and into Lower Broadway.

Suddenly I noticed that he was no longer at my side. I looked back and there he was biting into one sour tomato and holding a fresh one in the other hand, all ready to go. I had become a fancy guy by then and he was afraid he would embarrass me, but my mouth was watering, Broadway and all.

And then there were the permanent vendors—the soda-water stands. On nearly every corner a soda-water stand. These were the size and shape of the average newsstand you see in most of the big cities today. There was a soda fountain behind a narrow counter, and a rack for factory-made American candy, which was becoming increasingly popular, especially the Hershey bar. The fellow also sold cigarettes. No woman was ever seen smoking a cigarette in those days. The brands were Mecca, Hassan, Helmar, Sweet Caporal (which are still sold), Egyptian Deities, Moguls, Schinasi, Fifth Avenue, and Afternoons.

My father smoked Afternoons. Half the cigarette was a hard mouthpiece, or what the advertising boys today call a filter. I bought many a box of Afternoons and they were seven cents for ten cigarettes. I also bought whiskey. There was no inhibition about it and no sense of guilt. We had no drunks down there, and a kid could buy a bottle of whiskey for his father the same as he could buy a loaf of bread. I read the label many times on the way home, "Pennsylvania Rye Whiskey; we guarantee that this whiskey has been aged in the wood twenty years before bottling; signed, Park and Tilford." Cost, $1.80 for an imperial quart. No fancy "fifth-shmifth" business.

The fellow with the stand had a small marble counter on which he served his drinks and made change for candy and cigarettes. Along the counter were jars of preserves—cherry, raspberry, mulberry—for his mixed drinks. He also had a machine to make malted milks. How the immigrants took to the malted milk!

Like the other folks, my mother pronounced it "ah molta." But, of course, the big seller was seltzer (carbonated water), either plain or with syrup. A small glass of seltzer cost a penny—"Give me a small plain." That meant no syrup. And for the large glass you said, "Give me for two cents plain." For an extra penny he ladled out a spoonful of one of his syrups and mixed it with the seltzer. Here, too, there was plenty of bargaining. A fellow said, "Give me for two cents plain," and as the man was filling the glass with seltzer the customer said, casuallike, "Put a little on the top." This meant syrup, of course, and yet it did not mean the extra penny. You did not say, "Give me a raspberry soda." It was all in the way you said it, nonchalantly and in a sort of deprecating tone, "Put a little on the top." It meant that you were saving the fellow the trouble of even stirring the glass. Well, the man had already filled the glass with seltzer and what could he do with it unless you paid for it? So he "put a little on the top" but not the next time if he could help it. Often he would take the two cents first and give you a glass of plain. "I know my customers," he'd say. The man who had the stand on our corner was an elderly gent, "Benny," and once when I was playing around his counter, one of his jars fell down and the syrup got all over me. Every time I came near Benny's stand after that he took extra precautions; "Go way hard luck," he always said to me. Benny wore a coat he had brought from Europe and it reached down to his ankles. He would take a handful of that coat, feel it a while, and tell you whether it was going to rain the next day. People came from blocks around to get a weather forecast from Benny and his coat. He rarely missed.

And so you can hardly blame the young boy, the eating-days boy, when he quit the table of those home-cooked meals and went down into this world of pleasures and joys.

STUDY QUESTIONS

1. There is, of course, no question of the Jewish family's desire to help an eating-day fellow. But, what advantage did they take of him?

2. What is the thesis sentence of Golden's essay?

3. In the discussion of street vendors, are there any vendors who do not logically belong in this essay by virtue of the wares they peddle? What is the organizing principle for the two paragraphs on p. 49 beginning, "And then there were the permanent vendors—the soda-water stands." and "My father smoked Afternoons"? Do these paragraphs have topic sentences?

4. Golden uses parentheses rather freely. Why does he use them when he does?

5. How does the audience for whom Golden wrote, and the medium in which this essay appeared explain the tone and style of "For Two Cents Plain"?

Graham Greene

THE REVOLVER IN THE CORNER CUPBOARD

Graham Greene (1904–   ) was born in Berkhamstead, England, and educated at Balliol College, Oxford. He holds an honorary Litt.D. from Cambridge University. Although a well-known playwright, essayist, and short-story writer, he is most famous for his novels and "entertainments." These include *Babbling April* (1925), *It's a Battlefield* (1934), *A Gun for Sale* (1936), *Brighton Rock* (1938), *The Power and the Glory* (1940), *The Ministry of Fear* (1943), *The Heart of the Matter* (1948), *The Third Man* (1950), *The End of the Affair* (1951), *The Quiet American* (1955), *Our Man in Havana* (1958), *A Burnt-out Case* (1961), and *The Comedians* (1966). His *Collected Essays* were published in 1969.

I CAN remember very clearly the afternoon I found the revolver in the brown deal corner cupboard in the bedroom which I shared with my elder brother. It was the early autumn of 1922. I was seventeen and terribly bored and in love with my sister's governess—one of those miserable, hopeless, romantic loves of adolescence that set in many minds the idea that love and despair are inextricable and that successful love hardly deserves the name. At that age one may fall irrevocably in love with failure, and success of any kind loses half its savour before it is experienced. Such a love is surrendered once and for all to the singer at the pavement's edge, the bankrupt, the old school friend who wants to touch you for a dollar. Perhaps in many so conditioned it is the love for God that mainly survives, because in his eyes they can imagine themselves remaining always drab, seedy, unsuccessful, and therefore worthy of notice.

The revolver was a small genteel object with six chambers like a tiny egg stand, and there was a cardboard box of bullets. It has only recently occurred to me that they may have been blanks; I always assumed them to be live ammunition, and I never mentioned the discovery to my brother because I had realized the moment I saw the revolver the use I intended to make of it. (I don't to this day know why he possessed it; certainly he had no licence, and he was only three years older than myself. A large family is as departmental as a Ministry.)

My brother was away—probably climbing in the Lake District—and until he returned the revolver was to all intents mine. I knew what to do with it because I had been reading a book (the name Ossendowski comes to mind as the possible author) describing how the White Russian officers, condemned to inaction in South Russia at the tail-end of the counter-revolutionary war, used to invent hazards with which to escape boredom. One man would slip a charge into a revolver and turn the chambers at random, and his companion would put the revolver to his head and pull the trigger. The chance, of course, was six to one in favour of life.

How easily one forgets emotions. If I were dealing now with an imaginary character, I would feel it necessary for verisimilitude to make him hesitate, put the revolver back into the cupboard, return to it again after an interval, reluctantly and fearfully, when the burden of boredom became too great. But in fact I think there was no hesitation at all, for the next I can remember is crossing Berkhamstead Common, gashed here and there between the gorse bushes with the stray trenches of the first Great War, towards the Ashridge beeches. Perhaps before I had made the discovery, boredom had already reached an intolerable depth.

I think the boredom was far deeper than the love. It had always been a feature of childhood: it would set in on the second day of the school holidays. The first day was all happiness, and, after the horrible confinement and publicity of school, seemed to consist of light, space and silence. But a prison conditions its inhabitants. I never wanted to return to it (and finally expressed my rebellion by the simple act of running away), but yet I was so conditioned that freedom bored me unutterably.

The psycho-analysis that followed my act of rebellion had fixed the boredom as hypo fixes the image on the negative. I emerged from those delightful months in London spent at my analyst's house—perhaps the happiest months of my life—correctly orientated, able to take a proper extrovert interest in my fellows (the jargon rises to the lips), but wrung dry. For years, it seems to me, I could take no aesthetic interest in any visual thing at all: staring at a sight that others assured me was beautiful, I would feel nothing. I was fixed in my boredom. (Writing this I come on a remark of Rilke:

"Psycho-analysis is too fundamental a help for me, it helps you once and for all, it clears you up, and to find myself finally cleared up one day might be even more helpless than this chaos.")

Now with the revolver in my pocket I was beginning to emerge. I had stumbled on the perfect cure. I was going to escape in one way or another, and because escape was inseparably connected with the Common in my mind, it was there that I went.

The wilderness of gorse, old trenches, abandoned butts was the unchanging backcloth of most of the adventures of childhood. It was to the Common I had decamped for my act of rebellion some years before, with the intention, expressed in a letter left after breakfast on the heavy black sideboard, that there I would stay, day and night, until either I had starved or my parents had given in; when I pictured war it was always in terms of this Common, and myself leading a guerilla campaign in the ragged waste, for no one, I was persuaded, knew its paths so intimately (how humiliating that in my own domestic campaign I was ambushed by my elder sister after a few hours).

Beyond the Common lay a wide grass ride known for some reason as Cold Harbour to which I would occasionally with some fear take a horse, and beyond this again stretched Ashridge Park, the smooth olive skin of beech trees and the thick last year's quagmire of leaves, dark like old pennies. Deliberately I chose my ground, I believe without any real fear—perhaps because I was uncertain myself whether I was play-acting; perhaps because so many acts which my elders would have regarded as neurotic, but which I still consider to have been under the circumstances highly reasonable, lay in the background of this more dangerous venture.

There had been, for example, perhaps five or six years before, the disappointing morning in the dark room by the linen cupboard on the eve of term when I had patiently drunk a quantity of hypo under the impression that it was poisonous: on another occasion the blue glass bottle of hay fever lotion which as it contained a small quantity of cocaine had probably been good for my mood: the bunch of deadly nightshade that I had eaten with only a slight narcotic effect: the twenty aspirins I had taken before swimming in the empty out-of-term school baths (I can still remember the curious sensation of swimming through wool): these acts may have removed all sense of strangeness as I slipped a bullet into a chamber and, holding the revolver behind my back, spun the chambers round.

Had I romantic thoughts about the governess? Undoubtedly I must have had, but I think that at the most they simply eased the medicine down. Boredom, aridity, those were the main emotions. Unhappy love has, I suppose, sometimes driven boys to suicide, but this was not suicide, whatever a coroner's jury might have said of it: it was a gamble with six chances to one against an inquest. The romantic flavour—the autumn scene, the small heavy compact shape lying in the fingers—that perhaps was a tribute to adolescent love, but the discovery that it was possible to enjoy again the visible world by risking its total loss was one I was bound to make sooner or later.

I put the muzzle of the revolver in my right ear and pulled the trigger. There was a minute click, and looking down at the chamber I could see that the charge had moved into place. I was out by one. I remember an extraordinary sense of jubilation. It was as if a light had been turned on. My heart was knocking in its cage, and I felt that life contained an infinite number of possibilities. It was like a young man's first successful experience of sex— as if in that Ashridge glade one had passed a test of manhood. I went home and put the revolver back in the corner cupboard.

The odd thing about this experience was that it was repeated several times. At fairly long intervals I found myself craving for the drug. I took the revolver with me when I went up to Oxford and I would walk out from Headington towards Elsfield down what is now a wide arterial road, smooth and shiny like the walls of a public lavatory. Then it was a sodden unfrequented country lane. The revolver would be whipped behind my back, the chambers twisted, the muzzle quickly and surreptitiously inserted beneath the black and ugly winter tree, the trigger pulled.

Slowly the effect of the drug wore off—I lost the sense of jubilation, I began to gain from the experience only the crude kick of excitement. It was like the difference between love and lust. And as the quality of the experience deteriorated so my sense of responsibility grew and worried me. I wrote a very bad piece of free verse (free because it was easier in that way to express my meaning without literary equivocation) describing how, in order to give a fictitious sense of danger, I would "press the trigger of a revolver I already know to be empty." This piece of verse I would leave permanently on my desk, so that if I lost my gamble, there would be incontrovertible evidence of an accident, and my parents, I thought, would be less troubled than by an apparent suicide—or than by the rather bizarre truth.

But it was back at Berkhamstead that I paid a permanent farewell to the drug. As I took my fifth dose it occurred to me that I wasn't even excited: I was beginning to pull the trigger about as casually as I might take an aspirin tablet. I decided to give the revolver—which was six-chambered—a sixth and last chance. Twirling the chambers round, I put the muzzle to my ear for the last time and heard the familiar empty click as the chambers revolved. I was through with the drug, and walking back over the Common, down the new road by the ruined castle, past the private entrance to the gritty old railway station—reserved for the use of Lord Brownlow—my mind was already busy on other plans. One campaign was over, but the war against boredom had got to go on.

I put the revolver back in the corner cupboard, and going downstairs I lied gently and convincingly to my parents that a friend had invited me to join him in Paris.

STUDY QUESTIONS

1. Was Greene deliberately and repeatedly attempting suicide? Had he attempted suicide before?

2. How did the governess contribute to Greene's state of mind? Was she the main reason for it?

3. Earlier, why had Greene run away from school?

4. Why did he eventually stop playing his dangerous, solitary game?

5. What is the point of the lie he tells his parents?

6. Why is the first-person point-of-view particularly effective in this essay? Besides the obvious changes of pronouns and tenses, what changes would a third-person point-of-view have necessitated?

George Orwell

A HANGING

George Orwell (1903–1950) was the pen name of Eric Blair, who was born in Bengal, India. He graduated from Eton College, served with the Indian Imperial Police in Burma from 1922 to 1927, and then returned to England to begin his career as a writer. His works include *Burmese Days* (1934), *Homage to Catalonia* (1936) *Dickens, Dali, and Others* (1946), and *Shooting an Elephant* (1950). His fame, however, is primarily the result of *Animal Farm* (1946) and *1984* (1949), the former one of the most famous modern satires and the latter a classic novel of social protest. His *Collected Essays* were published in 1969.

I T WAS in Burma, a sodden morning of the rains. A sickly
light, like yellow tinfoil, was slanting over the high walls
into the jail yard. We were waiting outside the condemned
cells, a row of sheds fronted with double bars, like small animal cages. Each
cell measured about ten feet by ten and was quite bare within except for a
plank bed and a pot for drinking water. In some of them brown, silent men
were squatting at the inner bars, with their blankets draped round them.
These were the condemned men, due to be hanged within the next week or
two.

One prisoner had been brought out of his cell. He was a Hindu, a puny
wisp of a man, with a shaven head and vague liquid eyes. He had a thick,
sprouting moustache, absurdly too big for his body, rather like the moustache of a comic man on the films. Six tall Indian warders were guarding him
and getting him ready for the gallows. Two of them stood by with rifles and
fixed bayonets, while the others handcuffed him, passed a chain through his
handcuffs and fixed it to their belts, and lashed his arms tight to his sides.
They crowded very close about him, with their hands always on him in a
careful, caressing grip, as though all the while feeling him to make sure he
was there. It was like men handling a fish which is still alive and may jump
back into the water. But he stood quite unresisting, yielding his arms limply
to the ropes, as though he hardly noticed what was happening.

Eight o'clock struck and a bugle call, desolately thin in the wet air, floated
from the distant barracks. The superintendent of the jail, who was standing
apart from the rest of us, moodily prodding the gravel with his stick, raised
his head at the sound. He was an army doctor, with a grey toothbrush moustache and a gruff voice. "For God's sake hurry up, Francis," he said irri-
tably. "The man ought to have been dead by this time. Aren't you ready
yet?"

Francis, the head jailer, a fat Dravidian in a white drill suit and gold spectacles, waved his black hand. "Yes sir, yes sir," he bubbled. "All iss satisfactorily prepared. The hangman iss waiting. We shall proceed."

"Well, quick march, then. The prisoners can't get their breakfast till this
job's over."

We set out for the gallows. Two warders marched on either side of the
prisoner, with their rifles at the slope; two others marched close against him,
gripping him by arm and shoulder, as though at once pushing and supporting him. The rest of us, magistrates and the like, followed behind. Suddenly,
when we had gone ten yards, the procession stopped short without any order
or warning. A dreadful thing had happened—a dog, come goodness knows
whence, had appeared in the yard. It came bounding among us with a loud
volley of barks and leapt round us wagging its whole body, wild with glee at

finding so many human beings together. It was a large woolly dog, half Aire-dale, half pariah. For a moment it pranced round us, and then, before any-one could stop it, it had made a dash for the prisoner, and jumping up tried to lick his face. Everybody stood aghast, too taken aback even to grab the dog.

"Who let that bloody brute in here?" said the superintendent angrily. "Catch it, someone!"

A warder detached from the escort, charged clumsily after the dog, but it danced and gambolled just out of his reach, taking everything as part of the game. A young Eurasian jailer picked up a handful of gravel and tried to stone the dog away, but it dodged the stones and came after us again. Its yaps echoed from the jail walls. The prisoner, in the grasp of the two war-dens, looked on incuriously, as though this was another formality of the hanging. It was several minutes before someone managed to catch the dog. Then we put my handkerchief through its collar and moved off once more, with the dog still straining and whimpering.

It was about forty yards to the gallows. I watched the bare brown back of the prisoner marching in front of me. He walked clumsily with his bound arms, but quite steadily, with that bobbing gait of the Indian who never straightens his knees. At each step his muscles slid neatly into place, the lock of hair on his scalp danced up and down, his feet printed themselves on the wet gravel. And once, in spite of the men who gripped him by each shoulder, he stepped lightly aside to avoid a puddle on the path.

It is curious, but till that moment I had never realized what it means to destroy a healthy, conscious man. When I saw the prisoner step aside to avoid the puddle I saw the mystery, the unspeakable wrongness, of cutting a life short when it is in full tide. This man was not dying, he was alive just as we are alive. All the organs of his body were working—bowels digesting food, skin renewing itself, nails growing, tissues forming—all toiling away in solemn foolery. His nails would still be growing when he stood on the drop, when he was falling through the air with a tenth-of-a-second to live. His eyes saw the yellow gravel and the grey walls, and his brain still remem-bered, foresaw, reasoned—even about puddles. He and we were a party of men walking together, seeing, hearing, feeling, understanding the same world; and in two minutes, with a sudden snap, one of us would be gone— one mind less, one world less.

The gallows stood in a small yard, separate from the main grounds of the prison, and overgrown with tall prickly weeds. It was a brick erection like three sides of a shed, with planking on top, and above that two beams and a crossbar with the rope dangling. The hangman, a grey-haired convict in the white uniform of the prison, was waiting beside his machine. He greeted us with a servile crouch as we entered. At a word from Francis the two warders, gripping the prisoner more closely than ever, half led, half pushed him to the gallows and helped him clumsily up the ladder. Then the hangman climbed up and fixed the rope round the prisoner's neck.

We stood waiting, five yards away. The warders had formed in a rough circle round the gallows. And then, when the noose was fixed, the prisoner began crying to his god. It was a high, reiterated cry of "Ram! Ram! Ram! Ram!" not urgent and fearful like a prayer or cry for help, but steady, rhythmical, almost like the tolling of a bell. The dog answered the sound with a whine. The hangman, still standing on the gallows, produced a small cotton bag like a flour bag and drew it down over the prisoner's face. But the sound, muffled by the cloth, still persisted, over and over again: "Ram! Ram! Ram! Ram! Ram!"

The hangman climbed down and stood ready, holding the lever. Minutes seemed to pass. The steady, muffled crying from the prisoner went on and on, "Ram! Ram! Ram!" never faltering for an instant. The superintendent, his head on his chest, was slowly poking the ground with his stick; perhaps he was counting the cries, allowing the prisoner a fixed number—fifty, perhaps, or a hundred. Everyone had changed colour. The Indians had gone grey like bad coffee, and one or two of the bayonets were wavering. We looked at the lashed, hooded man on the drop, and listened to his cries— each cry another second of life; the same thought was in all our minds: oh, kill him quickly, get it over, stop that abominable noise!

Suddenly the superintendent made up his mind. Throwing up his head he made a swift motion with his stick. "Chalo!" he shouted almost fiercely.

There was a clanking noise, and then dead silence. The prisoner had vanished, and the rope was twisting on itself. I let go of the dog, and it galloped immediately to the back of the gallows; but when it got there it stopped short, barked, and then retreated into a corner of the yard, where it stood among the weeds, looking timorously out at us. We went round the gallows to inspect the prisoner's body. He was dangling with his toes pointed straight downwards, very slowly revolving, as dead as a stone.

The superintendent reached out with his stick and poked the bare brown body; it oscillated slightly. "*He's* all right," said the superintendent. He backed out from under the gallows, and blew out a deep breath. The moody look had gone out of his face quite suddenly. He glanced at his wrist-watch. "Eight minutes past eight. Well, that's all for this morning, thank God."

The warders unfixed bayonets and marched away. The dog, sobered and conscious of having misbehaved itself, slipped after them. We walked out of the gallows yard, past the condemned cells with their waiting prisoners, into the big central yard of the prison. The convicts, under the command of warders armed with lathis, were already receiving their breakfast. They squatted in long rows, each man holding a tin pannikin, while two warders with buckets marched round ladling out rice; it seemed quite a homely, jolly scene, after the hanging. An enormous relief had come upon us now that the job was done. One felt an impulse to sing, to break into a run, to snigger. All at once everyone began chattering gaily.

The Eurasian boy walking beside me nodded towards the way we had come, with a knowing smile: "Do you know, sir, our friend (he meant the dead man) when he heard his appeal had been dismissed, he pissed on the floor of his cell. From fright. Kindly take one of my cigarettes, sir. Do you not admire my new silver case, sir? From the boxwallah, two rupees eight annas. Classy European style."

Several people laughed—at what, nobody seemed certain.

Francis was walking by the superintendent, talking garrulously: "Well, sir, all hass passed off with the utmost satisfactoriness. It was all finished— flick! like that. It iss not always so—oah, no! I have known cases where the doctor wass obliged to go beneath the gallows and pull the prissoner's legs to ensure decease. Most disagreeable!"

"Wriggling about, eh? That's bad," said the superintendent.

"Ach, sir, it iss worse when they become refractory! One man, I recall, clung to the bars of hiss cage when we went to take him out. You will scarcely credit, sir, that it took six warders to dislodge him, three pulling at each leg. We reasoned with him, 'My dear fellow,' we said, 'think of all the pain and trouble you are causing to us!' But no, he would not listen! Ach, he wass very troublesome!"

I found that I was laughing quite loudly. Everyone was laughing. Even the superintendent grinned in a tolerant way. "You'd better all come out and have a drink," he said quite genially. "I've got a bottle of whisky in the car. We could do with it."

We went through the big double gates of the prison into the road. "Pulling at his legs!" exclaimed a Burmese magistrate suddenly, and burst into a loud chuckling. We all began laughing again. At that moment Francis' anecdote seemed extraordinarily funny. We all had a drink together, native and European alike, quite amicably. The dead man was a hundred yards away.

STUDY QUESTIONS

1. Why is the superintendent irritated by the delay in the hanging?

2. How does the incident with the dog contribute to the effectiveness of "A Hanging"?

3. Why does the prisoner's stepping aside to avoid a puddle bring Orwell to a full realization of the scene before him?

4. Why do the men feel an impulse to sing, to break into a run, to snigger after the hanging? Why does Orwell end his essay with, "The dead man was a hundred yards away"?

5. What is the tone of the essay? How does the narrator's attitude toward the hanging help determine the response elicited from the reader?

Section Two

Modern Social Problems

"Some Must Watch"

Ebony

WHAT WHITES CAN LEARN
FROM NEGROES

$\mathcal{T}$ROUBLE don't last always, says an old Negro spiritual, but according to screaming newspaper headlines, convulsed TV commentators and a frayed-nerved public, Old Man Trouble has pitched his teepee square in the middle of the twentieth century and settled down for a record run.

The whole world is on edge. Nations are bickering with nations. Races are pitted against races. Everybody seems beset by fears, overwrought by frustrations. They are jittery about the war in Viet Nam that had no beginning and the war that has no ending in the Dominican Republic and the cold war that occasionally gets mighty warm. They are hearing noises that do not exist, seeing objects that are not there.

In times like these, white people seeking a panacea for their problems might well take a lesson from the Negro on how to live in a troubled world. The Negro is an expert. He has known nothing but trouble all of his life. His grievances are multiple for he has all of the white man's fears and doubts plus the additional burden of being black. Yet the Negro can still smile, for the progress that he has made up from slavery to his present status—short of first class citizenship though it is—is one of the most remarkable advancements in the history of mankind. In the process he has learned to turn his liabilities into assets, to adjust to that over which he has no control and to have faith in his ability to overcome all of the other obstacles between himself and full equality.

The Philosophy of "If"

The way to tell a Negro from a white man when physical appearances failed, swore the old time armchair anthropologists, was to engage the suspect in conversation. Query him about his ambitions, his future plans, his

Reprinted from *The White Problem in America*. First published in *Ebony*, August 1965. With permission of the publishers.

next step. If he said he "hoped" to become a lawyer or a merchant, that he "wanted" to buy a car, spend his vacation in Canada, then that man was white. But if he prefaced his desire by the phrase: "If I live and nothing happens," he was colored. This homely philosophy with the built-in disaster clause allowed the Negro to take his setbacks and misfortunes in stride. It was this philosophy, born of heart-breaking experiences, which kept his insanity and suicide rates below those of his fair-skinned brothers. But today's Negro has added a positive dimension to a probable clause. If he lives, he will *make* something happen.

The white man stakes his all on a business venture or a political campaign. He will even put his life's savings in schemes that can pay off only with a hoped-for boom, and bet his last five dollars on a long-shot nag. If he loses he will have an opportunity to recoup and start all over again, but all too often, he is found below an open window or his last will and testament is contained in a brief note on the railing of a bridge.

The Negro, whose existence is riddled with reverses and disappointments, has learned not to put all of his eggs in one shopping bag or his complete trust in one man. He knows that if he fails, there is no second chance. For him there are no short cuts to success. Only through his own supreme efforts can he attain his cherished goal. When bad luck overtook him, he used to console himself with the adage that "everything happens for the best." Today, he does not wait for things to happen, and the best may not be good enough. Instead of taking his troubles to the window or the water, he is more likely to try them in the courts or dramatize them in the streets.

The Negro is particularly adept at making the best of a bad situation, not because of any inherent powers that he may have, but because he has had an abundance of practice and more bad situations than the white man. More put upon and less protected than any other ethnic group in our society except the Indian, he has been under the strain of racial tensions all of his life; has always been handicapped by patterns of prejudice and walls of discrimination. The Negro in America is kept so busy trying to live under the same flag as the Ku Klux Klan, the White Citizens Councils and other hate-Negro, hate-minority organizations, that he has little time to worry about communism in China or India's population explosion.

A nuclear bomb which he may never see is not nearly as imminent as an electric cattle prod he has felt. Wars in distant lands in which he too must fight, are not as personal as demonstrations in Chicago or boycotts in Birmingham. Although some white citizens would rather cloud the image of this country abroad than practice democracy here at home, the Negro remains loyal to America. He fights for it and he dies for it and he hopes fervently that it will soon be at peace, for he needs all his war-spent energies to earn his daily bread and a little butter. Now that his right to the ballot has been reaffirmed, he needs his war-spent strength to make things happen: to lead registration drives in the South and to discourage voter apathy in the North, to exercise his right to live where his money and desires dictate, to obtain better education for his children, to fit himself for a better job so that he can improve his standard of living. He knows that these things are now possible, but wishing alone will not make them so.

In the South and to some extent in the North, the Negro's very existence once depended upon his ability to get along with white people. The psychology of fear employed by race supremacists to frighten him into 100 years of submission is no longer applicable. His is the faith that overcomes, the courage that marches around bigots and laughs at the Klan. His is an example of faith and courage that other men might follow.

Trapped in a white-dominated world, the black man has learned to live with trouble. To yesterday's motto "don't get mad, get smart," he has added "do something!" If white men are to have peace of mind they must also stop getting mad and getting nervous and do something. For one thing, they must learn to live with men who are black and red and yellow and brown. They, too, must learn to become bedfellows with fear and frustration, to turn liabilities into assets, adjust to that which cannot be helped and change those things that are morally wrong.

To master the art of doing with and doing without is essential to all men. With very little of this world's goods the Negro has been able to an unbelievable degree to survive—even thrive—under oppressions, uncertainties and inconveniences. He has worn hand-me-down clothing, lived in second-class housing, worked at low-paying jobs. But those conditions were morally wrong and he found a way to change them. In doing so, he has transferred his disappointments into hopes and hopes into actions and actions into improvements which, if continued, will bring him the full equality and ultimate happiness all men seek.

If white people would profit by the Negro's ability to overcome, they can begin by cultivating his sense of humor. His public posture may be that of the angry young man, but his capacity to laugh at his troubles, even though he does so in the privacy of his race, is his means of releasing pent-up emotions. White people who would have peace of mind, must ease their guilty consciences. Like the Negro, they must put their trust in God and their shoulder to the wheel. Faith alone will not move mountains.

If the black man can make it by adding new dimensions to old adages, surely white men can follow his example. No people can have peace always nor can their prosperity continue unbroken. All of this country's citizens have worked hard and sacrificed much to make America the great nation that it is today. Surely those who by virtue of color have inherited the bulk of her many benefits can, like the Negro, learn to endure her limitations.

1. How does the author use comparison and contrast to develop his thesis?

2. What does the author mean by the philosophy of "if"?

3. According to the essay, how does the Negro's sense of humor serve him?

4. Do you regard the author's advice as practical? Is the white man prepared to follow such course of action as the author recommends?

5. Is the author's strategy to appeal to the reader's reason or his emotions?

William Styron

IT IS DONE
(Part IV, *The Confessions of Nat Turner*)

William Styron (1925–   ), well-known author, is a native of the Tidewater region of Virginia, the area where Nat Turner's revolt took place. Styron earned his college degree at Duke University. He has been honored by the American Academy of Arts and Letters and by the National Institute of Arts and Literature. Before writing *The Confessions of Nat Turner* (1967), he had published three novels: *Lie Down in Darkness* (1951), *The Long March* (1953), and *Set This House On Fire* (1960). In addition he has published numerous short stories and articles.

SURELY I COME QUICKLY . . .
           Cloudless sunlight suggesting neither hour nor season glows down upon me, wraps me with a cradle's warmth as I drift toward the river's estuary; the little boat rocks gently in our benign descent together toward the sea. On the unpeopled banks the woods are silent, silent as snowfall. No birds call; in windless attitudes of meditation the

crowd of green trees along the river shore stands drooping and still. This low country seems untouched by humanity, by past or future time. Beneath me where I recline I feel the boat's sluggish windward drift, glimpse rushing past eddies of foam, branches, leaves, clumps of grass all borne on the serene unhurried flood to the place where the river meets the sea. Faintly now I hear the oceanic roar, mark the sweep of sunlit water far-near, glinting with whitecaps, the ragged shoulder of a beach where sea and river join in a tumultuous embrace of swirling waters. But nothing disturbs me, I drowse in the arms of a steadfast and illimitable peace. Salt stings my nostrils. The breakers roll to shore, the lordly tide swells back beneath a cobalt sky arching eastward toward Africa. An unhurried booming fills me not with fear but only with repose and slumbrous anticipation—serenity as ageless as those rocks, in garlands of weeping seaweed, thrown up by the groaning waves.

Now as I approach the edge of land I look up for one last time to study the white building standing on its promontory high above the shore. Again I cannot tell what it is or what it means. Stark white, glittering, pure as alabaster, it rests on the precipice unravaged by weather or wind, neither temple nor monument nor sarcophagus but relic of the ages—of all past and all futurity—white inscrutable paradigm of a mystery beyond utterance or even wonder. The sun bathes its tranquil marble sides, its doorless façade, the arches that sweep around it, revealing no entry anywhere, no window; inside, it would be as dark as the darkest tomb. Yet I cannot dwell on that place too long, for again as always I know that to try to explore the mystery would be only to throw open portals on even deeper mysteries, on and on everlastingly, into the remotest corridors of thought and time. So I turn away. I cast my eyes toward the ocean once more, watch the blue waves and glitter of spume-borne light approaching, listen to the breaking surf move near as I pass, slowly, in contemplation of a great mystery, out toward the sea . . .

I come awake with a start, feeling the cedar plank cold beneath my back, the leg irons colder still—like encircling bands of ice. It is full dark, I can see nothing. I rise up on my elbows, letting the dream dwindle away from my mind, fade out—this one last time, and forever—from recollection. The chains at my feet chink in the morning's black silence. It is bitterly cold but the wind has died and I no longer shiver so; I draw the remnant of my ragged shirt close around my chest. Then I tap with my knuckles against the wall separating me from Hark. He sleeps deeply, his breath a jagged sigh as it rattles through his wound. *Tap-tap.* Silence. *Tap-tap* again, louder. Hark awakes. "Dat you, Nat?"

"It's me," I reply, "we go soon."

He is quiet for a moment. Then he says, yawning: "I knows it. Lawd, I wish dey would git on wid it. What time it is you reckon, Nat?"

"I don't know," I say, "they must be a couple hours more."

I hear the heavy thump of his feet and the sound of his chain-links clinking together, then the noise of a bucket scraping across the floor. Hark chuckles faintly. "Lawd me, Nat," he says. "Wisht I could move about. Hit hard enough to pee lyin' down in de daytime, at night I cain't hit dat bucket in no way." I hear a noisy spatter and splash and Hark's laughter again, low in his throat, rich, amused at himself. "Ain't nothin' mo' useless dan a twofifty-pound nigger dat cain't hardly move. Did you know, Nat, dey gwine hang me all roped up in a *chair?* Leastwise, dat's what dat man Gray done said. Dat sho' is *some* way to go."

I make no reply, the sound of flowing water ceases, and Hark's voice too falls still. Somewhere far off in the town a dog howls on and on without lull or respite, a continuous harsh lonely cry from the bowels of the dark morning, touching me with dread. *Lord,* I whisper to myself in anguish, *Lord?* And I clench my eyelids together in a sudden spasm, hoping to find some vision, some word or sign in the profounder darkness of my own mind, but there is still no answer. I will go without Him, I think, I will go without Him because He has abandoned me without any last sign at all. Was what I done wrong in His sight? And if what I done was wrong is there no redemption?

"Dat God durned dog," I hear Hark say. "Lissen at him, Nat. Dat sho de sign of somepn, awright. Lawd, dat dog done barked right on th'ough my dreams jes' now. Dreamed I was back home at Barnett's long long time ago when I was jes' a little ole thing 'bout knee-high to a duck. An' me an' my sister Jamie was gwine fishin' together down in de swamp. And we was walkin' along underneath dem wild cherry trees, jes' as happy as we could be, talkin' about all dem fish we was gwine catch. On'y dey dis yere dog a-barkin' at us an followin' us th'ough the woods. An' Jamie she done kep' sayin', 'Hark, how come dat dog make all dat holler?' An' I say back to Jamie, 'Don' bothah 'bout no dog, don' pay dat ole dog no nem'mine.' Den you done knock on de wall, Nat, and now here dat *same* dog a-barkin' way off in de road, and here *I* is, an' dis mornin' dey gwine hang me."

Then behold I come quickly . . .

I drowse off dreamless for a time, then I wake abruptly to see that morning approaches with the faintest tinge of pale frosty light, stealing through the barred window and touching the cedar walls with a glow barely visible, like ashes strewn upon a dying fire. Way off in the lowlands across the river, somewhere among the fields and frosty meadows, I hear the sad old blast of a horn as it rouses up the Negroes for work. Nearer there is a tinkle and a rustle, barely heard; the town stirs. A single horse passes *cloppetyclop* over the wooden bridge, and far away in the distance a cock crows, then another, and they cease suddenly; for a moment all is still and sleeping. Hark again slumbers, the air whistles from his wounded chest. I rise and make my way to the end of the chain, shuffling in a sideways motion toward the window. Then I lean forward against the freezing sill, and stand motionless in the still-encompassing dark. Against the rim of the heavens, high above the river and the towering wall of cypress and pine, dawn begins to rise in light of the softest blue. I raise my eyes upward. There alone amidst the blue, steadfast, unmoving, fiery marvel of brightness, shines the morning star. Never has that star seemed so radiant, and I stand gazing at it and do not move though the chill of the damp floor imprisons my feet in piercing ice-bound pain.

Surely I come quickly . . .

I wait for minutes at the window, looking out at the new day which is still dark. Behind me I hear a noise in the tiny corridor, hear Kitchen's keys jangling, and see against the walls a lantern's ruddy orange glow. Footsteps scrape on the floor with a gritty sound. I turn about slowly and find that it is Gray. But this time he does not enter the cell, merely stands outside the door as he peers in, then beckons me with his finger. With clumsy trouble I move across the floor, chain dragging between my feet. In the lantern light I see that he is clasping something in his hand; when I draw closer to the door I can tell that it is a Bible. For once Gray seems quiet, subdued.

"I brung you what you asked for, Reverend," he says in a soft voice. So composed does he seem, so tranquil, so gentle are his tones, that I almost take him for another man. "I done it against the will of the court. It's my doing, my risk. But you've been pretty fair and square with me, all in all. You can have this solace if you want it."

He hands the Bible to me through the bars of the door. For a long moment we gaze at each other in the flickering light and I have a strange sensation which passes almost as quickly as it comes, that never have I seen this man in my life. I say nothing to him in answer. At last he reaches through the bars and grasps my hand; as he does so I know by some strange and tentative feeling in his hasty grip that this is the first black hand he has ever shaken, no doubt the last.

"Good-bye, Reverend," he says.

"Good-bye, Mr. Gray," I reply.

Then he is gone, the lantern flame fades and dies out, and the cell again is filled with darkness. I turn and place the Bible down gently on the cedar plank. I know that I would not open it now even if I had the light to read it by. Yet its presence warms the cell and for the first time since I have been in jail, for the first time since I gazed into his irksome face, I feel a wrench of pity for Gray and for his mortal years to come. Again I move to the window, inhaling deeply the wintry morning air. It tastes of smoke, of burning apple

wood, and I am flooded with swift shifting memories, too sweet to bear, of
all distant childhood, of old time past. I lean against the sill of the window,
and gaze up at the morning star. *Surely I come quickly . . .*

Then behold I come quickly . . .
And as I think of her, the desire swells within me and I am stirred by a
longing so great that like those memories of time past and long-ago voices,
flowing waters, rushing winds, it seems more than my heart can abide. *Beloved, let us love one another: for love is of God; and everyone that loveth is
born of God, and knoweth God.* Her voice is close, familiar, real, and for an
instant I mistake the wind against my ear, a gentle gust, for her breath, and I
turn to seek her in the darkness. And now beyond my fear, beyond my dread
and emptiness, I feel the warmth flow into my loins and my legs tingle with
desire. I tremble and I search for her face in my mind, seek her young body,
yearning for her suddenly with a rage that racks me with a craving beyond
pain; with tender stroking motions I pour out my love within her; pulsing
flood; she arches against me, cries out, and the twain—black and white—
are one. I faint slowly. My head falls toward the window, my breath comes
hard. I recall a meadow, June, the voice a whisper: *Is it not true, Nat? Did
He not say, I am the root and the offspring of David, and the bright and
morning star?*

Surely I come quickly . . .
Footsteps outside the door jar me from my reverie, I hear white men's
voices. Again a lantern casts a bloom of light through the cell, but the half-
dozen men go past with thumping boots and stop at Hark's door. I hear jin-
gling keys and a bolt slides back with a thud. I turn and see the outline of two
men pushing the chair past my door. Its legs bump and clatter on the plank
floor, there is a heavy jolt as its arms strike against the doorjamb of Hark's
cell. "Raise up," I hear one of the men say to Hark. "Raise yore ass up, we
got to rope you in." There is silence, then a creaking sound. I hear Hark
begin to moan in pain. "Easy dar!" he cries out, gasping. *"Easy!"*
"Move his legs," I hear one of the white men order another.
"Grab him by the arms," says someone else.
Hark's voice becomes a wail of hurt and wild distress. The sound of
bumping and shoving fills the air.
"Easy!" Hark cries out, sobbing.
"Push him down!" says a voice.
I find myself hammering at the walls. *"Don't hurt him!"* I rage. "Don't
hurt him, you white sons of bitches! You've done hurt him enough! All his
life! Now God damn you don't hurt him no more!"

Silence descends as the men cease talking. In a long drawn-out breath Hark's wail dies away. Now I hear a hurried sound of snapping ropes as they tie him into the chair. Then the white men whisper and grunt while they strain beneath the weight of their burden and lift Hark out into the hallway. Shadows leap up and quiver in the lantern's brassy radiance. The white men shuffle in furious labor, gasping with the effort. Hark's bound and seated shape, like the silhouette of some marvelous black potentate borne in stately procession toward his throne, passes slowly by my door. I reach out as if to touch him, feel nothing, clutch only a handful of air.

"Dis yere some way to go," I hear Hark say. "Good-bye, ole Nat!" he calls.

"Good-bye, Hark," I whisper, "good-bye, good-bye."

"Hit gwine be all right, Nat," he cries out to me, the voice fading. "Ev'y-thin' gwine be all right! Dis yere ain't nothin', Nat, nothin' atall! Good-bye, ole Nat, good-bye!"

Good-bye, Hark, good-bye.

The edge of dawn pales, brightens; stars wink away like dying sparks as the night fades and dusty sunrise begins to streak the far sky. Yet steadfast the morning star rides in the heavens radiant and pure, set like crystal amid the still waters of eternity. Morning blooms softly upon the rutted streets of Jerusalem; the howling dog and the crowing roosters at last are silent. Somewhere behind me in the jail I hear a murmuration of voices; I sense a presence at my back, I feel the approach of gigantic, unrelenting footfalls. I turn and retrieve the Bible from the cedar plank and for one last time take my station by the window, breathing deeply in the apple-sweet air. My breath is smoke, I shudder in the cold newborn beauty of the world. The footsteps draw near, suddenly cease. There is a rattle of bolts and keys. A voice says: "Nat!" And when I do not answer, the same voice calls out: "Come!"

We'll love one another, she seems to be entreating me, very close now, *we'll love one another by the light of heaven above.* I feel the nearness of flowing waters, tumultuous waves, rushing winds. The voice calls again: "Come!"

Yes, I think just before I turn to greet him, *I would have done it all again. I would have destroyed them all. Yet I would have spared one. I would have spared her that showed me Him whose presence I had not fathomed or maybe never even known. Great God, how early it is! Until now I had almost forgotten His name.*

"Come!" the voice booms, but commanding me now: *Come, My son!* I turn in surrender.

Surely I come quickly. Amen.

Even so, come, Lord Jesus.

Oh how bright and fair the morning star . . .

The bodies of those executed, with one exception, were buried in a decent
and becoming manner. That of Nat Turner was delivered to the doctors,
who skinned it and made grease of the flesh. Mr. R. S. Barham's father
owned a money purse made of his hide. His skeleton was for many years in
the possession of Dr. Massenberg, but has since been misplaced.

—Drewry, *The Southampton Insurrection*

*   *   *

And he said unto me, It is done.
I am Alpha and Omega, the beginning and
the end. I will give unto him that is
athirst of the fountain of the water
of life freely. He that overcometh shall inherit
all things; and I will be his God and
he shall be my son.

STUDY QUESTIONS

1. What poetic qualities do you find in the language of Nat's dreams and
    reveries?

2. What can we surmise about Nat's character and personality from this
    selection? Note what he thinks, dreams, says, and does; note also the
    tone he employs in relating these.

3. What is the rhetorical effect of the repetitive "Then behold I come
    quickly" and "Surely I come quickly"?

4. What is the significance of the howling dog Nat hears in the distance?

5. Does this selection present a creditable portrayal of a condemned man
    in his final hours of life?

C. Vann Woodward

CONFESSIONS OF A REBEL: 1831

C. Vann Woodward (1908–   ) is an eminent historian who has received numerous honors and awards for his work in Southern history. He earned his undergraduate degree at Emory University, his M.A. at Columbia University and Oxford University, and his Ph.D. at the University of North Carolina. He has taught history at the University of Florida, the University of Virginia, Scripps College, Johns Hopkins University, Harvard University, the University of Chicago, Louisiana State University and the University of London. He was the Harnsworth Professor of American History at Oxford University and the Stirling Professor at Yale University. He has been accorded honors by the National Institute of Arts and Letters, the Social Science Research Council, and the American Council of Learned Societies. Among his books are the following: *Tom Watkins; Agrarian Rebel* (1938), *The Battle For Leyte Gulf* (1947), *Origins of the New South* (1951), *Reunion and Reaction* (1951), *The Burden of Southern History* (1960), and *The Comparative Approach to American History* (1960).

IN THE ANNALS of American slavery two figures stand out with unrivaled prominence among the very few who resorted to armed rebellion—John Brown and Nat Turner, one white and one black. The historical importance of their roles is roughly comparable and there is as much reason for enduring curiosity about the one as about the other. Of the two, Turner's rebellion was far more bloody, both in the lives it took and in the reprisals it evoked. As a threat to the security of a slave based society, Turner's conspiracy was more momentous than Brown's. John Brown's Raid never had the remotest chance of success.

Yet there is a remarkable disparity in the amount that is known and in what has been written about the two men and their deeds. On John Brown there exists a vast library, forty-odd biographies, massive monographs, scores of poems, plays, and works of fiction. This is partly explained by the relative abundance of source materials. Brown left extensive (though mis-leading) accounts of himself and a large mass of correspondence. He was acquainted with some of the most prominent writers of his day. A few intel-lectuals were personally involved and many were passionately interested in his conspiracy and left their own records. Two congressional hearings and a mountain of archival material multiply the sources.

In striking contrast, the sources on Nat Turner and the scholarly as well as creative writing about him are minuscule. Since there were no white par-ticipants in the rebellion and the life of no white witness of the massacres was spared by the rebels, the information about the conspiracy boils down largely to twenty-odd pages of Turner's "Confessions" in the stilted prose of the Virginia lawyer to whom he dictated them in prison. Mainly on this and on a pedestrian monograph or two rests all we know of the only slave rebel-lion of consequence in the largest slave society in the 19th-century world.

If there were ever a free hand for a novelist, this was it. Yet the obstacles were formidable. There were no models. The only major American novelist to treat a slave rebellion was Melville, and *Benito Cereno* is viewed entirely through the eyes of the white man. Nat's story would have to be seen from behind the black mask. That was the boldest decision William Styron made. There was little to go on beyond the author's imagination. What history tells us about slavery is mainly the white man's experience, not the black man's —what it was like to *have* slaves, not what it was like to *be* slaves. No one has more than an ill-informed guess about why the greatest slave republic in the New World had by far the fewest rebellions; why smaller and alleg-edly more benevolent slave societies bred vast insurrections, blood baths in-volving many thousands of slaves that lasted scores of years, and America had one that recruited seventy-five and petered out in three days; why ser-vility and submission were the rule and Sambo the stereotype and heritage of American slavery. And most of all, what explains the terrible enigma of Nat Turner, the other-worldly young carpenter of obscure origins and apoc-alyptic visions who at the age of thirty-one took the road to Jerusalem, Va., martyrdom, and immortality.

To complicate the enigma, the rebellion took place not in the brutal Delta cotton fields or the Louisiana sugar cane, but in mellowed, impoverished tidewater Virginia, where even Nat Turner thought there was "still an ebb and flow of human sympathy—no matter how strained and imperfect— between slave and master." And Nat himself was a product of benevolent, if unusual, paternalism at its best—fondly educated, trained in a craft, and promised liberation. The picture of Nat's life and motivation the novelist constructs is, but for a few scraps of evidence, without historical underpin-nings, but most historians would agree, I think, not inconsistent with any-thing historians know. It is informed by a respect for history, a sure feeling for the period, and a deep and precise sense of place and time.

Nat was the child of a house servant and grew up in the big house, familiar with "the chink of silver and china" as well as his "black Negro world" of the kitchen, but not with the toil of field and mill. His mistress taught him to read and gave him a Bible, of which he learned great parts by heart and knew better than the white preachers of the parish. He discovered his intelligence and his ability to charm, grew accustomed to love from all sides, and never encountered harshness or brutality. "I became in short a pet, the darling, the little black jewel of Turner's Mill. Pampered, fondled, nudged, pinched, I was the household's spoiled child." Toward his master, Samuel Turner, he felt a regard "very close to the feeling one should bear only toward the Divinity." Between them were "strong ties of emotion," in fact, "a kind of love." The master responded by giving encouragement, careful training, flattering responsibilities, and three years before Nat came of age, the intoxicating promise of freedom. Toward the field hands beyond the big house perimeter little Nat felt a contemptuous disdain, regarding them as "a lower order of people—a ragtag mob, coarse, raucous, clownish, uncouth." He identified completely with his master and looking back later realized that had this life continued he would have achieved in old age "a kind of purse-lipped dignity, known as Uncle Nat, well loved and adoring in return, a palsied stroker of the silken pates of little white grandchildren." But that life came to an end when Samuel Turner went bankrupt and moved to Alabama when Nat was twenty. Before leaving Virginia he placed Nat in the care of a poverty-ravaged, fanatical Baptist preacher under legal obligation to free his charge in a stated time. Instead, after giving Nat a year's taste of how degrading slavery could be, the preacher sold him for $460 to an illiterate brute named Moore, from whom he eventually passed into the hands of his last owner, Travis. Among the many harsh lessons these experiences taught Nat was "how greatly various were the moral attributes of white men who possessed slaves, how different each owner might be by way of severity or benevolence." They ranged "from the saintly," such as his first owner, "to a few who were unconditionally monstrous." Nat never fell into the hands of the last type, and his owner at the time of the rebellion generally behaved "like every slave's ideal master." Whatever accounts for Nat's rebellion, it was not the irrepressible rage of the intolerably oppressed. Instead, he observed, "the more tolerable and human white people became in their dealings with me, the keener was my passion to destroy them."

Nat was twenty and on the threshold of freedom before he suddenly realized what slavery was, "the *true* world in which a Negro moves and breathes. It was like being plunged into freezing water." A year later came his betrayal, the final shattering of the dream of freedom, and his submission to a master he knew to be his moral inferior, stupid, brutal, swinish. For nearly ten years his disciplined defense was to become "a paragon of rectitude, of alacrity, of lively industriousness, of sweet equanimity and uncomplaining obedience," the ideal slave. He had learned never to look a white man in the eye, how to smell danger, how like a dog "to interpret the *tone* of what is being said," how to assume "that posture of respect and deference it is wise for any Negro to assume" in the presence of a strange white man, and how to "merge faceless and nameless with the common swarm." He learned how, when necessary, to shuffle and scrape and adopt the egregious, gluey cornfield accents and postures of niggerness.

He became a discriminating connoisseur of Sambo types, those given to "wallowing in the dust at the slightest provocation, midriffs clutched in idiot laughter," those who "endear themselves to all, white and black, through droll interminable tales about ha'nts and witches and conjures," and at the other extreme those who "reverse this procedure entirely and in *their* niggerness are able to outdo many white people in presenting to the world a grotesque swagger," a posture suited to the black driver or the tyrannical kitchen mammy and butler, who were skilled in keeping "safely this side of insolence." For his own part, Nat "decided upon humility, a soft voice, and houndlike obedience." Yet he was always conscious of "the weird unnaturalness of this adopted role," always counseling himself "to patience, patience, *patience* to the end," biding his time.

As he watched the potential recruits for his divine mission of vengeance and liberation he often despaired. His black brothers, "half drowned from birth in a kind of murky mindlessness," drifted before him "mouths agape or with sloppy uncomprehending smiles, shuffling their feet." They would suddenly seem to him "as meaningless and as stupid as a barnful of mules," and he would "hate them one and all." But this hatred would alternate with "a kind of wild, desperate love for them." The ambivalence came out in his feelings about Hark (originally named Hercules) whom he intended to make one of his lieutenants. Hark had "the face of an African chieftain," a godlike frame and strength, and a mortal grievance against his master for selling his wife and child. "Yet the very sight of white skin cowed him, humbled him to the most servile abasement." He drove Nat to incoherent rage when in the presence of any white he unconsciously became "the unspeakable bootlicking Sambo, all giggles and smirks and oily, sniveling servility." Hark's defense was that he was overcome by "dat black-assed feelin'," and Nat admitted to himself that the expression perfectly expressed "the numbness and dread which dwells in every Negro's heart."

Nat labored desperately to quell this fear in his recruits and to instill pride and confidence and blind faith in their leader. He clung to his faith that in every Sambo was a Nat Turner, that while "most Negroes are hopelessly docile, many of them are filled with fury," and that servility was "but a form of self-preservation." In the more desperate of them he counted upon the common postulate that "nigger life ain't worth pig shit"—they had nothing to lose.

It is one mark of William Styron's genius that he deliberately threw away the Christ symbol, which would have been irresistible to many novelists. For Nat was strictly Old Testament, the stuff of Ezekiel, Daniel, Isaiah, and Jeremiah, the blood-stained righteousness of his somber Hebrew heroes, Joshua and David. He thought and spoke in the rhetoric of the Prophets and the Psalms and scriptural poetry weaves in and out of his ruminations. He fasted and prayed in the wilderness and waited for a sign. And the sign came: "Then swiftly in the very midst of the rent in the clouds I saw a black angel clothed in black armor with black wings outspread from east to west; gigantic, hovering, he spoke in a thunderous voice louder than anything I had ever heard: *'Fear God and give glory to Him for the Hour of His judgment is come. . .'.*"

Against the hour of the bloodbath Nat had steeled himself in apocalyptic hatred, "hatred so pure and obdurate that no sympathy, no human warmth, no flicker of compassion can make the faintest nick or scratch upon the stony surface of its being." He had achieved this exaltation, he thought, by "knowing the white man at close hand," by becoming "knowledgeable about the white man's wiles, his duplicity, his greediness, and his ultimate depravity," and most of all by "having submitted to his wanton and arrogant kindness." Then when the moment came and the dread axe was poised over his master's head, Nat's hand palsied and the blow missed. Again and again between violent seizures of vomitting he tried to kill and failed. Initiative fell to a demented black monster maddened by a master's brutality. The only life Nat was able to take, among the score slaughtered, was that of the one white person he still loved, a simple-hearted and sympathetic girl.

This is the most profound fictional treatment of slavery in our literature. It is, of course, the work of a skilled and experienced novelist with other achievements to attest his qualifications. It is doubtful, however, if the rare combination of talents essential to this formidable undertaking, a flawless command of dialect, a native instinct for the subtleties and ambivalences of race in the South, and a profound and unerring sense of place—Styron's native place as it was Nat Turner's—could well have been found anywhere else.

Charles V. Hamilton

OUR NAT TURNER AND
WILLIAM STYRON'S CREATION

Charles V. Hamilton is a professor in the Political Science Department at Columbia University, in New York. He was formerly head of the Political Science Departments at Roosevelt University, in Chicago, and at Lincoln University, in Pennsylvania. He is the co-author of *Black-Power*.

WILLIAM STYRON classifies his story, *The Confessions of Nat Turner,* as "a meditation on history." It is important for us, then, to view it in this sense and to see precisely what this means in terms of white America's ability or inability to come to terms with the black man in this country. This book is a best seller because it raises and treats all the problems of black people versus whites—the assertive black male, the white woman bugaboo, violence, freedom—and the ultimate treatment reinforces what white America wants to believe about black America. The treatment, in other words, turns out right for whites.

Black youth (and some not so youthful) today who are challenging the values and practices of this society, especially in regard to race, find Styron's book a prime example of the obstacles to overcome. Black youth on college campuses I visit across this country, who form black student associations and who insist on a redefinition of historical and educational legitimacy, can never and should never accept the portrayal (or is the word "betrayal"?) of Nat Turner as set forth by Styron. Granted, Styron is entitled to his literary license, but black people today cannot afford the luxury of having their leaders manipulated and toyed with. Nat Turner struck a blow for freedom; Nat Turner was a revolutionary who did *not* fail, but rather one who furthered the idea and cause of freedom precisely because he chose to act for

Reprinted from *William Styron's Nat Turner: Ten Black Writers Respond.* First appeared in Saturday Review (June 22, 1968), under the title "Nat Turner Reconsidered: The Fiction and the Reality." With permission of the author.

freedom. Black people today must not permit themselves to be divested of their historical revolutionary leaders. And it is incumbent upon blacks to make this clear to the Styrons and to all who read his book and are soothed.

We will not permit Styron's "meditation" to leave unchallenged an image of Nat Turner as a fanatical black man who dreams of going to bed with white women, who holds nothing but contempt for his fellow blacks, and who understands, somewhat, the basic human desire to be free but still believes in the basic humanity of some slaveholders.

We will not permit Styron to picture unchallenged Nat Turner as a leader who did not understand that the military defeat should not be confused with the ideological victory: i.e., a blow for freedom. The rebellion of 1831, led by Nat Turner, is important today for blacks to understand and whites to accept precisely because its lesson is that there will be leaders who *will* rise up—against all odds—to strike blows for freedom against an oppressive, inhumane system. And there can be no refuge in the thought that Turner felt himself devinely inspired or waited for signs from heaven, etc. The important thing is that the desire for human freedom resides in the black breast as well as in any other. No amount of explicating about the harshness of slavery or the gentleness of slavery, about the docility of the masses of slaves, etc., can keep that desire from exploding. Man—black or white or yellow or red—moves to maximize his freedom: *That* is the lesson of Nat Turner that Styron did not deal with.

Styron's literary mind can wander about homosexuality and the like, and his vast readership can have their stereotypes strengthened by an image of a black preacher who is irrational and weak (unable to kill, excepting some white woman he loves) and uncertain. But black people should reject this; and white people should not delude themselves.

Let us see how Styron's "meditation on history" fits perfectly with traditional, widely acclaimed historical accounts of the event and the institution of slavery. And in doing this, we will see how his book feeds the distortions of white America. I will cite two major historical texts, sources used widely in colleges and high schools. First—simply to observe the uses of history —note how Professor Thomas A. Bailey in his *The American Pageant: A History of the Republic* describes the American Revolution:

> The revolutionists were blessed with outstanding leadership. Washington was a giant among men; Benjamin Franklin was a master among diplomats, . . . The Americans, in addition, enjoyed the moral advantage that came from what they regarded as a just cause. . . . The brutal truth is that only a select minority of the American colonials attached themselves to the cause of independence with a spirit of selfless devotion. These were the dedicated souls who bore the burden of battle and the risks of defeat; these were the freedom-loving patriots who deserved the gratitude and approbation of generations yet unborn. Seldom have so few done so much for so many.

Now let us see how this same objective, white American scholar deals
with Nat Turner:

Fanatical Nat Turner, a semi-educated Negro preacher who had visions, organized a conspiracy which resulted in the butchering of about sixty white Virgin-
ians, mostly women and children. The outburst was speedily crushed, but an
understandable wave of hysteria swept over the South.

(When I taught at a southern Negro college, a black history professor
once told me: "Oh, I always use Bailey's *American Pageant*. It is simple and
clear and my students like it and find it easy to read.") To my knowledge,
Professor Bailey, then on the faculty at Stanford University, is not noted for
racist views.

One other source is useful: *The American Republic* (Vol. I, to 1865) by
Richard Hofstadter, William Miller, and Daniel Aaron. Note their treatment of slavery:

The kindliest slaveholder, either as a buyer or seller, was sometimes forced to
break up Negro families. In short, the slaveholder was frequently victimized by
the system.
But there is a brighter side of the picture. Even some of the anti-slavery men
acknowledged that ordinarily the slaves were adequately housed, clothed, and fed.
The slave's diet of pork, cornmeal, molasses, and greens was coarse and monot-
onous, and the slave quarters were unhygienic by modern standards. But many
poor-white farmers lived no better. Slaves worked no longer than many northern
agricultural and industrial laborers and, in areas where the "task" system was
employed, a slave might complete his assigned chores by early afternoon and
spend the rest of the day as he chose. Progressive planters encouraged their slaves
to cultivate truck gardens and keep pigs and chickens for their use or to sell. In-
centive payments, holidays, and entertainments alleviated the drudgery on some
plantations, and where the work became too exacting the slaves developed their
own slow-down techniques. House-servants found life much easier than field
hands, and some gifted slaves were rewarded with positions of trust and responsibility. It seems true enough that many white southerners treated their slaves affec-
tionately and that many slaves responded to this treatment with loyalty and
devotion.

Styron's novel is in this historical tradition. He does not assign to Nat
Turner a basic revolutionary desire to overcome oppression. In fact, Styron
clearly asserts that Turner and his followers needed specific traumatic acts
to galvanize them into action: being whipped unmercifully, being sold by a
"decent" owner to a tyrant, having one's wife and children taken. On the
other hand, Styron joins that school of thought which believes that the
kinder you treat the subjects, the more likely they are to rebel. This is related to the current notion of growing black militancy resulting from rising

expectations. Some of us black Americans view human bondage as bad per se, and we believe that Nat Turner, with his basically revolutionary temperament, had to strike out against that bondage. He was the real freedom-lover, the true freedom-fighter.

Styron dwells on the reason the slaves would kill those masters who were kinder to them—like Travis. This, indeed, should be a message. The focus is on the fact that they were "masters," not that they were kinder than other masters. And so the white liberal today tries to remove himself from the racism of the system, without understanding that he is part of the racist system, and those of us who are real live victims of that system cannot afford irrelevant distinctions. The white liberal feels that good intentions are sufficient to relieve him of responsibility. He is sadly mistaken. To him, the problem is abstract, academic. To us, it is real, tangible.

Styron imputes irony to the fact that "almost the only white man in the county who owned a truly illustrious reputation for cruelty to Negroes escaped the blade of [our] retribution." The implication being, of course, that all the violence still did not get the "right" ones, that the "good" whites suffered. And, thus, further evidence of failure. Nonsense! Then and now. The Nathaniel Francises in Styron's story exist precisely because of the support —covert or overt—of the "good white folk." No sensitive black man today confuses this point—even if Styron does.

It is perfectly clear why Styron's book would be a hit on the American market: it confirms white America's racist feelings. Here was an ungrateful slave, taught to read by his master, who repaid that "gift" by murder. (See what happens when you try to be a little kind to them.) Here was the fanatical black leader who held profound contempt for his own people and who led them into a senseless bloodbath destined to fail, all the while dreaming of copulating with "Miss Anne." (They are really incapable of sticking together or of being leaders. All they really want is to have sexual intercourse with our women.) Here was the visionary who frequently doubted himself and his venture. (They are little children who really must be led and brought along slowly—for their own sake.) And, of course, here was the final act of nobility on the part of the Great White Father—Gray, the attorney—who extends the hand of forgiveness through the bars. (We must be patient and understanding with these little savages. We must show them that we are big enough to forgive.)

If this is Styron's (and white America's) "meditation on history," let the record show that this is meditation mired in misinterpretation, and that this is history many black people reject.

Nat Turner is our hero, unequivocally understood. He is a man who had profound respect and love for his fellow blacks and who respected black womanhood and held utter contempt for those white slavemasters who violated the purity and beauty of our black women. Nat Turner *was a success* because he perpetuated the *idea* of freedom—freedom at all cost. He will not be denied his place in the revolutionary annals of black people by white people who—through the guise of art or otherwise—feel a conscious or subconscious need to belittle him. If white America feels a need to relieve its conscience, to soften *its* confession, let it be clear that it will not be done, unchallenged, at the expense of our black brothers—past or present. That day is done.

STUDY QUESTIONS

1. On what grounds do Hamilton and Woodward ("Confessions of a Rebel: 1831") judge *The Confessions of Nat Turner?*

2. What are the principal differences in their opinions of the book?

3. Of the two reviews, which one appears to be the more authoritative?

4. Hamilton contends that Styron's book "confirms white America's racist feelings," and he notes some of them. Is there any evidence of such feelings in the selection "It is Done"?

Eric Sevareid

THE WORLD STILL MOVES
OUR WAY

Eric Sevareid (1912–   ) is well-known to the American public for his work in broadcasting and reporting. He received his college degree from the University of Minnesota and started his career in journalism as a copy boy with the *Minneapolis Journal*. After working as a reporter for various other papers he became Paris editor of the *New York Herald-Tribune*. During World War II he was a foreign correspondent for the Columbia Broadcasting Company. His books include *Not So Wild A Dream* (1946), *In One Ear* (1952), *Small Sounds in the Night* (1956), *Candidates* (1960), and *This*

Is Eric Sevareid (1964). At present he is correspondent for Columbia Broadcasting Company and is a regular contributor to various magazines.

THERE ARE THOSE WHO SAY the dream is dead or dying, poisoned by self-interest, rotted by surfeit and indifference, maimed by violence. The great aspiration is ended, they tell us, and America is now only another crowded nation, not even able to maintain order; a Power, but not a society, not a culture. We have gone, almost directly, they would have us believe, from primitiveness to decadence, a far poorer record than that of Rome.

The fireworks of this July 4—which may well illuminate the scene, again, of whole urban blocks consumed by flames, from the Molotov cocktail, not the holiday sparkler—will give further force to this cry of the Cassandras.

But the cry is as old as the nation. It was sounded in Jefferson's time, when the states seemed ready to drift apart; in Lincoln's time, when they split apart; in Roosevelt's time, when, by the millions, husbands shuffled in soup lines; in Truman's time, when the Russians and Chinese were supposedly reordering the earth and Communist traitors were supposedly infesting the Government.

But this is not It—this is not our Armageddon, not the great day of judgment on America. For America is change, and the changes have come, often enough, in convulsive spasms. This country is the vast experimental laboratory in human relations for the twentieth century; it is, in a sense, defining and creating the twentieth century for much of the world.

Unless it is seen in this light, America cannot be understood at all. If many of our contemporary intellectuals, especially those communing with one another in New York City, almost a separate nation in spirit, do not understand it, this is partly because they do not understand themselves. As they attest in innumerable books, they do not know who they are. It may be news to them that the over-whelming majority of Americans *do* know who they are, do *not* feel alienated from their country or their generation.

This is not a "sick society." It is a deeply unsettled and bewildered society, and the reason is not merely the extraordinary changes in this last generation but the speed of these changes. It is the *rate* of change that is new. The life of Americans today resembles that of, say, Grant's time, less than life in Grant's time resembled life in ancient China. The nation is not over-populated, but the population has shifted out of balance. In the last 20 years alone, 18 million people, including, of course, the Negroes, have moved into the urban centers. This second industrial-scientific revolution has jammed us together, polluted much of our air and waters, smeared ugliness over much of our countryside, obliged us to work within greater economic units and increased the tensions of daily living.

Two other revolutions have been taking place in concert with the new industrial-scientific revolution. One is the communications revolution, which brings every social evil, every human tragedy and conflict immediately and intimately within everyone's ken. The other is the educational revolution, which adds millions every year to the ranks of those moved to add their investigation, articulation or actions to the processes of problem-solving and problem-creating.

We are not becoming less democratic but more democratic. It is not our individual freedom that is in jeopardy, in the first instance, but our public order. It could be argued that we are moving away from representative government in the direction, at least, of direct democracy, by no means an unmixed blessing. For the immediate future, the problem is not only the indifference or "apathy" of the much-abused middle class or any other group. It is also the problem of too many untrained cooks in the kitchen.

Many current phenomena to the contrary notwithstanding, Americans are the most natural workers-together in the world. We say we live by the system of individual enterprise, while we are the supreme cooperative society. Totalitarian countries say they are cooperative societies, while their regimes must coerce their people to work. It is absurd to believe that the races of men who turned an empty, forbidding continent into the most efficient engine of production and distribution ever seen, who created the first *mass* democracy with essential order and essential freedom will not solve the problems of crowding, poverty, pollution and ugliness. The solutions will create new problems, after which there will be new solutions, then new problems, and so our life will go on. Time is life. Were human problems ever totally solved, change would come to a stop, and we would begin to die.

American cynics and Cassandras see neither their own history nor the rest of the world with clarity. Violence? We have *always* had a high tolerance level for violence. Abraham Lincoln worried about what he called "the increasing disregard for law which pervades the country; the growing disposition to substitute the wild and furious passions, in lieu of the sober judgment of courts; and the worse than savage mobs, for the executive ministers of justice."

It is even to be doubted that crime is more prevalent than it was in the nineteenth century. Historian Arthur Schlesinger, Jr., reminds us that a century ago, every tenth person in New York City had a police record.

Alienated and irreverent youth? To a degree, youth is always alienated and to a degree ought to be. More than 2,000 years ago, Plato wrote that in a democracy, the father "accustoms himself to become like his child and to fear his sons. . . . The schoolmaster fears and flatters his pupils . . . the young act like their seniors, and compete with them in speech and action, while the old men condescend to the young. . . ." This happens because democratic life carries the in-built impulse to wish to please and accommodate to others.

The alarm over drug-taking is also exaggerated. There is far less use of dangerous drugs today than a half century ago, before narcotics control, when about one American in every four hundred was an addict of some harmful drug, ten times the present rate.

Americans, of course, are not spiritually geared to the past but to the future. It is a reflection of what John Steinbeck, speaking of the onpushing, haggard "Okies" in the dust-bowl years, called the "terrible faith," that we are constantly seized with concern for our children more than for ourselves. Yet it is not possible to see our society in perspective without these backward glances to what we once were, with the consequent realization that we are using different scales of measuring well-being today.

At the turn of the century, a newborn could expect to live about to the age of 50; today, the expectancy is about 70. Once, a mother had sound reason to fear giving birth; today, death in childbirth is regarded as intolerable. Once, a full high school education was the best achievement of a minority; today, it is the barest minimum for decent employment and self-respect. Once, the timber and mining barons stripped away the forests and topsoil wholesale; today, these companies are confronted by their communities at every other move.

One could cite hundreds of similar examples of how our standards of expectancy have risen, as they should, along with our standard of life. The truth is that we Americans are perfectionists, which simply means that we were not, are not and never will be satisfied either with the quantities or the qualities in our life.

By the year 2000, we will look back upon these present years not only as one of America's periodic convulsions but as a rather backward period. By then, the typical American family will have an income of around $20,000 a year or more; the typical American adult will have had at least two years of college, with far broader intellectual and aesthetic horizons. By then, the old urban centers will have been rebuilt, and many millions will live in satellite "new cities," part-urban, part-rural. The incurable diseases like cancer and arthritis will be under far better control.

The present explosion in books, theater, music and art will have transformed tastes and comprehension to an enormous degree. And already, according to the Englishman C. P. Snow, something like 80 percent of the advanced study of science in the Western world is going on in the United States of America. This is the heart reason for the "brain drain" from abroad to the U.S., not merely the higher pay. The facilities, the action, the creative excitement are increasingly here. None of this guarantees a single new Shakespeare, Rembrandt, Beethoven or Einstein, because genius is not developed (though even this may occur one day through selective breeding and cell transplant).

What it does guarantee is a great lifting of the massive center, of the "ordinary" people. This is the premise and the point about America—ours is the first organized dedication to *massive* improvement, to the development of a *mass* culture, the first attempt to educate *everyone* to the limit of his capacities. We have known for a long time that this can be done only through the chemistry of individual freedom. Soviet Russia is just now beginning to discover this for itself. I am unable to understand the thrust of the sufferings and strivings of Western man over the last thousand years save in terms of this kind of achievement.

The popular passion of Americans is not politics, baseball, money or material things. It is education. Education is now our biggest industry, involving more people even than national defense. The percentage of children in kindergarten has doubled in a rather short period; the percentage of youth in college climbs steeply upward. Today, even a Negro boy in the South has a better statistical chance of getting into college than an English youth. And there are about 44 million full- and part-time *adult* students pursuing some kind of formalized learning on their own!

Intelligent foreigners nearly everywhere understand the mountainous meaning of all this for the world as well as for America. They know that much of the world will be transformed in the American image, culturally if not politically. They know that struggle is really all over—it is the Western way of living and doing, our way and the way of Europe combined, that the world wants. It is North America and West Europe that make up the "in" world; Russia and China are still the outsiders trying to enter.

Communism already appears irrelevant, essentially passé. The more the Communist regimes educate their people, the more complex their life will become. They will struggle with the complexities the Western world confronts already, and they will discover that authoritarian direction from the top cannot cope with them. Only the essentially liberal society can manage twentieth-century life, even in practical terms. They will learn, as we have always known, that the effective, the lasting revolution lies in the West, particularly in America.

Why, then, are we in such a state of uproar in this year of Our Lord, and why is much of the world upset about the America of today? Because, as a philosopher once said, "nothing that is vast enters into the life of mortals without a curse," and America is struggling to rid itself of one old curse and one new one. The old curse is the Negro slavery Europeans fastened upon this land long ago, which continues in a hundred psychological, social and economic, if not legal, forms. The Negro Passion of today is a revolution within the continuing American revolution, and the one absolute certainty about it is that it is going to succeed, however long and distracting the agony for everyone. It will succeed not only because it has justice with it (justice has been suppressed before) but because there is a deep evangelical streak in the American people, a true collective conscience, and it has been aroused.

Racism exists in almost all societies on this globe, virulently so, incidentally, in Black Africa. It may be that race prejudice—the psychologists' "stranger hatred"—is an instinct tracing from our animal origins, and therefore ineradicable. Yet man is the only animal *aware* of his instincts; the only animal, therefore, capable of controlling, if not eliminating, his instincts. New law, enforced, compels new behavior. Behavior repeated daily comes to seem normal, and attitudes change. Illusions tend to vanish. The idea that a difference in skin color is an essential difference is an illusion. I am struck by an observation of McGeorge Bundy of the Ford Foundation. He said discrimination will end, partly because this college generation regards racial equality as natural, whereas the older generation regards it only as logical.

The twentieth-century war over racial injustice is now in its virulent stage. The nineteenth-century war in its virulent stage lasted four years. This one will last much longer because it is fought on a thousand narrow fronts, like guerrilla war, and because no grand climacteric is possible. But it is not going to "tear this country apart" or "burn America down" or anything of the sort. A tiny percentage of extremists among only 12 percent of the American population can do much, but they cannot do that.

The new curse has come with America's new military power. A form of Parkinson's Law operates here. The greater the power, the more the men who associate with it, extol it and find needs, real or sophistical, for its use. The use of available, flexible force becomes easier than hard thought; and the worst aspect of the curse is the gradual, almost unconscious identification of power with virtue. John Adams said, "Power always thinks it has a great soul and vast views beyond the comprehension of the weak. . . ."

We have fallen into this trap with the Vietnam intervention. For the first time, we have misused our power on a massive scale. But it does not mean that we are a "fascist" or aggressive people, any more than the racial mess means that we are a hating or oppressive people. Vietnam is not typical; it is a mistake, now recognized as such by most serious thinkers in this country. If millions of people in Europe (every province of which is soaked in blood) stand aghast at what we have done and reproach us bitterly, one unarticulated reason is that they *expect* the United States to act with humaneness and common sense. They do not shout advice to Russia and China, whatever their misdeeds, for the same reason that the crowd in the bullring does not shout advice to the bull but to the bullfighter.

The reassuring thing is not merely that we will get out of this trap and undo the damage as best we can but that we will do so because our own people demand it, not because the enemy is too strong, not because of foreign criticism. We could, if we would, lay North Vietnam totally waste. The American conscience will not permit it. We may not win a military victory in Vietnam, but we will win a victory in our own soul.

No—the humaneness of the American people is still here. The new problems have piled up too rapidly for our brains and our institutions to cope with at anything like the same rate, but the will for justice is as strong as ever—stronger, in my own belief, because thought and expression are freer today than ever before. This is why the Negro revolution has come now—not because conditions of life became worse, save for some, but because of a climate of free expression. In just such periods of great intellectual freedom have nearly all revolutions been generated.

It is a remarkable fact that great numbers of very ordinary people in distant lands understand all this about America better than some of our own intellectuals. If, by some magic, all barriers to emigration and immigration around the world were lifted tomorrow, by far the single biggest human caravan would start moving in one direction—our way.

One day recently, I asked a Cuban refugee why most Cubans like himself wanted to come to the United States rather than go to Latin Ameican countries with the same language and the same general culture. Was it just the thought of greater economic opportunity?

"No," he said, "many of us would have an easier time, economically, in a Latin country. It's just that we feel better here. We can feel like a human being. There seems to be something universal about this country."

This is living testimony, not abstract argument, from men who know the meaning of America in their bones and marrow. Of course, it is the truth. Of course, the dream lives on.

Let those who wish compare America with Rome. Rome lasted around a thousand years.

STUDY QUESTIONS

1. Describe Sevareid's method of presentation and note the advantages of such an approach.

2. What types of arguments does he use? Are there any that may be challenged as invalid or unconvincing?

3. According to Sevareid, how will America handle its old curse and its new curse?

4. What is the basic characteristic of the American people that informs Sevareid's optimism for the future of the country?

Section Three

Science

"Brave New World"

Ashley Montagu

INTRODUCING ANTHROPOLOGY

Ashley Montagu (1905–   ) was born in England and became a United States citizen in 1940. An anthropologist and social biologist, he was educated at the Universities of London and Florence, and received his Ph.D. from Columbia University in 1937. He has taught at New York University, Rutgers-The State University, and the New School for Social Research. Since 1930 he has served as a legal expert on scientific problems related to race and, in 1949, helped draft the UNESCO statement on race. Among his books are *Coming into Being Among Australian Aborigines* (1937), *Man's Most Dangerous Myth: The Fallacy of Race* (1942), *The Natural Superiority of Women* (1953), *Life Before Birth* (1964), *The Idea of Race* (1965), and *Man and His First Two Million Years: A Brief Introduction to Anthropology* (1969).

ANTHROPOLOGY is the science of man. That's a pretty broad definition. Let's try to draw a line around it so that we can really grasp what the science is concerned with. The word "anthropology" is derived from two Greek words, the one *anthropos* meaning "man," and the other *logos* meaning "ordered knowledge." So anthropology is the ordered knowledge of man. The fact is that anything relating to man is grist to the anthropologist's mill. Anthropology is divided into two great divisions: (1) cultural anthropology, and (2) physical anthropology.

Cultural Anthropology

Cultural anthropology is concerned with the study of man's cultures. By "culture" the anthropologist understands what may be called the man-made part of the environment: the pots and pans, the laws and institutions, the art, religion, philosophy. Whatever a particular group of people living together as a functioning population have learned to do as human beings, their way of life, in short, is to be regarded as culture. The cultural anthropologist studies different cultures and compares them with one another in order to learn how it is that people come to do what they do in so many different ways, and also to learn, wherever possible, the relationships of one culture to another. He tries to find those common elements in all cultures which can be summarized in terms of generalizations or laws which are true of all cultures. Where there are differences, he tries to find the causes of these differences.

The cultural anthropologist is interested in all the forms that human social behavior assumes in organized societies. He cannot remain contented with the mere description of these forms, for he desires to understand how they have come into being, and so the cultural anthropologist must often be quite as good a psychologist as he is anything else. Fundamentally what he is really interested in is the nature of human nature. Today there is quite a flourishing school of anthropologists known as the personality-in-culture school. These cultural anthropologists, such as Margaret Mead, Clyde Kluckhohn, John Honigmann, Francis Hsu, and many others, are interested in tracing the relationship of the cultures in which human beings are socialized, that is, brought up, to the kind of personalities they develop.

Other cultural anthropologists are interested as specialists in studying such aspects of the cultures of different peoples as their legal institutions, social organization, religion, mythology, language, and their material culture such as their art, pottery, basketry, implements, and the like. Some cultural anthropologists take whole tribes for their special study and spend from many months to many years attempting to study every aspect of their culture.

Traditionally the cultural anthropologist has studied the so-called "primitive peoples" of this earth, and the major part of the anthropologist's attention still continues to be devoted to the cultures of such peoples, but in more recent years anthropologists have been turning their attention to the study of the technologically more advanced peoples of the earth. Today we have good anthropological studies not only of the Australian aborigines and the Congo pygmies, but also of the Japanese, the Chinese, the Germans, the Americans, the English, the Norwegians, and many others.

Formerly the study of modern societies was left to the sociologist (sociology = the study of society). Today the methods of the cultural anthropologist have greatly influenced those of the sociologist, but the difference between the two disciplines remains: the sociologist studies modern societies in great detail; the anthropologist brings to the study of modern societies a method which is at once wider and deeper than that of the sociologist.

Today there are specialists who are known as *applied* anthropologists. These are essentially cultural anthropologists who bring their special methods to bear principally upon the problems of industry. They go into a plant and study the relationships between the workers and their employers, between the worker and his work, and they advise on the methods of improving these relationships.

There are cultural anthropologists who work in hospitals in collaboration with psychiatrists. They study the relationships within the hospital between patient and doctor, administration and staff, and they conduct collaborative studies of whole districts in order to throw light upon the genesis of mental illness and its possible prevention.

The collaboration between anthropologists and psychiatrists in the study of the cultures of different societies has been very fruitful indeed, and holds much promise for the future.

Another branch of cultural anthropology is *archaeology* (often unkindly called the moldier part of anthropology). Archaeology is the science which studies cultures that no longer exist, basing its findings on the study of cultural products and subsistence remains recovered by excavation and similar means. If anthropologists are "the glamour boys" of the social sciences, archaeologists are "the glamour boys" of anthropology. All of which means that their specialty can be a very exciting one indeed, even though it generally entails a great deal of hard work, with far too much sand in one's hair, one's boots, and one's dried-out sandwiches. What the archaeologist is interested in doing is not merely to disinter an extinct culture, but to trace its relationships to other cultures. In this way archaeologists have been able to solve many problems which would otherwise have remained puzzling and to link up cultures which in their present form hardly seem related.

Anthropological archaeologists are to be distinguished from classical archaeologists; the latter are interested in the extinct cultures of classical antiquity, such as those of Greece, Rome, Crete, Persia, and Palestine.

Physical Anthropology

Just as the cultural anthropologist is interested in studying man as a cultural being, so the physical anthropologist is interested in the comparative study of man as a physical being. The physical anthropologist studies the origin and evolution of man's physical characters and the diversity of forms which those physical characters may take. He tries to discover the means by which the likenesses and the differences between groups of human beings have been produced. He tries to discover how man, in his various physical shapes, got to be the way he is now.

There are all sorts of specialists in physical anthropology. There are those who study man's origin and evolution; these are called paleoanthropologists (paleo = old). They study the extinct remains of man and everything related to them. Then there are those who study the comparative anatomy of the primates, the classificatory group to which man in common with the apes and monkeys belongs. Here the primatologist, as he is called, is interested in discovering possible physical relationships between the large variety of types that constitute this group.

There are physical anthropologists who study growth and development. There are those who study physiology, and those who study the blood groups and blood types. There are those that study the so-called "races" of man, and there are a few who study all these subjects in the attempt to unify what they know into a consistent body of knowledge.

There are also applied physical anthropologists. These are largely concerned with the measurement of man, anatomically and physiologically, in order to determine, for example, standards for clothes, equipment in the armed forces, seats for railroad cars, hat sizes for men, shoe sizes for women, and the like.

There are also some constitutional physical anthropologists. These attempt to study the possible relationships between body-form and disease, body-form and personality, and even body-form and race.

Anthropology and Humanity

The anthropologist is first and foremost interested in human beings, no matter what the shape of their heads, the color of their skin, or the form of their noses. As a scientist he is interested in the facts about human beings, and as an anthropologist he knows that the facts are vastly more interesting than the fancies, the false beliefs, and the downright distortions of the facts, which some misguided persons seem always to have found it necessary to perpetrate. Humanity has a wonderfully interesting history, and it is the principal function of the anthropologist to reveal that history to the student as simply and as clearly as possible. This is what we shall now attempt to do in the following pages.

In concluding this introduction to anthropology I should like to quote the words of a great anthropologist, Thomas Henry Huxley (1825–95), writing in 1889 to a young man who later became a distinguished physical anthropologist at Cambridge University (Alfred Cort Haddon, 1855–1940). They are as true today as when they were written. Wrote Huxley: "I know of no department of natural science more likely to reward a man who goes into it thoroughly than anthropology. There is an immense deal to be done in the science pure and simple, and it is one of those branches of inquiry which brings one into contact with the great problems of humanity in every direction."

1. What are the main structural divisions of this essay? What part do defini-
   tions play in marking the points of division?

2. What does Montagu mean when he says: "Let's try to draw a line around
   it. . . ."?

3. How do you suppose a sociologist would react to Montagu's comment that
   anthropology has a method which is "wider and deeper" than that of
   sociology? Does Montagu provide any evidence for this statement?

4. Can you account for the departure from a badly objective prose style
   in the paragraph about anthropological archeologists ("All of which . . .
   sandwiches.")?

5. What does Montagu accomplish by quoting Thomas Henry Huxley in the last
   paragraph? Could this be considered a kind of name dropping?

Walter Van Tilburg Clark

HOOK

Walter Van Tilburg Clark (1901–   ) is a highly regarded writer and
teacher of creative writing, whose stories and novels about the West have
helped rescue Western fiction from the popularizers of the Western
"myth." His *The Ox-Bow Incident* (1940) is considered a classic Western
novel. Among his other well-known works are *The City of Trembling
Leaves* (1945), *The Track of the Cat* (1949), and *The Watchful Gods and
Other Stories* (1950). He has been in great demand as a teacher of writers.
He was Writer in Residence at the University of Nevada, Visiting Lecturer
at the Universities of Iowa, Utah, Wyoming, California, Washington, Ore-
gon, and Stanford University and Reed College. In 1945 he won the
O. Henry Memorial Award for *The Wind and the Snow of Winter*.

HOOK, the hawks' child, was hatched in a dry spring among the oaks, beside the seasonal river, and was struck from the nest early. In the drouth his single-willed parents had to extend their hunting ground by more than twice, for the ground creatures upon which they fed died and dried by the hundreds. The range became too great for them to wish to return and feed Hook, and when they had lost interest in each other they drove Hook down into the sand and brush and went back to solitary courses over the bleaching hills.

Unable to fly yet, Hook crept over the ground, challenging all large movements with recoiled head, erected, rudimentary wings, and the small rasp of his clattering beak. It was during this time of abysmal ignorance and continual fear that his eyes took on the first quality of a hawk, that of being wide, alert and challenging. He dwelt, because of his helplessness, among the rattling brush which grew between the oaks and the river. Even in his thickets and near the water, the white sun was the dominant presence. Except in the dawn, when the land wind stirred, or in the late afternoon, when the sea wind became strong enough to penetrate the half-mile inland to this turn in the river, the sun was the major force, and everything was dry and motionless under it. The brush, small plants and trees alike husbanded the little moisture at their hearts; the moving creatures waited for dark, when sometimes the sea fog came over and made a fine, soundless rain which relieved them.

The two spacious sounds of his life environed Hook at this time. One was the great rustle of the slopes of yellowed wild wheat, with over it the chattering rustle of the leaves of the California oaks, already as harsh and individually tremulous as in autumn. The other was the distant whisper of the foaming edge of the Pacific, punctuated by the hollow shoring of the waves. But these Hook did not yet hear, for he was attuned by fear and hunger to the small, spasmodic rustlings of live things. Dry, shrunken, and nearly starved, and with his plumage delayed, he snatched at beetles, dragging in the sand to catch them. When swifter and stronger birds and animals did not reach them first, which was seldom, he ate the small, silver fish left in the mud by the failing river. He watched, with nearly chattering beak, the quick, thin lizards pause, very alert, and raise and lower themselves, but could not catch them because he had to raise his wings to move rapidly, which startled them.

Only one sight and sound not of his world of microscopic necessity was forced upon Hook. That was the flight of the big gulls from the beaches, which sometimes, in quealing play, came spinning back over the foothills and the river bed. For some inherited reason, the big, shipbodied birds did not frighten Hook, but angered him. Small and chewed-looking, with his wide, already yellowing eyes glaring up at them, he would stand in an open place on the sand in the sun and spread his shaping wings and clatter his bill like shaken dice. Hook was furious about the swift, easy passage of gulls.

His first opportunity to leave off living like a ground owl came accidentally. He was standing in the late afternoon in the red light under the thicket, his eyes half-filmed with drowse and the stupefaction of starvation, when suddenly something beside him moved, and he struck, and killed a field mouse driven out of the wheat by thirst. It was a poor mouse, shriveled and lice ridden, but in striking, Hook had tasted blood, which raised nest memories and restored his nature. With started neck plumage and shining eyes, he tore and fed. When the mouse was devoured, Hook had entered hoarse adolescence. He began to seek with a conscious appetite, and to move more readily out of shelter. Impelled by the blood appetite, so glorious after his long preservation upon the flaky and bitter stuff of bugs, he ventured even into the wheat in the open sun beyond the oaks, and discovered the small trails and holes among the roots. With his belly often partially filled with flesh, he grew rapidly in strength and will. His eyes were taking on their final change, their yellow growing deeper and more opaque, their stare more constant, their challenge less desperate. Once during this transformation, he surprised a ground squirrel, and although he was ripped and wingbitten and could not hold his prey, he was not dismayed by the conflict, but exalted. Even while the wing was still drooping and the pinions not grown back, he was excited by other ground squirrels and pursued them futilely, and was angered by their dusty escapes. He realized that his world was a great arena for killing, and felt the magnificence of it.

The two major events of Hook's young life occurred in the same day. A little after dawn he made the customary essay and succeeded in flight. A little before sunset, he made his first sustained flight of over two hundred yards, and at its termination struck and slew a great buck squirrel whose thrashing and terrified gnawing and squealing gave him a wild delight. When he had gorged on the strong meat, Hook stood upright, and in his eyes was the stare of the hawk, never flagging in intensity but never swelling beyond containment. After that the stare had only to grow more deeply challenging and more sternly controlled as his range and deadliness increased. There was no change in kind. Hook had mastered the first of the three hungers which are fused into the single, flaming will of a hawk, and he had experienced the second.

The third and consummating hunger did not awaken in Hook until the following spring, when the exultation of space had grown slow and steady in him, so that he swept freely with the wind over the miles of coastal foothills, circling, and ever in sight of the sea, and used without struggle the warm currents lifting from the slopes, and no longer desired to scream at the range of his vision, but intently sailed above his shadow swiftly climbing to meet him on the hillsides, sinking away and rippling across the brush-grown canyons.

That spring the rains were long, and Hook sat for hours, hunched and angry under their pelting, glaring into the fogs of the river valley, and killed only small, drenched things flooded up from their tunnels. But when the rains had dissipated, and there were sun and sea wind again, the game ran plentiful, the hills were thick and shining green, and the new river flooded about the boulders where battered turtles climbed up to shrink and sleep. Hook then was scorched by the third hunger. Ranging farther, often forgetting to kill and eat, he sailed for days with growing rage, and woke at night clattering on his dead tree limb, and struck and struck and struck at the porous wood of the trunk, tearing it away. After days, in the draft of a coastal canyon miles below his own hills, he came upon the acrid taint he did not know but had expected, and sailing down it, felt his neck plumes rise and his wings quiver so that he swerved unsteadily. He saw the unmated female perched upon the tall and jagged stump of a tree that had been shorn by storm, and he stooped, as if upon game. But she was older than he, and wary of the gripe of his importunity, and banked off screaming, and he screamed also at the intolerable delay.

At the head of the canyon, the screaming pursuit was crossed by another male with a great wing-spread, and the light golden in the fringe of his plumage. But his more skillful opening played him false against the ferocity of the twice-balked Hook. His rising maneuver for position was cut short by Hook's wild, upward swoop, and at the blow he raked desperately and tumbled off to the side. Dropping, Hook struck him again, struggled to clutch, but only raked and could not hold, and, diving, struck once more in passage, and then beat up, yelling triumph, and saw the crippled antagonist side-slip away, half-tumble once, as the ripped wing failed to balance, then steady and glide obliquely into the cover of brush on the canyon side. Beating hard and stationary in the wind above the bush that covered his competitor, Hook waited an instant, but when the bush was still, screamed again, and let himself go off with the current, reseeking, infuriated by the burn of his own wounds, the thin choke-thread of the acrid taint.

On a hilltop projection of stone two miles inland, he struck her down, gripping her rustling body with his talons, beating her wings down with his wings, belting her head when she whimpered or thrashed, and at last clutching her neck with his hook and, when her coy struggles had given way to stillness, succeeded.

In the early summer, Hook drove the three young ones from their nest, and went back to lone circling above his own range. He was complete.

II

Throughout that summer and the cool, growthless weather of the winter, when the gales blew in the river canyon and the ocean piled upon the shore, Hook was master of the sky and the hills of his range. His flight became a lovely and certain thing, so that he played with the treacherous currents of the air with a delicate ease surpassing that of the gulls. He could sail for hours, searching the blanched grasses below him with telescopic eyes, gaining height against the wind, descending in mile-long, gently declining swoops when he curved and rode back, and never beating either wing. At the swift passage of his shadow within their vision, gophers, ground squirrels and rabbits froze, or plunged gibbering into their tunnels beneath matted turf. Now, when he struck, he killed easily in one hard-knuckled blow. Occasionally, in sport, he soared up over the river and drove the heavy and weaponless gulls downstream again, until they would no longer venture inland.

There was nothing which Hook feared now, and his spirit was wholly belligerent, swift and sharp, like his gaze. Only the mixed smells and incomprehensible activities of the people at the Japanese farmer's home, inland of the coastwise highway and south of the bridge across Hook's river, troubled him. The smells were strong, unsatisfactory and never clear, and the people, though they behaved foolishly, constantly running in and out of their built-up holes, were large, and appeared capable, with fearless eyes looking up at him, so that he instinctively swerved aside from them. He cruised over their yard, their gardens, and their bean fields, but he would not alight close to their buildings.

But this one area of doubt did not interfere with his life. He ignored it, save to look upon it curiously as he crossed, his afternoon shadow sliding in an instant over the chicken-and-crate-cluttered yard, up the side of the unpainted barn, and then out again smoothly, just faintly, liquidly rippling over the furrows and then over the stubble of the grazing slopes. When the season was dry, and the dead earth blew on the fields, he extended his range to satisfy his great hunger, and again narrowed it when the fields were once more alive with the minute movements he could not only see but anticipate.

Four times that year he was challenged by other hawks blowing up from behind the coastal hills to scud down his slopes, but two of these he slew in mid-air, and saw hurtle down to thump on the ground and lie still while he circled, and a third, whose wing he tore, he followed closely to earth and beat to death in the grass, making the crimson jet out from its breast and neck into the pale wheat. The fourth was a strong flier and experienced fighter, and theirs was a long, running battle, with brief, rising flurries of striking and screaming, from which down and plumage soared off.

Here, for the first time, Hook felt doubts, and at moments wanted to drop away from the scoring, burning talons and the twisted hammer strokes of the strong beak, drop away shrieking, and take cover and be still. In the end, when Hook, having outmaneuvered his enemy and come above him, wholly in control, and going with the wind, tilted and plunged for the death rap, the other, in desperation, threw over on his back and struck up. Talons locked, beaks raking, they dived earthward. The earth grew and spread under them amazingly, and they were not fifty feet above it when Hook, feeling himself turning toward the underside, tore free and beat up again on heavy, wrenched wings. The other, stroking swiftly, and so close to down that he lost wing plumes to a bush, righted himself and planed up, but flew on lumberingly between the hills and did not return. Hook screamed the triumph, and made a brief pretense of pursuit, but was glad to return, slow and victorious, to his dead tree.

In all these encounters Hook was injured, but experienced only the fighter's pride and exultation from the sting of wounds received in successful combat. And in each of them he learned new skill. Each time the wounds healed quickly, and left him a more dangerous bird.

In the next spring, when the rains and the night chants of the little frogs were past, the third hunger returned upon Hook with a new violence. In this quest, he came into the taint of a young hen. Others too were drawn by the unnerving perfume, but only one of them, the same with which Hook had fought his great battle, was a worthy competitor. This hunter drove off two, while two others, game but neophytes, were glad enough that Hook's impatience would not permit him to follow and kill. Then the battle between the two champions fled inland, and was a tactical marvel, but Hook lodged the neck-breaking blow, and struck again as they dropped past the treetops. The blood had already begun to pool on the gray, fallen foliage as Hook flapped up between branches, too spent to cry his victory. Yet his hunger would not let him rest until, late in the second day, he drove the female to ground among the laurels of a strange river canyon.

When the two fledglings of this second brood had been driven from the nest, and Hook had returned to his own range, he was not only complete, but supreme. He slept without concealment on his bare limb, and did not open his eyes when, in the night, the heavy-billed cranes coughed in the shallows below him.

III

The turning point of Hook's career came that autumn, when the brush in the canyons rustled dryly and the hills, mowed close by the cattle, smoked under the wind as if burning. One midafternoon, when the black clouds were torn on the rim of the sea and the surf flowered white and high on the rocks, raining in over the low cliffs, Hook rode the wind diagonally across the river mouth. His great eyes, focused for small things, stirring in the dust and leaves, overlooked so large and slow a movement as that of the Japanese farmer rising from the brush and lifting the two black eyes of his shotgun. Too late Hook saw and, startled, swerved, but wrongly. The surf muffled the reports, and nearly without sound, Hook felt the minute whips of the first shot, and the astounding, breath-taking blow of the second.

Beating his good wing, tasting the blood that quickly swelled into his beak, he tumbled off with the wind and struck into the thickets on the far side of the river mouth. The branches tore him. Wild with rage, he thrust up and clattered his beak, challenging, but when he had fallen over twice, he knew that the trailing wing would not carry, and then heard the boots of the hunter among the stones in the river bed and, seeing him loom at the edge of the bushes, crept back among the thickest brush and was still. When he saw the boots stand before him, he reared back, lifting his good wing and cocking his head for the serpent-like blow, his beak open but soundless, his great eyes hard and very shining. The boots passed on. The Japanese farmer, who believed that he had lost chickens, and who had cunningly observed Hook's flight for many afternoons, until he could plot it, did not greatly want a dead hawk.

When Hook could hear nothing but the surf and the wind in the thicket, he let the sickness and shock overcome him. The fine film of the inner lid dropped over his big eyes. His heart beat frantically, so that it made the plumage of his shot-aching breast throb. His own blood throttled his breathing. But these things were nothing compared to the lightning of pain in his left shoulder, where the shot had bunched, shattering the airy bones so the pinions trailed on the ground and could not be lifted. Yet, when a sparrow lit in the bush over him, Hook's eyes flew open again, hard and challenging, his good wing was lifted and his beak strained open. The startled sparrow darted piping out over the river.

Throughout that night, while the long clouds blew across the stars and the wind shook the bushes about him, and throughout the next day, while the clouds still blew and massed until there was no gleam of sunlight on the sand bar, Hook remained stationary, enduring his sickness. In the second evening, the rains began. First there was a long, running patter of drops upon the beach and over the dry trees and bushes. At dusk there came a heavier squall, which did not die entirely, but slacked off to a continual, spaced splashing of big drops, and then returned with the front of the storm. In long, misty curtains, gust by gust, the rain swept over the sea, beating down its heaving, and coursed up the beach. The little jets of dust ceased to rise about the drops in the fields, and the mud began to gleam. Among the boulders of the river bed, darkling pools grew slowly.

Still Hook stood behind his tree from the wind, only gentle drops reaching him, falling from the upper branches and then again from the brush. His eyes remained closed, and he could still taste his own blood in his mouth, though it had ceased to come up freshly. Out beyond him, he heard the storm changing. As rain conquered the sea, the heave of the surf became a hushed sound, often lost in the crying of the wind. Then gradually, as the night turned toward morning, the wind also was broken by the rain. The crying became fainter, the rain settled toward steadiness, and the creep of the waves could be heard again, quiet and regular upon the beach.

At dawn there was no wind and no sun, but everywhere the roaring of the vertical, relentless rain. Hook then crept among the rapid drippings of the bushes, dragging his torn sail, seeking better shelter. He stopped often and stood with the shutters of film drawn over his eyes. At midmorning he found a little cave under a ledge at the base of the sea cliff. Here, lost without branches and leaves about him, he settled to await improvement.

When, at midday of the third day, the rain stopped altogether, and the sky opened before a small, fresh wind, letting light through to glitter upon a tremulous sea, Hook was so weak that his good wing trailed also to prop him upright, and his open eyes were lusterless. But his wounds were hardened, and he felt the return of hunger. Beyond his shelter, he heard the gulls flying in great numbers and crying their joy at the cleared air. He could even hear, from the fringe of the river, the ecstatic and unstinted bubblings and chirpings of the small birds. The grassland, he felt, would be full of the stirring anew of the close-bound life, the undrowned insects clicking as they dried out, the snakes slithering down, heads half erect, into the grasses where the mice, gophers and ground squirrels ran and stopped and chewed and licked themselves smoother and drier.

With the aid of his hunger, and on the crutches of his wings, Hook came down to stand in the sun beside his cave, whence he could watch the beach. Before him, in ellipses on tilting planes, the gulls flew. The surf was rearing again, and beginning to shelve and hiss on the sand. Through the white foam-writing it left, the long-billed pipers twinkled in bevies, escaping each wave, then racing down after it to plunge their fine drills into the minute double holes where the sand crabs bubbled. In the third row of breakers two seals lifted sleek, streaming heads and barked, and over them, trailing his spider legs, a great crane flew south. Among the stones at the foot of the cliff, small red and green crabs made a little, continuous rattling and knocking. The cliff swallows glittered and twanged on aerial forays.

The afternoon began auspiciously for Hook also. One of the two gulls which came squabbling above him dropped a freshly caught fish to the sand. Quickly Hook was upon it. Gripping it, he raised his good wing and cocked his head with open beak at the many gulls which had circled and come down at once toward the fall of the fish. The gulls sheered off, cursing raucously.

Left alone on the sand, Hook devoured the fish and, after resting in the sun, withdrew again to his shelter.

IV

In the succeeding days, between rains, he foraged on the beach. He learned to kill and crack the small green crabs. Along the edge of the river mouth, he found the drowned bodies of mice and squirrels and even sparrows. Twice he managed to drive feeding gulls from their catch, charging upon them with buffeting wing and clattering beak. He grew stronger slowly, but the shot sail continued to drag. Often, at the choking thought of soaring and striking and the good, hot-blood kill, he strove to take off, but only the one wing came up, winnowing with a hiss, and drove him over onto his side in the sand. After these futile trials, he would rage and clatter. But gradually he learned to believe that he could not fly, that his life must now be that of the discharged nestling again. Denied the joy of space, without which the joy of loneliness was lost, the joy of battle and killing, the blood lust, became his whole concentration. It was his hope, as he charged feeding gulls, that they would turn and offer battle, but they never did. The sandpipers, at his approach, fled peeping, or, like a quiver of arrows shot together, streamed out over the surf in a long curve. Once, pent beyond bearing, he disgraced himself by shrieking challenge at the businesslike heron which flew south every evening at the same time. The heron did not even turn his head, but flapped and glided on.

Hook's shame and anger became such that he stood awake at night. Hunger kept him awake also, for these little leavings of the gulls could not sustain his great body in its renewed violence. He became aware that the gulls slept at night in flocks on the sand, each with one leg tucked under him. He discovered also that the curlews and the pipers, often mingling, likewise slept, on the higher remnant of the bar. A sensation of evil delight filled him in the consideration of protracted striking among them.

There was only half of a sick moon in a sky of running but far-separated clouds on the night when he managed to stalk into the center of the sleeping gulls. This was light enough, but so great was his vengeful pleasure that there broke from him a shrill scream of challenge as he first struck. Without the power of flight behind it, the blow was not murderous, and this newly discovered impotence made Hook crazy, so that he screamed again and again as he struck and tore at the felled gull. He slew the one, but was twice knocked over by its heavy flounderings, and all the others rose above him, weaving and screaming, protesting in the thin moonlight. Wakened by their clamor, the wading birds also took wing, startled and plaintive. When the beach was quiet again, the flocks had settled elsewhere, beyond his pitiful range, and he was left alone beside the single kill. It was a disappointing victory. He fed with lowering spirit.

Thereafter, he stalked silently. At sunset he would watch where the gulls settled along the miles of beach, and after dark he would come like a sharp shadow among them, and drive with his hook on all sides of him, till the beatings of a poorly struck victim sent the flock up. Then he would turn vindictively upon the fallen and finish them. In his best night, he killed five from one flock. But he ate only a little from one, for the vigor resulting from occasional repletion strengthened only his ire, which became so great at such a time that food revolted him. It was not the joyous, swift, controlled hunting anger of a sane hawk, but something quite different, which made him dizzy if it continued too long, and left him unsatisfied with any kill.

Then one day, when he had very nearly struck a gull while driving it from a gasping yellowfin, the gull's wing rapped against him as it broke for its running start, and, the trailing wing failing to support him, he was knocked over. He flurried awkwardly in the sand to regain his feet, but his mastery of the beach was ended. Seeing him, in clear sunlight, struggling after the chance blow, the gulls returned about him in a flashing cloud, circling and pecking on the wing. Hook's plumage showed quick little jets of irregularity here and there. He reared back, clattering and erecting the good wing, spreading the great, rusty tail for balance. His eyes shone with a little of the old pleasure. But it died, for he could reach none of them. He was forced to turn and dance awkwardly on the sand, trying to clash bills with each tormentor. They banked up quealing and returned, weaving about him in concentric and overlapping circles. His scream was lost in their clamor, and he appeared merely to be hopping clumsily with his mouth open. Again he fell sideways. Before he could right himself, he was bowled over, and a second time, and lay on his side, twisting his neck to reach them and clappering in blind fury, and was struck three times by three successive gulls, shrieking their flock triumph.

Finally he managed to roll to his breast, and to crouch with his good wing spread wide and the other stretched nearly as far, so that he extended like a gigantic moth, only his snake head, with its now silent scimitar, erect. One great eye blazed under its level brow, but where the other had been was a shallow hole from which thin blood trickled to his russet gap.

In this crouch, by short stages, stopping repeatedly to turn and drive the gulls up, Hook dragged into the river canyon and under the stiff cover of the bitter-leafed laurel. There the gulls left him, soaring up with great clatter of their valor. Till nearly sunset Hook, broken spirited and enduring his hardening eye socket, heard them celebrating over the waves.

When his will was somewhat replenished, and his empty eye socket had stopped the twitching and vague aching which had forced him often to roll ignominiously to rub it in the dust, Hook ventured from the protective lacings of his thicket. He knew fear again, and the challenge of his remaining eye was once more strident, as in adolescence. He dared not return to the beaches, and with a new, weak hunger, the home hunger, enticing him, made his way by short hunting journeys back to the wild wheat slopes and the crisp oaks. There was in Hook an unwonted sensation now, that of the ever-neighboring possibility of death. This sensation was beginning, after his period as a mad bird on the beach, to solidify him into his last stage of life. When, during his slow homeward passage, the gulls wafted inland over him, watching the earth with curious, miserish eyes, he did not cower, but neither did he challenge, either by opened beak or by raised shoulder. He merely watched carefully, learning his first lessons in observing the world with one eye.

At first the familiar surroundings of the bend in the river and the tree with the dead limb to which he could not ascend, aggravated his humiliation, but in time, forced to live cunningly and half-starved, he lost much of his savage pride. At the first flight of a strange hawk over his realm, he was wild at his helplessness, and kept twisting his head like an owl, or spinning in the grass like a small and feathered dervish, to keep the hateful beauty of the wind-rider in sight. But in the succeeding weeks, as one after another coasted his beat, his resentment declined, and when one of the raiders, a haughty year-ling, sighted his upstaring eye, and plunged and struck him dreadfully, and failed to kill him only because he dragged under a thicket in time, the second of his great hungers was gone. He had no longer the true lust to kill, no joy of battle, but only the poor desire to fill his belly.

Then truly he lived in the wheat and the brush like a ground owl, ridden with ground lice, dusty or muddy, ever half-starved, forced to sit for hours by small holes for petty and unsatisfying kills. Only once during the final months before his end did he make a kill where the breath of danger recalled his valor, and then the danger was such as a hawk with wings and eyes would scorn. Waiting beside a gopher hole, surrounded by the high, yellow grass, he saw the head emerge, and struck, and was amazed that there writhed in his clutch the neck and dusty coffin-skull of a rattlesnake. Holding his grip, Hook saw the great, thick body slither up after, the tip an erect, strident blur, and writhe on the dirt of the gopher's mound. The weight of the snake pushed Hook about, and once threw him down, and the rising and falling whine of the rattles made the moment terrible, but the vaulted mouth, gap-ing from the closeness of Hook's grip, so that the pale, envenomed sabers stood out free, could not reach him. When Hook replaced the grip of his beak with the grip of his talons, and was free to strike again and again at the base of the head, the struggle was over. Hook tore and fed on the fine, wat-ery flesh, and left the tattered armor and the long, jointed bone for the marching ants.

When the heavy rains returned, he ate well during the period of the first escapes from flooded burrows, and then well enough, in a vulture's way, on the drowned creatures. But as the rains lingered, and the burrows hung full of water, and there were no insects in the grass and no small birds sleeping in the thickets, he was constantly hungry, and finally unbearably hungry. His sodden and ground-broken plumage stood out raggedly about him, so that he looked fat, even bloated, but underneath it his skin clung to his bones. Save for his great talons and clappers, and the rain in his down, he would have been like a handful of air. He often stood for a long time under some bush or ledge, heedless of the drip, his one eye filmed over, his mind neither asleep or awake, but between. The gurgle and swirl of the brimming river, and the sound of chunks of the bank cut away to splash and dissolve in the already muddy flood, became familiar to him, and yet a torment, as if that great, ceaselessly working power of water ridiculed his frailty, within which only the faintest spark of valor still glimmered. The last two nights before the rain ended, he huddled under the floor of the bridge on the coastal highway, and heard the palpitant thunder of motors swell and roar over him. The trucks shook the bridge so that Hook, even in his famished lassitude, would sometimes open his one great eye wide and startled.

V

After the rains, when things became full again, bursting with growth and sound, the trees swelling, the thickets full of song and chatter, the fields, turning green in the sun, alive with rustling passages, and the moonlit nights strained with the song of the peepers all up and down the river and in the pools in the fields, Hook had to bear the return of the one hunger left him. At times this made him so wild that he forgot himself and screamed challenge from the open ground. The fretfulness of it spoiled his hunting, which was not entirely a matter of patience. Once he was in despair, and lashed himself through the grass and thickets, trying to rise when that virgin scent drifted for a few moments above the current of his own river. Then, breathless, his beak agape, he saw the strong suitor ride swiftly down on the wind over him, and heard afar the screaming fuss of the harsh wooing in the alders. For that moment even the battle heart beat in him again. The rim of his good eye was scarlet, and a little bead of new blood stood in the socket of the other. With beak and talon, he ripped at a fallen log, and made loam and leaves fly from about it.

But the season of love passed over to the nesting season, and Hook's love hunger, unused, shriveled in him with the others, and there remained in him only one stern quality befitting a hawk, and that the negative one, the remnant, the will to endure. He resumed his patient, plotted hunting, now along a field of the Japanese farmer, but ever within reach of the river thickets.

Growing tough and dry again as the summer advanced, inured to the fam-

ily of the farmer, whom he saw daily, stooping and scraping with sticks in
the ugly, open rows of their fields, where no lovely grass rustled and no life
stirred save the shameless gulls, which walked at the heels of the workers,
gobbling the worms and grubs they turned up, Hook became nearly content
with his shard of life. The only longing or resentment to pierce him was that
which he suffered occasionally when forced to hide at the edge of the mile-
long bean field from the wafted cruising and the restive, down-bent gaze of
one of his own kind. For the rest, he was without flame, a snappish, dust-
colored creature, fading into the grasses he trailed through, and suited to his
petty ways.

At the end of that summer, for the second time in his four years, Hook
underwent a drouth. The equinoctial period passed without a rain. The
laurel and the rabbit-brush dropped dry leaves. The foliage of the oaks
shriveled and curled. Even the night fogs in the river canyon failed. The
farmer's red cattle on the hillside lowed constantly, and could not feed on
the dusty stubble. Grass fires broke out along the highways, and ate fast in
the wind, filling the hollows with the smell of smoke, and died in the dirt of
the shorn hills. The river made no sound. Scum grew on its vestigial pools,
and turtles died and stank among the rocks. The dust rode before the wind,
and ascended and flowered to nothing between the hills, and every sunset
was red with the dust in the air. The people in the farmer's house quarreled,
and even struck one another. Birds were silent, and only the hawks flew
much. The animals lay breathing hard for very long spells, and ran and crept
jerkily. Their flanks were fallen in, and their eyes were red.

At first Hook gorged at the fringe of the grass fires on the multitudes of
tiny things that came running and squeaking. But thereafter there were the
blackened strips on the hills, and little more in the thin, crackling grass. He
found mice and rats, gophers and ground-squirrels, and even rabbits, dead
in the stubble and under the thickets, but so dry and fleshless that only a
faint smell rose from them, even on the sunny days. He starved on them. By
early December he had wearily stalked the length of the eastern foothills,
hunting at night to escape the voracity of his own kind, resting often upon
his wings. The queer trail of his short steps and great horned toes zigzagged
in the dust and was erased by the wind at dawn. He was nearly dead, and
could make no sound through the horn funnels of his clappers.

Then one night the dry wind brought him, with the familiar, lifeless dust,
another familiar scent, troublesome, mingled and unclear. In his vision-
dominated brain he remembered the swift circle of his flight a year past,
crossing in one segment, his shadow beneath him, a yard cluttered with
crates and chickens, a gray barn and then again the plowed land and the
stubble. Traveling faster than he had for days, impatient of his shrunken
sweep, Hook came down to the farm. In the dark wisps of cloud blown
among the stars over him, but no moon, he stood outside the wire of the

chicken run. The scent of fat and blooded birds reached him from the shelter, and also within the enclosure was water. At the breath of the water, Hook's gorge contracted, and his tongue quivered and clove in its groove of horn. But there was the wire. He stalked its perimeter and found no opening. He beat it with his good wing, and felt it cut but not give. He wrenched at it with his beak in many places, but could not tear it. Finally, in a fury which drove the thin blood through him, he leaped repeatedly against it, beating and clawing. He was thrown back from the last leap as from the first, but in it he had risen so high as to clutch with his beak at the top wire. While he lay on his breast on the ground, the significance of this came upon him.

Again he leapt, clawed up the wire, and, as he would have fallen, made even the dead wing bear a little. He grasped the top and tumbled within. There again he rested flat, searching the dark with quick-turning head. There was no sound or motion but the throb of his own body. First he drank at the chill metal trough hung for the chickens. The water was cold, and loosened his tongue and his tight throat, but it also made him drunk and dizzy, so that he had to rest again, his claws spread wide to brace him. Then he walked stiffly, to stalk down the scent. He trailed it up the runway. Then there was the stuffy, body-warm air, acrid with droppings, full of soft rustlings as his talons clicked on the board floor. The thick, white shapes showed faintly in the darkness. Hook struck quickly, driving a hen to the floor with one blow, its neck broken and stretched out stringily. He leaped the still pulsing body, and tore it. The rich, streaming blood was overpowering to his dried senses, his starved, leathery body. After a few swallows, the flesh choked him. In his rage, he struck down another hen. The urge to kill took him again, as in those nights on the beach. He could let nothing go. Balked of feeding, he was compelled to slaughter. Clattering, he struck again and again. The henhouse was suddenly filled with the squawking and helpless rushing and buffeting of the terrified, brainless fowls.

Hook reveled in mastery. Here was game big enough to offer weight against a strike, and yet unable to soar away from his blows. Turning in the midst of the turmoil, cannily, his fury caught at the perfect pitch, he struck unceasingly. When the hens finally discovered the outlet, and streamed into the yard, to run around the fence, beating and squawking, Hook followed them, scraping down the incline, clumsy and joyous. In the yard, the cock, a bird as large as he, and much heavier, found him out and gave valiant battle. In the dark, and both earthbound, there was little skill, but blow upon blow, and only chance parry. The still squawking hens pressed into one corner of the yard. While the duel went on, a dog, excited by the sustained scuffling, began to bark. He continued to bark, running back and forth along the fence on one side. A light flashed on in an uncurtained window of the farmhouse, and streamed whitely over the crates littering the ground.

Enthralled by his old battle joy, Hook knew only the burly cock before him. Now, in the farthest reach of the window light, they could see each other dimly. The Japanese farmer, with his gun and lantern, was already at the gate when the finish came. The great cock leapt to jab with his spurs and, toppling forward with extended neck as he fell, was struck and extinguished. Blood had loosened Hook's throat. Shrilly he cried his triumph. It was a thin and exhausted cry, but within him as good as when he shrilled in mid-air over the plummeting descent of a fine foe in his best spring.

The light from the lantern partially blinded Hook. He first turned and ran directly from it, into the corner where the hens were huddled. They fled apart before his charge. He essayed the fence, and on the second try, in his desperation, was out. But in the open dust, the dog was on him, circling, dashing in, snapping. The farmer, who at first had not fired because of the chickens, now did not fire because of the dog, and, when he saw that the hawk was unable to fly, relinquished the sport to the dog, holding the lantern up in order to see better. The light showed his own flat, broad, dark face as sunken also, the cheekbones very prominent, and showed the torn-off sleeves of his shirt and the holes in the knees of his overalls. His wife, in a stained wrapper, and barefooted, heavy black hair hanging around a young, passionless face, joined him hesitantly, but watched, fascinated and a little horrified. His son joined them too, encouraging the dog, but quickly grew silent. Courageous and cruel death, however it may afterward sicken the one who has watched it, is impossible to look away from.

In the circle of the light, Hook turned to keep the dog in front of him. His one eye gleamed with malevolence. The dog was an Airedale, and large. Each time he pounced, Hook stood ground, raising his good wing, the pinions newly torn by the fence, opening his beak soundlessly, and, at the closest approach, hissed furiously, and at once struck. Hit and ripped twice by the whetted horn, the dog recoiled more quickly from several subsequent jumps and, infuriated by his own cowardice, began to bark wildly. Hook maneuvered to watch him, keeping his head turned to avoid losing the foe on the blind side. When the dog paused, safely away, Hook watched him quietly, wing partially lowered, beak closed, but at the first move again lifted the wing and gaped. The dog whined, and the man spoke to him encouragingly. The awful sound of his voice made Hook for an instant twist his head to stare up at the immense figures behind the light. The dog again sallied, barking, and Hook's head spun back. His wing was bitten this time, and with a furious sideblow, he caught the dog's nose. The dog dropped him with a yelp, and then, smarting, came on more warily, as Hook propped himself up from the ground again between his wings. Hook's artificial strength was waning, but his heart still stood to the battle, sustained by a fear of such dimension as he had never known before, but only anticipated when the arrogant young hawk had driven him to cover. The dog, unable to find any point at which the merciless, unwinking eye was not watching him, the parted beak waiting, paused and whimpered again.

"Oh, kill the poor thing," the woman begged.

The man, though, encouraged the dog again, saying, "Sick him; sick him."

The dog rushed bodily. Unable to avoid him, Hook was bowled down, snapping and raking. He left long slashes, as from the blade of a knife, on the dog's flank, but before he could right himself and assume guard again, was caught by the good wing and dragged, clattering, and seeking to make a good stroke from his back. The man followed them to keep the light on them, and the boy went with him, wetting his lips with his tongue and keeping his fists closed tightly. The woman remained behind, but could not help watching the diminished conclusion.

In the little, palely shining arena, the dog repeated his successful maneuver three times, growling but not barking, and when Hook thrashed up from the third blow, both wings were trailing, and dark, shining streams crept on his black-fretted breast from the shoulders. The great eye flashed more furiously than it ever had in victorious battle, and the beak still gaped, but there was no more clatter. He faltered when turning to keep front; the broken wings played him false even as props. He could not rise to use his talons.

The man had tired of holding the lantern up, and put it down to rub his arm. In the low, horizontal light, the dog charged again, this time throwing the weight of his forepaws against Hook's shoulder, so that Hook was crushed as he struck. With his talons up, Hook raked at the dog's belly, but the dog conceived the finish, and furiously worried the feathered bulk. Hook's neck went limp, and between his gaping clappers came only a faint chittering, as from some small kill of his own in the grasses.

In this last conflict, however, there had been some minutes of the supreme fire of the hawk whose three hungers are perfectly fused in the one will; enough to burn off a year of shame.

Between the great sails the light body lay caved and perfectly still. The dog, smarting from his cuts, came to the master and was praised. The woman, joining them slowly, looked at the great wingspread, her husband raising the lantern that she might see it better.

"Oh, the brave bird," she said.

STUDY QUESTIONS

1. Clark's "Hook" is a short story. If you wished to convert "Hook" into an expository essay, what changes would you have to make?

2. Clark's story is divided into five sections. What major development of plot occurs in each of these sections?

3. How are Sections I and IV related?

4. When does Clark provide the first suggestion of Hook's approaching confrontation with the gulls? With the Japanese farmer?

5. In Section III, why does the farmer permit the hawk to live?

6. How do the reactions of the farmer and his wife to Hook's battle with the dog differ?

Loren C. Eiseley

THE BIRD AND THE MACHINE

Loren Eiseley (1907–   ) was born in Lincoln, Nebraska. He received his B.A. (1933) from the University of Nebraska, and his M.A. (1935) and Ph.D. (1937) from the University of Pennsylvania. He taught at the University of Kansas and Oberlin College before returning, in 1947, to the University of Pennsylvania where he is now University Professor in anthropology and history of science and head of the Department of the History and Philosophy of Science. A Guggenheim fellow, he has published widely in both popular periodicals and learned journals. *Darwin's Century* was given the Phi Beta Kappa science award in 1959, and *The Firmament of Time* (1960) received the John Burroughs medal and the Lecomte de Nouy award. His other books include *The Immense Journey* (1951), *Francis Bacon and the Modern Temper* (1952), and *Galapagos: The Flow of Wilderness* (1968).

I SUPPOSE THEIR little bones have years ago been lost among the stones and winds of those high glacial pastures. I suppose their feathers blew eventually into the piles of tumbleweed beneath the straggling cattle fences and rotted there in the mountain snows, along with dead steers and all the other things that drift to an end in the corners of the wire. I do not quite know why I should be thinking of birds over the *New York Times* at breakfast, particularly the birds of my youth half a continent away. It is a funny thing what the brain will do with memories and how it will treasure them and finally bring them into odd juxtapositions with other things, as though it wanted to make a design, or get some meaning out of them, whether you want it or not, or even see it.

It used to seem marvelous to me, but I read now that there are machines that can do these things in a small way, machines that can crawl about like animals, and that it may not be long now until they do more things—maybe even make themselves—I saw that piece in the *Times* just now. And then they will, maybe—well, who knows—but you read about it more and more with no one making any protest, and already they can add better than we and reach up and hear things through the dark and finger the guns over the night sky.

This is the new world that I read about at breakfast. This is the world that confronts me in my biological books and journals, until there are times when I sit quietly in my chair and try to hear the little purr of the cogs in my head and the tubes flaring and dying as the messages go through them and the circuits snap shut or open. This is the great age, make no mistake about it; the robot has been born somewhat appropriately along with the atom bomb, and the brain they say now is just another type of more complicated feedback system. The engineers have its basic principles worked out; it's mechanical, you know; nothing to get superstitious about; and man can always improve on nature once he gets the idea. Well, he's got it all right and that's why, I guess, that I sit here in my chair, with the article crunched in my hand, remembering those two birds and that bluemountain sunlight. There is another magazine article on my desk that reads "Machines Are Getting Smarter Every Day." I don't deny it, but I'll still stick with the birds. It's life I believe in, not machines.

Maybe you don't believe there is any difference. A skeleton is all joints and pulleys, I'll admit. And when man was in his simpler stages of machine building in the eighteenth century, he quickly saw the resemblances. "What," wrote Hobbes, "is the heart but a spring, and the nerves but so many strings, and the joints but so many wheels, giving motion to the whole body?" Tinkering about in their shops it was inevitable in the end that men would see the world as a huge machine "subdivided into an infinite number of lesser machines."

The idea took on with a vengeance. Little automatons toured the country —dolls controlled by clockwork. Clocks described as little worlds were taken on tours by their designers. They were made up of moving figures, shifting scenes and other remarkable devices. The life of the cell was unknown. Man, whether he was conceived as possessing a soul or not, moved and jerked about like these tiny puppets. A human being thought of himself in terms of his own tools and implements. He had been fashioned like the puppets he produced and was only a more clever model made by a greater designer.

Then in the nineteenth century, the cell was discovered, and the single machine in its turn was found to be the product of millions of infinitesimal machines—the cells. Now, finally, the cell itself dissolves away into an abstract chemical machine—and that into some intangible, inexpressible flow of energy. The secret seems to lurk all about, the wheels get smaller and smaller, and they turn more rapidly, but when you try to seize it the life is gone—and so, by popular definition, some would say that life was never there in the first place. The wheels and the cogs are the secret and we can make them better in time—machines that will run faster and more accurately than real mice to real cheese.

I have no doubt it can be done, though a mouse harvesting seeds on an autumn thistle is to me a fine sight and more complicated, I think, in his multiform activity, than a machine "mouse" running a maze. Also, I like to think of the possible shape of the future brooding in mice, just as it brooded once in a rather ordinary mousy insectivore who became a man. It leaves a nice fine indeterminate sense of wonder that even an electronic brain hasn't got, because you know perfectly well that if the electronic brain changes, it will be because of something man has done to it. But what man will do to himself he doesn't really know. A certain scale of time and a ghostly intangible thing called change are ticking in him. Powers and potentialities like the oak in the seed, or a red and awful ruin. Either way, it's impressive; and the mouse has it, too. Or those birds, I'll never forget those birds—yet before I measured their significance, I learned the lesson of time first of all. I was young then and left alone in a great desert—part of an expedition that had scattered its men over several hundred miles in order to carry on research more effectively. I learned there that time is a series of planes existing superficially in the same universe. The tempo is a human illusion, a subjective clock ticking in our own kind of protoplasm.

As the long months passed, I began to live on the slower planes and to observe more readily what passed for life there. I sauntered, I passed more and more slowly up and down the canyons in the dry baking heat of midsummer. I slumbered for long hours in the shade of huge brown boulders that had gathered in tilted companies out on the flats. I had forgotten the world of men and the world had forgotten me. Now and then I found a skull in the canyons, and these justified my remaining there. I took a serene cold interest in these discoveries. I had come, like many a naturalist before me, to view life with a wary and subdued attention. I had grown to take pleasure in the divested bone.

I sat once on a high ridge that fell away before me into a waste of sand dunes. I sat through hours of a long afternoon. Finally, as I glanced beside my boot an indistinct configuration caught my eye. It was a coiled rattlesnake, a big one. How long he had sat with me I do not know. I had not frightened him. We were both locked in the sleepwalking tempo of the earlier world, baking in the same high air and sunshine. Perhaps he had been there when I came. He slept on as I left, his coils, so ill discerned by me, dissolving once more among the stones and gravel from which I had barely made him out.

Another time I got on a higher ridge, among some tough little wind-warped pines half covered over with sand in a basin-like depression that caught everything carried by the air up to those heights. There were a few thin bones of birds, some cracked shells of indeterminable age, and the knotty fingers of pine roots bulged out of shape from their long and agonizing grasp upon the crevices of the rock. I lay under the pines in the sparse shade and went to sleep once more.

It grew cold finally, for autumn was in the air by then, and the few things that lived thereabouts were sinking down into an even chillier scale of time. In the moments between sleeping and waking I saw the roots about me and slowly, slowly, a foot in what seemed many centuries, I moved my sleep-stiffened hands over the scaling bark and lifted my numbed face after the vanishing sun. I was a great awkward thing of knots and aching limbs, trapped up there in some long, patient endurance that involved the necessity of putting living fingers into rock and by slow, aching expansion bursting those rocks asunder. I suppose, so thin and slow was the time of my pulse by then, that I might have stayed on to drift still deeper into the lower cadences of the frost, or the crystalline life that glistens pebbles, or shines in a snow-flake, or dreams in the meteoric iron between the worlds.

It was a dim descent, but time was present in it. Somewhere far down in that scale the notion struck me that one might come the other way. Not many months thereafter I joined some colleagues heading higher into a remote windy tableland where huge bones were reputed to protrude like boulders from the turf. I had drowsed with reptiles and moved with the century-long pulse of trees; now, lethargically, I was climbing back up some invisible ladder of quickening hours. There had been talk of birds in connection with my duties. Birds are intense, fast-living creatures—reptiles, I suppose one might say, that have escaped out of the heavy sleep of time, transformed fairy creatures dancing over sunlit meadows. It is a youthful fancy, no doubt, but because of something that happened up there among the escarpments of that range, it remains with me a lifelong impression. I can never bear to see a bird imprisoned.

We came into that valley through the trailing mists of a spring night. It was a place that looked as though it might never have known the foot of man, but our scouts had been ahead of us and we knew all about the abandoned cabin of stone that lay far up on one hillside. It had been built in the land rush of the last century and then lost to the cattlemen again as the marginal soils failed to take to the plow.

There were spots like this all over that country. Lost graves marked by unlettered stones and old corroding rim-fire cartridge cases lying where somebody had made a stand among the boulders that rimmed the valley. They are all that remain of the range wars; the men are under the stones now. I could see our cavalcade winding in and out through the mist below us: torches, the reflection of the truck lights on our collecting tins, and the far-off bumping of a loose dinosaur thigh bone in the bottom of a trailer. I stood on a rock a moment looking down and thinking what it cost in money and equipment to capture the past.

We had, in addition, instructions to lay hands on the present. The word had come through to get them alive—birds, reptiles, anything. A zoo somewhere abroad needed restocking. It was one of those reciprocal matters in which science involves itself. Maybe our museum needed a stray ostrich egg and this was the payoff. Anyhow, my job was to help capture some birds and that was why I was there before the trucks.

The cabin had not been occupied for years. We intended to clean it out and live in it, but there were holes in the roof and the birds had come in and were roosting in the rafters. You could depend on it in a place like this where everything blew away, and even a bird needed some place out of the weather and away from coyotes. A cabin going back to nature in a wild place draws them till they come in, listening at the eaves, I imagine, pecking softly among the shingles till they find a hole and then suddenly the place is theirs and man is forgotten.

Sometimes of late years I find myself thinking the most beautiful sight in the world might be the birds taking over New York after the last man has run away to the hills. I will never live to see it, of course, but I know just how it will sound because I've lived up high and I know the sort of watch birds keep on us. I've listened to sparrows tapping tentatively on the outside of air conditioners when they thought no one was listening, and I know how other birds test the vibrations that come up to them through the television aerials.

"Is he gone?" they ask, and the vibrations come up from below, "Not yet, not yet."

Well, to come back, I got the door open softly and I had the spotlight all ready to turn on and blind whatever birds there were so they couldn't see to get out through the roof. I had a short piece of ladder to put against the far wall where there was a shelf on which I expected to make the biggest haul. I had all the information I needed just like any skilled assassin. I pushed the door open, the hinges squeaking only a little. A bird or two stirred—I could hear them—but nothing flew and there was a faint starlight through the holes in the roof.

I padded across the floor, got the ladder up and the light ready, and slithered up the ladder till my head and arms were over the shelf. Everything was dark as pitch except for the starlight at the little place back of the shelf near the eaves. With the light to blind them, they'd never make it. I had them. I reached my arm carefully over in order to be ready to seize whatever was there and I put the flash on the edge of the shelf where it would stand by itself when I turned it on. That way I'd be able to use both hands.

Everything worked perfectly except for one detail—I didn't know what kind of birds were there. I never thought about it at all, and it wouldn't have mattered if I had. My orders were to get something interesting. I snapped on the flash and sure enough there was a great beating and feathers flying, but instead of my having them, they, or rather he, had me. He had my hand, that is, and for a small hawk not much bigger than my fist he was doing all right. I heard him give one short metallic cry when the light went on and my hand descended on the bird beside him; after that he was busy with his claws and his beak was sunk in my thumb. In the struggle I knocked the lamp over on the shelf, and his mate got her sight back and whisked neatly through the hole in the roof and off among the stars outside. It all happened in fifteen seconds and you might think I would have fallen down the ladder, but no, I had a professional assassin's reputation to keep up, and the bird, of course, made the mistake of thinking the hand was the enemy and not the eyes behind it. He chewed my thumb up pretty effectively and lacerated my hand with his claws, but in the end I got him, having two hands to work with.

He was a sparrow hawk and a fine young male in the prime of life. I was sorry not to catch the pair of them, but as I dripped blood and folded his wings carefully, holding him by the back so that he couldn't strike again, I had to admit the two of them might have been more than I could have handled under the circumstances. The little fellow had saved his mate by diverting me, and that was that. He was born to it, and made no outcry now, resting in my hand hopelessly, but peering toward me in the shadows behind the lamp with a fierce, almost indifferent glance. He neither gave nor expected mercy and something out of the high air passed from him to me, stirring a faint embarrassment.

I quit looking into that eye and managed to get my huge carcass with its fist full of prey back down the ladder. I put the bird in a box too small to allow him to injure himself by struggle and walked out to welcome the arriving trucks. It had been a long day, and camp still to make in the darkness. In the morning that bird would be just another episode. He would go back with the bones in the truck to a small cage in a city where he would spend the rest of his life. And a good thing, too. I sucked my aching thumb and spat out some blood. An assassin has to get used to these things. I had a professional reputation to keep up.

In the morning, with the change that comes on suddenly in that high country, the mist that had hovered below us in the valley was gone. The sky was a deep blue, and one could see for miles over the high outcroppings of stone. I was up early and brought the box in which the little hawk was imprisoned out onto the grass where I was building a cage. A wind as cool as a mountain spring ran over the grass and stirred my hair. It was a fine day to be alive. I looked up and all around and at the hole in the cabin roof out of which the other little hawk had fled. There was no sign of her anywhere that I could see.

"Probably in the next county by now," I thought cynically, but before beginning work I decided I'd have a look at my last night's capture.

Secretively, I looked again all around the camp and up and down and opened the box. I got him right out in my hand with his wings folded properly and I was careful not to startle him. He lay limp in my grasp and I could feel his heart pound under the feathers but he only looked beyond me and up.

I saw him look that last look away beyond me into a sky so full of light that I could not follow his gaze. The little breeze flowed over me again, and nearby a mountain aspen shook all its tiny leaves. I suppose I must have had an idea then of what I was going to do, but I never let it come up into consciousness. I just reached over and laid the hawk on the grass.

He lay there a long minute without hope, unmoving, his eyes still fixed on that blue vault above him. It must have been that he was already so far away in heart that he never felt the release from my hand. He never even stood. He just lay with his breast against the grass.

In the next second after that long minute he was gone. Like a flicker of light, he had vanished with my eyes full on him, but without actually seeing even a premonitory wing beat. He was gone straight into that towering emptiness of light and crystal that my eyes could scarcely bear to penetrate. For another long moment there was silence. I could not see. The light was too intense. Then from far up somewhere a cry came ringing down.

I was young then and had seen little of the world, but when I heard that cry my heart turned over. It was not the cry of the hawk I had captured; for, by shifting my position against the sun, I was now seeing further up. Straight out of the sun's eye, where she must have been soaring restlessly above us for untold hours, hurtled his mate. And from far up, ringing from peak to peak of the summits over us, came a cry of such unutterable and ecstatic joy that it sounds down across the years and tingles among the cups on my quiet breakfast table.

I saw them both now. He was rising fast to meet her. They met in a great soaring gyre that turned to a whirling circle and a dance of wings. Once more, just once, their two voices, joined in a harsh wild medley of question and response, struck and echoed against the pinnacles of the valley. Then they were gone forever somewhere into those upper regions beyond the eyes of men.

I am older now, and sleep less, and I have seen most of what there is to see and am not very much impressed any more, I suppose, by anything. "What Next in the Attributes of Machines?" my morning headline runs. "It Might Be the Power to Reproduce Themselves."

I lay the paper down and across my mind a phrase floats insinuatingly: "It does not seem that there is anything in the construction, constituents, or behavior of the human being which it is essentially impossible for science to duplicate and synthesize. On the other hand . . ."

All over the city the cogs in the hard, bright mechanisms have begun to turn. Figures move through computers, names are spelled out, a thoughtful machine selects the fingerprints of a wanted criminal from an array of thousands. In the laboratory an electronic mouse runs swiftly through a maze toward the cheese it can neither taste nor enjoy. On the second run it does better than a living mouse.

"On the other hand . . ." Ah, my mind takes up, on the other hand the machine does not bleed, ache, hang for hours in the empty sky in a torment of hope to learn the fate of another machine, nor does it cry out with joy nor dance in the air with the fierce passion of a bird. Far off, over a distance greater than space, that remote cry from the heart of heaven makes a faint buzzing among my breakfast dishes and passes on and away.

STUDY QUESTIONS

1. If any one sentence can be called the thesis sentence of this essay, which sentence is it? How effective is the transition between this sentence and the paragraph following it?

2. The introduction to this essay is set off from the body of the essay by extra spacing. Why isn't the conclusion similarly set off?

3. This essay is entitled "The Bird and the Machine." Does the essay compare birds and machines? Contrast them? Both compare and contrast them? What is the relationship of the episode of the bird to the thesis sentence?

4. What is your reaction to the conversation between the sparrows and the vibrations? Is Eiseley there too "cute"?

5. Why is Eiseley slightly embarrassed by the bird's glance? Why does he say, "I quit looking into that eye . . ." instead of "those eyes"?

Stephen Vincent Benét

WE AREN'T SUPERSTITIOUS

Stephen Vincent Benét (1898–1943) was born in Bethlehem, Pennsylvania, and was the younger brother of William Rose Benét. Among his
classmates at Yale, where he received an M.A., were Archibald MacLeish,
Philip Barry, and Thornton Wilder. *Heavens and Earth,* a book of poems,
was published in 1920, but Benét achieved real fame with two short stories
—"Johnny Pye and the Fool Killer" and "The Devil and Daniel Webster." With support from a Guggenheim Fellowship, he wrote *John
Brown's Body* (1928), the distinctly American classic that won a Pulitzer
Prize. Benét did propagandist work during World War II. His use of American history and folklore made him both a critical and popular success during his own lifetime, but his reputation has now diminished.

USUALLY, our little superstitious rituals and propitiations
don't hurt our daily lives. Usually. And then, on occasion,
a superstition—a belief—flares into crowd-madness and
kills and kills again before it has run its course. As it did in Salem Village, in
1692.

That story is worth retelling, as a very typical example of what wild belief
and crowd hysteria can do to an average community. For Salem Village, in
1691, was no different in any way, from any one of a dozen little New England hamlets. It didn't expect celebrity or notoriety and its citizens were the
average people of their day and age. There was the main road and the parsonage and the meeting house, the block house, the Ingersoll house where
travelers put up for the night, the eight or nine other houses that made up the
village. Beyond, lay the outlying farms with their hard working farmers—a
few miles away lay Salem Town itself—fifteen miles away, the overgrown
village that was Boston. King Philip's War had been over for some fourteen
years and the Colony recovering from the shock of it—there were still individual slayings by Indians but the real power of the Indian was very

largely broken. Men might look forward, with hope, to peace and thriving for a time.

And, as for the men and women of Salem Village—they were tough and knotty stock, if you like, not widely lettered, not particularly tolerant, especially in religion—but no different from their neighbors at Andover and Topsfield or in Boston itself. There were sensible men and stupid men among them, model housewives and slatterns, trouble makers and more peaceable folk. The names were the Puritan names that we are accustomed to reverence—Mercy and Abigail and Deborah, Nathaniel and Samuel and John. They lived a life of hard work and long winters, drank rum on occasion, took their religion with that mixture of grimness and enthusiasm that marked the Puritan, and intended, under God's providence, to beat wilderness and Indian, and wax and increase in the land. They were a great deal more human, crotchety and colorful than the schoolbook pictures of dour-faced men in steeple-crowned hats would suggest. In fact, if you want to find out how human they were, you have only to read Judge Sewall's diary. He was one of the judges at the Salem witch trials—and heartily sorry for it, later. But his Pepysian account of his own unsuccessful courtship of Madam Winthrop, and how he brought her gloves and sweets, is in the purest vein of unconscious farce.

And yet, to this ordinary community in the early Spring of 1692, came a madness that was to shake all Massachusetts before its fever was burned out. We are wiser, now. We do not believe in witches. But if, say, three cases of Asiatic cholera were discovered in your own hometown, and certified as such by the local board of health—and if your local newspaper promptly ran a boxed warning to all citizens on the front page—you would have some faint idea of how the average Salem Villager felt, when the "afflicted children" denounced their first victims.

For witchcraft, to almost all the New Englanders of 1692, was as definite, diagnosable and dangerous an evil as bubonic plague. It had its symptoms, its prognosis and its appalling results. Belief in it was as firmly fixed in most people's minds as belief in the germ theory of disease is in ours. Cotton Mather was one of the most able and promising young ministers of his day. But when, in 1688, in Boston, an eleven-year-old girl named Martha Goodwin accused an unhappy Irish Catholic laundress of bewitching her, Cotton Mather believed the eleven-year-old girl. In fact, he took the precocious brat into his own house, to study her symptoms and cure them by fasting and prayer, and wrote and published an elaborate, scientific account of his treatment of the case—which doubtless played its own part in preparing men's minds for the Salem madness.

True, there had been only some twenty witch trials in New England up to the Salem affair—compared to the hundreds and thousands of hangings, burnings, duckings, drownings, that had gone on in Europe and the British Isles during the last few centuries. But people believed in witches—why should they not? They were in the Bible—even the Bible itself said, "Thou shalt not suffer a witch to live." They were in every old wives' tale that was whispered about the winter fires. And, in 1692, they were in Salem Village.

Three years before, Salem Village had got a new minister—the Reverend Samuel Parris, ex-merchant in the West Indies. He seems to have been a self-willed, self-important man with a great sense of his own and the church's dignity, and, no sooner were he and his family well settled in the parsonage, than a dispute began as to whether the parsonage property belonged to him or to the congregation. But there was nothing unusual about that—Salem Village was a rather troublesome parish and two, at least, of the three previous ministers had had salary and other difficulties with the good folk of Salem. The quarrel dragged on like the old boundary dispute between Salem and Topsfield, creating faction and hard feeling, a typically New England affair. But there were boundary disputes elsewhere and other congregations divided in mind about their ministers.

But the most important thing about Samuel Parris was neither his self-importance nor his attempt to get hold of the parsonage property. It was the fact that he brought with him to Salem Village, two West Indian servants— a man known as John Indian and a woman named Tituba. And when he bought those two or their services in the West Indies, he was buying a rope that was to hang nineteen men and women of New England—so odd are the links in the circumstantial chain.

Perhaps the nine-year-old Elizabeth Parris, the daughter of the parsonage, boasted to her new friends of the odd stories Tituba told and the queer things she could do. Perhaps Tituba herself let the report of her magic powers be spread about the village. She must have been as odd and imagination-stirring a figure as a parrot or a tame monkey in the small New England town. And the winters were long and white—and any diversion a godsend.

In any case, during the winter of 1691–92, a group of girls and women began to meet nightly at the parsonage, with Tituba and her fortune-telling as the chief attraction. Elizabeth Parris, at nine, was the youngest—then came Abigail Williams, eleven and Ann Putnam, twelve. The rest were older—Mercy Lewis, Mary Wolcott and Elizabeth Hubbard were seventeen, Elizabeth Booth and Susan Sheldon, eighteen, and Mary Warren and Sarah Churchill, twenty. Three were servants—Mercy Lewis had been employed by the Reverend George Burroughs, a previous minister of Salem Village, and now worked for the Putnams—Mary Warren was a maid at the John Procters', Sarah Churchill at the George Jacobs'. All, except for Elizabeth Parris, were adolescent or just leaving adolescence.

The elder women included a pair of gossipy, superstitious busybodies—Mrs. Pope and Mrs. Bibber—and young Ann Putnam's mother, Ann Putnam, Senior, who deserves a sentence to herself.

For the Putnams were a powerful family in the neighborhood and Ann Putnam, married at seventeen and now only thirty, is described as handsome, arrogant, temperamental and high-strung. She was also one of those people who can cherish a grudge and revenge it.

The circle met—the circle continued to meet—no doubt with the usual giggling, whispering and gossip. From mere fortune-telling it proceeded to other and more serious matters—table-rapping, perhaps, and a little West Indian voodoo—weird stories told by Tituba and weird things shown, while the wind blew outside and the big shadows flickered on the wall. Adolescent girls, credulous servants, superstitious old women—and the two enigmatic figures of Tituba, the West Indian, and Ann Putnam, Sr.

But soon the members of the circle began to show hysterical symptoms. They crawled under tables and chairs, they made strange sounds, they shook and trembled with nightmare fears. The thing became a village celebrity—and more. Something strange and out of nature was happening—who had ever seen normal young girls behave like these young girls? And no one—certainly not the Reverend Samuel Parris—even suggested that a mixed diet of fortune-telling, ghost stories and voodoo is hardly the thing for impressionable minds during a long New England winter. Hysteria was possession by an evil spirit; pathological lying, the Devil putting words into one's mouth. No one suggested that even Cotton Mather's remedy of fasting and prayer would be a good deal better for such cases than widespread publicity. Instead the Reverend Samuel became very busy. Grave ministers were called in to look at the afflicted children. A Dr. Gregg gave his opinion. It was almost too terrible to believe, and yet what else could be believed? Witchcraft!

Meanwhile, one may suppose, the "afflicted children," like most hysterical subjects, enjoyed the awed stares, the horrified looks, the respectful questions that greeted them, with girlish zest. They had been unimportant girls of a little hamlet—now they were, in every sense of the word, spot news. And any reporter knows what that does to certain kinds of people. They continued to writhe and demonstrate—and be the center of attention. There was only one catch about it, If they were really bewitched—somebody must be doing the bewitching—

On the 29th of February, 1692, in the midst of an appropriate storm of thunder-and-lightning, three women, Sarah Good, Sarah Osburn and Tituba, were arrested on the deadly charge of bewitching the children.

The next day, March 1, two Magistrates, Justice Hathorne and Justice Corwin, arrived with appropriate pomp and ceremony. The first hearing was held in the crowded meetinghouse of the Village—and all Salem swarmed to it, as crowds in our time have swarmed to other sleepy little villages, suddenly notorious.

The children—or the children and Tituba—had picked their first victims well. Sarah Good and Sarah Osburn were old women of no particular standing in the community. Sarah Good had been a beggar and a slattern— her husband testified, according to report and with a smugness that makes one long to kick him, that she "either was a witch or would be one very quickly," ending "I may say, with tears, that she is an enemy to all good." As for Sarah Osburn, she had married a redemptioner servant after the death of her former husband and probably lost caste in consequence. Also, she had been bedridden for some time and therefore not as regular in her church attendance as a good Christian should be.

We can imagine that meetinghouse—and the country crowd within it— on that chill March day. At one end was the majesty of the law—and the "afflicted children" where all might see them and observe. Dressed in their best, very likely, and with solicitous relatives near at hand. Do you see Mercy Lewis? Do you see Ann Putnam? And then the whole crowd turned to one vast, horrified eye. For there was the accused—the old woman—the witch!

The justices—grim Justice Hathorne in particular—had, evidently, arrived with their minds made up. For the first question addressed to Sarah Good was, bluntly:

"What evil spirit have you familiarity with?"

"None," said the piping old voice. But everybody in the village knew worthless Sarah Good. And the eye of the audience went from her to the deadly row of "afflicted children" and back again.

"Have you made no contracts with the devil?" proceeded the Justice.

"No."

The Justice went to the root of the matter at once.

"Why do you hurt these children?"

A rustle must have gone through the meetinghouse at that. Aye, that's it—the Justice speaks shrewdly—hark to the Justice! Aye, but look, too! Look at the children! Poor things, poor things!

"I do not hurt them. I scorn it," said Sarah Good, defiantly. But the Justice had her, now—he was not to be brushed aside.

"Who then do you employ to do it?"

"I employ nobody."

"What creature do you employ then?" For all witches had familiars.

"No creature, but I am falsely accused." But the sweat must have been on the old woman's palms by now.

The Justice considered. There was another point—minor but illuminating.

"Why did you go away muttering from Mr. Parris, his house?"

"I did not mutter but I thanked him for what he gave my child."

The Justice returned to the main charge, like any prosecuting attorney. "Have you made no contract with the devil?"

"No."

It was time for Exhibit A. The Justice turned to the children. Was Sarah Good one of the persons who tormented them? Yes, yes!—and a horrified murmur running through the crowd. And then, before the awe-stricken eyes of all, they began to be tormented. They writhed, they grew stiff, they contorted, they were stricken moaning or speechless. Yet, when they were brought to Sarah Good and allowed to touch her, they grew quite quiet and calm. For, as everyone knew, a witch's physical body was like an electric conductor—it reabsorbed, on touch, the malefic force discharged by witchcraft into the bodies of the tormented. Everybody could see what happened —and everybody saw. When the meetinghouse was quiet, the Justice spoke again.

"Sarah Good, do you not see now what you have done? Why do you not tell us the truth? Why do you torment these poor children?"

And with these words, Sarah Good was already hanged. For all that she could say was, "I do not torment them." And yet everyone had seen her, with their own eyes.

The questions went on—she fumbled in her answers—muttered a bit of prayer. Why did she mutter? And didn't you see how hard it was for her to pronounce the name of God? Pressed and desperate, she finally said that if anyone tormented the children, it must be Sarah Osburn—she knew herself guiltless. The pitiful fable did not save her. To Boston Jail.

Sarah Osburn's examination followed the same course—the same prosecutor's first question—the same useless denial—the same epileptic feats of the "afflicted children"—the same end. It was also brought out that Sarah Osburn had said that "she was more like to be bewitched than to be a witch"—very dangerous that!—and that she had once had a nightmare about "a thing all black like an Indian that pinched her in the neck."

Then Tituba was examined and gave them their fill of marvels, prodigies and horrors.

The West Indian woman, a slave in a strange land, was fighting for her life and she did it shrewdly and desperately. She admitted, repentantly, that she had tormented the children. But she had been forced to do so. By whom? By Goody Good and Goody Osburn and two other witches whom she hadn't yet been able to recognize. Her voodoo knowledge aided her—she filled the open ears of Justices and crowd with tales of hairy familiars and black dogs, red cats and black cats and yellow birds, the phantasm of a woman with legs and wings. And everybody could see that she spoke the truth. For, when she was first brought in, the children were tormented at her presence, but as soon as she had confessed and turned King's evidence, she was tormented herself, and fearfully. To Boston Jail with her—but she had saved her neck.

The hearing was over—the men and women of Salem and its outlying farms went broodingly or excitedly back to their homes to discuss the fearful workings of God's providence. Here and there a common-sense voice murmured a doubt or two—Sarah Good and Sarah Osburn were no great losses to the community—but still, to convict two old women of heinous crime on the testimony of greensick girls and a West Indian slave! But, on the whole, the villagers of Salem felt relieved. The cause of the plague had been found —it would be stamped out and the afflicted children recover. The Justices, no doubt, congratulated themselves on their prompt and intelligent action. The "afflicted children" slept, after a tiring day—they were not quite so used to such performances as they were to become.

As for the accused women, they went to Boston Jail—to be chained there, while waiting trial and gallows. There is an item of, "To chains for Sarah Good and Sarah Osburn, 14 shillings," in the jailor's record. Only, Sarah Osburn was not to go to the gallows—she died in jail instead, some five and a half weeks later, at a recorded expense to the Colony of one pound, three shillings and five-pence for her keep. And Tituba stayed snugly in prison till the madness collapsed—and was then sold by the Colony to defray the expenses of her imprisonment. One wonders who bought her and whether she ever got back to the West Indies. But, with that, her enigmatic figure disappears from the scene.

Meanwhile, on an outlying farm, Giles Corey, a turbulent, salty old fellow of 81, began to argue the case with his wife, Martha. He believed, fanatically, in the "afflicted children." She did not, and said so—even going so far as to say that the magistrates were blinded and she could open their eyes. It was one of those marital disputes that occur between strong-willed people. And it was to bring Martha Corey to the gallows and Giles Corey to an even stranger doom.

Yet now there was a lull, through which people whispered.

As for what went on in the minds of "the afflicted children," during that lull, we may not say. But this much is evident. They had seen and felt their power. The hearing had been the greatest and most exciting event of their narrow lives. And it was so easy to do—they grew more and more ingenious with each rehearsal. You twisted your body and groaned—and grown people were afraid.

Add to this, the three girl-servants, with the usual servants' grudges against present or former masters. Add to this, that high-strung, dominant woman, Ann Putnam, Sr., who could hold a grudge and remember it. Such a grudge as there might be against the Towne sisters, for instance—they were all married women of the highest standing, particularly Rebecca Nurse. But they'd taken the Topsfield side in that boundary dispute with

Salem. So suppose—just suppose—that one of them were found out to be a witch? And hadn't Tituba deposed that there were other women, besides Good and Osburn, who made her torment the children?

On March 19, Martha Corey and Rebecca Nurse were arrested on the charge of witchcraft. On March 21, they were examined and committed. And, with that, the real reign of terror began.

For if Martha Corey, notably religious and Godfearing, and Rebecca Nurse, saintly and thoughtful, could be witches, no one in Salem or New England was safe from the charge. The examinations were brutally unfair —the "children" yet bolder and more daring. They would interrupt questions now to shout that "a black man" was whispering in the prisoner's ear —if the accused stood still, they were tormented, if she moved her hands, they suffered even greater agonies. Their self-confidence became monstrous—there was no trick too fantastic for them to try. When Deodat Lawson, a former minister of Salem and a well-educated and intelligent man, came to Ingersoll's on March 19, he first saw Mary Wolcott who "as she stood by the door was bitten, so that she cried out of her wrist, and, looking at it, we saw apparently the marks of teeth, both upper and lower set, on each side of her wrist." It would not have deceived a child—but Mary Wolcott was one of the "afflicted children" and her words and self-bitings were as gospel. He then went to the parsonage, where Abigail Williams, another afflicted child, put on a very effective vaudeville-act indeed, throwing firebrands around the house, crying "Whish, whish, whish!" and saying that she was being tormented by Rebecca Nurse who was trying to make her sign the Devil's book.

After that, there was, obviously, nothing for the Reverend Lawson to do but to preach a thunderous sermon on the horrors of witchcraft— interrupted by demonstrations and cries from "the afflicted"—and thus do his little bit toward driving the madness on. For by now, Salem Village, as a community, was no longer sane.

Let us get the rest of it over quickly. The Salem witches ceased to be Salem's affair—they became a matter affecting the whole colony. Sir William Phips, the new governor, appointed a special court of Oyer and Terminer to try the cases. And the hangings began.

On January 1, 1692, no one, except possibly the "Circle children" had heard of Salem witches. On June 10, Bridget Bishop was hanged. She had not been one of the first accused, but she was the first to suffer. She had been married three times, kept a roadhouse on the road to Beverley where people drank rum and played shovelboard, and dressed, distinctively for the period, in a "black cap and black hat and red paragon bodice broidered and looped with diverse colors." But those seem to have been her chief offences. When questioned, she said "I never saw the Devil in my life."

All through the summer, the accusations, the arrest, the trials came thick and fast till the jails were crowded. Nor were those now accused friendless old beldames like Sarah Good. They included Captain John Alden (son of Miles Standish's friend) who saved himself by breaking jail, and the wealthy and prominent Englishes who saved themselves by flight. The most disgraceful scenes occurred at the trial of the saintly Rebecca Nurse. Thirty-nine citizens of Salem were brave enough to sign a petition for her and the jury brought in a verdict of "not guilty." The mob in the sweating courtroom immediately began to cry out and the presiding judge as much as told the jury to reverse their verdict. They did so, to the mob's delight. Then the Governor pardoned her. And "certain gentlemen of Salem"—and perhaps the mob—persuaded him into reversing his pardon. She was hanged on Gallows Hill on July 19 with Sarah Good, Sarah Wilds, Elizabeth How and Susanna Martin.

Susanna Martin's only witchcraft seems to have been that she was an unusually tidy woman and had once walked a muddy road without getting her dress bedraggled. No, I am quoting from testimony, not inventing. As for Elizabeth How, a neighbor testified, "I have been acquainted with Goodwife How as a naybor for nine or ten years and I never saw any harm in her but found her just in her dealings and faithful to her promises . . . I never heard her revile any person but she always pitied them and said, 'I pray God forgive them now'," But the children cried, "I am stuck with a pin. I am pinched," when they saw her—and she hanged.

It took a little more to hang the Reverend George Burroughs. He had been Salem Village's second minister—then gone on to a parish in Maine. And the cloth had great sanctity. But Ann Putnam and Mercy Lewis managed to doom him between them—with the able assistance of the rest of the troupe. Mr. Burroughs was unfortunate enough to be a man of unusual physical strength—anyone who could lift a gun by putting four fingers in its barrel, must do so by magic arts. Also, he had been married three times. So when the ghosts of his first two wives, dressed in winding-sheets, appeared in a sort of magic-lantern show to Ann Putnam and cried out that Mr. Burroughs had murdered them—the cloth could not save him then. Perhaps one of the most pathetic documents connected with the trials is the later petition of his orphaned children. It begins, "We were left a parcel of small children, helpless—"

Here and there, in the records, gleams a flash of frantic common sense. Susanna Martin laughs when Ann Putnam and her daughter go into convulsions at her appearance. When asked why, she says, "Well I may, at such folly. I never hurt this woman or her child in my life." John Procter, the prosperous farmer who employed Mary Warren, said sensibly, before his arrest, "If these girls are left alone, we will all be devils and witches. They ought all to be sent to the whipping-post." He was right enough about it— but his servant helped hang him. White-haired old George Jacobs, leaning on his two sticks, cried out, "You tax me for a wizard, you might as well tax me for a buzzard!" Nevertheless, he hanged. A member of the Nurse family testifies, "Being in court this 29th June, 1692, I saw Goodwife Bibber pull pins out of her clothes and hold them between her fingers and clasp her hands around her knee and then she cried out and said Goodwife Nurse pinched her." But such depositions did not save Rebecca Nurse or her sister, Mary Easty.

Judge, jury and colony preferred to believe the writhings of the children, the stammerings of those whose sows had died inexplicably, the testimony of such as Bernard Peach who swore that Susanna Martin had flown in through his window, bent his body into the shape of a "whoope" and sat upon him for an hour and a half.

One hanging on June 10, five on July 19, five on August 19, eight on September 22, including Mary Easty and Martha Corey. And of these the Reverend Noyes remarked, with unction, "What a sad thing it is to see eight firebrands of hell hanging there!" But for stubborn Giles Corey a different fate was reserved.

The old man had begun by believing in the whole hocus-pocus. He had quarreled with his wife about it. He had seen her arrested as a witch, insulted by the magistrates, condemned to die. Two of his sons-in-law had testified against her—he himself had been closely questioned as to her actions and had made the deposition of a badgered and simple man. Yes, she prayed a good deal—sometimes he couldn't hear what she said—that sort of thing. The memory must have risen to haunt him when she was condemned. Now, he himself was in danger.

Well, he could die as his wife would. But there was the property—his goods, his prospering lands. By law, the goods and property of those convicted of witchcraft were confiscated by the State and the name attainted. With a curious, grim heroism, Giles Corey drew up a will leaving that property to the two sons-in-law who had not joined in the prevailing madness. And then at his trial, he said "I will not plead. If I deny, I am condemned already in courts where ghosts appear as witnesses and swear men's lives away."

A curious, grim heroism? It was so. For those who refused to plead either guilty or not guilty in such a suit were liable to the old English punishment called *peine forte et dure*. It consisted in heaping weights or stones upon the unhappy victim till he accepted a plea—or until his chest was crushed. And exactly that happened to old Giles Corey. They heaped the stones upon him until they killed him—and two days before his wife was hanged, he died. But his property went to the two loyal sons-in-law, without confiscation— and his name was not attainted. So died Giles Corey, New England to the bone.

And then, suddenly and fantastically as the madness had come, it was gone.

Not without other victims. At Andover, for instance, the wife of a citizen had fallen unaccountably ill. The first thought had been to call in two of the "afflicted children" as experts on witchcraft. As a result, something like fifty people were arrested and several hanged. But, after the hangings of September 22, the special court of Oyer and Terminer did not meet again—though the jails were crowded with accused and condemned.

The "afflicted children," at long last, had gone too far. They had accused the Governor's lady. They had accused Mrs. Hall, the wife of the minister at Beverley and a woman known throughout the colony for her virtues. And there comes a point when driven men and women revolt against blood and horror. It was that which ended Robespierre's terror—it was that which ended the terror of the "afflicted children." The thing had become a *reductio ad absurdum*. If it went on, logically, no one but the "afflicted children" and their protégées would be left alive.

So the madness died. In January, 1693, the Superior Court brought twenty-one to trial and condemned three. But no one was executed. In May, 1693, a proclamation emptied the jails.

So it ended. And Cotton Mather published *Wonders of the Invisible World* to prove it had all been true and Robert Calef, of Boston, promptly replied with *More Wonders of the Invisible World,* confuting and attacking Cotton Mather. And, in 1706, Ann Putnam made public confession that she had been deluded by the Devil in testifying as she had. She had testified in every case but one. And in 1711, the colony of Massachusetts paid 50 pounds to the heirs of George Burroughs, 21 pounds to the heirs of Giles Corey—578 pounds in all to the heirs of various victims. An expensive business for the colony, on the whole.

What happened to the survivors? Well, the Reverend Samuel Parris quit Salem Village to go into business in Boston and died at Sudbury in 1720. And Ann Putnam died in 1716 and from the stock of the Putnams sprang Israel Putnam, the Revolutionary hero. And from the stock of the "witches," the Nurses and the others, sprang excellent and distinguished people of service to State and nation. And hanging Judge Hathorne's descendant was Nathaniel Hawthorne. And Cotton Mather remained a brilliant minister, but his ambitions, on the whole, did not prosper as he thought they should. While as for the sanctimonious Dr. Noyes who spoke so unctuously of the "eight firebrands of hell," according to legend, he got his just deserts. For the legend goes that Sarah Good cursed him, saying, "I am no witch and because you say I am, God will give you blood to drink"—and he is supposed to have died of a hemorrhage of the throat. But Mercy Lewis and the rest of the "afflicted children" did not die so. They went on and lived their lives.

And I have not even spoken of the fifty-five who actually confessed to being witches—or the solemn examination of a five-year-old child for witchcraft—or of how two of the Carrier boys were hung up by the heels to make them testify against their mother—or of the time when Benjamin Hutchinson and Eleazer Putnam went stabbing with their rapiers at invisible cats and were solemnly assured they had slain three witches, equally invisible.

We have no reason to hold Salem up to obloquy. It was a town, like another, and a strange madness took hold of it. But it is no stranger thing to hang a man for witchcraft than to hang him for the shape of his nose or the color of his skin. We are not superstitious, no. Well, let us be a little sure we are not. For persecution follows superstition and intolerance as fire follows the fuse. And, once we light that fire, we cannot foresee where it will end or what it will consume—any more than they could in Salem, two hundred and forty-five years ago.

STUDY QUESTIONS

1. Why does Benét feel that this historical narrative has relevance in a twentieth-century society? Do you agree?

2. Why did the "afflicted" children pretend they were bewitched? What does Benét mean when he says that the children "had picked their victims well"?

3. How did Giles Cory triumph over his judges?

4. Does the last paragraph seem an integral part of the essay? Why?

5. What words, sentences, paragraphs most clearly reveal Benét's attempt to sway the reader's emotions and even his judgment?

Newsweek

THE NEW MEDICINE
AND ITS WEAPONS

*C*ALL HIM Harry Wilson, a 46-year-old sales executive. He had just strolled out of a restaurant with his wife when he felt a sudden crushing pressure on his chest and slumped to the sidewalk, the victim of a heart attack.

A clot had formed in an artery of his heart, part of the heart muscle was no longer pumping blood, blood pressure had fallen and his skin was already cold. In a matter of minutes an ambulance was rushing him to the hospital—and the beginning of a month-long battle to save his life.

The oldest of human emotions would be exposed in that time: a man struck down in his prime, a wife alone, children wondering if they would ever see their father again. But these fears would be met by the newest creations of human ingenuity. There is, of course, no "right" time to have a coronary, but for Wilson and literally thousands of others who fall victim to heart attacks, liver disorders, kidney failures and other killer diseases, something extra is now working to sustain their lives today. Doctors and nurses bring not only their traditional skills and time-tested drugs to the battle but also an extraordinary array of life-saving mechanical and electronic aids that didn't exist a few years ago.

Some items represent fallout from military research, the space program and even the atomic bomb; still others are the products of new alliances between industrial giants and hospitals. Lockheed and the Mayo Clinic, for example, are collaborating on a new computerized system of hospital care; North American Aviation is working on an emphysema belt that makes the breath of life easier for men and women suffering lung damage. In some modern operating rooms where the New Medicine is practiced, the technicians manning the machines and monitors often outnumber the doctors.

Alarm: In hospitals from Newport News, Va., to Mountain View, Calif., heart patients like Wilson are taken to coronary intensive-care units where electrodes similar to those used by the Gemini astronauts are placed on their chest and legs so that technicians can monitor their electrocardiogram, pulse and blood pressure around the clock. Three hours after Wilson was admitted, an alarm flashed on the central control desk—his heart had stopped beating. Within seconds, a nurse had wheeled a cart to the bedside. Called the Max (for Maximum Care), the cart was equipped with everything needed for cardiac resuscitation. Quickly a doctor placed two plunger-like electrodes on Wilson's chest and gave him a 100-watt shock that started his heart going again.

Sometimes coronaries are followed by a pulmonary embolism—a clot lodged in a blood vessel in the lung. As soon as he coughed blood—a telltale sign—Wilson was wheeled to the nuclear-medicine lab and given an injection of radioactive albumin particles. When the particles passed through the tiny capillaries in the lung, a scanner outside the chest picked up the radiation and printed out a picture of the lung in black dots. A wedge-shaped blank in the scan pinpointed the portion of the lung not receiving blood, confirming the doctors' diagnosis. Wilson was given anticoagulant drugs.

The physicians also checked for clots with a thermograph. This distant relative of the U.S. Army's sniperscope and of space satellite detectors measures the heat given off in the form of infra-red radiations by various parts of the body. Variations in the intensity of the infra-red appear as "hot" and "cold" spots on film. The area of a clot—with its seriously diminished blood supply—is cold, and shows up much darker than the normal areas on the thermograph.

Four weeks after the attack that struck him down, Wilson, 20 pounds lighter and the drug digitalis in his pocket, walked out of the hospital. But he wasn't beyond the ministrations of the New Medicine yet. The heart attack had damaged the nerve center—or pacemaker—that controls the regularity of the heartbeat; he could suffer from heart block culminating in heart failure. To prevent this, surgeons supplied him with an artificial pacemaker made possible by advances in miniaturized computer parts.

The pacemaker comes in several models. Wilson's is a 2½-inch plastic, battery-powered generator installed under the skin high on the chest. It is connected to the heart with a plastic-coated wire threaded through a vein under the collarbone and into the right pumping chamber, or ventricle. Over a three-year period, the generator releases minibursts of electricity to keep the heart beating at a steady rate. When the generator wears out, it can be easily replaced during a relatively simple chest operation. A two-speed model comes with a magnetized actuator shaped like a ball-point pen. "If the wearer wants to increase his heart rate in order to play a set of tennis or run to catch a train," explains James Nelson of GE's X-ray department in Milwaukee, "he simply passes the pen over the spot on his body where the battery is implanted to speed the impulse."

Innovations: Nothing, it seems, is so far out that it can't be applied in the New Medicine. A NASA metal alloy, originally used for bearings, is being tested for artificial hip and elbow joints. An accelerometer intended to measure the impact of micrometeorites against spacecraft has been converted into a means of measuring minute muscle tremors in diagnosing neurologic disease. And the lunar walker, developed for unmanned exploration of the moon's surface, has been adapted as a walking wheelchair to allow paraplegics to climb stairs by manipulating manual or chin-strap controls.

So much is happening in the field of biomedical engineering that a group of doctors and manufacturers recently formed the Association for Advancement of Medical Instrumentation as a clearinghouse for information. "The big firms are loaded with technicians who can help us solve our problems," says Harvard's Dr. John P. Merrill, a pioneer in the use of the artificial kidney and kidney transplants. Merrill visualizes the day when artificial kidneys and other hardware will be subjected to government tests by some sort of Federal Spare Parts Administration similar to the way medications are policed by the Food and Drug Administration.

The Federal government's involvement in the biomedical field is already large. In the fiscal year ending in June, expenditures for applied research are estimated at $832 million. And only last week, the U.S. Public Health Service awarded more than $2.5 million—the largest grant since passage of the 1946 Hill-Burton program for hospital construction—to the University of Southern California to develop an automated system for diagnosis, continuous monitoring and treatment of the critically ill.

But the New Medicine still leaves many old problems unsolved. Gadgetry and special-care untis add to the already soaring costs of medical care. A heart-lung machine costs $15,000 and the average open-heart operation may cost $3,000. A cobalt unit for deep cancer therapy can run as high as $95,000 and the charge for each treatment may be $15 or $20. The cost of the hardware is only part of the price the patient must pay, of course. For each new device, a technician with the skills to run it must be found—and medical technologists of all kinds are in short supply. And sometimes the shortage of skilled hands spells disaster. Just three months ago, three patients at Hennepin County General Hospital in Minneapolis died of salt and mineral depletion while being "run" on the hospital's artificial kidney machine because of an improper mixture of the solution used in the machine.

Personal Touch: Moreover, the huge radiotherapy units, glowing oscilloscopes and snake-like catheters characteristic of the New Medicine can have a frightening effect on patients. "You can put in all the machinery you want," says a doctor at the National Institutes of Health, "but the patient wants some attention from a person, not a machine."

Sometimes, too, physicians become bedazzled and overly dependent on the machine gadgetry of their surroundings. One NIH official recalls a brain surgeon who balked at proceeding with a relatively routine operation when an electrical defeat occurred in one of the operating-room monitors. After his initial dismay, he was persuaded to go on without the monitor. "I think there is a tyranny of technology," says Dr. Irving S. Cooper of New York's St. Barnabas Hospital. "The machine is not the message."

Still, an estimated 12,000 persons are living useful lives today wearing implanted heart pacemakers. Hundreds have been saved by artificial heart valves made of metal and plastic. And rapidly, even these experimental methods of treatment are being supplanted by more ingenious techniques. Some of the newest weapons of the New Medicine:

Gas Endarterectomy

Heart attacks kill about 525,000 Americans annually. They occur because fatty deposits of atherosclerosis clog the coronary arteries feeding the heart muscle. Although surgeons have learned how to remove or clear obstructed blood vessels elsewhere in the body, few have successfully operated on the delicate coronaries. Recently, Doctors Philip Sawyer, Martin Kaplitt and Sol Sobel of the State University of New York Downstate Medical Center in Brooklyn have developed a way of clearing the coronaries with injections of carbon dioxide.

The procedure, called a gas endarterectomy, imitates the destructive pattern of the disease known as dissecting aneurysm. The surgeons insert a fine hypodermic needle attached to a carbon-dioxide cylinder into the wall of the artery. A few jets of the gas tear the lining away from the artery wall, at the same time loosening the fatty core of atherosclerosis. A small incision is then made in the artery and another burst of gas frees the deposit completely. Then the surgeons simply remove the core with forceps.

The Laser Knife

The laser started out as a possible death ray; its military uses are still untested, but its role as a tool of surgery is being demonstrated daily. Lasers produce bursts of light millions of times brighter than sunlight when electrical energy strikes a gas such as argon and makes it emit light which is amplified and reflected repeatedly. The result is light of one pure wave length instead of the usual jumble of waves from the whole spectrum. This "coherent" light can be focused in a narrow beam with enough heat to cut through diamonds and the precision to raise a blister on a single red blood cell.

To date, lasers have been used most successfully in medicine to repair small tears and defects in the retina, the lining at the back of the eye. Through a focusing scope, the ophthalmologist aims the laser at the defect and fires a brief burst of energy. The beam passes harmlessly through the lens of the eye, but it burns the layer of blood vessels behind the retina. This layer, called the choroid, oozes a thick substance that hardens, gluing the retina to the back of the eye. Hundreds of cases have been treated satisfactorily by laser at New York's Columbia-Presbyterian Medical Center.

Lasers have been used to destroy skin cancers. And since laser light tends to be absorbed more readily by dark tissue than by light tissue, lasers are being tried experimentally in the destruction of malignant melanoma, a darkly pigmented and usually lethal form of cancer. In some cases the beam has destroyed individual growths, usually on the skin, but no one has yet reported any complete cures. Some researchers fear the use of lasers in cancer surgery because the beams may splatter cancer cells from the tumor and hasten spread of the disease to other parts of the body.

Cryosurgery

The most promising of the new surgical methods is cryosurgery, destruction of tissue by freezing. The technique was pioneered by Dr. Irving Cooper, director of neurosurgery at St. Barnabas, to relieve the rigidity and uncontrollable tremors of Parkinson's disease by freezing a tiny cluster of nerve cells inside the brain. The patient is given a local anesthetic and a dime-size hole is cut in his skull. Guided by a series of Polaroid X-rays, Cooper inserts a probe the size of a crochet needle into the thalamus, about 2½ inches deep in the brain. He then circulated liquid nitrogen at temperatures ranging from—94 to—58 degrees Fahrenheit through the probe, controlling the temperature at the uninsulated tip by the rate of flow. The rest of the probe is vacuum-insulated, Thermos-bottle fashion, to avoid damage to normal tissue as it rests in the brain.

A ball of frozen tissue gradually forms around the tip and, since the patient is conscious, Cooper can gauge the effect by observing his hand movements. The procedure is safe, because if the ice ball grows too large and the patient shows signs of paralysis, he has 30 seconds to raise the probe temperature and avert permanent damage.

Cryosurgery is being tested increasingly in other types of surgery. Cooper, for example, has frozen brain tumors that are too deep in the brain to be removed by conventional methods. After destruction by freezing, the dead tumor breaks down and is removed by the blood stream. "It looks very promising," Cooper notes, "but I don't want to shout about it yet." At Buffalo VA hospital, Dr. Andrew Gage has frozen bone tumors by wrapping a freezing coil around the bone shaft. The dead bone forms a structure around which new bone forms, Gage reports. Dr. Maurice J. Gonder, also of Buffalo VA, and his associate Dr. Ward A. Soanes have found the cryosurgical probe a good way to remove the prostate gland with relatively little pain and blood loss. And Dr. William G. Cahan of New York's Memorial Hospital has used cryosurgery to remove tonsils, to stop abnormal uterine bleeding (by destroying the lining of the uterus) and to control bleeding and relieve pain from large incurable tumors. Cryosurgery, Cahan notes, "bids well for becoming the most versatile modality in medicine."

Treatment Under Pressure

Hyperbaric oxygen chambers look like huge submarines moored improbably to hospital basement floors. The resemblance is apt; patients undergoing open-heart surgery in the chambers are given pure oxygen to breathe while the chamber pressure is raised to about three times normal atmospheric pressure. This saturates their blood and body tissues with up to fifteen times the normal concentration of oxygen—giving the surgeon more time to operate.

Chicago's Lutheran General Hospital has three chambers ranging in size from 23 feet to 41 feet long; one contains a fully equipped operating room, another, a six-bed intensive-care unit, and the third is used for research and isolation of patients with severe infections. Together they cost more than $1.1 million to install. In addition to heart surgery, hyperbaric therapy has proved its worth in the treatment of tetanus and gas gangrene, because the bacteria causing these diseases are killed by oxygen in heavy concentration.

Some researchers have found that hyperbaric oxygen treatments improve a stroke victim's chances of recovery by compensating for the impaired blood supply to the brain; the chambers have also averted the need for amputation in patients with injuries or atherosclerotic deposits that cut off circulation to the arms or legs. Finally, they are widely used in operations to repair heart defects in infants, whose circulatory systems are often too tiny to be hooked to the tubes of a heart-lung machine.

A novel variation of high-pressure therapy has been devised by Doctors W. James Gardner and John Storer of Cleveland's Huron Road Hospital. They adapted the principle of the flyer's G-suit to treat shock and abdominal bleeding. In shock, blood pressure drops, causing blood to drain from the brain and lungs to pool in the abdomen. When shock patients are placed in the inflatable plastic suit, the pressure forces blood back into the upper part of the body. The suit also can reduce internal hemorrhage by closing the bleeding vessels. Gardner and Storer have also developed a plastic G-splint that works on the same pressure principle. The inflated splint holds an injured arm or leg on a cushion of air and protects it from infection at the same time.

Super-Clean Care

Control of infection remains one of the biggest problems in U.S. hospitals, especially for patients with severe burns or cancer patients receiving drugs that suppress their ability to produce antibodies against disease. The space program's experience with "White Rooms" made dustfree by elaborate controls demonstrates what can be done to create a super-clean area. The medical version is the "life island," a transparent plastic canopy that completely engulfs the patient's bed. A filtered ventilating unit at the foot of the bed provides fresh air nearly 100 per cent free of bacteria and dust particles. Before being placed in the life island, the patient showers with hexachlorophene solution twice a day for three days and takes antibiotics to rid his body of bacteria.

Sterile Food: The patient's meals come from cans and are passed through an ultraviolet-treated portal on prewrapped, sterilized plates; even his razor and toothbrush are sterilized. Doctors and nurses tend the patient through plastic sleeves constructed in the canopy wall. At the National Institutes of Health in Bethesda, Md., an electronic stethoscope is being used to take readings of the patient's chest sounds from a distance. Among the life island's most promising uses: patients may be able to take higher doses of cancer-killing drugs without threat of infection.

NIH is now planning entire clean rooms built around the laminar-flow principle. Conceived initially for dust-free aerospace processes such as satellite assembly and checkout, laminar flow protects the patient with a curtain of air. In one laminar-flow room, air is filtered into the end where the patient's bed is located and is expelled at the other. Visitors entering at the exit end are, in effect, standing downstream and unable to contaminate the patient.

Ultrasonic Treatment

To relieve bronchial and lung congestion in infants with such disorders as pneumonia and cystic fibrosis, an inherited disease that clogs the lungs with mucus, physicians at Chicago's Children's Memorial Hospital have devised an ultrasonic nebulizer adapted by Dr. David Allen from a paint sprayer. A decongestant fog to break up the mucus is brewed in a container with a quartz crystal in the bottom. When the crystal is set in vibration at ultrasound frequencies, the water breaks up into fine particles that are then pumped into a plastic canopy over the child's bed. The size of the particles is controlled by changing the crystal frequency. Since the distance the mist will travel down into the baby's chest is determined by particle size—the smallest go farthest—physicians can aim treatment at any level—from the windpipe to the lungs. For most infections, a child spends all day in the fog tent for three or four days; Allen is convinced that the ultrasonic fog therapy shortens time in the hospital.

Atomic Attack

Radiation therapy and drugs are standard treatment for adult forms of leukemia, but both can damage normal tissue while combating the cancer. Researchers have recently begun experiments with extracorporeal blood irradiators. The irradiator at the Brookhaven National Laboratory, Upton, N.Y., is a 5-foot-high steel dome containing a core of cobalt 60, a potent source of gamma rays. The leukemia patient is attached to the irradiator by means of plastic tubes permanently placed in an artery and a vein in the forearm; the tubes are joined together when not in use. During irradiation, in effect, all the patient's blood is shipped outside his body for treatment. As his blood flows into the device, the cancerous white cells are exposed to the radio-cobalt source, while his body is shielded by lead and steel shielding (the red cells are less vulnerable to radiation). Two patients are treated at a time, lying in beds on either side of the irradiation unit.

At Boston's Massachusetts General Hospital, Dr. Benjamin Barnes has tested a way of irradiating a 48-year-old leukemia patient's blood with an irradiator worn on the wrist. Plastic tubes in the blood vessels in his arm conduct blood through a plastic capsule that is about an inch long and contains a small cylinder of strontium 90. This radioactive isotope produces beta rays which pass no further than the walls of the capsule. During a month of treatment, Barnes reports, the patient's lymphocytes (the white cells involved in one form of leukemia) dropped from a count of 40,000 to 1,000. Treatment was stopped because the effect of further loss of lymphocytes might be dangerous. Barnes reports that his patient seems "substantially" improved after wrist-irradiator treatment.

Max Care

At least a third of the patients rushed to hospitals after heart attacks die despite the best medical care. Usually the cause of death is a disturbance in the electrical system that regulates the heartbeat; the ventricles, or pumping chambers, may fibrillate—flutter uncontrollably—and fail to pump blood properly. Or the heart may stop beating entirely. Coronary-care units rapidly being established in a growing number of hospitals are beginning to reduce the death toll from arrhythmias.

In a typical unit, the patient is monitored continuously by electrocardiographs, blood-pressure and pulse recorders at his bed and at a central control console. At the first sign of serious abnormality in the heart rhythm, an alarm sounds at the control desk and at key stations throughout the hospital. While the patient is given oxygen, his heartbeat may be returned to normal by plunger-like electrodes that deliver a shock through the chest wall. In some units, "demand pacemakers" are attached to the patient's chest and back to restore automatically normal heart rate if it should slow down or speed up.

For hospitals that don't have separate coronary-care units, Dr. Joel J. Nobel of Philadelphia's Graduate Pain Research Foundation and biomedical engineer Richard M. Rauch designed the Max emergency cart. A rolling operating table, the cart is equipped with defibrillator, mechanical cardiac-massage pump, oxygen mask, EKG oscilloscope and blood-pressure recorder, drugs and surgical instruments.

Coronary intensive care, some experts believe, can cut heart-attack deaths in the U.S. by 50,000 a year. At Philadelphia's Presbyterian Medical Center, the survival rate of patients admitted after coronaries has increased by a third. But most cardiologists agree that the record could be even better if serious arrhythmias could be prevented from occurring in the first place. Of the 130 patients admitted to the coronary unit at Boston's Peter Bent Brigham Hospital during the first year of operation none has died from serious arrhythmias, mainly because the staff was trained to look for early-warning changes in the EKG and gave the patients drugs to prevent trouble.

Artificial Kidneys

The artificial kidney, the first mechanical substitute for a human organ, has been used since the 1940s to help patients with infections, shock or some types of high blood pressure get over the crisis of kidney failure. But in the last seven years, doctors have started using artificial kidneys to sustain the lives of patients afflicted with renal disease. The patients, wearing permanently attached plastic tubes in their arms or legs, report to the hospital once or twice a week for dialysis—having their blood cleansed of accumulated wastes.

The Washington VA hospital has one of the most modern kidney centers, capable of handling ten patients at a time. The fluid that removes poisons from the patient's blood is mixed automatically and delivered from a central storage tank to five bedside units, each serving two patients. The center can treat up to 25 patients a week.

Unfortunately, there are still not enough artificial kidneys to go around. Approximately 700 patients are receiving treatment in hospitals or in their homes, yet at least 5,000 Americans develop a form of renal disease each year that could be treated by chronic dialysis—if machines were available. One of the main reasons for the kidney gap is cost. Some kidneys cost $3,-000; just changing coils costs $25 per treatment. For the hospital, staffing a kidney machine may cost $10,000 to $25,000 a year per patient, while the cost for a dialysis in special home units may range from $5,000 to $15,000. Recently, Dr. Willem Kloff, who developed the first artificial kidney more than two decades ago, has ingeniously fashioned a cheaper artificial kidney unit out of an old washing machine. The whole rig cost $350, and each dialysis costs $16.

Scanning the Body

The use of radioactive isotopes to trace diseases throughout the body was one of the most dramatic postwar developments in medical diagnosis. Radioactive iodine, one of the oldest diagnostic isotopes, travels to the thyroid gland; a radio-sensitive scanner records radiation from the isotope and prints a map of the gland. A light area on the map might be a cancer. Radioactive gold collects in the liver, acting as a way of detecting a malignancy or the scar tissue of cirrhosis. More sensitive scanners and isotopes that produce better pictures while exposing the patient to less radiation are rapidly becoming available.

One of the best scanners is the "gamma camera," developed at the University of California's Donner Lab. Gamma rays emitted from an isotope create faint flashes of light on a crystal that are then amplified by phototubes. A computer relays the flashes to a picture tube where they can be recorded on Polaroid film as a series of white dots, showing the distribution of the isotope in the patient's body. After administration of technetium, for example, a patient can be examined for a brain tumor in three minutes, as compared with up to one hour for older scanning equipment. The camera also can provide a rapid series of Polaroid shots to trace the flow of blood to reveal, for example, where a stroke has occluded the blood supply to the brain.

Ultrasound, working on the same principle as naval sonar, is another important diagnostic tool. Ultrasonic scanners emit sound waves, measure the time they take to echo from tissues inside the body and record the "contacts" on an oscilloscope. An ultrasonic probe attached to a tweezer device has been used to locate and remove a tiny metal fragment inside the eye. Sound waves can also locate brain tumors by showing that the midline membrane separating the two halves of the cerebrum has been squeezed to one side. And they can measure the size of a baby's head inside the womb, helping the obstetrician decide whether a Caesarean section is necessary without X-rays —a radiation hazard to mother or child.

A Spare Heart

The grand achievement in medical technology within the next few years will be the artificial heart. The National Heart Institute is spending $7 million this year to support artificial-heart research; some experts believe the goal could be reached by 1970. Just last year, Dr. Michael E. DeBakey of

Houston's Baylor University College of Medicine and Dr. Adrian Kantrowitz of the State University of New York Downstate Medical Center in Brooklyn were able to implant partial replacements for the heart in critically ill patients.

Both devices are made of plastic and synthetic fabric. They are actually air-driven pumps to take over part of the work of the left ventricle—the heart's main pumping chamber. One of DeBakey's patients, a 37-year-old woman with rheumatic heart disease, recovered after a ten-day boost from the pump.

The DeBakey auxiliary heart, designed with the aid of Rice University engineers, is a plastic globe about the size of a grapefruit containing a double lining of plastic fabric. It is installed on the left side of the chest, the top half protruding above the ribs. The Kantrowitz auxiliary ventricle is a curved Dacron tube containing a flexible rubber lining and was designed by an Avco-Everett Research Laboratory team led by physicist Arthur Kantrowitz, the surgeon's brother. The device is placed entirely inside the chest.

Kantrowitz points out that the left ventricle is the first to fail in serious heart disease, and that a perfected ventricle booster would adequately serve 98 per cent of heart patients. As for a completely artificial heart, the Brooklyn surgeon says: "I want to leave that to the next generation."

Priority: The Cleveland Clinic's Willem Kolff has constructed several models intended to replace the heart—and they are startlingly like the real thing and have four chambers. The hearts are made of silicone or natural rubber, have a synthetic valve system and a right ventricle to pump blood to the lungs, as well as a left one to send blood to the body. Air-driven from outside the body, like the DeBakey and Kantrowitz ventricles, one of Kolff's hearts kept a calf alive for two days until blood clots formed.

Kolff must solve the clotting problem and perfect the valves that open and close the chambers before it is ready for use in people. Moreover, sensitive controls are needed for regulating blood flow in and out of the heart. With the aid of NASA's Lewis Research Center, Kolff and his colleagues are experimenting with a mechanical control system that would simulate the pumping pattern of the natural heart and help the artificial heart's four chambers work in harmony. "Naturally," says Kolff, "I believe that the artificial heart is the major priority for the immediate future."

What about the more distant future? The era of collaboration between doctor and engineer is just getting under way. Other parts of the body will be constructed. Researchers at Western Reserve and the Case Institute are working on computerized artificial arms. Researchers at Baylor are trying to devise synthetic skin to cover burns. And many technologists speak seriously of an artificial liver, stomach, intestine and pancreas, made of exotic plastics, metals and ingenuity. Indeed, miniaturized computers might even make possible a synthetic brain. "We cannot duplicate God's work," says one member of Kolff's team, "but we can come very close."

STUDY QUESTIONS

1. According to *Newsweek,* the newest weapons against illness and disease are the result of alliances between medicine and what two unlikely sources?

2. What old problems has the "New Medicine" left unsolved?

3. What does *Newsweek* predict will be medicine's "grand achievement"? What artificial organ has already proven successful?

4. The *Newsweek* article is replete with technical jargon. Can you define *cryosurgery, the life island, Max,* and *the laminar-flow principle* after a single reading?

5. Do the divisions and their headings clarify either the structure or informational content of the essay?

Rachel Carson

THE OBLIGATION TO ENDURE

Rachel Carson (1907–1964) was born in Springdale, Pennsylvania and attended Pennsylvania College for Women and Johns Hopkins University. She was awarded honorary doctorates by Oberlin College, the Drexel Institute of Technology, and Smith College. She received the George Westinghouse AAAS Science Writing Award (1950), a Guggenheim Fellowship (1951), the John Burroughs Medal (1952), and the Page-One Award (1952). Her books include *Under the Sea Wind* (1941), *The Sea Around Us* (1951), *The Edge of the Sea* (1956), and *Silent Spring* (1962). *Silent Spring* became one of the most controversial books of the past decade.

$\mathcal{T}$HE HISTORY of life on earth has been a history of interaction between living things and their surroundings. To a large extent, the physical form and the habits of the earth's vegetation and its animal life have been molded by the environment. Considering the whole span of earthly time, the opposite effect, in which life actually modifies its surroundings, has been relatively slight. Only within the moment of time represented by the present century has one species—man—acquired significant power to alter the nature of his world.

During the past quarter century this power has not only increased to one of disturbing magnitude but it has changed in character. The most alarming of all man's assaults upon the environment is the contamination of air, earth, rivers, and sea with dangerous and even lethal materials. This pollution is for the most part irrecoverable; the chain of evil it initiates not only in the world that must support life but in living tissues is for the most part irreversible. In this now universal contamination of the environment, chemicals are the sinister and little-recognized partners of radiation in changing the very nature of the world—the very nature of its life. Strontium 90, released through nuclear explosions into the air, comes to earth in rain or drifts down as fallout, lodges in soil, enters into the grass or corn or wheat grown there, and in time takes up its abode in the bones of a human being, there to remain until his death. Similarly, chemicals sprayed on croplands or forests or gardens lie long in soil, entering into living organisms, passing from one to another in a chain of poisoning and death. Or they pass mysteriously by underground streams until they emerge and, through the alchemy of air and sunlight, combine into new forms that kill vegetation, sicken cattle, and work unknown harm on those who drink from once pure wells. As Albert Schweitzer has said, "Man can hardly even recognize the devils of his own creation."

It took hundreds of millions of years to produce the life that now inhabits the earth—eons of time in which that developing and evolving and diversifying life reached a state of adjustment and balance with its surroundings. The environment, rigorously shaping and directing the life it supported, contained elements that were hostile as well as supporting. Certain rocks gave out dangerous radiation; even within the light of the sun, from which all life draws its energy, there were short-wave radiations with power to injure. Given time—time not in years but in millennia—life adjusts, and a balance has been reached. For time is the essential ingredient; but in the modern world there is no time.

The rapidity of change and the speed with which new situations are created follow the impetuous and heedless pace of man rather than the deliberate pace of nature. Radiation is no longer merely the background radiation of rocks, the bombardment of cosmic rays, the ultraviolet of the sun that have existed before there was any life on earth; radiation is now the unnatural creation of man's tampering with the atom. The chemicals to which life is asked to make its adjustment are no longer merely the calcium and silica and copper and all the rest of the minerals washed out of the rocks and carried in rivers to the sea; they are the synthetic creations of man's inventive mind, brewed in his laboratories, and having no counterparts in nature.

To adjust to these chemicals would require time on the scale that is nature's; it would require not merely the years of a man's life but the life of generations. And even this, were it by some miracle possible, would be futile, for the new chemicals come from our laboratories in an endless stream; almost five hundred annually find their way into actual use in the United States alone. The figure is staggering and its implications are not easily grasped—500 new chemicals to which the bodies of men and animals are required somehow to adapt each year, chemicals totally outside the limits of biologic experience.

Among them are many that are used in man's war against nature. Since the mid-1940's over 200 basic chemicals have been created for use in killing insects, weeds, rodents, and other organisms described in the modern vernacular as "pests"; and they are sold under several thousand different brand names.

These sprays, dusts, and aerosols are now applied almost universally to farms, gardens, forests, and homes—nonselective chemicals that have the power to kill every insect, the "good" and the "bad," to still the song of birds and the leaping of fish in the streams, to coat the leaves with a deadly film, and to linger on in soil—all this though the intended target may be only a few weeds or insects. Can anyone believe it is possible to lay down such a barrage of poisons on the surface of the earth without making it unfit for all life? They should not be called "insecticides," but "biocides."

The whole process of spraying seems caught up in an endless spiral. Since DDT was released for civilian use, a process of escalation has been going on in which ever more toxic materials must be found. This has happened because insects, in a triumphant vindication of Darwin's principle of the survival of the fittest, have evolved super races immune to the particular insecticide used, hence a deadlier one has always to be developed—and then a deadlier one than that. It has happened also because, for reasons to be described later, destructive insects often undergo a "flareback," or resurgence, after spraying, in numbers greater than before. Thus the chemical war is never won, and all life is caught in its violent crossfire.

Along with the possibility of the extinction of mankind by nuclear war, the central problem of our age has therefore become the contamination of man's total environment with such substances of incredible potential for harm—substances that accumulate in the tissues of plants and animals and even penetrate the germ cells to shatter or alter the very material of heredity upon which the shape of the future depends.

Some would-be architects of our future look toward a time when it will be possible to alter the human germ plasm by design. But we may easily be doing so now by inadvertence, for many chemicals, like radiation, bring about gene mutations. It is ironic to think that man might determine his own future by something so seemingly trivial as the choice of an insect spray.

All this has been risked—for what? Future historians may well be amazed by our distorted sense of proportion. How could intelligent beings seek to control a few unwanted species by a method that contaminated environment and brought the threat of disease and death even to their own kind? Yet this is precisely what we have done. We have done it, moreover, for reasons that collapse the moment we examine them. We are told that the enormous and expanding use of pesticides is necessary to maintain farm production. Yet is our real problem not one of *overproduction?* Our farms, despite measures to remove acreages from production and to pay farmers *not* to produce, have yielded such a staggering excess of crops that the American taxpayer in 1962 is paying out more than one billion dollars a year as the total carrying cost of the surplus-food storage program. And is the situation helped when one branch of the Agriculture Department tries to reduce production while another states, as it did in 1958, "It is believed generally that reduction of crop acreages under provisions of the Soil Bank will stimulate interest in use of chemicals to obtain maximum production on the land retained in crops."

All this is not to say there is no insect problem and no need of control. I am saying, rather, that control must be geared to realities, not to mythical situations, and that the methods employed must be such that they do not destroy us along with the insects.

The problem whose attempted solution has brought such a train of disaster in its wake is an accompaniment of our modern way of life. Long before the age of man, insects inhabited the earth—a group of extraordinarily varied and adaptable beings. Over the course of time since man's advent, a small percentage of the more than half a million species of insects have come into conflict with human welfare in two principal ways: as competitors for the food supply and as carriers of human disease.

Disease-carrying insects become important where human beings are crowded together, especially under conditions where sanitation is poor, as in time of natural disaster or war or in situations of extreme poverty and deprivation. Then control of some sort becomes necessary. It is a sobering fact, however, as we shall presently see, that the method of massive chemical control has had only limited success, and also threatens to worsen the very conditions it is intended to curb.

Under primitive agricultural conditions the farmer had few insect problems. These arose with the intensification of agriculture—the devotion of immense acreages to a single crop. Such a system set the stage for explosive increases in specific insect populations. Single-crop farming does not take advantage of the principles by which nature works; it is agriculture as an engineer might conceive it to be. Nature has introduced great variety into the landscape, but man has displayed a passion for simplifying it. Thus he undoes the built-in checks and balances by which nature holds the species within bounds. One important natural check is a limit on the amount of suitable habitat for each species. Obviously then, an insect that lives on wheat can build up its population to much higher levels on a farm devoted to wheat than on one in which wheat is intermingled with other crops to which the insect is not adapted.

The same thing happens in other situations. A generation or more ago, the towns of large areas of the United States lined their streets with the noble elm tree. Now the beauty they hopefully created is threatened with complete destruction as disease sweeps through the elms, carried by a beetle that would have only limited chance to build up large populations and to spread from tree to tree if the elms were only occasional trees in a richly diversified planting.

Another factor in the modern insect problem is one that must be viewed against a background of geologic and human history: the spreading of thousands of different kinds of organisms from their native homes to invade new territories. This worldwide migration has been studied and graphically described by the British ecologist Charles Elton in his recent book *The Ecology of Invasions*. During the Cretaceous Period, some hundred million years ago, flooding seas cut many land bridges between continents and living things found themselves confined in what Elton calls "colossal separate nature reserves." There, isolated from others of their kind, they developed many new species. When some of the land masses were joined again, about 15 million years ago, these species began to move out into new territories— a movement that is not only still in progress but is now receiving considerable assistance from man.

The importation of plants is the primary agent in the modern spread of species, for animals have almost invariably gone along with the plants, quarantine being a comparatively recent and not completely effective innovation. The United States Office of Plant Introduction alone has introduced almost 200,000 species and varieties of plants from all over the world. Nearly half of the 180 or so major insect enemies of plants in the United States are accidental imports from abroad, and most of them have come as hitchhikers on plants.

In new territory, out of reach of the restraining hand of the natural enemies that kept down its numbers in its native land, an invading plant or animal is able to become enormously abundant. Thus it is no accident that our most troublesome insects are introduced species.

These invasions, both the naturally occurring and those dependent on human assistance, are likely to continue indefinitely. Quarantine and massive chemical campaigns are only extremely expensive ways of buying time. We are faced, according to Dr. Elton, "with a life-and-death need not just to find new technological means of suppressing this plant or that animal"; instead we need the basic knowledge of animal populations and their relations to their surroundings that will "promote an even balance and damp down the explosive power of outbreaks and new invasions."

Much of the necessary knowledge is now available but we do not use it. We train ecologists in our universities and even employ them in our governmental agencies but we seldom take their advice. We allow the chemical death rain to fall as though there were no alternative, whereas in fact there are many, and our ingenuity could soon discover many more if given ŏpportunity.

Have we fallen into a mesmerized state that makes us accept as inevitable that which is inferior or detrimental, as though having lost the will or the vision to demand that which is good? Such thinking, in the words of the ecologist Paul Shepard, "idealizes life with only its head out of water, inches above the limits of toleration of the corruption of its own environment . . . Why should we tolerate a diet of weak poisons, a home in insipid surroundings, a circle of acquaintances who are not quite our enemies, the noise of motors with just enough relief to prevent insanity? Who would want to live in a world which is just not quite fatal?"

Yet such a world is pressed upon us. The crusade to create a chemically sterile, insect-free world seems to have engendered a fanatic zeal on the part of many specialists and most of the so-called control agencies. On every hand there is evidence that those engaged in spraying operations exercise a ruthless power. "The regulatory entomologists . . . function as prosecutor, judge and jury, tax assessor and collector and sheriff to enforce their own orders," said Connecticut entomologist Neely Turner. The most flagrant abuses go unchecked in both state and federal agencies.

It is not my contention that chemical insecticides must never be used. I do content that we have put poisonous and biologically potent chemicals indiscriminately into the hands of persons largely or wholly ignorant of their potentials for harm. We have subjected enormous numbers of people to contact with these poisons, without their consent and often without their knowledge. If the Bill of Rights contains no guarantee that a citizen shall be secure against lethal poisons distributed either by private individuals or by public officials, it is surely only because our forefathers, despite their considerable wisdom and foresight, could conceive of no such problem.

I contend, furthermore, that we have allowed these chemicals to be used with little or no advance investigation of their effect on soil, water, wildlife, and man himself. Future generations are unlikely to condone our lack of prudent concern for the integrity of the natural world that supports all life.

There is still very limited awareness of the nature of the threat. This is an era of specialists, each of whom sees his own problem and is unaware of or intolerant of the larger frame into which it fits. It is also an era dominated by industry, in which the right to make a dollar at whatever cost is seldom challenged. When the public protests, confronted with some obvious evidence of damaging results of pesticide applications, it is fed little tranquilizing pills of half truth. We urgently need an end to these false assurances, to the sugar coating of unpalatable facts. It is the public that is being asked to assume the risks that the insect controllers calculate. The public must decide whether it wishes to continue on the present road, and it can do so only when in full possession of the facts. In the words of Jean Rostand, "the obligation to endure gives us the right to know."

STUDY QUESTIONS

1. What does Rachel Carson feel is the central problem of our age?

2. According to Miss Carson, how has the history of man's relationship to his environment changed in the twentieth century?

3. How has the chemical contamination of man's environment upset the balance of nature?

4. In what way is man's experimenting with the atom "unnatural"?

5. How has Darwin's principle of the survival of the fittest escalated the production of toxic materials?

6. What two factors have increased the effectiveness of insect invasions?

Loren C. Eiseley

USING A PLAGUE TO FIGHT A PLAGUE

Loren Eiseley (1907–   ) was born in Lincoln, Nebraska. He received his B.A. (1933) from the University of Nebraska, and his M.A. (1935) and Ph.D. (1937) from the University of Pennsylvania. He taught at the University of Kansas and Oberlin College before returning, in 1947, to the University of Pennsylvania where he is now University Professor in anthropology and history of science and head of the Department of the History and Philosophy of Science. A Guggenheim fellow, he has published widely in both popular periodicals and learned journals. *Darwin's Century* was given the Phi Beta Kappa science award in 1959, and *The Firmament of Time* (1960) received the John Burroughs medal and the Lecomte de Nouy award. His other books include *The Immense Journey* (1951), *Francis Bacon and the Modern Temper* (1952), and *Galapagos: The Flow of Wilderness* (1968).

A FEW DAYS ago I stood amidst the marshes of a well-known wildlife refuge. As I studied a group of herons through my glasses, there floated by the margin of my vision the soapy, unsightly froth of a detergent discharged into the slough's backwaters from some source upstream. Here nature, at first glance, seemed green and uncontaminated. As I left, however, I could not help wondering how long it would be before seeping industrial wastes destroyed the water-life on which those birds subsisted—how long it would be before poisonous and vacant mudflats had replaced the chirping frogs and waving cattails I loved to visit. I thought also of a sparkling stream in the Middle West in which, as a small boy, I used to catch sunfish, but which today is a muddy, lifeless treacle filled with oil from a nearby pumping station. No living thing now haunts its polluted waters.

These two episodes out of my own experience are trifling, however, com-

Reprinted by permission of the author. First published in *Saturday Review*. Copyright © 1962.

pared with that virulent facet of man's activities treated in Rachel Carson's latest book. It is a devastating, heavily documented, relentless attack upon human carelessness, greed, and irresponsibility—an irresponsibility that has let loose upon man and the countryside a flood of dangerous chemicals in a situation which, as Miss Carson states, is without parallel in medical history. "No one," she adds, "yet knows what the ultimate consequences may be."

Silent Spring is her account of those floods of insecticides and well-intentioned protective devices which have indiscriminately slaughtered our wildlife of both forest and stream. Such ill-considered activities break the necessary food chains of nature and destroy the livelihood of creatures not even directly affected by the pesticides. The water run-off from agricultural and forested areas carries to our major rivers and to the seas chemicals which may then impregnate the food we eat. We have no assurance that we are not introducing into nature heavy concentrates of non-natural substances whose effects are potentially as dangerous as those that came to light in the dramatic medical episode that shocked the public in recent weeks. I refer, of course, to the foetal monsters produced by the sleep drug Thalidomide. Imperfect though the present legal controls in the field of direct medical experiment may be, they are less inadequate than in the domain of agricultural chemistry, where aerial spraying is cascading a rain of poison over field and farmland.

D'Arcy Thompson, the great British biologist of the late nineteenth century, commented astutely in 1897 that the increasing tempo of human cultural evolution produces a kind of evolution of chance itself—an increasing dissonance and complexity of change beyond what one finds in the world before man came. Though this evolution of chance arises within the human domain, it does not long remain confined to it. Instead, the erratic and growingly unpredictable fantasies created in the human mind invade nature itself. Tremendous agricultural productivity is correlated with the insatiable demands of ever-growing populations. Wastes in the air and wastes polluting the continental arteries increasingly disrupt the nature that we have taken for granted since the first simple hunters wandered out of the snowy winter of the Ice Age and learned to live in cities.

Man's sanitary engineering, in western civilization, never amounted to much until the middle phase of the industrial revolution and the discovery of the relation of bacteria to disease. Now it is apparent that man must learn to handle more wisely the products of his own aspiring chemistry. He is faced with the prospect of learning to be a creative god in nature without, at the same time, destroying his surroundings and himself through thoughtless indifference to the old green world out of which he has so recently emerged and to which (though he forgets) he is as indissolubly bound in his own way as the herons that stalked before my field glasses.

Essentially there are two ways of approaching the control of noxious insects: a natural and a chemical means. I am deliberately confining my remarks here, not to the effect of man's accidental industrial wastes upon his environment—a subject worthy of attention in itself—but to his deliberate and largely post-World War II use of peculiar carbon compounds in crop dusting and other forms of insect control. DDT is an excellent and spectacular example. With the passage of time the chemical industries have pressed more and more such substances upon the receptive public. Extensive research has been carried on in this field, frequently with results, at first glance, of an impressive character. That there may be other results, less favorable when viewed over a longer time span, is not always so well publicized.

The reason that Rachel Carson has chosen the more conservative biological approach to the problem of insect control lies in the following facts: Ill or uncontrolled spraying with deadly chemicals destroys beneficial as well as undesirable forms of life; furthermore, the poisonous residues may and do find their way into human food. Secondly, because insect generations are short and their numbers large, they rapidly become immune to the poisons that originally decimated them. By contrast, birds and the higher mammals, including man, cannot rapidly develop this selective immunity. They are eventually threatened not only by tougher and more formidable insect disease-carriers, but also by progressively dangerous chemicals devised against the mounting numbers of insects that refuse to succumb but whose natural enemies—the birds and fish—are being slaughtered in growing numbers by these same chemicals. The normal balance of life is thus increasingly disrupted. Man is whetting the cutting edge of natural selection, but its edge is turned against himself and his allies in the animal world.

In case after case, Miss Carson succeeds in documenting her thesis with complete adequacy. It is not pleasant to learn of the casual spraying of the landscape with chemicals capable of mutagenic effects and regarded by some authorities as representing as great a menace as high levels of radiation. Nor is it reassuring to read that the hydrocarbons have an affinity for mammalian germ cells. At present there is no law on the statute books that requires manufacturers to demonstrate the genetic effects, as distinguished from the toxicity, of their concoctions. Nor is there any way of controlling what the average uninformed farmer may do with his insecticides. An equally ill-educated and impatient public wants its weeds, gnats, and mosquitoes eliminated in one fell blow. It is not sophisticated enough to trouble over the looming demise of our beautiful national bird, the bald eagle, nor to connect the return of many supposedly eliminated pests with the fact that the newer generation may be able to flourish in a sack of DDT and thus be twice as formidable.

The biological controls which Miss Carson favors, along with other in-formed biologists, are not just more careful and discreet use of pesticides, but also such clever natural manipulations as the release of sterilized screw worm flies, causing a greater reduction in the population of this parasite than any insecticide would have achieved. Successful experiments such as this depend upon precise knowledge of the life history of an organism. They strike directly at the heart of the problem. They do not leave poisonous resi-dues or resistant life-strains, nor do they result in the mass killing that fre-quently destroys valuable food chains on which even man is in the long run dependent.

All of these facts Rachel Carson has set forth sensibly in the quiet, ra-tional prose for which she is famous. If her present book does not possess the beauty of *The Sea Around Us,* it is because she has courageously chosen, at the height of her powers, to educate us upon a sad, an unpleasant, an un-beautiful topic, and one of our own making. *Silent Spring* should be read by every American who does not want it to be the epitaph of a world not very far beyond us in time.

STUDY QUESTIONS

1. What episodes from his own experience does Eiseley use in support of Miss Carson's thesis?

2. What two basic means of approaching the control of noxious insects are open to men?

3. According to Eiseley, what facts led Miss Carson to choose the more con-servative of these two approaches?

William J. Darby

SILENCE, MISS CARSON

William J. Darby (1913–   ) was born in Galloway, Arkansas, and re-ceived his B.S. (1936) and M.D. (1937) from the University of Arkansas and his M.S. (1941) and Ph.D. (1942) from the University of Michigan. He

A review of *Silent Spring* by Rachel Carson. Reprinted from *Chemical and Engineer-ing News,* Vol. 40, October 1, 1962, pp. 60–63. Copyright 1962 by The American Chemical Society and reprinted by permission.

is now head of the Department of Biochemistry and director of the Division of Nutrition, School of Medicine, at Vanderbilt University. He has served with the National Research Council and the World Health Organization. Darby is coauthor of *Nutrition and Diet in Health and Disease* and codiscoverer of vitamin M and the activity of pteroylglutamic acid in sprue.

S*ilent Spring* starts with a bit of dramatic description of a situation which the author then acknowledges does not actually exist. It then orients the reader to its subject matter by stating that "only within . . . the present century has man . . . acquired significant power to alter the nature of his world." It identifies as irrecoverable and "for the most part irreversible" the effects of "this now universal contamination of the environment (in which) chemicals are the sinister and little recognized partners of radiation in changing the very nature of the world, the very nature of life itself." Man has, according to Miss Carson, now upset that ideal state of "adjustment and balance" of life on this planet through "synthetic creations of man's inventive mind, brewed in his laboratory, and having no counterpart in nature." These products, the reader is told, are "staggering in number," have "power to kill," have "incredible potential for harm," represent a "train of disaster," result in a "chemical death rain," and are being used with "little or no advance investigation of their effect on soil, water, wildlife, and man himself." She further warns the reader that all of these sinister chemicals will not only extinguish plant life, wild life, aquatic life, and man, but they will produce cancer, leukemia, sterility, and cellular mutations.

There are 297 pages devoted to reiteration of these views. There then follows a 55-page "list of principal sources" designed to impress the reader with the extent of the support for Miss Carson's views. This list uses an extender and is artificially colored and flavored. Its apparent bulk is made one third greater through devoting a line of type to identify each page on which a source bears, and by repeating in full the title of each source in relation to recurrent pages. Its bulk will appeal to those readers who are as uncritical as the author, or to those who find the flavor of her product to their taste. These consumers will include the organic gardeners, the antifluoride leaguers, the worshipers of "natural foods," those who cling to the philosophy of a vital principle, and pseudo-scientists and faddists.

The flavor of this product is indicated in part by the source list. She refers frequently to testimony given at 1950, 1951, and 1952 Congressional hearings, seldom to later years, and to the opinions of Morton S. Siskind and W. C. Hueper.

The author ignores the sound appraisals of such responsible, broadly knowledgeable scientists as the President of the National Academy of Sciences, the members of the President's Scientific Advisory Committee, the

Presidents of the Rockefeller Foundation and Nutrition Foundation, the several committees of the National Academy of Sciences-National Research Council (including the Food and Nutrition Board, the Agricultural Board, the Food Protection Committee) who have long given thoughtful study to these questions, and the special advisory committees appointed by the governors of California and Wisconsin. The latter committees were chaired by two distinguished scientist-presidents of universities, Dr. Emil Mrak and the late Dr. Conrad A. Elvehjem.

All of these groups of scientists have recognized the essentiality of use of agricultural chemicals to produce the food required by the expanding world population and to sustain an acceptable standard of living and health. They have recognized the safety of proper use of agricultural chemicals and, indeed, the benefits to the consumer which accrue from their proper use in food and agricultural production.

Miss Carson's book adds no new factual material not already known to such serious scientists as those concerned with these developments, nor does it include information essential for the reader to interpret the knowledge. It does confuse the information and so mix it with her opinions that the uninitiated reader is unable to sort fact from fancy. In view of the mature, responsible attention which this whole subject receives from able, qualified scientific groups such as those identified in the foregoing (and whom Miss Carson chooses to ignore); in view of her scientific qualifications in contrast to those of our distinguished scientific leaders and statesmen, this book should be ignored.

Logically, it should be possible to terminate this review here. Unfortunately, however, this book will have wide circulation on one of the standard subscription lists. It is doubtful that many readers can bear to wade through its high-pitched sequences of anxieties. It is likely to be perused uncritically, to be regarded by the layman as authoritative (which it is not), and to arouse in him manifestations of anxieties and psychoneuroses exhibited by some of the subjects cited by the author in the chapter "The Human Price." Indeed, the author's efforts at appraising psychologic evidence concerning the effects of substances reveal a remarkable lack of competence as a psychiatrist, even as great a lack in the area of toxicology or even knowledge of existing regulatory controls. The obvious effect of all of this on the reader will be to aggravate unjustifiably his own neurotic anxiety.

Her thesis is revealed by the dedicatory quotations: "Man has lost the capacity to foresee and to forestall. He will end by destroying the earth." (Albert Schweitzer) "Our approach to nature is to beat it into submission. We would stand a better chance of survival if we accommodated ourselves to this planet and viewed it appreciatively instead of skeptically and dictatorially." (E. B. White)

Such a passive attitude as the latter coupled with such pessimistic (and to this reviewer, unacceptable) philosophy as the former, means the end of all human progress, reversion to a passive social state devoid of technology, scientific medicine, agriculture, sanitation, or education. It means disease, epidemics, starvation, misery, and suffering incomparable and intolerable to modern man. Indeed, social, educational, and scientific development is prefaced on the conviction that man's lot will be and is being improved by greater understanding of and thereby increased ability to control or mold those forces responsible for man's suffering, misery, and deprivation.

The author's motivation is not quite so evident, but the emotional call to write the book is revealed by her acknowledgment that "In a letter written in January 1958, Olga Owens Huckins told me of her own bitter experience of a small world made lifeless, and so brought my attention sharply back to a problem with which I had long been concerned. I then realized *I must write this book*" (italics are the reviewer's).

So impelled, Miss Carson has effectively used several literary devices to present her thesis and make it appear to be a widely held scientific one. She "name-drops" by quoting or referring to renowned scientists out of context. A statement divorced from its original meaning is then approximated to an opinion of the author or else to a question posed by her with an implied answer. The reader is led to conclude thereby that the authority mentioned is in accord with the author's position. Nobel prize winners are recognized as especially useful names for such a purpose.

Another device used is that of confusion of the reader with (to him) unintelligible scientific jargon or irrelevant discussions of cellular processes.

Miss Carson's failure to distinguish between the occupational and residue hazards is common to almost all popular writers on this subject. The occupational hazard associated with the manufacture and application of agricultural chemicals is similar to that of other work and can, should be, and is being reduced. That accidents have occurred is well known, but this is no more reason to ban useful chemicals than is the lamentable occurrence of preventable automobile or airplane accidents reason to ban these modern modes of transportation. Despite all of the implications of harm from residues on foods, Miss Carson has not produced one single example of injury resulting to man from these residues.

Miss Carson is infatuated with biologic control and the balance of nature. Despite her statement that the really effective control of insects is that applied by nature, one must observe that the very ineffectiveness of such control is the raison d'être of chemical pesticides.

She commits the scientifically indefensible fallacy of considering that any substance which in any quantity is toxic must per se be a poison. By such a definition almost everything—water, salt, sugar, amino acids, minerals, vitamins A or D, etc.—is a poison. She gives the reader a mistaken concept of tolerances. Tolerances are not ill-defined levels of maximum quantities which can be ingested without acute harm. They are minimum amounts of a substance which should exist when the chemical has been employed in good and proper beneficial practice. They are based on extensive use data and toxicologic testing in animals and frequently metabolic studies in man. They include a very wide margin of safety, usually being set at 100 times the *minimum* amount of the substance which induces any physiologic effect in the most sensitive of at least two species of animals for lifetime or two- to four-year periods.

The benefit of use of chemicals, charges Miss Carson, is for the producer. She ignores the requirement under the Miller bill that a chemical must be *effective,* which means benefit to the consumer. She fails to recognize that "the consumer" includes the producer, farmer, wholesaler, retailer, equipment manufacturer, their families, and even the scientists who evaluate the chemicals. The toxicologists in industry, in the Food and Drug Administration, in our universities and research institutes have, as consumers, equal stake in protecting the nation's health as does Miss Carson—and I believe, are better qualified to assume this protection.

Her ignorance or bias on some of the considerations throws doubt on her competence to judge policy. For example, she indicates that it is neither wise nor responsible to use pesticides in the control of insect-borne diseases. The July–August 1962 *World Health* (WHO publication) reports that a malaria eradication program in Mexico has since 1957 reduced the malaria area from 978,185 sq. km. with 18 million inhabitants to 224,500 sq. km. with 1.5 million inhabitants. "In most areas the simple technique of indoor spraying of houses proved effective . . ."; where bedbugs were resistant to DDT, an insecticide mixture was successfully used. "As a result of the campaign, the Mexican Government is expanding its agricultural programme, distributing land, and undertaking irrigation and hydroelectric schemes." It is most doubtful that Miss Carson really is ignorant of these and other facts which any objective appraisal of this subject demands. Instead, it seems that a call to write a book has completely outweighed any semblance of scientific objectivity.

The public may be misled by this book. If it stimulates the public to press for unwise and ill-conceived restrictions on the production, use, or development of new chemicals, it will be the consumer who suffers. If, on the other hand, it inspires some users to read and heed labels more carefully, it may aid in the large educational effort in which industry, government, colleges, and many other groups are engaged (despite Miss Carson's implication that they are not.)

The responsible scientist should read this book to understand the ignorance of those writing on the subject and the educational task which lies ahead.

STUDY QUESTIONS

1. What does Darby seek to accomplish by the numerous quotations in the
    first paragraph?

2. What objections does he raise to Miss Carson's bibliography?

3. What significance does Darby find in Miss Carson's reference to testimony
    given in 1950–1952 Congressional hearings? Is this significance ex-
    plicit or implicit?

4. What effect does Darby feel *Silent Spring* will have on the layman?

5. How does Darby explain Miss Carson's having ignored the statistics he
    presents?

Section Four

Language

"The Soul of Wit"

George Orwell

POLITICS AND THE
ENGLISH LANGUAGE

George Orwell (1903–1950) was the pen name of Eric Blair, who was born in Bengal, India. He graduated from Eton College, served with the Indian Imperial Police in Burma from 1922 to 1927, and then returned to England to begin his career as a writer. His works include *Burmese Days* (1934), *Homage to Catalonia* (1936), *Dickens, Dali, and Others* (1946), and *Shooting an Elephant* (1950). His fame, however, is primarily the result of *Animal Farm* (1946) and *1984* (1949), the former one of the most famous modern satires and the latter a classic novel of social protest. His *Collected Essays* were published in 1969.

Most people who bother with the matter at all would admit that the English language is in a bad way, but it is generally assumed that we cannot by conscious action do anything about it. Our civilization is decadent and our language—so the argument runs—must inevitably share in the general collapse. It follows that any struggle against the abuse of language is a sentimental archaism, like preferring candles to electric light or hansom cabs to aeroplanes. Underneath this lies the half-conscious belief that language is a natural growth and not an instrument which we shape for our own purposes.

Now, it is clear that the decline of a language must ultimately have political and economic causes: it is not due simply to the bad influence of this or that individual writer. But an effect can become a cause, reinforcing the original cause and producing the same effect in an intensified form, and so on indefinitely. A man may take to drink because he feels himself to be a failure, and then fail all the more completely because he drinks. It is rather the same thing that is happening to the English language. It becomes ugly and inaccurate because our thoughts are foolish, but the slovenliness of our language makes it easier for us to have foolish thoughts. The point is that the process is reversible. Modern English, especially written English, is full of bad habits which spread by imitation and which can be avoided if one is willing to take the necessary trouble. If one gets rid of these habits one can think more clearly, and to think clearly is a necessary first step towards political regeneration: so that the fight against bad English is not frivolous and is not the exclusive concern of professional writers. I will come back to this presently, and I hope that by that time the meaning of what I have said here will have become clearer. Meanwhile, here are five specimens of the English language as it is now habitually written.

These five passages have not been picked out because they are especially bad—I could have quoted far worse if I had chosen—but because they illustrate various of the mental vices from which we now suffer. They are a little below the average, but are fairly representative samples. I number them so that I can refer back to them when necessary:

"(1) I am not, indeed, sure whether it is not true to say that the Milton who once seemed not unlike a seventeenth-century Shelley had not become, out of an experience ever more bitter in each year, more alien [*sic*] to the founder of that Jesuit sect which nothing could induce him to tolerate."

Professor Harold Laski
(Essay in *Freedom of Expression*).

"(2) Above all, we cannot play ducks and drakes with a native battery of idioms which prescribes such egregious collocations of vocables as the Basic *put up with* for *tolerate* or *put at a loss* for *bewilder*."

Professor Lancelot Hogben (*Interglossa*).

"(3) On the one side we have the free personality: by definition it is not neurotic, for it has neither conflict nor dream. Its desires, such as they are, are transparent, for they are just what institutional approval keeps in the forefront of consciousness; another institutional pattern would alter their number and intensity; there is little in them that is natural, irreducible, or culturally dangerous. But *on the other side,* the social bond itself is nothing but the mutual reflection of these self-secure integrities. Recall the definition of love. Is not this the very picture of a small academic? Where is there a place in this hall of mirrors for either personality or fraternity?"

Essay on psychology in *Politics* (New York).

"(4) All the 'best people' from the gentlemen's clubs, and all the frantic fascist captains, united in common hatred of Socialism and bestial horror of the rising tide of the mass revolutionary movement, have turned to acts of provocation, to foul incendiarism, to medieval legends of poisoned wells, to legalize their own destruction of proletarian organizations, and rouse the agitated petty-bourgeoisie to chauvinistic fervour on behalf of the fight against the revolutionary way out of the crisis."

Communist pamphlet.

"(5) If a new spirit *is* to be infused into this old country, there is one thorny and contentious reform which must be tackled, and that is the humanization and galvanization of the B.B.C. Timidity here will bespeak cancer and atrophy of the soul. The heart of Britain may be sound and of strong beat, for instance, but the British lion's roar at present is like that of Bottom in Shakespeare's *Midsummer Night's Dream*—as gentle as any sucking dove. A virile new Britain cannot continue indefinitely to be traduced in the eyes or rather ears, of the world by the effete languors of Langham Place, brazenly masquerading as 'standard English.' When the Voice of Britain is heard at nine o'clock, better far and infinitely less ludicrous to hear aitches honestly dropped than the present priggish, inflated, inhibited, school-ma'amish arch braying of blameless bashful mewing maidens!"

Letter in *Tribune*.

Each of these passages has faults of its own, but, quite apart from avoidable ugliness, two qualities are common to all of them. The first is staleness of imagery: the other is lack of precision. The writer either has a meaning and cannot express it, or he inadvertently says something else, or he is almost indifferent as to whether his words mean anything or not. This mixture of vagueness and sheer incompetence is the most marked characteristic of modern English prose, and especially of any kind of political writing. As soon as certain topics are raised, the concrete melts into the abstract and no one seems able to think of turns of speech that are not hackneyed: prose consists less and less of *words* chosen for the sake of their meaning, and more and more of *phrases* tacked together like the sections of a prefabricated hen-house. I list below, with notes and examples, various of the tricks by means of which the work of prose-construction is habitually dodged:

Dying Metaphors. A newly invented metaphor assists thought by evoking a visual image, while on the other hand a metaphor which is technically "dead" (e.g. *iron resolution*) has in effect reverted to being an ordinary word and can generally be used without loss of vividness. But in between these two classes there is a huge dump of worn-out metaphors which have lost all evocative power and are merely used because they save people the trouble of inventing phrases for themselves. Examples are: *Ring the changes on, take up the cudgels for, toe the line, ride roughshod over, stand shoulder to shoulder with, play into the hands of, no axe to grind, grist to the mill, fishing in troubled waters, on the order of the day, Achilles' heel, swan song, hotbed.* Many of these are used without knowledge of their meaning (what is a "rift," for instance?), and incompatible metaphors are frequently mixed, a sure sign that the writer is not interested in what he is saying. Some metaphors now current have been twisted out of their original meaning without those who use them even being aware of the fact. For example, *toe the line* is sometimes written *tow the line*. Another example is *the hammer and the anvil*, now always used with the implication that the anvil gets the worst of it. In real life it is always the anvil that breaks the hammer, never the other way about: a writer who stopped to think what he was saying would be aware of this, and would avoid perverting the original phrase.

Operators or *Verbal False Limbs*.   These save the trouble of picking out appropriate verbs and nouns, and at the same time pad each sentence with extra syllables which give it an appearance of symmetry. Characteristic phrases are: *render inoperative, militate against, make contact with, be subjected to, give rise to, give grounds for, have the effect of, play a leading part (role) in, make itself felt, take effect, exhibit a tendency to, serve the purpose of, etc., etc.* The keynote is the elimination of simple verbs. Instead of being a single word, such as *break, stop, spoil, mend, kill*, a verb becomes a *phrase*, made up of a noun or adjective tacked on to some general-purposes verb such as *prove, serve, form, play, render*. In addition, the passive voice is wherever possible used in preference to the active, and noun constructions are used instead of gerunds (*by examination of* instead of *by examining*). The range of verbs is further cut down by means of the *-ize* and *de-* formation, and the banal statements are given an appearance of profundity by means of the *not un-* formation. Simple conjunctions and prepositions are replaced by such phrases as *with respect to, having regard to, the fact that, by dint of, in view of, in the interests of, on the hypothesis that;* and the ends of sentences are saved from anticlimax by such resounding commonplaces as *greatly to be desired, cannot be left out of account, a development to be expected in the near future, deserving of serious consideration, brought to a satisfactory conclusion*, and so on and so forth.

Pretentious Diction.   Words like *phenomenon, element, individual* (as noun), *objective, categorical, effective, virtual, basic, primary, promote, constitute, exhibit, exploit, utilize, eliminate, liquidate*, are used to dress up simple statements and give an air of scientific impartiality to biased judgments. Adjectives like *epoch-making, epic, historic, unforgettable, triumphant, age-old, inevitable, inexorable, veritable*, are used to dignify the sordid processes of international politics, while writing that aims at glorifying war usually takes on an archaic colour, its characteristic words being: *realm, throne, chariot, mailed fist, trident, sword, shield, buckler, banner, jackboot, clarion*. Foreign words and expressions such as *cul de sac, ancien régime, deus ex machina, mutatis mutandis, status quo, gleichschaltung, weltanschauung,* are used to give an air of culture and elegance. Except for the useful abbreviations *i.e., e.g.,* and *etc.,* there is no real need for any of the hundreds of foreign phrases now current in English. Bad writers, and especially scientific, political and sociological writers, are nearly always haunted by the notion that Latin or Greek words are grander than Saxon ones, and unnecessary words like *expedite, ameliorate, predict, extraneous, deracinated, clandestine, subaqueous* and hundreds of others constantly gain ground from their Anglo-Saxon opposite numbers.[1] The jargon peculiar to Marxist writing (*hyena, hangman, cannibal, petty bourgeois, these gentry, lacquey, flunkey, mad dog, White Guard,* etc.) consists largely of words and phrases translated from Russian, German or French; but the normal way of coining a new word is to use a Latin or Greek root with the appropriate affix and, where necessary, the -ize formation. It is often easier to make up words of this kind (*deregionalize, impermissible, extramarital, nonfragmentatory* and so forth) than to think up the English words that will cover one's meaning. The result, in general, is an increase in slovenliness and vagueness.

Meaningless Words.   In certain kinds of writing, particularly in art criticism and literary criticism, it is normal to come across long passages which are almost completely lacking in meaning.[2] Words like *romantic, plastic, values, human, dead, sentimental, natural, vitality,* as used in art criticism, are strictly meaningless in the sense that they not only do not point to any discoverable object, but are hardly ever expected to do so by the reader. When one critic writes, "The outstanding feature of Mr. X's work is its living quality," while another writes, "The immediately striking thing about Mr. X's work is its peculiar deadness," the reader accepts this as a simple difference of opinion. If words like *black* and *white* were involved, instead of the jargon words *dead* and *living,* he would see at once that language was being used in an improper way. Many political words are similarly abused. The word *Fascism* has now no meaning except in so far as it signifies "something not desirable." The words *democracy, socialism, freedom, patriotic, realistic, justice,* have each of them several different meanings which cannot

---

[1] An interesting illustration of this is the way in which the English flower names which were in use till very recently are being ousted by Greek ones, *snapdragon* becoming *antirrhinum, forget-me-not* becoming *myosotis,* etc. It is hard to see any practical reason for this change of fashion: it is probably due to an instinctive turning-away from the more homely word and a vague feeling that the Greek word is scientific.

[2] Example: "Comfort's catholicity of perception and image, strangely Whitmanesque in range, almost the exact opposite in aesthetic compulsion, continues to evoke that trembling atmospheric accumulative hinting at a cruel, an inexorably serene timelessness . . . Wrey Gardiner scores by aiming at simple bull's-eyes with precision. Only they are not so simple, and through this contented sadness runs more than the surface bitter-sweet of resignation." (*Poetry Quarterly.*)

be reconciled with one another. In the case of a word like *democracy,* not only is there no agreed definition, but the attempt to make one is resisted from all sides. It is almost universally felt that when we call a country democratic we are praising it: consequently the defenders of every kind of régime claim that it is a democracy, and fear that they might have to stop using the word if it were tied down to any one meaning. Words of this kind are often used in a consciously dishonest way. That is, the person who uses them has his own private definition, but allows his hearer to think he means something quite different. Statements like *Marshal Pétain was a true patriot, The Soviet Press is the freest in the world, The Catholic Church is opposed to persecution,* are almost always made with intent to deceive. Other words used in variable meanings, in most cases more or less dishonestly, are: *class, totalitarian, science, progressive, reactionary, bourgeois, equality.*

Now that I have made this catalogue of swindles and perversions, let me give another example of the kind of writing that they lead to. This time it must of its nature be an imaginary one. I am going to translate a passage of good English into modern English of the worst sort. Here is a well-known verse from *Ecclesiastes:*

"I returned and saw under the sun, that the race is not to the swift, nor the battle to the strong, neither yet bread to the wise, nor yet riches to men of understanding, nor yet favour to men of skill; but time and chance happeneth to them all."

Here it is in modern English:

"Objective considerations of contemporary phenomena compels the conclusion that success or failure in competitive activities exhibits no tendency to be commensurate with innate capacity, but that a considerable element of the unpredictable must invariably be taken into account."

This is a parody, but not a very gross one. Exhibit (3), above, for instance, contains several patches of the same kind of English. It will be seen that I have not made a full translation. The beginning and ending of the sentence follow the original meaning fairly closely, but in the middle the concrete illustrations—race, battle, bread—dissolve into the vague phrase "success or failure in competitive activities." This had to be so, because no modern writer of the kind I am discussing—no one capable of using phrases like "objective consideration of contemporary phenomena"—would ever tabulate his thoughts in that precise and detailed way. The whole tendency of modern prose is away from concreteness. Now analyse these two sentences a little more closely. The first contains forty-nine words but only sixty syllables, and all its words are those of everyday life. The second contains thirty-eight words of ninety syllables: eighteen of its words are from Latin roots, and one from Greek. The first sentence contains six vivid images, and only one phrase ("time and chance") that could be called vague. The second contains not a single fresh, arresting phrase, and in spite of its ninety syllables it gives only a shortened version of the meaning contained in the first. Yet without a doubt it is the second kind of sentence that is gaining ground in modern English. I do not want to exaggerate. This kind of writing is not yet universal, and outcrops of simplicity will occur here and there in the worst-written page. Still, if you or I were told to write a few lines on the uncertainty of human fortunes, we should probably come much nearer to my imaginary sentence than to the one from *Ecclesiastes*.

As I have tried to show, modern writing at its worst does not consist in picking out words for the sake of their meaning and inventing images in order to make the meaning clearer. It consists in gumming together long strips of words which have already been set in order by someone else, and making the results presentable by sheer humbug. The attraction of this way of writing is that it is easy. It is easier—even quicker, once you have the habit—to say *In my opinion it is a not unjustifiable assumption that* than to say *I think*. If you use ready-made phrases, you not only don't have to hunt about for words; you also don't have to bother with the rhythms of your sentences, since these phrases are generally so arranged as to be more or less euphonious. When you are composing in a hurry—when you are dictating to a stenographer, for instance, or making a public speech—it is natural to fall into a pretentious, Latinized style. Tags like *a consideration which we should do well to bear in mind* or *a conclusion to which all of us would readily assent* will save many a sentence from coming down with a bump. By using stale metaphors, similes and idioms, you save much mental effort, at the cost of leaving your meaning vague, not only for your reader but for yourself. This is the significance of mixed metaphors. The sole aim of a metaphor is to call up a visual image. When these images clash—as in *The Fascist octopus has sung its swan song, the jackboot is thrown into the melting pot*—it can be taken as certain that the writer is not seeing a mental image of the objects he is naming; in other words he is not really thinking. Look again at the examples I gave at the beginning of this essay. Professor Laski (1) uses five negatives in fifty-three words. One of these is superfluous, making nonsense of the whole passage, and in addition there is the slip *alien* for akin, making further nonsense, and several avoidable pieces of clumsiness which increase the general vagueness. Professor Hogben (2) plays ducks and drakes with a battery which is able to write prescriptions, and, while disapproving of the everyday phrase *put up with,* is unwilling to look *egregious* up in the dictionary and see what it means. (3), if one takes an uncharitable attitude towards it, is simply meaningless: probably one could work out its intended meaning by reading the whole of the article in which it occurs. In (4), the writer knows more or less what he wants to say, but an accumulation of stale phrases chokes him like tea leaves blocking a sink. In (5), words and meaning have almost parted company. People who write in this manner usually have a general emotional meaning—they dislike one

thing and want to express solidarity with another—but they are not interested in the detail of what they are saying. A scrupulous writer, in every
sentence that he writes, will ask himself at least four questions, thus: What
am I trying to say? What words will express it? What image or idiom will
make it clearer? Is this image fresh enough to have an effect? And he will
probably ask himself two more: Could I put it more shortly? Have I said
anything that is avoidably ugly? But you are not obliged to go to all this
trouble. You can shirk it by simply throwing your mind open and letting the
ready-made phrases come crowding in. They will construct your sentences
for you—even think your thoughts for you, to a certain extent—and at
need they will perform the important service of partially concealing your
meaning even from yourself. It is at this point that the special connection
between politics and the debasement of language becomes clear.

In our time it is broadly true that political writing is bad writing. Where it
is not true, it will generally be found that the writer is some kind of rebel,
expressing his private opinions and not a "party line." Orthodoxy, of whatever colour, seems to demand a lifeless, imitative style. The political dialects to be found in pamphlets, leading articles, manifestos, White Papers and
the speeches of under-secretaries do, of course, vary from party to party, but
they are all alike in that one almost never finds in them a fresh, vivid, home-
made turn of speech. When one watches some tired hack on the platform
mechanically repeating the familiar phrases—*bestial atrocities, iron heel,
bloodstained tyranny, free peoples of the world, stand shoulder to shoulder*
—one often has a curious feeling that one is not watching a live human
being but some kind of dummy: a feeling which suddenly becomes stronger
at moments when the light catches the speaker's spectacles and turns them
into blank discs which seem to have no eyes behind them. And this is not
altogether fanciful. A speaker who uses that kind of phraseology has gone
some distance towards turning himself into a machine. The appropriate
noises are coming out of his larynx, but his brain is not involved as it would
be if he were choosing his words for himself. If the speech he is making is
one that he is accustomed to make over and over again, he may be almost
unconscious of what he is saying, as one is when one utters the responses in
church. And this reduced state of consciousness, if not indispensable, is at
any rate favourable to political conformity.

In our time, political speech and writing are largely the defence of the
indefensible. Things like the continuance of British rule in India, the Russian purges and deportations, the dropping of the atom bombs on Japan, can
indeed be defended, but only by arguments which are too brutal for most
people to face, and which do not square with the professed aims of political
parties. Thus political language has to consist largely of euphemism,
question-begging and sheer cloudy vagueness. Defenceless villages are
bombarded from the air, the inhabitants driven out into the countryside, the

cattle machine-gunned, the huts set on fire with incendiary bullets: this is called *pacification*. Millions of peasants are robbed of their farms and sent trudging along the roads with no more than they can carry: this is called *transfer of population* or *rectification of frontiers*. People are imprisoned for years without trial, or shot in the back of the neck or sent to die of scurvy in Arctic lumber camps: this is called *elimination of unreliable elements*. Such phraseology is needed if one wants to name things without calling up mental pictures of them. Consider for instance some comfortable English professor defending Russian totalitarianism. He cannot say outright, "I believe in killing off your opponents when you can get good results by doing so." Probably, therefore, he will say something like this:

"While freely conceding that the Soviet régime exhibits certain features which the humanitarian may be inclined to deplore, we must, I think, agree that a certain curtailment of the right to political opposition is an unavoidable concomitant of transitional periods, and that the rigours which the Russian people have been called upon to undergo have been amply justified in the sphere of concrete achievement."

The inflated style is itself a kind of euphemism. A mass of Latin words falls upon the facts like soft snow, blurring the outlines and covering up all the details. The great enemy of clear language is insincerity. When there is a gap between one's real and one's declared aims, one turns as it were instinctively to long words and exhausted idioms, like a cuttlefish squirting out ink. In our age there is no such thing as "keeping out of politics." All issues are political issues, and politics itself is a mass of lies, evasions, folly, hatred and schizophrenia. When the general atmosphere is bad, language must suffer. I should expect to find—this is a guess which I have not sufficient knowledge to verify—that the German, Russian and Italian languages have all deteriorated in the last ten or fifteen years, as a result of dictatorship.

But if thought corrupts language, language can also corrupt thought. A bad usage can spread by tradition and imitation, even among people who should and do know better. The debased language that I have been discussing is in some ways very convenient. Phrases like *a not unjustifiable assumption, leaves much to be desired, would serve no good purpose, a consideration which we should do well to bear in mind,* are a continuous temptation, a packet of aspirins always at one's elbow. Look back through this essay, and for certain you will find that I have again and again committed the very faults I am protesting against. By this morning's post I have received a pamphlet dealing with conditions in Germany. The author tells me that he "felt impelled" to write it. I open it at random, and here is almost the first sentence that I see: "(The Allies) have an opportunity not only of achieving a radical transformation of Germany's social and political structure in such a way as to avoid a nationalistic reaction in Germany itself, but at the same time of laying the foundations of a co-operative and unified

Europe." You see, he "feels impelled" to write—feels, presumably, that he has something new to say—and yet his words, like cavalry horses answering the bugle, group themselves automatically into the familiar dreary pattern. This invasion of one's mind by ready-made phrases (*lay the foundations, achieve a radical transformation*) can only be prevented if one is constantly on guard against them, and every such phrase anaesthetizes a portion of one's brain.

I said earlier that the decadence of our language is probably curable. Those who deny this would argue, if they produced an argument at all, that language merely reflects existing social conditions, and that we cannot influence its development by any direct tinkering with words and constructions. So far as the general tone or spirit of a language goes, this may be true, but it is not true in detail. Silly words and expressions have often disappeared, not through any evolutionary process but owing to the conscious action of a minority. Two recent examples were *explore every avenue* and *leave no stone unturned,* which were killed by the jeers of a few journalists. There is a long list of flyblown metaphors which could similarly be got rid of if enough people would interest themselves in the job; and it should also be possible to laugh the *not un-* formation out of existence,[3] to reduce the amount of Latin and Greek in the average sentence, to drive out foreign phrases and strayed scientific words, and, in general, to make pretentiousness unfashionable. But all these are minor points. The defence of the English language implies more than this, and perhaps it is best to start by saying what it does *not* imply.

To begin with it has nothing to do with archaism, with the salvaging of obsolete words and turns of speech, or with the setting up of a "standard English" which must never be departed from. On the contrary, it is especially concerned with the scrapping of every word or idiom which has outworn its usefulness. It has nothing to do with correct grammar and syntax, which are of no importance so long as one makes one's meaning clear, or with the avoidance of Americanisms, or with having what is called a "good prose style." On the other hand it is not concerned with fake simplicity and the attempt to make written English colloquial. Nor does it even imply in every case preferring the Saxon word to the Latin one, though it does imply using the fewest and shortest words that will cover one's meaning. What is above all needed is to let the meaning choose the word, and not the other way about. In prose, the worst thing one can do with words is to surrender to them. When you think of a concrete object, you think wordlessly, and then, if you want to describe the thing you have been visualizing you probably hunt about till you find the exact words that seem to fit. When you think of something abstract you are more inclined to use words from the start, and

[3] One can cure oneself of the *not un-* formation by memorizing this sentence: *A not unblack dog was chasing a not unsmall rabbit across a not ungreen field.*

unless you make a conscious effort to prevent it, the existing dialect will come rushing in and do the job for you, at the expense of blurring or even changing your meaning. Probably it is better to put off using words as long as possible and get one's meaning as clear as one can through pictures or sensations. Afterwards one can choose—not simply *accept*—the phrases that will best cover the meaning, and then switch round and decide what impression one's words are likely to make on another person. This last effort of the mind cuts out all stale or mixed images, all prefabricated phrases, needless repetitions, and humbug and vagueness generally. But one can often be in doubt about the effect of a word or a phrase, and one needs rules that one can rely on when instinct fails. I think the following rules will cover most cases:

(i)   Never use a metaphor, simile or other figure of speech which you are used to seeing in print.
(ii) Never use a long word where a short one will do.
(iii) If it is possible to cut a word out, always cut it out.
(iv) Never use the passive where you can use the active.
(v)   Never use a foreign phrase, a scientific word or a jargon word if you can think of an everyday English equivalent.
(vi) Break any of these rules sooner than say anything outright barbarous.

These rules sound elementary, and so they are, but they demand a deep change of attitude in anyone who has grown used to writing in the style now fashionable. One could keep all of them and still write bad English, but one could not write the kind of stuff that I quoted in those five specimens at the beginning of this article.

I have not here been considering the literary use of language, but merely language as an instrument for expressing and not for concealing or preventing thought. Stuart Chase and others have come near to claiming that all abstract words are meaningless, and have used this as a pretext for advocating a kind of political quietism. Since you don't know what Fascism is, how can you struggle against Fascism? One need not swallow such absurdities as this, but one ought to recognize that the present political chaos is connected with the decay of language, and that one can probably bring about some improvement by starting at the verbal end. If you simplify your English, you are freed from the worst follies of orthodoxy. You cannot speak any of the necessary dialects, and when you make a stupid remark its stupidity will be obvious, even to yourself. Political language—and with variations this is true of all political parties, from Conservatives to Anarchists—is designed to make lies sound truthful and murder respectable, and to give an appearance of solidity to pure wind. One cannot change this all in a moment, but one can at least change one's own habits, and from time to time one can

even, if one jeers loudly enough, send some worn-out and useless phrase—
some *jackboot, Achilles' heel, hotbed, melting pot, acid test, veritable inferno* or other lump of verbal refuse—into the dustbin where it belongs.

STUDY QUESTIONS

1. What do each of the five examples illustrate that Orwell finds objection-
   able?

2. What is a dying metaphor? Can you add examples to those Orwell gives?

3. According to Orwell, what is the connection between politics and the debasement of language?

4. In what ways does language corrupt thought, and thought corrupt language?

H. L. Mencken

HELL AND ITS OUTSKIRTS

Henry Louis Mencken (1880–1956), editor, critic, columnist, and scholar,
was born in Baltimore, Maryland. For many years he was editor and columnist for the *Baltimore Sun,* and then later literary critic and editor of
Smart Set magazine. He gained a reputation as a master of wit and invective. The American public, particularly the middle class, became his special
target. He helped to found *The American Mercury,* a magazine devoted to
satire and comment on American life, politics, and customs. He is well
known among students of the English language for his scholarly *The American Language* (1919) and its two supplements. Titles of his other books are
The Philosophy of Friedrich Nietzsche (1908), *In Defense of Women*
(1918), *Prejudices* (in six series, 1919–1927), *Treatise on the Gods* (1930),
Treatise on Right and Wrong (1934), and *A Mencken Chrestomathy*
(1949).

> It doesn't matter what they preach,
>   Of high or low degree:
> The old Hell of the Bible
>   Is Hell enough for me.
>
> 'Twas preached by Paul and Peter;
>   They spread it wide and free;
> 'Twas Hell for old John Bunyan
>   And it's Hell enough for me.

THE AUTHOR of these elegiac strophes, Frank Lebby Stanton, has been moldering in the red clay of Georgia for a long, long while, but what he wrote went straight to the hearts of the American people, and there it still glows warmly. Hell remains the very essence not only of their dogmatic theology but also of their everyday invective. They employ it casually more than any other *Kulturvolk,* and perhaps more than all others put together. They have enriched it with a vast store of combinations, variations, licks, breaks, and riffs. They have made it roar and howl, and they have made it coo and twitter. It helps to lift them when supersonic waves of ecstasy rush through their lymphatic systems, and it soothes them when they roll in the barbed wire of despair. To find its match, you must go to the Buddhist *Om mani padma Hum,* meaning anything you please, or the Moslem *al-hamdu lil'lah,* meaning the same, or the ancient Mesopotamian Word from the Abyss, *Muazagagu-abzu.* Even so, *hell* is far ahead, for, compared to it, all these ejaculations have a pale and pansy cast, as does *hell* itself in nearly every other language; e.g., *enfer* in French, *inferno* in Spanish, *helvede* in Danish, *jigoku* in Japanese, and *Hölle* in German. So long ago as 1880, in the appendix on "The Awful German Language" to "A Tramp Abroad," Mark Twain derided *Hölle* as "chipper, frivolous and unimpressive" and marveled that anyone invited to go there could "rise to the dignity of feeling insulted." He had never heard, apparently, of the even more flaccid Finnish *manala,* which in These States would be the name of an infant food or perhaps of a female infant among the Bible-searchers of the Dust Bowl.

   Hell is one of the most ancient and honorable terms in English, and etymologists in their dusty cells have traced it to the first half of the ninth century. It is thus appreciably older than either *home* or *mother* and nearly five centuries older than its great rival, *damn.* But it was not until Shakespeare's time that it began to appear in the numerous blistering phrases that now glorify it—e.g., *go to hell, to hell with, hell to pay, hell is loose, hellcat,* and so on—and even then it rose only to be knocked down, for Shakespeare's time also saw the beginnings of the Puritan murrain, and once the bluenoses were in power they put down all strong language with a brutal hand. At the

Restoration, of course, it was reliberated, but only in a spavined state. The
Cavaliers, male and female, were great swearers, but their oaths were nearly
all cautious and cushioned. Such examples as *gadzooks, zounds, 'sdeath,
'sblood, by'r Lady, a plague on't, rat me, split my windpipe, marry,* and *burn
me* are heard in America today, when they are heard at all, only among candidates in theology and Boy Scouts. The English, indeed, have never recovered from the blight of Puritanism, and their swearing strikes all other civi-
lized peoples as puny. They are constantly working up a pother over such
forms as *bloody,* which to the rest of the world are quite innocuous. *Good
gracious,* which appeared in Oliver Goldsmith's "Good Natur'd Man" in
1768, seems to have been regarded in that day as pretty pungent, and *mercy,*
which preceded it by some years, was frowned upon as blasphemous. "Our
armies," says Uncle Toby in *Tristram Shandy,* "swore terribly in Flanders,"
but at home such virtuosity was rare, even among the military. In the wars of
our own time, the swearing of the English has provoked the contempt of
both their allies and their enemies. In both World War I and World War II,
they depended mainly upon a couple of four-letter words that are obscene
but not profane, and what they made of them showed little ingenuity or
imagination. The American military borrowed these terms in a spirit probably more derisory than admiring, and dropped them the instant they were
restored to Mom.

But as the brethren of the Motherland lost their Elizabethan talent for
wicked words it was transferred to these shores. Even the Puritans of New
England, once they settled down, took to cussing out one another in a violent
manner, and thousands of them were sent to the stocks or whipping post for
it by their baffled magistrates. The heroes of the Revolution not only swore
in all the orthodox forms but also invented a new expletive, *tarnation,* which
survived until the Mexican War. As Dr. Louise Pound has demonstrated
with great learning, both *tarnation* and *darn* were derived from *eternal* and
the former preceded the latter in refined use. George Washington himself
cut loose with *hell* and *damn* whenever the imbecilities of his brass went too
far. But it was the great movement into the West following the War of 1812
that really laid the foundations of American profanity and got *hell* firmly on
its legs. Such striking forms as *to raise hell, to hell around, hell-bent for
election, to be hell on, to play hell with, what the hell, heller, merry hell,
hellish, hellcat, hell on wheels, hell and high water, from hell to breakfast, a
hoot in hell, the hell of it, hell's a-poppin', the hell you say, hell with the lid
off,* and *the hinges of hell* were then invented by the gallant fellows, many of
them fugitives from Eastern sheriffs, who legged it across the great plains to
die for humanity at the hands of Indians, buffalo, catamounts, rattlesnakes,
bucking broncos, and vigilance committees. For nearly two generations nine-
tenths of the new terms in America, whether profane or not, came from the
region beyond Wheeling, West Virginia, and were commonly called West-

ernisms. It was not until after the Civil War that the newspaper wits of the
East began to contribute to the store, and not until after World War I that
concocting such things became the monopoly of Hollywood press agents,
radio mountebanks, and Broadway columnists.

The great upsurge of *hell* that rose to a climax in the Mexican War era
naturally upset the contemporary wowsers, and they busied themselves
launching euphemistic surrogates. Some of these seem to have been imported from the British Isles, along with Dundreary whiskers, soda water,
and bathing; for example, *by heck,* which originated there as a substitute for
by Hector, itself a substitute for *by God,* but was already obsolete at home
by the time it appeared in America. Here it not only flourished among the
prissy in its prototypical form but also moved over into the domain of *hell*
and gave birth to *a heck of a, to raise heck, to run like heck, colder than
heck, to play heck with, to beat heck, what the heck,* and *go to heck.* Other
deputies for *hell* were invented on American soil, notably *thunder and
blazes. Go to thunder* in the sense of *go to hell* is traced by the "Dictionary of
American English" to 1848 and marked an Americanism, and at about the
same time *thunderaction* began to be used for *damnation.* But soon *thunderaction* was used in place of *hell,* as in *what the thunderation.* It is possible
that German immigration helped to spread it in its various forms, for a favorite German expletive in those days was *Donnerwetter;* i.e., thundery
weather. But this is only a guess, and, like all other learned men, I am suspi-
cious of guessing.

After the Civil War there was another great upsurge of wowserism, culminating in the organization of the Comstock Society in 1873 [1] and of the
Woman's Christian Temperance Union the year following. Neither organization devoted itself specifically to profanity, but the moral indignation that
radiated from both of them soon began to affect it, and by 1880 it was being
denounced violently in thousands of far-flung evangelical pulpits. In this
work, the leader was the Reverend Sam Jones, who had been converted and
ordained a Methodist clergyman in 1872. Sam roared against cussing as he
roared against boozing, but the Devil fetched him by seducing him into
using stronger and stronger language himself, and toward the end of his life
I more than once heard him let go with objurgations that would have
cheered a bouncer clearing out a Sailor's Bethel. Even the Catholics, who
ordinarily never mistake the word for the deed, joined the crusade, and in
1882 they were reviving the Holy Name Society, which had been organized
back in 1274 and then forgotten. This combined assault had some effect; indeed, it probably had much more effect than it has been given credit for. At
all events, the lush profanity of the Civil War era began to shrink and pale,

[1] Its legal name was The New York Society for the Suppression of Vice. In 1947 that
name was changed to the Society to Maintain Public Decency. Old Anthony Comstock
was snatched up to Heaven in 1915 and succeeded by John S. Sumner.

and such unearthly oaths as *Jesus Christ and John Jacob Astor, by the high heels of St. Patrick,* and *by the double-barreled jumping Jiminetty* began to vanish from the American repertory. *God damn* kept going downhill throughout my youth in the eighties and nineties, and by the time I came of age I seldom used it. Many new euphemisms took the places of the forthright oaths of an earlier day, and one of them, *hully gee,* quickly became so innocuous that when Edward W. Townsend introduced it into "Chimmie Fadden," in 1895, it fell almost as flat as the four-letter words with which the lady novelists now pepper their pages.

But *hell* and *damn* somehow survived this massacre—maybe because the new euphemisms left a man choking and gasping when the steam really rose in his gauges, or maybe because some amateur canon lawyer discovered that in their naked state, uncoupled to sacred names, they are not officially blasphemous. Whatever the reason, American profanity was saved, and to this day it revolves around them and recruits itself from their substance. *Damn* is plainly the feebler of the two, despite its crashing effect when used by a master. *Hell* is enormously more effective, if only because it is more protean. For one phrase embodying the former there are at least forty embodying the latter, and many of them are susceptible to elegant and ingenious permutations. It is impossible for *damn* to bust loose, or to freeze over; it is impossible to knock it out of anyone, or to give it to anyone, or to beat it, or to raise it, or to think of a snowball or a bat in it, or to link it to high water, or to be *damn*-bent for election, or to plunge from *damn*-to-breakfast, or to *damn* around, or to get the *damn* out of any place, or to pull its lid off, or to think of it as having hubs or hinges. There is no such thing as a *damn*-hound, a *damn*cat, a *damn*hole, or a *damn*ion. Nothing is as black as *damn,* as busy as *damn,* as hot (or cold) as *damn,* or as deep, crazy, dumb, clever, cockeyed, crooked, touchy, dead, drunk, nervous, dull, expensive, scared, funny, hungry, lonely, mad, mean, poor, real, rotten, rough, serious, sick, smart, or sore as *damn. Damn* is a simple verb and its only child is a simple adjective, but *hell* ranges over all the keys of the grammatical scale and enters into combinations as avidly as oxygen.

There was a time when men learned in the tongues turned trembling backs upon such terms, but in recent years they have shown a libido for studying them, and the result is a rising literature. One of the earliest of the new monographs upon the subject—and still one of the best—was published in *American Speech* in August, 1931, by Dr. L. W. Merryweather. Probing scientifically, he discovered a great deal about *hell* that no one had ever noticed before. It can be slung about, he found, through nearly all the parts of speech. It can be used to represent almost every shade of meaning from yes to no, so that *hell of a time* may mean both the seraphic felicity of a police sergeant in a brewery and the extreme discomfort of a felon in the electric chair. A thing may be either *hotter than hell* or *colder than hell.* A *hellcat* may be either a woman so violent that her husband jumps overboard or nothing worse than a college cheerleader. *What in hell* is a mere expression of friendly interest, but *who the hell says so* is a challenge to fight. Merryweather threw out the suggestion that the upsurge and proliferation of *hell* in the Old West may have been due to Mormon influence. The Saints, he said, were very pious fellows and avoided the vain use of sacred names, but they were also logicians and hence concluded that the use of terms of precisely opposite connotation might be allowable, and even praise-worthy. At all events, they began to swear *by hell* and to call ordinary Christians *hellions* and *sons of hell,* and these terms were quickly borrowed by the miners, trappers, highwaymen, and others who invaded their Zion, and out of them flowed some of the most esteemed terms in *hell* of today. Whether Merryweather was right here I do not presume to say, but in another of his conclusions he undoubtedly slipped, as even savants sometimes do. "Today," he said, *"hell* fills so large a place in the American vulgate that it will probably be worn out in a few years more, and will become obsolescent." We all know now that nothing of the sort has happened. *Hell,* in fact, is flourishing as never before. I have many hundreds of examples of its use in my archives, and new ones are being added almost every day.

A large number of swell ones were assembled into a monograph by another scholar, Dr. Bartlett Jere Whiting, published in *Harvard Studies and Notes in Philology and Literature,* Vol. XX, 1938. Whiting, a sequestered philologian interested chiefly in Old and Middle England, sought his material not in the market place but in books—mostly novels of the 1920–37 period. But even within this narrow and somewhat dephlogisticated field he found enough phrases based on *hell* to fill twenty-four pages of the austere journal in which he wrote. I have space for only a few examples: *holy hell, fifteen kinds of hell, to batter hell into, assorted hell, the seven hinges of hell, thicker than fiddlers in hell, four naked bats out of hell, like a shot out of hell, the chance of a celluloid collar in hell, three hurrahs in hell, hell's own luck, hell up Sixth Street, hell on toast, from hell to Harvard, hell gone from nowhere, like a hangman from hell, hell's half acre, hell-for-leather,* and *what the red* (or *bloody*) *hell.* Whiting duly noted *hell of a business, hurry, jam, job, life, mess, place, note, row, time,* and *way* but overlooked George Ade's *hell of a Baptist.* He added some euphemisms for *hell*—for example, *billy-be-damned, billy-ho,* and *blazes*—but he had to admit that these "makeshifts and conscience-easers," as he called them, were all pretty feeble.

Robert Southey, more than a century ago, investigated the names of the principal devils of Hell, and not only printed a list of them in one of his books but also suggested that some might be useful as cuss words; e.g., *Lacahabarrutu, Buzache, Knockadawe, Baa,* and *Ju.* There were, however, no takers for his suggestion and he got no further with the subject. In Harlem, according to Zora Neale Hurston, the dark geographers have discovered that there is a hotter Hell lying somewhat south of the familiar Christian resort, and have given it the name of *Beluthahatchie*. So far, not much has been learned about its amperage, sociology, or public improvements, but its temperature has been fixed tentatively somewhere between that of a blast furnace and that of the sun. These Afro-American explorers also believe that their spectroscopes have found three suburbs of Hell proper, by name *Diddy-wah-diddy, Ginny Gall,* and *West Hell.* Unhappily, not much is known about them, though several ghosts returned to earth report that *Diddy-wah-diddy* is a sort of Long Island, given over mainly to eating houses and night clubs, and that *West Hell* lies beyond the railroad tracks and is somewhat tacky.

STUDY QUESTIONS

1. According to Mencken, what is the early history of the word *hell?* What is the effect of his noting that it is older than either *home* or *mother?*

2. What evidence does he cite for the growth of the use of *hell* in this country?

3. Look up the meaning of the word *wowser.* What, according to Mencken, did the wowsers have to do with the history of the word *hell* in this country?

4. To Mencken, *hell* is much stronger and more effective than *damn.* How does he support his opinion? Do you agree?

5. Can you add any phrases based on *hell* to the list Mencken gives as collected by Dr. Whiting? What is the status of *hell* and phrases based on it today?

6. Examine Mencken's diction. It has been called vigorous. Can you cite his use of particular words that justify this? How does he use certain words to make judgments?

Wallace E. Stegner

"GOOD-BYE TO ALL T--T"

Wallace Stegner is a well-known writer and teacher of writers at Stanford
University, where he heads a creative writing program. He earned his
undergraduate degree at the University of Utah and his M.A. and Ph.D.
degrees at the University of Iowa. He has taught at Augustana College, the
Universities of Utah and Wisconsin, and Harvard University. He was
awarded Guggenheim Fellowships in 1950, 1952, and 1959, and has won
the O'Henry First Prize for Short Stories. His books include *The Woman
on the Wall* (1950), *The Preacher and the Slave* (1950), *Beyond the Hun-
dredth Meridian* (1954), *The City of the Living* (1956), *A Shooting Star*
(1961), *Wolf Willow* (1962), *The Gathering of Zion* (1964) and *All the Little Live Things* (1967). He has also written numerous articles and short
stories.

N̲OT EVERYONE who laments what contemporary novelists
have done to the sex act objects to the act itself, or to its
mention. Some want it valued higher than fiction seems
to value it; they want the word "climax" to retain some of its literary meaning. Likewise, not everyone who has come to doubt the contemporary freedom of language objects to strong language in itself. Some of us object precisely because we value it.

I acknowledge that I have used four-letter words familiarly all my life,
and have put them into books with some sense that I was insisting on the
proper freedom of the artist. I have applauded the extinction of those d----d
emasculations of the Genteel Tradition and the intrusion into serious fiction
of honest words with honest meanings and emphasis. I have wished, with
D. H. Lawrence, for the courage to say shit before a lady, and have sometimes had my wish.

Words are not obscene: naming things is a legitimate verbal act. And
"frank" does not mean "vulgar," any more than "improper" means "dirty."
What vulgar does mean is "common"; what improper means is "unsuit-

able." Under the right circumstances, any word is proper. But when any sort of word, especially a word hitherto taboo and therefore noticeable, is scattered across a page like chocolate chips through a tollhouse cookie, a real impropriety occurs. The sin is not the use of an "obscene" word; it is the use of a loaded word in the wrong place or in the wrong quantity. It is the sin of false emphasis, which is not a moral but a literary lapse, related to sentimentality. It is the sin of advertisers who so plaster a highway with neon signs that you can't find the bar or liquor store you're looking for. Like any excess, it quickly becomes comic.

If I habitually say shit before a lady, what do I say before a flat tire at the rush hour in Times Square or on the San Francisco Bay Bridge? What do I say before a revelation of the inequity of the universe? And what if the lady takes the bit in her teeth and says shit before *me?*

I have been a teacher of writing for many years and have watched this problem since it was no bigger than a man's hand. It used to be that with some Howellsian notion of the young-girl audience one tried to protect tender female members of a mixed class from the coarse language of males trying to show off. Some years ago Frank O'Connor and I agreed on a system. Since we had no intention whatever of restricting students' choice of subject or language, and no desire to expurgate or bowdlerize while reading their stuff aloud for discussion, but at the same time had to deal with these young girls of an age our daughters might have been, we announced that any stuff so strong that it would embarrass us to read it aloud could be read by its own author.

It was no deterrent at all, but an invitation, and not only to coarse males. For clinical sexual observation, for full acceptance of the natural functions, for discrimination in the selection of graffiti, for boldness in the use of words that it should take courage to say before a lady, give me a sophomore girl every time. Her strength is as the strength of ten, for she assumes that if one shocker out of her pretty mouth is piquant, fifty will be literature. And so do a lot of her literary idols.

Some acts, like some words, were never meant to be casual. That is why houses contain bedrooms and bathrooms. Profanity and so-called obscenities are literary resources, verbal ways of rendering strong emotion. They are not meant to occur every ten seconds, any more than—Norman Mailer to the contrary notwithstanding—orgasms are.

So I am not going to say shit before any more ladies. I am going to hunt words that have not lost their sting, and it may be I shall have to go back to gentility to find them. Pleasant though it is to know that finally a writer can make use of any word that fits his occasion, I am going to investigate the possibilities latent in restraint.

I remember my uncle, a farmer who had used four-letter words ten to the sentence ever since he learned to talk. One day he came too near the circular saw and cut half his fingers off. While we stared in horror, he stood watching the bright arterial blood pump from his ruined hand. Then he spoke, and he did not speak loud. "Aw, the dickens," he said.

I think he understood, better than some sophomore girls and better than some novelists, the nature of emphasis.

STUDY QUESTIONS

1. According to Stegner, the sin of false emphasis is related to sentimentality. Explain.

2. What are the premises of the argument in the third paragraph. Is this a valid argument?

3. What is the objection to "those d----d" emasculations of the Genteel Tradition"?

4. Why do writers today have license to use words that were formerly taboo?

5. Does Stegner give any consideration to taste in the use of certain words?

Mark Twain

BUCK FANSHAW'S FUNERAL

Mark Twain, pen name for Samuel Langhorne Clemens (1835–1910), internationally known humorist and satirist, was born in Florida, Missouri, and spent his boyhood in Hannibal, Missouri. In his youth and early manhood he worked at a variety of occupations—journeyman printer, steamboat pilot, newspaper reporter, prospector, free-lance writer, and lecturer. His experiences gave him a lifetime of material for his writings. In his own time he enjoyed an international reputation as a wit and social commentator. In his later years he became bitterly cynical, but by most Americans he is remembered as the author of *Tom Sawyer* (1876) and *The Adventures of Huckleberry Finn* (1884).

Chapter VI in *Roughing It* by Mark Twain. Reprinted by permission of Harper & Row, publishers.

SOMEBODY has said that in order to know a community, one must observe the style of its funerals and know what manner of men they bury with most ceremony. I cannot say which class we buried with most éclat in our "flush times," the distinguished public benefactor or the distinguished rough—possibly the two chief grades or grand divisions of society honored their illustrious dead about equally; and hence, no doubt, the philosopher I have quoted from would have needed to see two representative funerals in Virginia before forming his estimate of the people.

There was a grand time over Buck Fanshaw when he died. He was a representative citizen. He had "killed his man"—not in his own quarrel, it is true, but in defense of a stranger unfairly beset by numbers. He had kept a sumptuous saloon. He had been the proprietor of a dashing helpmeet whom he could have discarded without the formality of a divorce. He had held a high position in the fire department and been a very Warwick in politics. When he died there was great lamentation throughout the town, but especially in the vast bottom-stratum of society.

On the inquest it was shown that Buck Fanshaw, in the delirium of a wasting typhoid fever, had taken arsenic, shot himself through the body, cut his throat, and jumped out of a four-story window and broken his neck—and after due deliberation, the jury, sad and tearful, but with intelligence unblinded by its sorrow, brought in a verdict of death "by the visitation of God." What could the world do without juries?

Prodigious preparations were made for the funeral. All the vehicles in town were hired, all the saloons put in mourning, all the municipal and fire-company flags hung at half-mast, and all the firemen ordered to muster in uniform and bring their machines duly draped in black. Now—let us remark in parentheses—as all the peoples of the earth had representative adventurers in the Silverland, and as each adventurer had brought the slang of his nation or his locality with him, the combination made the slang of Nevada the richest and the most infinitely varied and copious that had ever existed anywhere in the world, perhaps, except in the mines of California in the "early days." Slang was the language of Nevada. It was hard to preach a sermon without it, and be understood. Such phrases as "You bet!" "Oh, no, I reckon not!" "No Irish need apply," and a hundred others, became so common as to fall from the lips of a speaker unconsciously—and very often when they did not touch the subject under discussion and consequently failed to mean anything.

After Buck Fanshaw's inquest, a meeting of the short-haired brotherhood was held, for nothing can be done on the Pacific coast without a public meeting and an expression of sentiment. Regretful resolutions were passed and various committees appointed; among others, a committee of one was deputed to call on the minister, a fragile, gentle, spiritual new fledgling from an Eastern theological seminary, and as yet unacquainted with the ways of the mines. The committeeman, "Scotty" Briggs, made his visit; and in after days it was worth something to hear the minister tell about it. Scotty was a stalwart rough, whose customary suit, when on weighty official business, like committee work, was a fire-helmet, flaming red flannel shirt, patent-leather belt with spanner and revolver attached, coat hung over arm, and pants stuffed into boot-tops. He formed something of a contrast to the pale theological student. It is fair to say of Scotty, however, in passing, that he had a warm heart, and a strong love for his friends, and never entered into a quarrel when he could reasonably keep out of it. Indeed, it was commonly said that whenever one of Scotty's fights was investigated, it always turned out that it had originally been no affair of his, but that out of native good-heartedness he had dropped in of his own accord to help the man who was getting the worst of it. He and Buck Fanshaw were bosom friends, for years, and had often taken adventurous "pot-luck" together. On one occasion, they had thrown off their coats and taken the weaker side in a fight among strangers, and after gaining a hard-earned victory, turned and found that the men they were helping had deserted early, and not only that, but had stolen their coats and made off with them. But to return to Scotty's visit to the minister. He was on a sorrowful mission, now, and his face was the picture of woe. Being admitted to the presence he sat down before the clergyman, placed his fire-hat on an unfinished manuscript sermon under the minister's nose, took from it a red silk handkerchief, wiped his brow and heaved a sigh of dismal impressiveness, explanatory of his business. He choked, and even shed tears; but with an effort he mastered his voice and said in lugubrious tones:

"Are you the duck that runs the gospel-mill next door?"

"Am I the—pardon me, I believe I do not understand?"

With another sigh and a half-sob, Scotty rejoined:

"Why you see we are in a bit of trouble, and the boys thought maybe you would give us a lift, if we'd tackle you—that is, if I've got the rights of it and you are the head clerk of the doxology-works next door."

"I am the shepherd in charge of the flock whose fold is next door."

"The which?"

"The spiritual adviser of the little company of believers whose sanctuary adjoins these premises."

Scotty scratched his head, reflected a moment, and then said:

"You ruther hold over me, pard. I reckon I can't call that hand. Ante and pass the buck."

"How? I beg pardon. What did I understand you to say?"

"Well, you've ruther got the bulge on me. Or maybe we've both got the bulge, somehow. You don't smoke me and I don't smoke you. You see, one of the boys has passed in his checks, and we want to give him a good send-off, and so the thing I'm on now is to roust out somebody to jerk a little chin-music for us and waltz him through handsome."

"My friend, I seem to grow more and more bewildered. Your observations are wholly incomprehensible to me. Cannot you simplify them in some way? At first I thought perhaps I understood you, but I grope now. Would it not expedite matters if you restricted yourself to categorical statements of fact unencumbered with obstructing accumulations of metaphor and allegory?"

Another pause, and more reflection. Then, said Scotty:

"I'll have to pass, I judge."

"How?"

"You've raised me out, pard."

"I still fail to catch your meaning."

"Why, that last lead of yourn is too many for me—that's the idea. I can't neither trump nor follow suit."

The clergyman sank back in his chair perplexed. Scotty leaned his head on his hand and gave himself up to thought. Presently his face came up, sorrowful but confident.

"I've got it now, so's you can savvy," he said. "What we want is a gospel-sharp. See?"

"A what?"

"Gospel-sharp. Parson."

"Oh! Why did you not say so before? I am a clergyman—a parson."

"Now you talk! You see my blind and straddle it like a man. Put it there!" —extending a brawny paw, which closed over the minister's small hand and gave it a shake indicative of fraternal sympathy and fervent gratification.

"Now we're all right, pard. Let's start fresh. Don't you mind my snuffling a little—becuz we're in a power of trouble. You see, one of the boys has gone up the flume—"

"Gone where?"

"Up the flume—throwed up the sponge, you understand."

"Thrown up the sponge?"

"Yes—kicked the bucket—"

"Ah—has departed to that mysterious country from whose bourne no traveler returns."

"Return! I reckon not. Why, pard, he's *dead!*"

"Yes, I understand."

"Oh, you do? Well I thought maybe you might be getting tangled some more. Yes, you see he's dead again—"

"*Again!* Why, has he ever been dead before?"

"Dead before? No! Do you reckon a man has got as many lives as a cat?

But you bet you he's awful dead now, poor old boy, and I wish I'd never seen this day. I don't want no better friend than Buck Fanshaw. I knowed him by the back; and when I know a man and like him, I freeze to him—you hear *me*. Take him all round, pard, there never was a bullier man in the mines. No man ever knowed Buck Fanshaw to go back on a friend. But it's all up, you know, it's all up. It ain't no use. They've scooped him."

"Scooped him?"

"Yes—death has. Well, well, well, we've got to give him up. Yes, indeed. It's a kind of a hard world, after all, *ain't* it? But pard, he was a rustler! You ought to seen him get started once. He was a bully boy with a glass eye! Just spit in his face and give him room according to his strength, and it was just beautiful to see him peel and go in. He was the worst son a thief that ever drawed breath. Pard, he was *on* it! He was on it bigger than an Injun!"

"On it? On what?"

"On the shoot. On the shoulder. On the fight, you understand. *He* didn't give a continental for *any*body. *Beg* your pardon, friend, for coming so near saying a cuss-word—but you see I'm on an awful strain, in this palaver, on account of having to cramp down and draw everything so mild. But we've got to give him up. There ain't any getting around that, I don't reckon. Now if we can get you to help plant him—"

"Preach the funeral discourse? Assist at the obsequies?"

"Obs'quies is good. Yes. That's it—that's our little game. We are going to get the thing up regardless, you know. He was always nifty himself, and so you bet you his funeral ain't going to be no slouch—solid-silver door-plate on his coffin, six plumes on the hearse, and a nigger on the box in a biled shirt and a plug hat—how's that for high? And we'll take care of *you,* pard. We'll fix you all right. There'll be a kerridge for you; and whatever you want, you just 'scape out and we'll 'tend to it. We've got a shebang fixed up for you to stand behind, in No. 1's house, and don't you be afraid. Just go in and toot your horn, if you don't sell a clam. Put Buck through as bully as you can, pard, for anybody that knowed him will tell you that he was one of the whitest men that was ever in the mines. You can't draw it too strong. He never could stand it to see things going wrong. He's done more to make this town quiet and peaceable than any man in it. I've seen him lick four Greasers in eleven minutes, myself. If a thing wanted regulating, *he* warn't a man to go browsing around after somebody to do it, but he would prance in and regulate it himself. He warn't a Catholic. Scasely. He was down on 'em. His word was, 'No Irish need apply!' But it didn't make no difference about that when it came down to what a man's rights was—and so, when some roughs jumped the Catholic boneyard and started in to stake out town lots in it he *went* for 'em! And he *cleaned* 'em, too! I was there, pard, and I seen it myself."

"That was very well indeed—at least the impulse was—whether the act was strictly defensible or not. Had deceased any religious convictions? That is to say, did he feel a dependence upon, or acknowledge allegiance to a higher power?"

More reflection.

"I reckon you've stumped me again, pard. Could you say it over once more, and say it slow?"

"Well, to simplify it somewhat, was he, or rather had he ever been connected with any organization sequestered from secular concerns and devoted to self-sacrifice in the interests of morality?"

"All down but nine—set 'em up on the other alley, pard."

"What did I understand you to say?"

"Why, you're most too many for me, you know. When you get in with your left I hunt grass every time. Every time you draw, you fill; but I don't seem to have any luck. Let's have a new deal."

"How? Begin again?"

"That's it."

"Very well. Was he a good man, and—"

"There—I see that; don't put up another chip till I look at my hand. A good man, says you? Pard, it ain't no name for it. He was the best man that ever—pard, you would have doted on that man. He could lam any galoot of his inches in America. It was him that put down the riot last election before it got a start; and everybody said he was the only man that could have done it. He waltzed in with a spanner in one hand and a trumpet in the other, and sent fourteen men home on a shutter in less than three minutes. He had that riot all broke up and prevented nice before anybody ever got a chance to strike a blow. He was always for peace, and he would *have* peace—he could not stand disturbances. Pard, he was a great loss to this town. It would please the boys if you could chip in something like that and do him justice. Here once when the Micks got to throwing stones through the Methodis' Sunday-school windows, Buck Fanshaw, all of his own notion, shut up his saloon and took a couple of six-shooters and mounted guard over the Sunday-school. Says he, 'No Irish need apply!' And they didn't. He was the bulliest man in the mountains, pard! He could run faster, jump higher, hit harder, and hold more tanglefoot whisky without spilling it than any man in seventeen counties. Put that in, pard—it'll please the boys more than anything you could say. And you can say, pard, that he never shook his mother."

"Never shook his mother?"

"That's it—any of the boys will tell you so."

"Well, but why *should* he shake her?"

"That's what *I* say—but some people does."

"Not people of any repute?"

"Well, some that averages pretty so-so."

"In my opinion the man that would offer personal violence to his own mother, ought to—"

"Cheese it, pard; you've banked your ball clean outside the string. What I was a drivin' at, was, that he never *throwed off* on his mother—don't you see? No indeedy. He give her a house to live in, and town lots, and plenty of money; and he looked after her and took care of her all the time; and when she was down with the smallpox I'm d—d if he didn't set up nights and nuss her himself! *Beg* your pardon for saying it, but it hopped out too quick for yours truly. You've treated me like a gentleman, pard, and I ain't the man to hurt your feelings intentional. I think you're white. I think you're a square man, pard. I like you, and I'll lick any man that don't. I'll lick him tell he can't tell himself from a last year's corpse! Put it *there!*" [Another fraternal handshake—and exit.]

The obsequies were all that "the boys" could desire. Such a marvel of funeral pomp had never been seen in Virginia. The plumed hearse, the dirge-breathing brass-bands, the closed marts of business, the flags drooping at half-mast, the long, plodding procession of uniformed secret societies, military battalions and fire companies, draped engines, carriages of officials, and citizens in vehicles and on foot, attracted multitudes of spectators to the sidewalks, roofs, and windows; and for years afterward, the degree of grandeur attained by any civic display in Virginia was determined by comparison with Buck Fanshaw's funeral.

Scotty Briggs, as a pall-bearer and a mourner, occupied a prominent place at the funeral, and when the sermon was finished and the last sentence of the prayer for the dead man's soul ascended, he responded, in a low voice, but with feeling:

"AMEN. No Irish need apply."

As the bulk of the response was without apparent relevancy, it was probably nothing more than a humble tribute to the memory of the friend that was gone; for, as Scotty had once said, it was "his word."

Scotty Briggs, in after days, achieved the distinction of becoming the only convert to religion that was ever gathered from the Virginia roughs; and it transpired that the man who had it in him to espouse the quarrel of the weak out of inborn nobility of spirit was no mean timber whereof to construct a Christian. The making him one did not warp his generosity or diminish his courage; on the contrary it gave intelligent direction to the one and a broader field to the other. If his Sunday-school class progressed faster than the other classes, was it matter for wonder? I think not. He talked to his pioneer small-fry in a language they understood! It was my large privilege, a month before he died, to hear him tell the beautiful story of Joseph and his brethren to his class "without looking at the book." I leave it to the reader to fancy what it was like, as it fell, riddled with slang, from the lips of that

grave, earnest teacher, and was listened to by his little learners with a con-
suming interest that showed that they were as unconscious as he was that
any violence was being done to the sacred proprieties!

STUDY QUESTIONS

1. In addition to Scotty's and the minister's language, we have the lan-
    guage of the author, who introduces the story and concludes it. Compare
    his manner of speech with that of the other two.

2. Make note of the many different expressions Scotty and the minister use
    for death and funeral. Can you add to these?

3. Some of Scotty's expressions are current today. What are some of them?

Max Beerbohm

HOW SHALL I WORD IT?

Max Beerbohm (1872–1956), well-known critic and satirist, was born in
London. He received his A.B. degree from Merton College, Oxford. After
gaining an early reputation for his satirical essays in the famous *Yellow
Book,* he succeeded George Bernard Shaw as drama critic of the *Saturday Review.* In addition to countless essays published in magazines, he
wrote *The Happy Hypocrite* (1897), *More* (1899), *Yet Again* (1907), *And
Even Now* (1920), *A Variety of Things* (1928), *Mainly on the Air* (1946),
and *Around Theatres* (1953). He was knighted in 1939.

IT WOULD SEEM that I am one of those travellers for whom
the railway bookstall does not cater. Whenever I start on
a journey, I find that my choice lies between well-printed
books which I have no wish to read, and well-written books which I could

not read without permanent injury to my eyesight. The keeper of the bookstall, seeing me gaze vaguely along his shelves, suggests that I should take
Fen Country Fanny or else *The Track of Blood* and have done with it. Not
wishing to hurt his feelings, I refuse these works on the plea that I have read
them. Whereon he, divining despite me that I am a superior person, says
"Here is a nice little handy edition of More's *Utopia*" or "Carlyle's *French
Revolution*" and again I make some excuse. What pleasure could I get from
trying to cope with a masterpiece printed in diminutive grey-ish type on a
semi-transparent little grey-ish page? I relieve the bookstall of nothing but a
newspaper or two.

The other day, however, my eye and fancy were caught by a book entitled
How Shall I Word It? and sub-entitled *A Complete Letter Writer for Men
and Women*. I had never read one of these manuals, but had often heard that
there was a great and constant "demand" for them. So I demanded this one.
It is no great fun in itself. The writer is no fool. He has evidently a natural
talent for writing letters. His style is, for the most part, discreet and easy. If
you were a young man writing "to Father of Girl he wishes to Marry" or
"thanking Fiancée for Present" or "reproaching Fiancée for being a Flirt,"
or if you were a mother "asking Governess her Qualifications" or "replying
to Undesirable Invitation for her Child," or indeed if you were in any other
one of the crises which this book is designed to alleviate, you might copy out
and post the specially-provided letter without making yourself ridiculous in
the eyes of its receiver—unless, of course, he or she also possessed a copy
of the book. But—well, can you conceive any one copying out and posting
one of these letters, or even taking it as the basis for composition? You cannot. That shows how little you know of your fellow-creatures. Not you nor I
can plumb the abyss at the bottom of which such humility is possible. Nevertheless, as we know by that great and constant "demand," there the abyss is,
and there multitudes are at the bottom of it. Let's peer down . . . No, all is
darkness. But faintly, if we listen hard, is borne up to us a sound of the
scratching of innumerable pens—pens whose wielders are all trying, as the
author of this handbook urges them, to "be original, fresh, and interesting"
by dint of more or less strict adherence to sample.

Giddily you draw back from the edge of the abyss. Come!—here is a
thought to steady you. The mysterious great masses of helpless folk for
whom *How Shall I Word It?* is written are sound at heart, delicate in feeling,
anxious to please, most loth to wound. For it must be presumed that the
author's style of letter-writing is informed as much by a desire to give his
public what it needs, and will pay for, as by his own beautiful nature; and in
the course of all the letters that he dictates you will find not one harsh word,
not one ignoble thought or unkind insinuation. In all of them, though so
many are for the use of persons placed in the most trying circumstances, and
some of them are for persons writhing under a sense of intolerable injury,

sweetness and light do ever reign. Even "yours truly, Jacob Langton," in his "letter to his Daughter's Mercenary Fiancé," mitigates the sternness of his tone by the remark that his "task is inexpressibly painful." And he, Mr. Langton, is the one writer who lets the post go out on his wrath. When Horace Masterton, of Thorpe Road, Putney, receives from Miss Jessica Weir, of Fir Villa, Blackheath, a letter "declaring her Change of Feelings," does he upbraid her? No; "it was honest and brave of you to write to me so straightforwardly and at the back of my mind I know you have done what is best. . . . I give you back your freedom only at your desire. God bless you, dear." Not less admirable is the behaviour, in similar case, of Cecil Grant (14, Glover Street, Streatham). Suddenly, as a bolt from the blue, comes a letter from Miss Louie Hawke (Elm View, Deerhurst), breaking off her betrothal to him. Haggard, he sits down to his desk; his pen traverses the notepaper—calling down curses on Louie and on all her sex? No; "one cannot say good-bye for ever without deep regret to days that have been so full of happiness. I must thank you sincerely for all your great kindness to me. . . . With every sincere wish for your future happiness," he bestows complete freedom on Miss Hawke. And do not imagine that in the matter of self-control and sympathy, of power to understand all and pardon all, the men are lagged behind by the women. Miss Leila Johnson (The Manse, Carlyle) has observed in Leonard Wace (Dover Street, Saltburn) a certain coldness of demeanour; yet "I do not blame you; it is probably your nature"; and Leila in her sweet forbearance is typical of all the other pained women in these pages: she is but one of a crowd of heroines.

Face to face with all this perfection, the not perfect reader beings to crave some little outburst of wrath, of hatred or malice, from one of these imaginary ladies and gentleman. He longs for—how shall he word it?—a glimpse of some bad motive, of some little lapse from dignity. Often, passing by a pillar-box, I have wished I could unlock it and carry away its contents, to be studied at my leisure. I have always thought such a haul would abound in things fascinating to a student of human nature. One night, not long ago, I took a waxen impression of the lock of the pillar-box nearest to my house, and had a key made. This implement I have as yet lacked either the courage or the opportunity to use. And now I think I shall throw it away. . . . No, I shan't. I refuse, after all, to draw my inference that the bulk of the British public writes always in the manner of this handbook. Even if they all have beautiful natures they must sometimes be sent slightly astray by inferior impulses, just as are you and I.

And, if err they must, surely it were well they should know how to do it correctly and forcibly. I suggest to our author that he should sprinkle his next edition with a few less righteous examples, thereby both purging his book of its monotony and somewhat justifying its subtitle. Like most people who are in the habit of writing things to be printed, I have not the knack of writing really good letters. But let me crudely indicate the sort of thing that our manual needs. . . .

LETTER FROM POOR MAN TO OBTAIN MONEY FROM RICH ONE.

[*The English law is particularly hard on what is called blackmail. It is therefore essential that the applicant should write nothing that might afterwards be twisted to incriminate him.*—ED.]

DEAR SIR,

To-day, as I was turning out a drawer in my attic, I came across a letter which by a curious chance fell into my hands some years ago, and which, in the stress of grave pecuniary embarrassment, had escaped my memory. It is a letter written by yourself to a lady, and the date shows it to have been written shortly after your marriage. It is of a confidential nature, and might, I fear, if it fell into the wrong hands, be cruelly misconstrued. I would wish you to have the satisfaction of destroying it in person. At first I thought of sending it on to you by post. But I know how happy you are in your domestic life; and probably your wife and you, in your perfect mutual trust, are in the habit of opening each other's letters. Therefore, to avoid risk, I would prefer to hand the document to you personally. I will not ask you to come to my attic, where I could not offer you such hospitality as is due to a man of your wealth and position. You will be so good as to meet me at 3.0 A.M. (sharp) to-morrow (Thursday) beside the tenth lamp-post to the left on the Surrey side of Waterloo Bridge; at which hour and place we shall not be disturbed.

I am, dear Sir,

Yours respectfully,

JAMES GRIDGE.

LETTER FROM YOUNG MAN REFUSING TO PAY HIS TAILOR'S BILL.

Mr. Eustace Davenant has received the half-servile, half-insolent screed which Mr. Yardley has addressed to him. Let Mr. Yardley cease from crawling on his knees and shaking his fist. Neither this posture nor this gesture can wring one bent farthing from the pockets of Mr. Davenant, who was a minor at the time when that series of ill-made suits was supplied to him and will hereafter, as in the past, shout (without prejudice) from the house-tops that of all the tailors in London Mr. Yardley is at once the most grasping and the least competent.

LETTER TO THANK AUTHOR FOR INSCRIBED COPY OF BOOK

DEAR MR EMANUEL FLOWER,
It was kind of you to think of sending me a copy of your new book. It would have been kinder still to think again and abandon that project. I am a man of gentle instincts, and do not like to tell you that "A Flight into Arcady" (of which I have skimmed a few pages, thus wasting two or three minutes of my not altogether worthless time) is trash. On the other hand, I am determined that you shall not be able to go around boasting to your friends, if you have any, that this work was not condemned, derided, and dismissed by your sincere well-wisher, WREXFORD CRIPPS.

LETTER TO MEMBER OF PARLIAMENT UNSEATED AT GENERAL ELECTION

DEAR MR. POBSBY-BURFORD,
Though I am myself an ardent Tory, I cannot but rejoice in the crushing defeat you have just suffered in West Odgetown. There are moments when political conviction is overborne by personal sentiment; and this is one of them. Your loss of the seat that you held is the more striking by reason of the splendid manner in which the northern and eastern divisions of Odgetown have been wrested from the Liberal Party. The great bulk of the newspaper-reading public will be puzzled by your extinction in the midst of our party's triumph. But then, the great mass of the newspaper-reading public has not met you. I have. You will probably not remember me. You are the sort of man who would not remember anybody who might not be of some definite use to him. Such, at least, was one of the impressions you made on me when I met you last summer at a dinner given by our friends the Pelhams. Among the other things in you that struck me were the blatant pomposity of your manner, your appalling flow of cheap platitudes, and your hoggish lack of ideas. It is such men as you that lower the tone of public life. And I am sure that in writing to you thus I am but expressing what is felt, without distinction of party, by all who sat with you in the late Parliament.

The one person in whose behalf I regret your withdrawal into private life is your wife, whom I had the pleasure of taking in to the aforesaid dinner. It was evident to me that she was a woman whose spirit was well-nigh broken by her conjunction with you. Such remnants of cheerfulness as were in her I attributed to the Parliamentary duties which kept you out of her sight for so very many hours daily. I do not like to think of the fate to which the free and independent electors of West Odgetown have just condemned her. Only, remember this: chattel of yours though she is, and timid and humble, she despises you in her heart.

> I am, dear Mr. Pobsby-Burford,
> Yours very truly,
> HAROLD THISTLAKE.

LETTER FROM YOUNG LADY IN ANSWER TO INVITATION FROM OLD SCHOOLMISTRESS.

MY DEAR MISS PRICE,

How awfully sweet of you to ask me to stay with you for a few days but how *can* you think I may have forgotten you for of course I think of you so very often and of the three ears I spent at your school because it is such a joy not to be there any longer and if one is at all down it bucks one up derectly to remember that *thats* all over atanyrate and that one has enough food to nurrish one and not that awful monottany of life and not the petty fogging daily tirrany you went in for and I can imagin no greater thrill and luxury in a way than to come and see the whole dismal grind still going on but without me being in it but this would be *rather* beastly of me wouldnt it so please dear Miss Price dont expect me and do excuse mistakes of English Composition and Spelling and etcetra in your affectionate old pupil,

> EMILY THÉRÈSE LYNN-ROYSTON.

ps, I often rite to people telling them where I was edducated and highly reckomending you.

LETTER IN ACKNOWLEDGEMENT OF WEDDING PRESENT.

DEAR LADY AMBLESHAM,

Who gives quickly, says the old proverb, gives twice. For this reason I have purposely delayed writing to you, lest I should appear to thank you more than once for the small, cheap, hideous present you sent me on the occasion of my recent wedding. Were you a poor woman, that little bowl of ill-imitated Dresden china would convict you of tastelessness merely; were you a blind woman, of nothing but an odious parsimony. As you have normal eyesight and more than normal wealth, your gift to me proclaims you at once a Philistine and a miser (or rather did so proclaim you until, less than ten seconds after I had unpacked it from its wrappings of tissue paper, I took it to the open window and had the satisfaction of seeing it shattered to atoms on the pavement). But stay! I perceive a possible flaw in my argument. Perhaps you were guided in your choice by a definite wish to insult me. I am sure, on reflection, that this was so. *I shall not forget.*

Yours, etc.,

CYNTHIA BEAUMARSH.

PS. My husband asked me to tell you to warn Lord Amblesham to keep out of his way or to assume some disguise so complete that he will not be recognised by him and horsewhipped.

PPS. I am sending copies of this letter to the principal London and provincial newspapers.

LETTER FROM . . .

But enough! I never thought I should be so strong in this line. I had not foreseen such copiousness and fatal fluency. Never again will I tap these deep dark reservoirs in a character that had always seemed to me, on the whole, so amiable.

STUDY QUESTIONS

1. In the opening paragraph, what does Beerbohm indirectly tell us about himself?

2. What is Beerbohm's criticism of the models in the letter-writing manual? What does he see as the rhetorical strategy in these letters?

3. Examine each of the letters he writes and determine his rhetorical strategy.

Section Five

Education

"*Unwillingly to School*"

Hugh Kenner

DON'T SEND JOHNNY TO COLLEGE

Hugh Kenner (1923–   ) was born in Petersborough, Canada. He received his B.A. and M.A. from the University of Toronto and his Ph.D. from Yale University. He is professor of English at the University of California, Santa Barbara. Mr. Kenner has received fellowships from the American Council of Learned Societies and the Guggenheim foundation. In 1950 he won the Porter Prize at Yale. He is an outstanding scholar and the author of numerous articles on contemporary literature. In addition to his studies on T. S. Eliot and Samuel Beckett, he is the author of *The Poetry of Ezra Pound, Wyndham Lewis,* and *Dublin's Joyce.* His most recent book is *Counterfeiters: An Historical Comedy* (1968).

JOHNNY GOES BY the official title of "student." Yet Johnny's is the face every professor would prefer to see anywhere but in his classroom, where it blocks with its dreary smile, or its stoical yawn, the educational process on which we are proud to spend annually billions of dollars. By his sheer inert numbers he is making the common pursuit of professors and students—real students—impossible.

No one, least of all his professor, wills Johnny an injustice. Even the dean of students, whose lot he renders abysmal, finds it impossible not to like him, though some miraculous multiplication of loafers and fish sends Johnnies in an endless column trooping past the dean's receptionist, to stammer out their tale of dragging grades and just not digging the stuff.

Johnnies by the thousand, by the hundred thousand, clutter up every college in the land, where they long ago acquired a numerical majority. If you have a teenager in your home, thinking of college, the chances are you have Johnny. On behalf of my 400,000 colleagues in the academic profession, I'd be grateful if you'd keep him home.

Though Johnny is by definition multitudinous and anonymous, bits of Johnnyism stick in every teacher's mind. I remember the set neon smile that greeted me class after class for three whole weeks from a front-row seat just next to the door. The smile's owner and operator—let's call her Jonnie—never said a word, never took a note, never turned a page in her copy of *Gulliver's Travels*. Then, the day after I assigned a paper, the smile was gone, and so was she, apparently for good.

A month later, having heard that I would welcome some explanation, Jonnie turned up in my office, smiling. No, she couldn't do papers at all, not at all. Then what, pray, had brought her to a university, where, as everyone knows, one does papers? Well, she had enrolled on the advice of her psychiatrist. He had said the College Experience would be good therapy. Unwilling to monkey with therapy, I referred her, smile and all, to the dean. I've forgotten what he decided. There are so many Johnnies and Jonnies.

And there is no end to what their mentors and counselors, not to say psychiatrists, expect a university to do. Teach Johnny to behave like a gentleman. Prevent his simultaneous presence with Jonnie in parked cars after 10 P.M. Help him (her) get to know girls (boys). Improve his work habits. Open his mind (he has nothing but prejudices). Shut his mouth (he does nothing but talk). Tighten his morals. Loosen his imagination. Spread beneath his slack chin the incredible banquet of Western Civilization. And discharge him fit to earn a better living, make a better marriage and digest (Lord help him) *The New York Times*.

The parents and mentors who expect all this expect it not of the college but of the College Experience, which is turning, accordingly, into the experience of living in a whole cityful of Johnnies. (I've just been told by a Sunday supplement that within 35 years many colleges with enrollments of 100,000 to 200,000 will have become cities in their own rights.)

Johnny (Jonnie) expects none of the wonders of the College Experience, except in *re* girls (boys). Johnny is amiably devoid of expectations. One might say that he goes where he's shoved. One might affirm with more tact that he lends himself amiably to the College Experience, having no better plans. That is what marks him as Johnny, not as a student. A student has a vocation for study. But there's really nothing that Johnny comes to campus burning to learn about.

"Real education," wrote Ezra Pound 30 years ago, "must ultimately be limited to men who INSIST on knowing; the rest is mere sheepherding."

The mind that insists on knowing is (alas) not to be identified by tests, which explains why, despite the well-publicized vigilance of admissions officers, the number of campus Johnnies keeps rising. A mind that insists on knowing has begun to focus its energies by the time it has been in the world 16 years. By 17 or 18—the age of a college freshman—it has learned the taste of knowledge and the sensation of reaching for more. It may spell erratically, if it is served (like Yeats) by a deficient visual memory. It may calculate imperfectly, if it is (like Einstein) more at home with concepts than with operations. There may be strange gaps in its information, since a young mind cannot be everywhere at once.

But what it does not know it will encounter with pleasure. And it *must* learn, as a cat must eat. It may not yet know where its need for knowledge is meant to be satisfied. It may tack about, sails taut, without regard for curricular symmetry, changing majors perhaps more than once. But its tireless curiosity is unmistakable. In time, if all goes well, it will accept training, and the lifelong responsibilities of keeping itself trained.

But Johnny has no such appetite, no such momentum. When Johnny applies his brand-new ball-point to his first blue book, each sentence comes out smudged with his unmistakable pawprint. "Newspaper comics are good because they put a rosy glow on the grayish realities of the mind": There you have Johnny ingenuously expressing the state of *his* mind—a gray place which Pogo can occasionally animate, and a place of Good Things and Bad Things where Pogo is a Good Thing.

"The three main groups of people are the well-educated, semieducated and semiuneducated." There is all mankind characterized (a feat that taxed Aristotle), complete with a category for Johnny himself; he never forgets himself.

I am not inventing these examples. A colleague of mine gleaned a dozen like them in a single afternoon, from freshman themes at a university that accepts only the top one-eighth of the high-school crop. What they illustrate isn't primarily the "inability to express oneself," i.e., technical difficulties with the English language. What they illustrate is something deeper, probably irremediable; a happy willingness to emulate the motions of thought, since a teacher is standing there expecting such motions, along with a nearly total want of experience of what the process of thinking feels like.

"And this is why we should have no prejudice against Negroes and other lower races." That mind, we may say with some confidence, doesn't insist upon knowing. It doesn't know even its own most blatant contradictions. "To analyze this theory, it can be broken down into two parts: men and women." That's what men and women are, for the nonce—they are the parts of Johnny's theory. "The result is a ridiculous fiasco under which the roof falls in." It is indeed, and one does not know whether to marvel more at the oppressive weight of that fiasco, crashing through the roof like a half-ton bear, or at the innocent ease with which Johnny, supposing ideas to be weightless, pats them to and fro like bubbles.

But examples don't define a problem which by its very nature arises out of sheer multitudinousness. The amiable dumbbell has for decades been a part of campus folklore, like the absentminded professor. It is when you multiply him by a million that he grows ominous, swamping the campus as with creeping molasses. His uncle of 40 years ago, Joe College, had no more interest in learning than Johnny has, but none of Johnny's baleful power. With a certain talent for grotesque stylization, he conducted his entertaining ballet of raccoon coats, hip flasks, and whiffenpoofery, while the business of the academy, a considerably more modest business than today, went on.

What has created the Johnny problem isn't some freakish metamorphosis of Joe College into numberless protozoa, but rather the nearly universal conviction that everybody ought to spend four years at college if it can possibly be managed.

Johnny's parents, needless to say, believe this. His state legislator, despite the fantastic costs, tries to believe it, since his constituents seem to. The prospective employer believes it: let Johnny check "none" where the personnel blank inquires after "college record," and Johnny will be lucky to be issued a pick and shovel, let alone a sample kit. Even the college, caught in competitions for funds (which tend to hinge on enrollments), has come to believe it believes it.

Meanwhile B.A.'s grow so common that employers who once demanded them now demand M.A.'s, and the Master's requirement in some fields (not just the academic) has been upgraded to the Ph. D. In the years since Robert M. Hutchins sardonically proposed that we achieve our desires with less trouble by granting every American citizen a B.A. at birth, we have moved closer and closer to a utopia in which everyone receives it at 21, in return for doing classroom time. One already hears talk of attendance being compulsory through age 20. In California, where problems tend to surface before New England need worry about them, the state population rose 50 percent in one decade, and the college population 82 percent. It grows easy to foresee the day when 50 percent of the population of California (and, after a suitable time lag, of Massachusetts, of New York, of Illinois and, yes of Montana) will be employed at teaching the other 50 percent, perhaps changing ends at the half.

Clearly something has got to bust, and no one doubts what: the idea of a university. As an institution for (in Thomas Jefferson's words) "the instruction of those who will come after us," it's already being trampled out of recognizable existence by hordes of Johnnies.

The real student, struggling against suffocation of the soul, draws back, or beefs about how "the class" is holding things up, or starts feeling superior (and energy expended in nourishing a feeling of superiority is wholly lost). At worst, from being eager he turns merely "sensitive," and allows his zeal to be leached away. He is deprived, and can rightfully resent being deprived, of the kind of company he deserves to expect at a place where, often at considerable sacrifice, he has elected to invest four years of his life.

The professors suffer too. For one thing, they are coming off the production line too rapidly (though the harried trustees, looking wildly around at teaching machines and television hookups say "Not rapidly enough!"). Since there's no way of growing scholars at a pace keyed to the amoebalike increase of Johnnies, substitutes have begun to be manufactured. As real students are swamped by Johnnies, real professors must coexist with a swarm of Johnny-professors.

And like the real students, the real professors grow obsessed with futility, and unless they succeed, as some do, in isolating themselves with advanced students, fall victim to the real occupational hazard of the profession: an inability to believe that anybody can be taught anything. I once heard of a man who was so startled by the discovery of a real student that, lest she slip over his horizon, he divorced his wife and married her. I don't believe that story, but it's indicative; the professor who told it to me found it believable.

There's no doubt that as a nation we settle for only the side effects and the fringe benefits of what we invest in universities: the products of physics labs and research stations, and the economic advantages, to which our economy has been attuned ever since the G. I. Bill, of keeping several million young people off the labor market as long as possible. We are getting even this, though, at the price of a colossal wastage of time and spirit—the time and spirit of the real students on whose behalf the system is allegedly being run. If by the year 2000, as President Clark Kerr of California expects, educational institutions will be the largest single force in the economy, and if attendance to the age of 20 is compulsory, as Dr. Dwayne Orton of I.B.M. expects, why then the economy will in the lifetime of most of us have begun devoting its principal energies to the maintenance of huge concentration camps for keeping Johnnies by the multimillion agreeably idle.

So do we kick out Johnny? Alas, things will never be that simple again. Our social and economic system has come to depend on Johnny, B.A., in ways that can probably never be unstitched. Moreover, the College Experience probably *is* the most important event in the lives of most of the people who undergo it, even of the hundreds of thousands who learn very little. It is their time of access to the intellectual traffic patterns that define the quality of American life. A Kansan and a Georgian who have both been to college —merely been there—will have more to say to one another than a Vermonter who has and a Vermonter who hasn't. The College Experience is our folk ritual for inducting our adolescents into the 20th century. As part of our established religion, it must be treated as immune from curtailment.

Very well, then: the College Experience for Johnny, in his Johnny-classrooms. But let us, in the name of sanity, allow the real students to have *their* version of the College Experience. That means either separate-but-equal facilities, or (better, I think), some college equivalent of the two-track high schools that already exist.

One way of arranging a two-track college with minimum disruption is to permit only the real students to pursue majors. The University of Toronto has been doing that for more than half a century. Two decades ago I was one of a group of 40 freshman English majors there. In the sophomore year there were 20 of us, in the junior year 10; there the ruthless cutting stopped. But the missing 30 were not slung out of school. All but a few hopeless cases were "permitted," as the official formula had it, "to transfer to the pass course," which meant that, if they wanted to stay on at college, they abandoned the major and enrolled in "pass arts."

Pass arts was a three-year humanities mixture, leading to the degree of B.A. And it wasn't a ghetto for dropouts; many students enrolled in it to start with. Its degree satisfied employers, parents and the Ontario College of Education. It satisfied Johnny just fine. It gave the university all the advantages of bigness, as the quality of the library testified. It wasn't conducive to snobbery or segregation; every honor student took a couple of pass courses a year, in subjects peripheral to his major.

It was, in short, a two-track system, with the tracks parallel, and with means for switching laggards onto the slow track.

Everyone, we agree, should have access to all the education he can absorb. Everyone who can absorb education deserves, I would add, a chance to absorb it, free from the distracting tramp of the million-footed Johnny. As colleges now operate, the idea that everybody should be sent to them is nonsense. The only hope is to start operating them differently, detached from the dogma that Johnny is by birthright a student. He needs, in fact, explicit treatment as a nonstudent. There's no inherent reason why the nation's universities shouldn't make special curricular arrangements for several million nonstudents, any more than there's an inherent reason why one of the nation's universities shouldn't be the world's largest purveyor of white mice. (One of them is.)

STUDY QUESTIONS

1. According to Kenner, what has created the Johnny problem?

2. In what ways is Johnny different from the real student?

3. Do you judge Kenner's proposal for the "Johnny problem" a practical solution? Would you be willing to take a "Johnny-curriculum"?

4. Compare Kenner's proposal with Hutchins' proposal ("Colleges Are Obsolete").

5. This essay originally appeared in a magazine designed for the general public. In what ways did Kenner direct his essay to this audience? Note the diction, sentence structure, organization, and general structure.

Clark Kerr

THE EXAGGERATED GENERATION

Clark Kerr (1911–   ), economist, university professor, and former university administrator, earned degrees from Swarthmore, Stanford University, and the University of California (Berkeley). After teaching in a number of universities, he became chancellor of the University of California (Berkeley) in 1952, and president in 1958. Resigning his office in 1967 at the height of the "free speech" movement on the Berkeley campus, he became Professor of Economics. In addition to his services to universities, he served both the Eisenhower and Kennedy administrations as an expert in labor and management affairs. He has written a number of books on labor relations and industrial management, including *Labor and Management in an Industrial Society* (1964). His influential *Uses of the University* was published in 1963.

THE CURRENT generation of college and university students is the most-berated, the most-praised—certainly the most talked-about—in America's history. The names are varied, even contradictory. They tend to reveal more of the biases of the observers than of the nature of the students.

To conservatives, this is a "discontented" generation—even though youth never had it so good; or a "distrustful" generation—distrustful of its elders, the schools, the Government, the Establishment, distrustful of all the elements that have brought the good life to Americans, and to young Americans in particular. University students of today are seen as "difficult" at best and "radical" at worst, disrupting society.

To liberals, students of today constitute a "generation of conscience" in a nation that badly needs a conscience; or a "prophetic minority" pointing the way for an evil society to evolve. Or they are said to be "committed" to reform and good works; or to constitute a "New Left," presumably carrying on the torch for the tired Old Left which sees in this new generation proof that it really was not defeated permanently and completely. Paul Goodman has called the students of today the "New Aristocrats"—"America's emergent power elite."

From a more neutral point of observation, today's youth has been called "cool" or "activist" or "alienated" or "permissive." The current generation is many of these things to some extent some of the time. It is, for example, certainly occasionally difficult; often committed to some cause or another; to a degree alienated. There are many facets to this generation, perhaps more than to any earlier generation. It is going in more directions and at a faster pace. Thus, any simple designation may hold an element of truth but not the whole truth.

Exaggeration is one word that figs this new generation. It has exaggerated itself. It has been exaggerated by the news media. It has been exaggerated and also used, for their own purposes, by the left and the right. And, as a result, seldom in history have so many people feared so much for so little reason from so few.

The exaggeration is the work of many people. The students themselves are responsible in the first instance; some of them have wanted it that way. A few highly visible minorities, on a relatively small number of campuses, have become symbolic to the public at large of a whole generation. The dress has, at times, been outlandish. The speech, on a few occasions, has been without taste. The behavior of some, with sex and drugs, has been outside established norms. These characteristics have created an impression of widespread Bohemianism distasteful to large elements of the public. To distaste has been added actual fear and anger over actions of the political activists.

The student activists might be called the "McLuhan Generation." Their style is geared to the TV cameras and the flashbulbs, the bullhorn, the microphone and the walkie-talkie. Electricity powers this new student guerrilla warfare. It pulls in information, sends out instructions and carries the message of dissident views to a huge audience.

The media have also played their role in the exaggeration. Berkeley in the fall of 1964 and again in December, 1966, offered an example. The crowds were uniformly reported as being far larger than they were. Herbert Jacobs, a lecturer in journalism at Berkeley, has compared TV and press reports with analyses of photographs of the crowds. Thus, when reports said that 8,000 or 10,000 students voted to strike in Sproul Hall Plaza in December, 1966, the actual number of people there was 2,000—and this number included wives, curious onlookers and nonstudents. Another count, on another occasion, showed a count of 2,400 actually present, when 6,000 to 7,000 had been reported.

"Crowdsmanship," as Jacobs calls it, is a game played by the sponsor, the police and the media alike. They all have an interest in raising the score.

Thus a demonstration becomes bigger and more violent than it really was. A sit-in becomes a riot, then a rebellion and finally the "revolution" at Berkeley.

I once said to some TV executives that, in the course of reporting history, they were changing it. They agreed, but said this was what their competition did—and what the public wanted.

Exaggerated accounts have, on occasion, produced exaggerated reactions. The Old Left has picked up each episode of campus protest around the nation and made it another omen of the second coming of the American Revolution. Its spokesmen saw these protests as involving more students, the students as more radical, the tactics as more effective and the "movement" as more permanent than the facts would seem to warrant. Some liberals went along, for they liked the goals, if not the methods; they wore their hearts on other people's picket signs.

The New Right, rising to the right of the Old Establishment, saw the long arm of Marx and trumpeted its discovery. The Old Establishment was the power structure and it did not like being pushed around; it liked law and order, and it did little to correct the exaggerations.

The middle class tended to be shocked. What it thought it saw of students disturbed it greatly—the biggest scare since the Korean war and Senator McCarthy. Politicians entered the game in more than one state to add their own misrepresentations. In California, "treason, drugs and sex" were said to be a part of the curriculum offered to the students on one campus, and student behavior was highlighted as involving an orgy."

Amid these exaggerations, efforts to identify "cultures" and "typologies" of students are precarious at best. My own observation is that there are three main student types now vying to set the tone of campus life—Political Activists, Bohemians and the New Collegiates. These types, singly and together, constitute a minority of all students but contribute a majority of the off-campus impressions and impact of the modern generation.

The Political Activists: The protest element of issue-by-issue demonstrations first arose out of opposition to the House Un-American Activities Committee, atomic testing, capital punishment and other similar issues in the late nineteen-fifties and early nineteen-sixties, but particularly reflects in its style and content the civil-rights movement and then the opposition to the war in Vietnam. It rises and falls as issues rise and fall, and it attracts more or fewer or different people as the issues change. The radical element on campus finds its origins particularly in the Depression of the nineteen-thirties and the more recent developments in Cuba and China, and its fractionalization relates to the historical point of origin of each of its components. It has been undergoing a current revival particularly as a corollary to the rise in protest sentiment. The protest element and the radical element together constitute the political activitists.

The activist students have wanted to influence the Establishment but have often ended up, partly because of exaggeration on all sides, by energizing the right, giving ammunition to their worst enemies. They have been, on some occasions, self-defeating prophets, better in the long run at building resistance than getting results, more adept at bringing the counterrevolution than at getting basic reforms, fated to achieve minor successes and major failures. A few of the activists, on the far left, wanted it this way, since they believed that destruction must precede reconstruction. But the great majority of activists wanted to do good things with and for the existing society.

The Bohemians: The Bohemian element in American universities is largely a product of the post-World War II period. It is basically incompatible, in its temperament and use of time, with hard academic work, and superficial evidence is a poor test of the real hold that this culture has on students. Yet this element is certainly growing and, given the conditions out of which it arises in modern society, it is almost bound to keep on growing. More fragmentation of life and less sense of purpose in the mass industrial society leads to more such behavior.

(Here we must note a subgroup, outside the campus itself but related to it. This comprises the nonstudents. It is a deviant group—deviant on politics, deviant on attitudes toward sex, morality, religion. Its members are children of affluence who often can make a life without having to make a living. They reflect the attraction of a large campus with its cultural programs, its political activism, its sense of freedom. They reflect the desire for the excitement without the hard work of intellectual pursuits. They reflect both Bohemianism and political activism—both of which reject the middle class. The period between emancipation from adult control and assumption of full adult responsibility can be prolonged almost indefinitely through nonstudent status. Left Banks are now found around a few of the great American universities. They will be found around more, and they will grow in size.)

The New Collegiates: Traditional collegiate culture took on its modern form before and after World War I with the development of intercollegiate athletics, formal student governments, debating clubs and the like. But, in terms of adherents, it has been losing ground rapidly since the G.I.'s came back to the campuses after World War II. What distinguishes the new collegiate culture is a sense of community service. It was hardly known in the nineteen-thirties and is particularly a product of the current decade, during which it has grown enormously.

In my student days at Swarthmore during the depths of the Depression, there were only two of us in my senior class who went to a Negro school in Philadelphia one morning a week to work on a Quaker project. Last fall, at the University of California, 8,000 students, or nearly 10 per cent of the total student body, engaged in projects such as these: tutoring Negro children in West Oakland; volunteer teaching in Watts; running a camp in the San Bernardino Mountains for disadvantaged children; serving as "Amigos Anonymous" in villages in Mexico; cleaning up freeways and parks as a beautification project around Berkeley; teaching in San Quentin prison; running summer schools for the children of migratory workers in the San Joaquin and Sacramento Valleys; helping to construct an orphanage in Baja California; working with delinquents in Riverside; providing free dental care to disadvantaged families in Northern California; "adopting" two orphanages in South Vietnam.

The report we issued on these and other projects was called "The Untold Story." The overtold story was about the "filthy nine" (only four of them students) who constituted the totality of the much-publicized Filthy Speech Movement on the Berkeley campus.

This generation, as a whole, has some characteristics that mark the influences that have shaped it. No one today would describe students, as Philip Jacobs did in 1957, as "gloriously contented" and "self-centered" and satisfied with the "American assembly line." They might better be described as "aggressive"—at home, on the campus, off the campus; "concerned"—about the meaning of life and the quality of society; "serious"—about their studies and their actions; "experimental"—in their way of life and their attack on problems; "impatient"—with an education that sometimes lacks relevance and a society that often practices hypocrisy.

This is a generation that was born under the sign of the bomb and suckled at the breast of TV. The bomb created a feeling that there was a time limit on getting a better world. Some students have another sense of urgency—to get something done before they disappear forever into the flatland of the suburb and the wasteland of the corporation.

TV brought to this generation at an early age, as the newspapers never did to children and young people in the past, a view of the whole world and all aspects of it. It became interested in all the world, including Mississippi and Vietnam, and saw vividly that participation was not something to be postponed until adult life. The means were there, through the electronic revolution, for students to be citizens, to be informed and to participate.

This generation was raised at home according to new manuals that stressed permissiveness, and at school under new views that stressed participation. Too often, its members arrived at colleges and universities which still reflected the old manuals and the old views, and both the students and the colleges were unprepared for the meeting.

The quality of education has been improved all along the line, particularly in the high schools and particularly since Sputnik I. There is a new emphasis on grades and on going into graduate work. The meritocracy is taking hold and school is the way to move up to avoid being moved down. The pressure is greater at all levels and students are better educated. Among other things, they are better educated in basic American principles like equality, freedom and the pursuit of happiness. And they see around them discrimination, restrictions on their freedoms, and poverty. They are troubled by the gap between aspiration and attainment. They were told all through high school about the sins of omission of the apathetic generation and the conformity of the "organization man" and exhorted to do otherwise. They are doing otherwise.

American society is now, by and large, affluent—students stay in school longer and fewer of them support themselves while going to school. One result is to reduce their dependence on the world of work and the sense of reality that goes with it. As Eric Hoffer said, "They haven't raised a blade of grass, they haven't laid a brick." They are also, frequently, less oriented toward getting a job after graduation, since that is taken for granted. Thus, materialistic considerations and pressures are less evident now that materialistic welfare is taken more or less for granted and also given a lower value.

The American society of the future troubles them. They have read "1984," "Brave New World," "Animal Farm," and they know about I.B.M. cards and automation. The sense of a world in which the individual counts for less and less weighs heavily. Conformity to Big Brother and to science is not so very far off. There is a countermove toward individuality as against the requirements of "the system." This move toward individuality is speeded as the new religion and the new anthropology remove some of the restraints on personal behavior.

The Rebel, to use the terminology of Camus, accepts society but wants to improve it. He accepts restraint but not the status quo. He rejects the absolutism of much of the left but not the need for reform. He rejects violence and seeks the possible. Part of his motivation is religious; part relates to a desire for a better future. The Rebel approach is at the heart of the community-service element as well as of the protest tendency among college students.

Confrontation politics, which has often been the special form of student protest, seems to be becoming a less significant weapon. Civil-rights victories are farther in the background. The radicals have taken over much of the guidance of confrontations, and conservative, religious and moderate support has dropped away. Vietnam, of course, remains an issue over which protest can easily be organized, but the great wave of student confrontations now seems to be passing. The sense of protest will continue, and may even rise in intensity, but it will find expression less through confrontation and more through other means.

New leaders are arising from what I have characterized as the New Collegiate group. The New Collegiate type has as one of its characteristics devotion to the campus and willingness to work with and through the campus power structure. The New Collegiate leaders, including those active in fraternities and sororities, are pushing academic reform instead of athletics, political discussion instead of activities, community projects instead of dances—and they appeal to the new interests of the students. They do not wish to bring a campus to a grinding halt, but to halt neglect of students and give voice to community and national concerns. The New Collegiate leaders reflect the student interest in service and protest and give organized expression to it. And then a number of them go overseas and become Peace Corps participants.

Nobody pays much attention to them, but in my opinion they are setting the tone of this generation. The campus revolutionaries are never going to win; this is not a revolutionary country. And the alienated Bohemians are parasites. What is most significant about this generation is the very high proportion of the Peace Corps type.

Society faces the campus just as the campus faces society. A reappraisal by society of the new generation is in order—a reappraisal which recognizes the diversity and the essential goodwill of the students of today. The communications media have a special responsibility to present the facts for this reappraisal. The public should read and hear and see the news about university students with sophistication and some tolerance. The excesses of youth are nothing new in history.

Aristotle once wrote: "They [young people] have exalted notions, because they have not yet been humbled by life or learned its necessary limitations; moreover, their hopeful disposition makes them think themselves equal to great things—and that means having exalted notions. They would always rather do noble deeds than useful ones: Their lives are regulated more by moral feeling than by reasoning—all their mistakes are in the direction of doing things excessively and vehemently. They overdo everything—they love too much, hate too much, and the same with everything else."

STUDY QUESTIONS

1. Kerr describes three student types that create the off-campus impression of the modern generation. Do these descriptions apply to types on your campus? Are there other types on your campus that are more influential than the ones Kerr notes?

2. From your perspective as a member of the modern generation, can you think of a more accurate name for your generation than the one Kerr uses?

3. Kerr notes that the Bohemian group is growing and that unless conditions change it will continue to grow. Does this appear to be the case on your campus?

4. Does Kerr's tone indicate his approval or disapproval of the modern generation or of any types in it?

5. Does Kerr use any unsupported generalizations you could challenge?

Paul Woodring

EROS ON THE CAMPUS

Paul Woodring (1917–   ) is Distinguished Service Professor of the College of Western Washington State College and Editor-at-Large of the *Saturday Review*. He earned his undergraduate degree at Bowling Green University and his M.A. and Ph.D. degrees at Ohio State University. He taught in the public schools in Ohio before joining the ranks of college teachers. Before joining the staff of Western Washington State College he taught at Ohio State University. From 1960–1966 he was Education Editor of *Saturday Review*. He has written numerous articles and books about education; the latter includes *Let's Talk Some About Our Schools* (1953), *A Fourth of the Nation* (1957), and *New Directions in Teacher Education* (1965). Published in 1968, his latest book is *The Higher Learning in America: A Reassessment*.

Has There Been a Sexual Revolution?

FOR AS LONG as I can remember—and my memory for such things goes back into the 1920s—we have been hearing about something called a "sexual revolution." Students of the flapper era, who identified themselves with the "lost generation," dated the revolt from World War I. Undergraduates of the thirties believed that it began with the Depression, when many young people found marriage impossible and consequently looked for other sexual outlets. Those of the

From *The Higher Learning in America:* A Reassessment by Paul Woodring. Copyright © 1968 by Paul Woodring. Used with permission of McGraw-Hill Book Company.

fifties thought the sexual revolution was an aftermath of World War II and began when returning veterans encountered patriotic coeds. Today's undergraduates firmly believe that the revolt started about 1960 when they were in junior high and that it somehow is related to both the threat of nuclear war and the invention of the pill.

All these views reveal the innocence of youth, for neither sexual activity nor the open discussion of it is as new as many students believe. In 1721, Harvard students formally debated the question "Whether it be fornication to lye with one's Sweetheart before Marriage." It is unlikely that there has ever been a generation of students to which sex was not a major interest or that did not include many individuals who violated the rules laid down for them by their elders and demanded that the rules be changed.

It requires no great knowledge of history to know that the sexual mores are no more relaxed today than they have been at many other times in man's long past and that the loosening and tightening of the restrictions on sexual activity go in cycles of irregular length that are related to a wide variety of social forces.

The present trend toward a loosening of restraints dates roughly from the beginning of the twentieth century. It is not so much a revolution as a persistent and growing reaction against the restrictive sexual morality that has variously and somewhat carelessly been described as "Puritanical," "Victorian," or "middle-class." The trend was accelerated by the invention of the automobile, improvement in the techniques of birth control, the dislocation of families resulting from the move from farms to cities, and the two world wars that took many young men away from the restraining influences of their home communities. Freer sexual activity was made to seem more necessary by careless reading of Freud and more normal (at least statistically) by careful reading of Kinsey. It both gave rise to and fed upon the literature, motion pictures, and television programs of the twentieth century.

By 1920 students had discovered that a date in an automobile could be something quite different from one in the front parlor with Mother hovering in the background. Their parents were shocked to learn that young people were parking on country roads for purposes other than enjoying the moonlight. But the students who first made this discovery, and now are parents and grandparents, are shocked in turn to learn that students now have dates in dormitory rooms while the Dean of Women looks the other way. Perhaps the activities in either case do not differ greatly from what happened on back porches and in lawn swings in the nineties, but it seems to be generally agreed that the frequency has increased and that a larger proportion of today's adolescents participate freely in what has always been the favorite sport of the human race.

Whatever the change in activity—and no statistics on such a subject can be reliable—there has been a vast change in the kind of advice given to adolescents. A half-century ago the books of intimate advice for boys and girls told readers that any sexual activity outside marriage was sinful, and that premarital activity precluded the possibility of a happy marriage because no man respected a girl who allowed what were then called "liberties." Girls were advised that anything more intimate than handholding aroused the baser passions in a man and could lead to no good.

The books of advice read by teen-agers today are equally moral in their own way but the morality is different. Some sternly advise against all premarital intercourse, but the reasons given are often practical rather than ethical. Nearly all agree that some modest degree of petting and fondling is a normal way of showing deep affection and that such preliminary activities are a necessary prelude to a happy marriage. And every teen-ager has read at least one book in which a psychiatrist, psychologist, or possibly a minister sagely pontificates that while caution is advisable, no activity between two consenting adults is really sinful or necessarily harmful. Any reader over sixteen feels certain that he is an adult and that the consent can be obtained —if necessary with the aid of the book, which can be discussed on the next date.

Students are also aware that many "respectable" adults of this and other centuries, including quite possibly their own parents, have at times violated the conventional codes and seem to be none the worse for it. They have read the biographies of the mistresses of famous men and stories of clandestine affairs between individuals who have played a conspicuous part in history. They are aware of a conspicuous gap between the publicly announced morality and the actual behavior of men and women. Consequently they are not inclined to accept the restrictions that adults attempt to place upon their activities.

The Dilemma

The dilemma faced by young people is clear enough. Males reach their period of greatest sexual vigor and desire at a time preceding marriage, when the doors to socially approved sexual activity are officially closed to them. But these doors, which have never been successfully locked and barred, have now been set aside by a more permissive society. Now that the fears of pregnancy and disease have been substantially reduced, there is even greater need than before for a code of ethics to guide behavior. But, in our pluralistic society, there is no clear-cut moral code for young people to follow.

The dilemma faced by girls is different but no less perplexing. Though some girls of college age have strong sexual urges, most of them are motivated more by the desire to be popular with boys and often by the desire to please one particular boy. They do not want to be considered old-fashioned, moralistic, or stuffy. When they find that other girls among their associates are engaging in sexual activities, and that the boys expect it, they find it difficult to give a socially acceptable reason for refusing.

Many of today's students would like to be conventional and law-abiding, but first they want the conventions and the laws changed to conform to the current practices. They are convinced that the older generation hypocritically gives lip service to a code in which it does not really believe and which it does not always follow. They differ from the students of the twenties and thirties in that while the earlier generation took pleasure in breaking the rules, the new generation demands that the rules be changed. Another difference is that among the older generation, even those who defended premarital sex insisted that it was justifiable only between two individuals deeply committed emotionally to each other, and that it should be of a continuing nature, while some of the college students today hold that neither commitment nor emotional involvement is necessary to sexual enjoyment. The thing to do, they say, is play it cool, avoid involvement, and live for the pleasure of the moment.

It is unlikely that so hedonistic a philosophy will be widely accepted, particularly by girls, most of whom see sex as a step toward a stable family life. Perhaps the younger generation eventually will develop its own code, though by the time it has done so it will probably have become the older generation and will experience the same difficulty older people always have faced in passing their own moral code on to the young.

The New Morality

The new morality, if it is to be acceptable to a substantial majority of the people who are young today, must be one that appeals to people of many religious faiths as well as to those who are indifferent to religion. It must be acceptable to Catholics, Jews, Protestants of many denominations ranging from the Episcopalians to the fundamentalists, as well as to the agnostics and atheists who are found in substantial numbers on today's campuses. It must also be consistent with the knowledge now available from psychology, sociology, anthropology, and biology.

The fact that this seems a large order probably explains why a new morality to replace the old has been so slow in emerging. But unless it does, we are faced with the prospects of moral chaos, for the older sexual morality, based as it was on a combination of religion, tradition, and fears of pregnancy and disease, is not acceptable to most of the people in college today. No student who has studied the sexual practices that prevail in this and other cultures and that have prevailed at different times in history is likely to believe that monogamous marriage is the only outlet for sex that can be defended. He is almost certain to reject the view that all premarital or extramarital sex inevitably leads to guilt feelings, unhappiness, or neurosis. He knows that whether or not one will feel guilty about any kind of behavior depends on what he has been taught and what he has learned from previous experience. He knows that pregnancy can now be prevented by any intelligent adult willing to plan ahead, and he has more confidence than may be justified in his own ability to do the planning.

The view that men want to marry virgins is not nearly so popular with today's college boys as it is with men of lower cultural levels or as it was in Grandfather's day. Girls who know this no longer fear that premarital sexual experience will be a barrier to a happy marriage. No amount of lecturing on the part of older people is likely to change their conviction that some amount of premarital sex is both permissible and quite possibly a necessary prelude to a happy marriage. This does not mean that most of today's young people are or want to be promiscuous. Most of them believe that sex ought to mean something beyond the purely physical and that it ought to be a part of a continuing relationship. But they are convinced that sexual activities involving consenting adults should not be governed by law and that neither college officials nor the police and courts have a moral right to interfere, whatever the law may say. They are determined to bring about a change in the laws and regulations that are inconsistent with their views. And they have a considerable amount of support from older people, including many who are in responsible positions. The laws in England and in several of the United States are already undergoing change in the direction of greater permissiveness. Greater changes will come when those who are now in college reach voting age.

The Kinsey reports revealed that while adolescents, particularly boys, who lack a college education engage in overt sex earlier and more frequently than do those who go to college, the college students of both sexes much more often engage in "heavy petting" which leads to orgasm without actual intercourse. Some writers have said that such petting is the distinctive feature of dating behavior in the present generation, but anyone old enough to remember the flapper era of the twenties will recall that this term was used even then and that it meant just about what it does now. Petting, light or heavy, has been a part of dating behavior for a long time, but it probably is true that there has been a statistical increase in the variety called "heavy" and less moral opposition to it.

Insofar as they draw their conclusions from the printed word, today's students are influenced by the works of Albert Ellis, Kinsey, the Kronhausens, such recent medical reports as those of W. H. Masters and V. E. Johnson, and Hugh Hefner's "*Playboy* philosophy" of recreational sex far more than they are by the now-antiquated views of Havelock Ellis, Krafft-Ebing, Sigmund Freud, and Bertrand Russell. Older people who wish to guide them should be aware of these new sources of enlightenment even though it obviously would be difficult for anyone to devise a workable code of behavior from such an assortment of literary contributions.

Though a new code for sexual conduct clearly is needed, it cannot safely be constructed by adolescents alone; for, as Richard Hettlinger reminds us in *Living with Sex:* "There is no field of human activity in which it is so easy to deceive oneself and to be convinced by arguments which are in fact nothing but rationalizations of clamant desires." In planning the new morality, young people will need all the advice they can get from older people whose desires presumably have cooled a bit and who can take a longer view. But, being young, they are not likely to take it.

The new code must be based upon a clear recognition of the fact that most educated and enlightened people of all ages look upon sexual desire as biologically, socially, and psychologically normal rather than as something evil, dirty, or shameful. They reject as ridiculous the view that the desire to produce offspring is the only legitimate motivation for sexual activities. Because they accept adolescent petting as normal and know that sex takes many forms, they place less emphasis than their ancestors on the importance of technical virginity. They are aware that sexual desire is strong in youth and that efforts to postpone sexual activities until marriage are at best futile and perhaps both unnecessary and undesirable.

But there is no agreement on what the new code should be, for there is a solid nucleus of more conservative people on every college campus, and a still larger number off campus, who think that it is essential that we preserve some aspects of the traditional morality. Students holding such views and living up to the older code can be found even on the campuses reputed to be most liberal in their attitudes; a Reed professor recently was quoted as saying "There's a lot more virginity around here than you might expect."

One thing seems clear: the new code, to be acceptable, must grant equal freedom to both sexes even though it still is true that it is the girls who have the babies. Throughout the eighteenth and nineteenth centuries it was customary for college boys to have their first sexual experience with "town girls" or prostitutes and then look for virgins of their own social class to marry. Co-education has changed that. Today most of the college boys who have premarital sex have it with girls of their own social and educational level, often with the girls they eventually marry. The double standard is no longer acceptable to either sex.

Early marriage, when it is combined with early parenthood, seems to create as many problems as it solves; the divorce rate among those who marry in their teens is substantially higher than among those who marry later. But it might be possible to provide for a new kind of temporary marriage that would enable young couples to live together during their college years without subterfuge or hypocrisy and would provide a legitimate outlet for sexual urges without all the responsibilities of conventional marriage.

Forty years ago, Judge Ben Lindsey of the juvenile courts of Denver proposed what he called "Companionate Marriage" whereby young couples might legally live together for a time with the understanding that divorce could be obtained by mutual consent so long as there were no children. The world was not ready for so drastic a solution; though Lindsey's plan was applauded by some it was roundly condemned by many and led to no action. But when Margaret Mead recently suggested a somewhat similar plan she met with much less opposition. Perhaps the nation is almost ready to accept such an arrangement, but it will surely take several decades to get the necessary laws through the state legislatures. In any case a good many of today's young people want a greater degree of freedom to experiment than would be provided for by any form of monogamous marriage.

Unless some solution is found we shall undoubtedly see a continued relaxation of standards, a growing contempt for the traditional rules and laws governing sexual activities, and still more confusion on the part of young people as to what is and what is not acceptable. If our society takes a downward trend, historians and archeologists of the future who dig up the remnants of our culture will probably conclude that a decline of sexual morality was a major cause of the deterioration. But if the culture continues to survive and flourish despite a greater degree of sexual freedom, tomorrow's historians will call attention to the fact that sexual freedom has been a characteristic of many of the greatest periods of human achievement. And they will find many examples to cite.

STUDY QUESTIONS

1. Be prepared to discuss the author's claim that young people face a dilemma because there is no longer a clear cut moral code for them to follow. Do you agree with his position?

2. Why, according to the author, has a new morality been so slow in emerging?

3. This selection contains a number of unsupported generalizations about attitudes toward sex and sexual morality. Be prepared to challenge those you find invalid or misleading.

4. To what extent do you find the selection authoritative in tone and substance?

5. What are the basic differences between the attitudes of the older and the modern generation toward sex and morality?

Herbert Gold

LETTER FROM A FAR FRAT

Herbert Gold (1924–   ) is a teacher who turned to a career in writing. He earned both his B.A. and M.A. degrees at Columbia University and has been awarded a Guggenheim Fellowship and an American Institute of Arts and Letters Award. As a visiting professor, he has taught at Cornell University, the University of California (Berkeley) and Harvard University. His novels include *Birth of a Hero* (1951), *The Prospect Before Me* (1954), *The Man Who Was Not With It* (1956), *The Optimist* (1958), *Therefore Be Bold* (1961), *Salt* (1963), and *Fathers* (1967). His short stories and articles have appeared in various magazines.

If this is the era for assaulting university presidents and prancing nude in Harvard houses, can life in a typical college fraternity still be the same? To the hop-flavored surprise of Mr. Gold, author of FATHERS, THE MAN WHO WAS NOT WITH IT, and other novels, the answer—at Chapel Hill, North Carolina, in any case—proved to be, Yes.

WELL, THE Fraternity House still exists. I almost thought it went out of fashion with Dick Powell and Jack Oakie and the great homecoming games of early MGM musicals, but by golly, the old beer-spraying, girl-harvesting, ear-splitting article can still be found on, say, the campus of the University of North Carolina at Chapel Hill, which is an excellent school with high standards. Because I was a guest in the house, I'll invent a name for the occupants, Kappa Lambda Pi.

OK, on a Saturday night the fine old lovingly demolished mansion is surrounded by MG's, Sprites, American convertibles; the lawn is covered with heartbreakingly—beautiful? well, cute—it's covered with girls, and weaving about the girls are the boys, casting their spell, making time. The band is an amplified rock group, good strong sound, tough and nonpsychedelic, out of Carrboro or the country surrounding—black, of course, and no one else is. The hospitality is immense and genuine. They are lovingly demolishing the place by hand; it's a local craft. Echo says, and echo replies: "Have a beer, have a brew. Here, have a swig. Hey, sir, have a drink of mine. Aw, come on, have fun with us, sir."

The boys of KLP are celebrating losing a game. On other nights they celebrate winning the game, or rush week, or the water shortage, or exam week, or the visit of Spiro T. Agnew to Raleigh, or it doesn't make any difference. The faucet in the kitchen is never turned off. Since there has been a prolonged drought and a crucial water shortage which threatens to shut down the school, it has seemed a fine joke to some good old boy to get out of various academic problems by doing his best to drain the lake. Some of the would-be adults in the house think this is childish behavior, he hadn't ought to do like that, but it's a matter of *esprit de corps*. It would be finking on a good buddy to interfere. When one fellow twisted the faucet shut, his good brother got red-eyed and sore, silent; but that's the limit of it. Well, it really means something to him, that water-lover. Hurtie tough-titty feelings. Anyway, they might get the emergency pipeline from Chapel Hill to Durham in time to relieve the reservoir. And in a democracy every man should be free, shouldn't he, to decide whether or not the town has any water?

During the festivities which I attended, sex and politics were the prime subjects. So far, so good. I've heard of them. Water and studying were a distraction from real life. The future is a slightly disagreeable consequence of the present, following it by association as "liver" follows "cirrhosis of the." The smell of beer, which I thought had disappeared from campuses, is making its last stand in North Carolina. Beer was a stranger to me (I've spent a lot of time at California colleges). A tall, sandy, snob-nosed brother called Boyce explained about things: "we can't be too cool, man. We can't operate like them Ivies, you know, smoke a joint and then zap her upstairs. We got to plan and work out a three-stage campaign, not like those Ivies up north, man. I prepped at Lawrenceville, I skied in Colorado, so I had that experience, those Ivies. We got to work a three-stage campaign, not cool, man, not like those Ivies, man, sir."

"I understand," I said, almost understanding.

"First stage, we got to dance a little, get 'em a little slushed up, you know, hot, not like those Ivies. That's first stage. Love 'em up a little. Then second stage: into the car. Sir, let me explain, that's trouble, getting 'em out of here and across the parking lot into the car. Now they want it as much as we do, don't misunderstand me, sir, just like those Ivy girls, they want it, but they stumble, they make it tough crossing the parking—OK, into the car, man. Then we have these apartments in town—"

"You mean you can't take the girls upstairs?"

He looked at me, shocked at my presumption. He offered me a swig from his can. He defended Southern womanhood. "Here?" he asked. "In the house? In front of all everybody?"

"I'm sorry," I said.

"Well, we drag 'em out the door and through the parking lot. Course lots of times they yell and scream and laugh and throw up a lot, but we get 'em out, because they want to as much as we do, you know, that's human nature. So then we get 'em to our apartments in town, oh, maybe three, four of us share an apartment, and then . . ." A grin lit up his face. It was like the sun rising over Georgia. "Man, can I just tell you what I did to that little girl over there—see, that one? No, not that one, sir—you like her? Cindy?—no, the one next to Cindy."

He pointed to a little flower of Southern womanhood stubbing out her cigarette against the veneered wood atop the TV.

"You don't know her, do you? so it's all right if I tell you. But listen, sir, if you'd like to meet her . . ."

First, however, he described stage four in the three-stage plan.

I was also interested in his political views, but first we got involved about this girl.

Oh, well, I have prurient interest, too.

"Come here, honey," Boyce called to the girl (not Cindy). She came over, mussed and sulky, with a great hair-collector's mane of yellow hair, and then shot me that marvelous easeful flirty Southern smile which nice girls down there give not only their men but also girlfriends, pregnant ladies, small animals, and the short-answer questions on a nursing exam. She had liquid brown eyes, lovely, hysteric eyes, soft stalks with contact lenses perched atop the irises. "I just been telling him what we did t'other night, honey."

"Went to the movies," she said.

"No, not that night—"

"Saw *Disaster Angels,* with a revival of camp classic *Suddenly Last Summer*—"

"No, the next night, night we had the party—"

"Oh, Boyce, you're a, you're a, you're a—"

He grinned while she suffered her failure of vocabulary. But she seemed about to cry—hysteric, remember?—so he apologized gently, saying, "Aw, honey, don't carry on like that. I didn't show him the Polaroids."

I was getting mired in interpersonal relations. It would be better all the way around, including my development as a thinking human being and a visiting writer, if I heard some of their views on wider topics.

Floyd Jones is an activist. He has been to Europe on his summer vacation. He thinks about local option and states' rights (positive). Hair and hippies mash around in his emotions (negative). In Europe he noticed the happy faces in West Berlin, the unhappy ones in East Berlin, and that settled Communism for him. It was all clear now, roger and over, and this led him straight back to American politics. "I met these German men in a bar," he told me, "good old boys, spoke good English, said why don't we kick the shit out of those hippies and draft-card burners." He had discussed everything from Vietnam to race with those happy faces, and they compacted together that Communism must be stopped.

Our conversation took place during the heat of the last political campaign, just after a Northerner, Curtis LeMay, native of my home state of Ohio, had been chosen to assist George Wallace in his mission. "He's a good old boy," said Floyd, as the dancers flailed about us. The cigarettes were falling into the carpet, the fastidious were drinking out of plastic-foam cups, the forthright were drinking out of their cans, and the group had me backed against the color TV. The sound was turned off, but the light show flickered and spattered against the screen. I reached behind to turn it off so that the radiation wouldn't catch me behind while the vocal emanations and renditions took me afront.

Floyd is the only man I know who was overjoyed by the three major candidates for the presidency. Hubie was a good old boy, loyal to London, a virtue all in itself, and of course Wallace had the clearest and finest ideas, but he personally was voting for Mr. Nixon. It's a class thing, he felt; a duty to live up to the word "responsible"; and Mr. Nixon's speeches nearly brought tears to his eyes. They were that sincere. Also, he hoped he'd kick the shit out of those draft-card burners and long-haired hippies.

"You really like all the candidates?"

"They're loyal Americans, aren't they? That's what I ask of a man."

I offered some objections to Floyd and the others, but mainly I tried to play Socratic Method—questions: Is this a happy country? Do you really think more weapons for the police are the "answers" to law and order? What is your conception of America's role? One very tall, horn-rimmed young man, with a look of poetic angularity about him, hung on my words, and I thought I had an ally. He too seemed puzzled by America circa 1968. He suddenly burst out: "Wha yo so gol-darned negative? What is this negative bit?" Astonished by his own anger, he added: "Sir?"

A few girls had joined us. One of them was Cindy—eyes afire, that old golf club menace in them. There was some kicking and giggling going on below the level of the conversation. It was stage one and a half of the campaign, I decided, not like those Ivies.

I must have asked a question, because the sensitive-looking brother burst out, "Course I wouldn't kick the shit out of 'em! I just say that!" Then he smiled shyly. "Wouldn't want to get my shoes dirty," and nudged me. "Aw, sir, I just say that. They got the right to free speech, too, so long as they don't go tearing down this country. You're not always so negative, are you, sir?"

It was time to be their buddy, I decided. I too had done my term at Fort Bragg and elsewhere, though this was before their birth. I reminisced about Fayetteville, North Carolina, which we called Fagleberg.

"You mean Fayettenam?" Floyd asked. "When they call me there, I'm going. If they cancel my deferment, sir, I'm going. But I'm going to try to finish my education first, and get into a good position, and if the Lord is good to me, I won't have to fight. I can tell what you're thinking, sir. I got strong feelings. But like I already explained, killing's just not in the American line."

He was wearing tight maroon pants and a white button-down short-sleeve shirt with notched vents at the sleeve. One of his Hush Puppies was unlaced. He leaned on me a little, partly out of friendship and desire to be understood, saying, "Now don't get me wrong, hear? They call me, I go. I got this deferment, no gol-darned evasion."

"I'm not a pacifist either," I said.

"But I never did meet any Marine from Veetnam committed an atrocity who enjoyed it, hear? Hear me, sir? We just got to defend the American perimeter, it's as simple as that. So I'll go, I'll go, sir, soon as they call me."

When it came time to part, two of the brothers insisted on walking me home to the Carolina Inn. It had rained gleaming Burgie flip-top friendship rings on the Carolina earth. The brothers scuffed along, bumping and uneasy about the discussion. The men of the KLP house have a complex feeling about life—a minority on this campus, a majority in their own hometowns, but are they a majority in America and the world? It is no longer easy to find the tides of right and float back and forth on them. Kappa Lambda Pi is in trouble as a way of life.

There was a shy moment in the fragrant Indian summer evening, hot rods and flowering trees and sweet echo of amplified rock from the Carrboro Rhythm Ramblers. Something had been left unsaid. Some generation gap had been left ajar, some culture gap unclosed, some stony silence in the metaphysics. We all wanted to be close and warm, and yet we were not close and warm. We had kidded around, but what else? In a world of making out OK, and getting bugged by it, we had made out all right, and gotten bugged by each other, just like the Ivies; and yet there must be something more than paltry victories in love and politics. There might be, for example, real victories. Stage five. Stage six. Stage seven.

On another part of the campus the 1 A.M. showing of underground art flicks was just beginning, and the Dandelion, a head shop, was just closing, and the Racial Confrontation group was continuing out under the famous Davie poplar. As we walked by, a tall black man in a denim suit, a refugee from Resurrection City, a pioneer of Freedom City, was smiling and saying softly, We're sick of trickeration, we won't stand still for extermination, so we got to have communication; and an earnest young white student said, But we got to talk it all out first so's not to frighten the other people; and the man from Resurrection City said, Son, that's trickeration . . .

One of my escorts shook his head, grinning. "Man, oh, man," he said to me. Some of these jerks were beyond his comprehension.

All over the campus the gritty Indian summer smell of autumn leaves was helping lovers and celebrants and reformers and late-night scholars fix the memory in their hearts, whether they knew it or not: *This is it, this was college in my time.*

As we walked along, beer fizzing in the jiggled cans, a member of my honor guard said, "It's just, sir, we didn't want you to get the one-sided impression about this school."

"I appreciate your hospitality," I said.

We were standing near the rocking chairs on the porch of the Carolina Inn (widows, conferences, and faculty visitors). "Don't get us wrong," he said. "We have strict rules at the house. We don't always live up to them, but we try not to be litterbugs. We might be Tarheels and we got a lousy team, but we have fun, too, sir." He gazed wearily back across campus to the traditional Davie poplar, famed in song and story. Chapel Hill's little Berkeley was still strolling and consulting near that spot. "Just didn't want you to go away thinking we're all a bunch of stupid intellectuals."

Study Questions

1. What characterizes the tone of this selection? Note details that reveal Gold's attitude toward his subject.

2. What would you say is the sexual morality code of the Kappa Lambda Pi's?

3. How does Gold's method of presentation serve his purpose better than a straight expository approach would?

4. What is the serious purpose underlying Gold's playful account?

5. What is the rhetorical effect of the last sentence in the essay?

Sidney Hook

ACADEMIC FREEDOM
AND STUDENT RIOTS

Sidney Hook (1902–   ), philosopher and educator, was born in New
York. At The City College of New York, where he received his B.S., he won
the Ward Medal for Logic. He received his M.A. and Ph.D. from Columbia
University. Currently he is chairman of the philosophy department at
Washington Square College, New York University. He has been an active
member of the Commission on Cultural Freedom and the Conference on
Methods and Philosophies, and he has been a recipient of a Guggenheim
fellowship.

AMERICANS ARE accustomed to reading about universities
as storm centers of political disturbance in Latin and Asiatic countries. In a country like the United States, how-
ever, most criticism of student bodies in the past has been directed against
their political apathy. The fact, therefore, that a building was seized by students at the Berkeley campus of the University of California, bringing all
administrative activities to a halt, that a strike was declared, paralyzing
teaching, and that the governor of the most populous state in the union, after
the arrest of some 800 students, felt it necessary to appeal for problems to be
solved "by evolution not revolution," should give not only educators but all
reflective citizens pause. It has focused attention upon a question of considerable complexity—the rights, and the responsibilities, of students.

Since so much of the controversy and agitation swirls around the slogans
of freedom, the first question to be asked is: Do students enjoy the right of
academic freedom? This depends on what is meant by academic freedom.
Perhaps the best short definition was offered by Arthur O. Lovejoy, founder,
together with John Dewey, of the American Association of University Professors.

"Academic freedom," he wrote, "is the freedom of the teacher or research

worker in higher institutions of learning to investigate and discuss the problems of his science and to express his conclusions, whether through publications or the instruction of students, without interference from political or
ecclesiastical authority, or from the administrative officials of the institution
in which he is employed, unless his methods are found by qualified bodies of
his own profession to be clearly incompetent or contrary to professional
ethics."

A number of interesting implications may be drawn from this definition.
First, academic freedom exists primarily for "teachers"—in the most com-
prehensive sense of that term. Strictly speaking, it makes no sense to talk of
"academic freedom" for students. Students have a right to freedom to learn.
The best guarantee of freedom to learn is academic freedom for those who
teach them. Where teachers are deprived of academic freedom, students are
ipso facto deprived of the freedom to learn.

The converse, however, is not true. It is simply false both in logic and in
fact to assert that freedom to teach and freedom to learn are indivisible.
Many things may interfere with the student's freedom to learn—poverty,
racial discrimination, inadequate transportation—which have no direct relevance to academic freedom. The latter may flourish in institutions to
which students are unjustly denied the opportunity to enter. The movement
to abolish poverty, discrimination and other social evils in order to give students access to education and to effective freedom to learn flows from their
moral rights as persons and from their *civil* rights as citizens. They are not
corollaries of academic freedom. To deny this would make the university responsible for the entire state of society and its reform.

Second, academic freedom is not a civil right like freedom of speech. A
teacher who is dropped or refused a post on grounds of incompetence, because, say, he indoctrinates his students with the belief that the earth is flat,
or that the Elders of Zion are engaged in a conspiracy to destroy America, or
that Communists are twentieth-century Jeffersonian democrats, is not being
deprived of freedom of speech. He can still proclaim his discovery from the
house tops. As a citizen he can talk nonsense without let or hindrance. But
in order to talk "nonsense" in the academy with impunity—and strange
things *can* be heard within it!—a teacher must win the right to do so by
certification from his peers that he is competent and by having acquired tenure. What may sound like nonsense to the plain citizen may be the birth of a
revolutionary discovery.

The same consideration applies to the student.

There is no direct connection between the student's freedom to learn and
his freedom of speech. The controlling consideration must be his freedom to
learn. If restrictions are placed on freedom of speech—aside from those
which exist on the freedom of *all* citizens—they must be justified by the

educational needs of the student and reasonable institutional provisions for its expression. It is one thing to set up a miniature Hyde Park on some corner of the campus and encourage students to use it; it is another to allow them to call a mass meeting on Prexy's lawn at dawn.

Third, responsibility for the certification of a teacher's competence, and for interpreting and applying the rules of tenure, must ultimately lie in the hands of the faculty. The faculty should also set the educational standards which students are required to measure up to. Students may be free to learn but sometimes they don't learn enough. Students too, therefore, must earn the right to continue as students. Higher education is not a civil right like the right to a fair trial or other Bill of Rights freedoms that do not have to be earned.

Fourth, an important aspect of the faculty's responsibility for the entire educational enterprise is ultimate control over the classrooms, meeting halls and other educational facilities of the campus and over the conditions of their use. This has a bearing, as we shall see, on some crucial questions.

The extent to which these principles are applied is affected by the fact that legal authority in American higher institutions of learning is vested either in boards of regents or in corporate boards of laymen. While there is no practicable way of reversing this historical trend, immense progress has been made in winning over those with legal authority to the acceptance of enlightened principles of academic freedom which in effect entrust educational policy to the faculties. This has been a gradual and sometimes painful development, but today academic freedom is in a more flourishing state than ever before in its history. It is only when one remembers how many and onerous were the religious, political and social restrictions upon the teacher's freedom in the past that one can grasp the remarkable progress that has been made.

What is true of the teacher's academic freedom is also true of the student's freedom to learn. My own lifetime spans a period from relative tyranny in the classroom to open inquiry. During my freshman year in college, I gave two reports in a class in political science. In the first, I defended Charles A. Beard's approach to the Constitution—to the manifest disapproval of the teacher. In the second, I argued that Calhoun's logic was superior to Webster's in their famous debates. This was too much for the instructor who ejected me from the class with the indignant observation: "When you aren't preaching sedition you are preaching secession!" That could hardly happen today. Although conditions are not uniform, almost everywhere the climate of opinion and practice is healthier than it used to be.

The issues that agitate campuses today are more likely to arise from the behavior of students than from actions of the faculty. Of these, some stem from rules governing the students' personal and social behavior, and some from efforts to regulate their extracurricular political activities both on and off campus.

Confusion, and sometimes needless controversy, arise from a failure to distinguish between the area of conduct in which students may justifiably exercise their rights as individual citizens and that which is related to the specific function of the college and to the business which presumably brings the student to school. To indicate the relevance of this distinction, let us examine some of the concrete issues that have provoked controversy in recent years.

The first concerns the personal morality of students. Unfortunately, personal morality for many people refers exclusively to sexual behavior, but, properly understood, it embraces every form of individual conduct whose consequences have some bearing on the welfare of others. On the assumption that in institutions of higher learning we are not dealing with children, standards of personal deportment should initially be left to the students themselves. In the interests of safety, however, it is necessary to establish rules and regulations governing the use of cars, liquor, smoking and visits to dormitories, but, wherever possible, these rules should be administered by the students themselves. Anything students can properly do for themselves as adults should be left to them. To student self-government, broad-based and representative, can be entrusted many of the functions incidental to organized student life in the college community—although the faculty cannot forgo exercising some oversight as a kind of appeals body to see that fair play is done.

Should students be permitted to organize political groups on campus or invite speakers of extremist political views to address them? This kind of problem has occasioned far more bitter controversy than problems of purely personal behavior. And failure to define the issue properly has prevented the right kind of questions from being asked and the relevant considerations brought to bear.

A student request which may have considerable *educational* validity may be wrongfully denied because it is mistakenly put forward as a political demand. This is particularly true with respect to who should be allowed to speak on a university campus. This has nothing to do with questions of free speech or academic freedom. Political speakers can reach students in many ways. If the faculties do not permit the use of college facilities to individuals outside of the academic community, they are not denying the civil right of freedom of speech to speakers, who can easily address students off-campus, or the civil right of freedom to listen to students, who can attend their meetings off-campus. This is a false issue.

The genuine issue is the *educational* one. It is on educational, not political, grounds that a valid case can be made for permitting recognized student organizations to invite speakers of their choice to the campus to discuss any topic, no matter how controversial. The educational process cannot and should not be confined merely to the classroom. Students should be encouraged to pursue their educational interests on their own initiative, and contemporary issues which convulse society are legitimate subjects of inquiry.

Faculties and administrations often suffer from educational timidity. They are unduly fearful when a speaker of extremist views is invited to the campus. If a college is doing its job properly, it doesn't require Fascists or Communists to instruct its students about Fascism or Communism. But so long as students want to hear such speakers—often to see them in the flesh and to find out how they tick mentally—there can be no reasonable educational objection to their appearance—particularly if it is made clear that such speakers do not represent the views of the student body or faculty.

If students and faculty cannot cope with the "arguments" of the Lincoln Rockwells and Gus Halls, then the college is failing badly in its educational task. In an open and honest forum, the cause of freedom and democracy can triumph over all challengers. And as for the vaunted "public image" (horrid phrase!) of the college, the prolonged controversy and newspaper publicity attendant upon banning a speaker is usually far more damaging than the one-day sensation provided by his appearance. For one thing seems assured by experience. A prolonged controversy over an invitation to an extremist almost always guarantees him an overflow audience when he does finally appear.

In the rare cases in which the need for control of student activities does arise, failure on the part of the faculty to draw the line means that it has abdicated from its educational responsibilities. For example, students, sometimes unfortunately abetted by junior faculty personnel, will occasionally try to break up meetings of speakers with whom they disagree. A self-respecting faculty cannot tolerate such activities. Similarly, if outside groups send professional organizers onto the campuses of large metropolitan universities to recruit students or to provoke incidents with the administration or faculties, they should be barred from access.

Then, too, small groups of students, zealots in some cause, will occasionally violate the rules of fair discussion and honest advocacy. I could fill a volume describing stratagems of this kind I have observed over a lifetime. A few students, for example, will organize a "Free Speech Forum" or something else with a libertarian flavor. Their first speaker will be Lincoln Rockwell or someone of his kidney. Thereafter, featured as "a reply" to Fascism, will come a succession of Communist speakers, sometimes paid from general student or school funds. The "educational" point of the forum is to build up Communism in its various disguises as the only real answer to Fascism.

Complaints about the absence of liberal speakers are met with the statement that liberals have been invited but refused to come. The evidence? A carbon copy of a letter to a liberal figure 2,000 miles or more distant, the original of which he may never have received. Where representatives of the student body are unable to prevent dishonest practices of this kind, the faculty is justified in stepping in.

The same general principles should govern student publications. On educational grounds, students should be encouraged to publish their own newspapers, periodicals and pamphlets, exchanging ideas, commenting on great issues, testing and challenging their teachers' views. But it would be ridiculous to say that this freedom is absolute and exempts them from restraints against slander and libel. Particularly obnoxious is the circulation of anonymous literature on campus defaming members of the student body or faculty.

Only those who believe it is possible to be liberal without being intelligent will affirm that the content of speech is always privileged irrespective of its effects.

The very fact that speech can be used not only for advocacy—which is permissible—but for incitement, defamation and slander—which is not —shows how absurd it is to hold that speech should never be restricted. There should be no prior censorship, of course, unless there is convincing evidence that a speaker plans to incite to violence. We do not have to wait for a mob actually to move to lynch someone before we stop the agitator inciting it.

The irony of the situation is that students in our mass institutions of learning suffer today far more from the failure of faculties to attend to the students' individual educational needs than from alleged suppressions of their freedom of speech. The students' freedom to learn is frustrated by crowding, inferior staffing and by the indifference of many faculties to the best methods of classroom teaching. Colleges still operate on the absurd assumption that anyone who knows anything can teach it properly. It is an open scandal that the worst teaching in the American system of education takes place at the college level.

In some universities, large introductory courses where skillful teaching is of critical importance in arousing student interest are turned over to young, inexperienced graduate assistants at the outset of their careers who stumble along by trial and error and groping imitation of the models of teaching they vaguely remember. No wonder they sometimes play up to students, joining them in their vague resentments against the educational establishment in a kind of compensatory camaraderie. Some observers believe that unless conditions change the real revolt on campus will some day be directed against the shoddy educational treatment to which students have been subjected. As the numbers of students grow the situation deteriorates.

A sense of proportion, a pinch of humor and a draft of common sense are wonderful specifics against friction, but they vanish when either students or faculty resort to ultimatums. Both sides have a mutual interest in keeping the educational enterprise going. When problems and difficulties arise they must be routed through recognized channels of petition, complaint and protest. The officially elected representatives of the student body should meet periodically with representatives of the faculty which, when grave issues are at stake, should sit as a committee of the whole.

Attempts by any group, even when it feels it has a legitimate grievance, to short-circuit official channels, to appeal over the heads of the representative student body for mass demonstrations or strikes, to threaten force and violence or to resort to so-called passive resistance should be condemned by both students and faculty. Such tactics are not only destructive of the atmosphere in which teaching and learning can take place, they prejudice the chances for reaching mutually satisfactory settlements.

The student "Free Speech Movement" at the University of California had every right to press for modification of university rules governing campus and off-campus activities. What was shocking, however, was its deliberate boycott and by-passing of the Associated Students, the elected representative organization of the student body. It neither used all the existing channels of protest nor sought to avail itself of the remedies open to it.

Even more shocking was the demagogic and odious comparison drawn by some students between the situation at the University, which, despite its restrictions, is still far more liberal than most, and the situation in Mississippi. And worst of all was the resort to tactics of mass civil disobedience which could only be justified in extreme situations in behalf of basic principles of freedom. Except in such situations, changes in the laws of a democratic community must be urged by practices within the law.

Almost as shocking as the action of the students in seizing University property was the failure of the faculty at Berkeley to condemn the action. Indeed, by failing to couple its call for an amnesty for students with a sharp rebuke for their actions, the faculty seemed to condone indirectly the students' behavior. Apparently those who wanted to be heroes were to be spared the consequences of their heroism.

The administration of the University also seems at fault in not anticipating developments on campus. Signs of student unrest and dissatisfaction were apparent many months ago. The faculty, therefore, should have been brought into the picture much earlier and entrusted with the formulation of rules of conduct, in consultation with official representatives of the student body, and with their subsequent enforcement.

The really disquieting aspect of the situation at the University of California, however, was the extremism of the student leaders, the lengths to which they were willing to go—at one point, bloodshed and possible loss of life seemed imminent—and the contemptuous and disingenuous account they gave of their behavior. One of them described their activities as "controversial measures to begin a dialogue." Student concern with the content and method of their education is sure to grow and should be encouraged. But if they are going to lie down, seize buildings and call strikes whenever their demands are not granted by faculty and administration, it bodes ill for the future.

Even before the events at Berkeley, I read literature distributed by a strong student group at the University of California calling for "the total elimination of course, grade and unit system of undergraduate learning" and urging other proposals—not all of them as silly. But what was definitely not silly or funny in the light of what has happened was the injunction to students to resort ultimately to "civil disobedience" to get their way! It is a safe bet to anyone who knows the psychology of students that once they get away with the tactic of civil disobedience in protesting a minor rule, their demands—and their conduct—will grow wilder and more unreasonable.

No service is done to students by flattering them or by giving them the impression they can acquire an education in any other way than by hard intellectual discipline—by accepting the logic of ideas and events. They cannot be encouraged too much to broaden their intellectual interests, and they certainly must not be discouraged from giving expression to their generous enthusiasms for civil rights, for human welfare, for peace with freedom. But good works off campus cannot be a substitute for good work on campus. Ultimately, the good causes our society always needs have a better chance of triumphing if their servitors equip themselves with the best education our colleges and universities can give them.

STUDY QUESTIONS

1. According to Hook, are there any restrictions on the students' right to learn? If so, what are they?

2. What should be the criteria for allowing student organizations to invite speakers to the campus? What possible problems could arise from using this criteria?

3. In his criticism of the Free Speech Movement at the University of California, what does Hook say about the faculty and the administration?

4. How is it that the students' freedom to learn depends on the academic freedom of the faculty but the converse is not true?

5. In Hook's view, why is it unreasonable to give students unrestricted freedom
of speech?

Leo Rosten

TO AN ANGRY YOUNG MAN

Leo Rosten (1908–   ), author and political scientist, earned his under-
graduate and his graduate degrees at the University of Chicago. He has
taught at the University of Chicago and the University of California
(Berkeley). At present he is a special correspondent and education adviser
for *Look* magazine. His books include *The Washington Correspondents*,
The Education of Hyman Kaplan, *The Straight Places*, *Hollywood: the
Movie Colony*, *The Movie Makers*, *The Dark Corner*, *The Return of
Hyman Kaplan*, *Captain Newman, M.D.*, *The Story Behind the Painting*,
The Many Worlds of Leo Rosten, and *A Most Private Intrigue*. A prolific
and versatile writer, as this list of books indicate, Rosten also is a regular
contributor to journals and magazines.

I HAVE BEEN GETTING lusty cheers and jeers for a rueful little paragraph I recently wrote about student riots. The
most eloquent (and savage) letter ended: "Drop dead!!!"
Another diatribe was signed "Columbia Senior." I wish I knew where to
send this reply to both:

Dear?:
It will upset you to learn that I agree with many things you said. For instance: "Don't question our sincerity!" I don't. You are about as sincere as
anyone can be. You are sincerely unhappy, sincerely frustrated and sincerely confused. You are also sincerely wrong about the few facts you cite,
and sincerely illogical in the violent conclusions you reach. Besides, what
does "sincerity" have to do with issues? Any insane asylum is full of sincere

patients. Hitler was undoubtedly sincere. So are the followers of Voliva, who think the world is sincerely flat.

I sadly agree that your college courses have been "outrageously irrelevant to the times"—because your letter reveals that you could not pass a freshman exam in at least three fields in which you pass such sweeping judgments: economics, history, political theory.

You say, "Destroy a system that has not abolished unemployment, exploitation and war!" By the same reasoning, you should blow up all hospitals (and perhaps execute all doctors, biologists and researchers): they have not abolished disease.

Before you destroy a system, propose another that *will* solve (not hide, shift or disguise) unemployment, "exploitation," war. Anyone can promise Utopia—without specifying a program. Tom Hayden, idol of the New Left, has said: "First we'll make the revolution—then we'll find out what for." Would you employ a plumber who rips out all the pipes in your house before he learned how to repair a leak?

You say, "The mass media are not telling us the truth." Then how and from whom did *you* learn the "evils" you correctly deplore? After all, your information comes from one or another organ of—the mass media.

"This society is only interested in higher prices and profits!" You apparently do not understand this society, or *a* society, or the function of prices (and profits) in *any* economy. Has it never occurred to you that the marketplace is a polling booth? That buying is voting? That no economic system is possible without *some* form of pricing, without some measure of efficacy or worth? Has it never occurred to you that profits are a form of *proof* (that something gives satisfaction to those who pay for it)? Perhaps you should examine the public *uses* that we make of private profits—through taxation.

The countries that follow your platitude, "production for use," *without exception* produce far less for their people to enjoy, of much shoddier quality, at much higher prices (measured by the hours of work needed to buy something). Don't you know that "Socialist" countries are smuggling "capitalist" incentives into their systems? Has it not dawned on you that wherever and whenever there is no free market, there is no free thought, no free art, no free politics, no free life?

You rage against "a heartless country in which the poor get poorer." Alas, poor Yoricks: The *decline* in poverty in the U.S. is among the more astonishing and hopeful facts of human history. (In 1900, about 90% of our population was poor; in 1920—50%; in 1930—34%; in 1968—15%). You will cry that 15% is outrageous. Agreed. The question is: How best abolish it? (A negative income tax makes more sense than anything your colleagues propose.)

"The middle class exploits the unemployed." Please examine that cliché. Would the middle class be worse off or better off if all the unemployed magically disappeared? Obviously, *much* better off: Think of the enormous saving in taxes, the enormous improvement in public services, the enormous benefits from refocused energies now used to ameliorate poverty's abominable toll.

You say your generation "wants to be understood." Well, so does mine. How much have you tried to understand others? You pillory us for injustices not of our making, frictions not of our choice, dilemmas that history (or our forebears or the sheer intractability of events) presented to us. You say we "failed" because you face so many awful problems. Will you then accept blame for all the problems that exist (and they will) when you are 20 years older? And how do you know that all problems are soluble? Or soluble swiftly? Or soluble peacefully? Or soluble, given the never-infinite resources, brains and experience any generation is endowed with?

I say that *you* are failing *us*—in failing to learn and respect discomforting facts; in failing to learn how to *think* (it is easier to complain); in using violence to shut down colleges; in shamefully denying the freedom of others to study and to teach; in barbarously slandering and abusing and shouting down those who disagree with you; in looting, stealing and defiling; in failing to see how much more complicated social problems are than you blindly assume; in acting out of an ignorance for which idealism is no excuse, and a hysteria for which youth is no defense. "Understanding"? You don't even understand that when you call me a "mother ------" you are projecting your unresolved incestuous wishes onto me. The technical name for such projection, in advanced form, is paranoia.

Again and again, you say, "the American people want" or "demand" or "insist." How do you know? *Every poll I have seen puts your position in a minority.* You just say, "the American people demand"—then add whatever *you* prefer. This is intellectually sloppy at best, and corrupt at worst.

You want to "wreck this slow, inefficient democratic system." It took the human race centuries of thought and pain and suffering and hard experiment to devise it. Democracy is not a "state" but a process; it is a way of solving human problems, a way of hobbling power, a way of protecting every minority from the awful, fatal tyranny of either the few or the many.

Whatever its imperfections, democracy is the only system man has discovered that makes possible *change without violence.* Do you really prefer bloodshed to debate? Quick dictates to slow law? This democracy made possible a great revolution in the past 35 years (a profound transfer of power, a distribution of wealth, an improvement of living and health) without "liquidating" millions, without suppressing free speech, without the obscenities of dogma enforced by terror.

This "slow, inefficient" system protects people like me against people like you; and (though you don't realize it) protects innocents like you against those "reactionary . . . fascist forces" you fear: They, like you, prefer "action to talk." As for "security"—at what price? The most "secure" of human institutions is a prison; would you choose to live in one?

You want "a society in which the young speak their minds against the Establishment." Where have the young more freely, recklessly and intransigently attacked "the Establishment"? (*Every* political order has one.) Wherever "our heroes—Marx, Mao, Ché" have prevailed, students, writers, teachers, scientists have been punished with hard labor or death—for what? For their opinions. Where but in "fake democracies" are mass demonstrations possible, or your bitter (and legitimate) dissent televised?

You rail against "leaders crazed with power," who "deceive the people." Your leaders are self-dramatizers who demand that power, which would craze them, and they deceive you in not telling you how they plan your "confrontations"—to force the police to use force, whose excesses I hate more than you do. *I,* unlike you, want no one put "up against the wall." No "cheap politician" more cynically deceived you than fanatical militants did—and will. Your support feeds their neurotic (because extremist) needs. Washington's " 'Non-Violent' Coordinating Committee" has engaged in gunfire for three days as I write this.

You say Marcuse "shows that capitalist freedom actually enslaves." (He doesn't "show"—he only *says.*) He certainly does not sound enslaved. And does mouthing fragments of 19th-century ideology (Marx, Bakunin) really liberate? And is not Marcuse 40 years "older than 30," your cutoff on credibility? Incidentally, would you trust your life to a surgeon under 30—who never finished medical school?

Your irrationality makes me wonder how you were ever admitted *into* Columbia. You confuse rhetoric with reasoning. Assertions are not facts. Passion is no substitute for knowledge. Slogans are not solutions. Your idealism takes no brains. And when you dismiss our differences with contempt, you become contemptible.

Very sincerely yours,
LEO ROSTEN

P.S. Please don't take any more courses in sociology, which seduces the immature into thinking they understand a problem if they discuss it in polysyllables. Jargon is not insight. Vocabulary is the opiate of radicals.

STUDY QUESTIONS

1. What characterizes the author's tone in this selection? Does it appear that his intention is to antagonize?

2. The author employs a fairly conventional strategy in establishing his positions. What are the advantages of such strategy? What are the dangers?

3. If you were the Columbia Senior, what rebuttal could you offer to his reasoning in the fourth, fifth, and sixth paragraphs?

4. Does Rosten support any of his positions with arguments you find invalid or false?

Jeremy Larner

ANOTHER PLANE IN ANOTHER SPHERE: THE COLLEGE DRUG SCENE

Jeremy Larner (1937–   ) was born in Olean, New York. He completed his undergraduate work at Brandeis University and attended the Graduate College of the University of California at Berkeley. He teaches at New York State University at Stony Brook, Long Island. His writings have appeared in the *Atlantic, Holiday, Nation,* and *Dissent.* He is coauthor of *The Addict in the Street.* His novel *Drive, He Said* won the Delta Award in 1965. His most recent books are *Answer* (1968), and *Poverty: Views From the Left* (1968), which he edited with Irving Howe.

Why do we try drugs? We really feel like we're limited so much. And we want to do so much. And we're always told we should try things and grow. It's part of the liberal arts education. It seems hypocritical of older people to tell us not to try certain things. We feel we can take care of ourselves.

Whilst there are no significant statistics—any more than there are on virginity, and for the same reason—drug-taking is becoming increasingly popular on American campuses. A variety of drugs can now be easily obtained at any college which draws its students from metropolitan areas—which means that the problem is most acute at the biggest and best universities and at some of the most prestigious small colleges. Marijuana is generally the drug of choice: a young man from an Eastern college claims, "I have yet to see a college party anywhere in the last two years where at least one-third of the kids have not been turned on."

The local marijuana connection is usually a fellow classmate. But if a student wants other drugs, or if he uses marijuana in large quantities, he need not seek further than the circle of hangers-on who live in the university community without attending college. In brief, availability is such that nearly every contemporary student must make up his mind whether or not he wants to try drugs—because he will certainly have the chance.

For most students, marijuana is something to be tried once or twice, to see what it's like. Those who consider themselves hip with smoke reefers "socially," in the same spirit in which executives drink martinis. Of these social smokers, a few will get to the point where they are turning on every day; and it is these few who will also try other drugs—for example, amphetamine "pep pills" in quantities that can cause psychotic distortions, berserk outbreaks, and even cerebral hemorrhage. Heroin, barbiturates, and other "hard narcotics" are also available for the self-destructive; but as a rule the hip thing is to take drugs for "exploration" rather than escape.

When drug use first comes to light on a given campus, college officials tend to protect the school's reputation by expelling the culprits and even by turning them over to the police. Experienced administrators, however, are learning to make a distinction between trying drugs and selling them, and in the former case are more likely to use probation or a psychiatric referral as a means of correction. The fact that drugs are illegal does not in itself serve as a deterrent. Students of all generations have traditionally sought out forbidden activities as a valuable part of their college education. Thus choosing one's drug, or no drugs, is regarded as a personal decision, like choosing friends, books, or clothes, to be made on personal grounds quite apart from the opinions or threats of authorities.

The modern student will accept responsibility for the effects his actions have on others, but beyond that he sees all arbitrary limits as impositions of the status quo. Personal responsibility, to him, implies the freedom to take risks that involve only himself and his development. He feels that if parents and school officials really believe in that "free inquiry" which is supposedly the ideal of a liberal education, they must respect his right to conduct his own quest by his own rules.

The drugs most talked about in terms of questing are the powerfully mind-disturbing hallucinogens (peyote, mescaline, psilocybin, LSD). Most of the daily pot-smokers will sooner or later try the hallucinogens. Other students are also curious to try them, partly for "kicks," partly because they feel challenged, and partly because they are attracted by claims of mystic and psychological revelation. The most extravagant of these claims emanate from grown-up enthusiasts who are devoting their careers to popularizing the hallucinogens.

For many young Americans, college represents four years of free experiment between the restrictions of the parental family and the responsibilities of the marital family. The student is aware that every choice he makes—both occupationally and personally—may have a telling effect on the adult he will become. He is under pressure to "find himself"—and quickly.

Like other Americans, the college student may look for his "self" in the products he consumes. Universities that are organized like supermarkets will only encourage such unsatisfying searches. Students, moreover, are susceptible to an existentialist strain of the disease called "conspicuous consumption." Rerouting the pursuit of the material, they seek to consume pure experience. They hope that by choosing the right activities they can create an external confirmation of the power and beauty they would like to feel within.

Drugs, as we shall see, are products that supply the illusion of choice while they simultaneously minister to the anxieties that choosing creates. The increasing use of drugs may be seen as a reflection of an unconscious belief in the commercials that pound home the connection between a judicious drug choice and the relief of any mental or physical "symptom." Such assumptions are not easily overcome by a generation that is, after all, the first whose members are lifelong TV viewers, bombarded from infancy by suggestions of false needs.

Marijuana

To us a muggle wasn't any more dangerous or habit-forming than those other great American vices, the five-cent Coke and the ice-cream cone, only it gave you more kicks for your money.

Us vipers began to know that we had a gang of things in common: we ate like starved cannibals who finally latch on to a missionary, and we laughed a whole lot and lazed around in an easygoing way, and we all decided that the muta had some aphrodisiac qualities too. . . . All the puffed-up strutting little people we saw around, jogging their self-important way along so chesty and chumpy, plotting and scheming and getting more wrinkled and jumpy all the time, made us all howl. . . . We were on another plane in another sphere compared to the musicians who were bottle babies, always hitting the jug and then coming up brawling after they got loaded. We liked things to be easy and relaxed, mellow and mild, not loud or loutish, and the scowling chin-out tension of the lushhounds with their false courage didn't appeal to us.

This classic description—from *Really the Blues* (1946) by Mezz Mezzrow and Bernard Wolfe—will serve to convey the general relaxation of the marijuana high and the good fellowship which prevails in the society of satisfied vipers. The *LaGuardia Report*—published in 1944 and still the standard scientific text on the subject—confirms that marijuana is non-addicting. The *Report* warns that marijuana taken in excess may produce anxiety as well as pleasant feelings, and that psychotic episodes are not unheard-of when the batch is strong and the smoker sensitive. The pleasurable response to pot is to some extent learned, and an experienced smoker will not continue once he has obtained the desired sensations. To quote the *Report:* "The description of the 'tea-pad parties' brings out clearly the convivial effect . . . and the absence of any rough or antagonistic behavior."

Obviously college administrators could not sanction pot, even if it were legal, any more than they sanction drinking. But students are contemptuous of the usual line about marijuana leading to heroin addiction. Since heroin is a depressant, its effects are entirely different from those described above, and are sought after by a different kind of person, one who is characteristically dissatisfied with marijuana. Commentators may fasten on the fact that heroin addicts "began" with pot, but it is just as accurate to say that they "began" with liquor. For most heroin addicts have at one time tried liquor as well as pot—and rejected both.

Since pot is outlawed, however, sooner or later a pot-smoker will come in contact with a connection who has other drugs for sale. This, to many students, represents the crucial difference between alcohol and marijuana. One drug is surrounded by accepted rituals, while consumption of the other is ipso facto connected with lawbreaking. Many feel that if marijuana were legalized, society would develop appropriate and enjoyable attitudes toward it. They feel that the comparison with alcohol is all in marijuana's favor. The White House Conference on Narcotic and Drug Abuse referred to alcohol as "the outstanding addictive drug in the United States." The country's five million alcoholics suffer from cirrhosis, nervous diseases, and even brain damage. Nicotine, too, has addictive properties, and cigarettes made from tobacco can cause lung cancer; whereas the *LaGuardia Report* tells us that "those who have been smoking marijuana for a period of years showed no mental or physical deterioration which may be attributed to the drug."

The upshot of misinformed fulminations about marijuana is that students in the know feel a certain superiority. They're entitled to smile when subjected to the liquor industry's 200-million-dollar annual barrage of advertising designed to link alcoholic intake with happiness, youth, and social power. They feel their product is better, cheaper, and less dangerous. And once they've tried pot and discovered that official warnings are based more on panic than fact, they are in a position to discredit apprehensions about any drug whatever.

The Hallucinogens

The hallucinogens—of which the laboratory synthetic LSD is by far the most powerful—produce a stunning impact on the mind. Distortions of time and space, intense color phenomena, and delusions of death and grandeur are commonly experienced. All sorts of thoughts, feelings, memories, fears, dreams, and images are released, often with an overlay of euphoria. Some psychiatrists see the hallucinogens as potentially useful in the treatment of various mental disorders, though most regard the experimental work in this field to date as inconclusive. Psychoanalysts have for years rejected techniques of artificial release—such as hypnotism and "truth serums"—on the grounds that psychoanalysis is not identical with the mere unearthing of material.

LSD cultists feel that under the effect of a hallucinogen, the mind activates inborn knowledge long "repressed" by civilization, knowledge which reveals the mystic "oneness" of the universe. The individual personality is supposedly dissolved in "The Void," where space and time vanish and all is impersonal "ecstasy." This experience, along with the emergence of "repressed" psychic material, is supposed to help the individual gain a transcendent perspective with which to reorient himself to the "illusory" world of earthbound humanity.

It is claimed that the regular use of LSD increases individual development and lovingness toward others, and that therefore the drug should be freely available. An LSD millennium is seen as inevitable, bringing with it the dissolution of human conflict and the recognition of the cult leaders as prophets of a scientific, philosophic, and historical "breakthrough."

Most psychiatrists, however, are wary of dangerous reactions to the hallucinogens. There are many verified reports of students in whom a hallucinatory drug touched off a latent psychosis so severe that hospitalization was required. Prolonged psychotic states, depression, recurring hallucinations, and suicide attempts (some successful) have resulted from the use of LSD—in some cases months after the drug was taken. As for the effects of LSD on the personality, medical investigators have noted the following: 1) dissociation and detachment, 2) personal insensitivity, superiority, 3) religious and philosophical solipsism, 4) impulsivity, poor judgment.

These observations, to be sure, depend on the observer's point of view. One of the chief concerns of the dedicated drug-taker is precisely to repudiate the values, judgments, and most basic perceptions of the persons he believes to represent a monolithic and repressive authority. He does his best to perceive school officials, scientists, teachers, psychiatrists, and indeed anyone who does not appreciate "the drug experience," as an organized "Establishment" conspiring to suppress individual "freedom."

The Dedicated Drug-User

It is now possible for a disaffected youngster to assume a highly developed role as drug-user. He usually begins with the perfection of a "cool" manner. The world is "too much"; his coolness announces that the cool one is invulnerable to involvement. He has taken the cure well in advance of the disease. To put it in consumer terms: desire is a weakness, because it expresses unfulfilled need. The cool one has found and taken the products that he needs.

To blow one's cool, then, is to reveal—to oneself as well as others—an inner lack. To maintain one's cool is to signify, "I've had it." The double meaning is intentional; for the cool one claims no great worldly future. He knows that his gestures are stylized; his pride is the masterly knowledge that in this world of appearances, style is all that matters. Unlike others whom he sees as self-deluded, the cool one suits his actions to his ideas. He has found a philosophy simple enough to live by (almost). In this sense, he alone has achieved the academic ideal.

There is, after all, a twisted idealism involved in submitting oneself to drug experiments. Erik Erikson, in "The Problem of Ego Identity," tells us that some young people respond to environmental pressures by trying to create a "negative identity." According to Erikson, "many a late adolescent, if faced with continuing diffusion, would rather *be nobody or somebody bad, or indeed, dead—and this totally, and by free choice—than be not-quite somebody.*" (Italics his.) Drugs, in these terms, provide the idealist with a chance to control his own destiny and to go all the way. There is a distorted testing mechanism at work here; Erikson speaks of "a radical search for the rock bottom . . . a deliberate search"—as if the searcher could master a sense of unworthiness by seeking out and inflicting upon himself certain selected dangers. Drugs are like Russian roulette: if you survive, you must have something going for you. It shouldn't surprise us that one of the most common, popular, and easily induced drug delusions is the fantasy of rebirth.

If one is to be reborn, one needs replacements for the mortal, fallible parents and family whose existence dictates unendurable limitations. Says Erikson, "Young people often indicate in rather pathetic ways a feeling that only a merging with a 'leader' could save them. . . . the late adolescent wants to be an apprentice or a disciple, a follower, sex mate, or patient." The contemporary campus is replete with drug-givers who will gladly initiate the yearningly incomplete student into all of the above roles. The novice is then equipped with drug priests for parents and fellow acolytes for siblings. The members of the drug family are connected not by birth and mortality, but by destiny and salvation. They reinforce their new improved personalities with ceremonial rituals, an in-group language, and—above all—the taking of the sacrament.

Before long the initiate drug-taker is in turn initiating others. Their desire directed toward him helps to confirm him in his role of "holder" and to convince him that he is indeed in possession of something worthwhile. It is to his advantage that expectation and suggestibility play a tremendous role in an individual's reaction to drugs. He himself is no longer surprised by the sensations produced by powerful drugs; he has learned to enjoy them and to interpret them in accordance with his own desires. Therefore he can guide the initiate who is panicky under his first dose of, say, a hallucinogen, can calm him with lofty wisdom, and help him explain his experience in the language of the drug ideology.

As the drug-taker becomes drug-giver, he cultivates a transcendent personality. He views the world with the secret superiority of one who has access to something better. All of you are playing a game, he says in his every gesture, but you could be saved if you'd follow me. Reality for him is no longer the uncertainty of the ordinary world but the heightened visions he experiences when high. Should his would-be disciples reject their own visions as drug-induced delusions, he informs them that they are tied up in "ego games." For him, the only criteria for interpreting drug phenomena are the phenomena themselves.

The transcendent personality is particularly useful for a student supported by his parents or a technician performing a job he despises. Ordinarily such a situation would raise a crisis of identity centered around the problem of achieving independence and self-respect. But for the true holder, serving his drug postpones the questions, Who am I? and What can I do?

Further, those dedicated to drugs have avoided the ambiguities of democratic face-to-face personal relations. Clinging to an in-group solidarity, they divide the world into sages and fools, saints and devils, holders and seekers. Richard Blum, in his book *The Utopiates,* speculates that drug proselytizers are particularly afraid of seeking and being denied. So they reverse the process, becoming tempters and rejecters. For this writer, the essential point is that both seekers and tempters are still caught up in the infantile drama of power-testing. Unable to bear a grown-up world without absolute power, they have invented that power—and invested it both in drugs and in the parental figures who oppose drugs.

Getting Hung Up

"David" is a brilliant student at an excellent college, well aware of the advantages he's had, and aware also that much is expected of him. Here, David tells of a recent experience which caused him to give up drugs entirely:

At the beginning of this year, I felt really low, I got completely bored with school, and I felt the teachers weren't giving me anything. I had been involved with a girl, but it ended at the end of the summer. And that was one of the things that really depressed me, you know, that I couldn't find anybody. Sex became a real drive, but since none of the chicks meant anything to me, sex itself became meaningless. I just didn't know what to do with myself. So I started smoking pot every day—to the point where I was high every minute.

Grass had become a crutch all of a sudden. I turned on before I went to class, before dinner, before skiing. I felt that everything could be better. It wasn't just music and girls; it was everything.

But after a few months, I got so I was tired all the time, my mouth was dry. I wasn't doing anything but getting high, and I couldn't get high anymore. I'd been dependent on getting high, and I wanted something to change. There had to be something that would *shake* me. No people were shaking me, no ideas were shaking me, and no course was shaking me. And no experiences were shaking me, so I said, what can shake me? LSD, maybe. So I thought I'd try LSD, to see if it shakes me into something new.

At this point David contacted a disturbed young friend who had been taking drugs heavily since he was fourteen. When David arrived, his friend had taken four times what is considered a heavy dose of LSD and had been hallucinating for five days. He gave David a black market sugar cube and told him it contained a heavy dose of LSD. After swallowing the cube, David found out that it held *twice* a heavy dose. "I think he was so far out of it he knew he wasn't coming back, and he wanted to take me with him."

So I took the cube. For a while it was nice, I'd lie down on the bed, hear some music, the music would sound nice, I'd see pretty colors dancing on the wall. But the fact that new and completely different, if not contradictory, ideas kept popping up in my mind, gradually began to depress me. I kept thinking I had the Answer to Life. I'd jump into one thing, then I'd say No, that's wrong; then another thing, then No, that's wrong . . . and finally I saw that the answers were just as illusory as the colors I saw on the wall.

And when I started to feel my mind flipping out of my body, I thought, Jesus Christ, I don't care how simple the pleasures would be, I'd rather be *back there*. I'd rather be in a boring state than where I am now, because I cannot live this way, I don't want to be like this. I'll commit suicide if necessary. I thought that this was going to go on continually, and I just couldn't cope with it.

Though inside himself David felt desperately hysterical, his outer manner was so remote that he couldn't convince the college doctor he needed help. Finally, after three days of hallucinations, David found a doctor who administered an antidote.

The LSD experience caused David to reconsider his way of using marijuana:

I realized afterwards that, as a result of smoking grass, the things that had been important to me were not only no longer important, I was incapable of doing them. I couldn't write, I couldn't think. I couldn't carry on normal relations with people. I saw how much time I'd been wasting. I mean, I sort of knew it all along. But when I took the LSD, I just had three days of intense fear and running around and nervous energy, and when I was brought back to earth, I said, God, your whole last few years have been like this! You haven't been doing anything; you've just been running around—and heading in toward a dead end. I hadn't been developing at all; I was just completely stagnant.

After telling his story, David gets into an argument with his roommate about a mutual friend who was once a brilliant musician but who now does nothing but stay high on pot all day long. David's roommate refers him to a long list of first-rate jazz musicians who are well-known vipers. David is forced to admit that the problem resides not in the marijuana itself but in the immaturity of his friend, who is "a weak, dependent person needing a crutch." The roommate presses further: isn't their musician friend just as well off staying high all day as he would be playing the piano? As long as he feels good, does it make any difference how he gets that way? David replies with some warmth:

No, my friend does *not* feel good—he could be happier with music than with pot. Because music never ceases to move and develop. Pot, instead of broadening and deepening, just becomes less than it was at the beginning. You could say the same about any drug: it's a dead end.

The Mystique
of "The Creative Experience"

Thousands of students would passionately object to David's separation of drugs and art. They would insist that drugs are indispensable for the understanding and creation of modern poetry, painting, music, fiction, and sculpture.

For reasons of social dislocation which the campus only mirrors, masses of the most confused, aimless, and sensitive young people are drawn to the arts and humanities. A common theme in the humanities is reverence for art—a reverence crudely reinforced by a society which has discovered the commodity value of culture. The student finds "great" art painstakingly analyzed by teachers who are masters of academic method. If he is not satisfied with mere learning, the student may be tempted to transcend the analysis and identify with the projected image of the artist. Art raises the possibility that one is possessed of a nonintellectual, unmeasurable, mysterious *something* that defies all academic categories. Under the circumstances, it is natural for the artistic student to be overly impressed with the notion that art is inspired by irrational mental states—even to the point where he regards insanity as a divine visitation.

For the would-be artist, drugs are a magic product advertising the separation of art from talent, time, judgment, and work. One turns on, and one has Visions. One digs music and painting with drug-heightened attention, and one has Revelations. If one tries to paint or write under the influence of drugs, the results are invariably disorganized and disappointing. Still, one has somehow been "creative." All that is necessary to call oneself an artist is to replace palpable creation with the notion of "the creative experience."

The trouble with "the creative experience" is that anyone can have it. But for those who cannot produce art itself, the drug ideology offers membership in an artistic consumer elite.

I recently met a young engineer who feels greater rapport with his girl when both are high. Every night they turn on while watching a TV movie and "really dig it." The engineer feels that everyone should smoke pot. "When I go out in the world looking for friends, the first question I ask myself is, do they smoke? Because if they don't they look at me like I'm a drug addict."

The engineer insists that he turns on not for escape but for "insight—to learn things about myself." As an example of his insight, he states that "ordinarily I have a masochistic streak: I let people get away with saying things they shouldn't. But when I'm high, I know what to answer."

The engineer's girl friend is an art student who claims she paints better when high. "I can paint and take in everything going on in the room at the same time." She enjoys the fact that so many of her friends use drugs. "You feel you're privileged—you're part of an artists' community."

College drug use reaches a peak at big city art schools. It's worth noting that at the art colleges young people in training to become fashion illustrators and advertising directors are exposed to a highly pretentious milieu. They make contact with future artists—and form an alliance between art and advertising which has proved effective in bringing visual art, more than any other, into the consumer market place. To be hip in the art world, one must now consume the newest thing in art in the same way one consumes drugs—for the latest sensation. Like "creative experience," the fabrication of "pop" art is within reach of anyone. And art fashions, like drug fashions, offer their consumers the justification of an in-group ideology.

The American Dream

Ever since the discovery of the New World and the Frontier, Americans have been looking for an absolute truth. This truth is thought to be natural and good, yet often it is to be attained through technical developments. Our politicians reflect these assumptions whenever they resort to the apocalyptic view of history, in which the United States is to play a divinely ordained dramatic role in directing the "progress" of the rest of the world.

D. H. Lawrence once described Americans as "Some insisting on the plumbing, and some on saving the world: these being the two great American specialties." The LSD missionaries are out to do both at the same time —to save the world by tinkering with the internal plumbing. As in the drug ads, the idea is happiness and fulfillment through the ingestion of a synthesized additive. If drug evangelists combine proselytism with claims of mystic serenity, it's not because of any profound "paradox," but because they are, at bottom, American innocents.

Another American tradition—which can be encountered in any decent course in American literature—is the myth of the New Self. The myth is that a powerful experience can purge a hero of his past and release innate powers which have been hitherto suppressed by an unnatural society. The desire is to rid oneself entirely of fear and guilt. For the American student, drugs are the latest platform from which the New Self may be announced. The young user may rejoice in a mode of being which seems utterly to by-pass his everyday problems in coming to terms with the world. He can occupy, for a while, "another plane in another sphere"—where everything depends upon himself and what he puts into his mouth.

Newness, by its nature, is temporary. Before long there may be a letdown, an impingement of the dreary "old" self who has survived somehow after all—then a need, as David puts it, for something to "shake" one. That something, for the modern student, is closer than the campus drugstore. It will be ready for him as often as he has to have it.

Eventually he may wonder why. Speaking of "insight"—as young "heads" are so prone to do—the deepest insight one could gain from drugs would be to discover, not one's essential greatness, but the reason one needed to take drugs in the first place. This knowledge comes from life rather than manufactured chemicals. As a matter of fact, there is a tendency for collegiate drug-users, such as David, to reach a peak and then abruptly leave the drug scene. But until an individual can understand his drug need in terms of his own psychology, drug use for him will continue to be one of those symptoms that perpetuates its causes.

STUDY QUESTIONS

1.   What is the rhetorical effect of the way Larner begins and ends his essay?

2.   Would you describe Larner's prose voice as one that speaks with authority? How is the authority established and maintained?

3. Do you believe he is correct in his account of why students try drugs?

4. The author observes that most psychiatrists are wary of dangerous reactions to the hallucinogens. What are some of these reactions?

5. What are popular views about the connection between the use of drugs and the understanding of poetry, music, and painting? What are Larner's opinions on this?

Popular Culture

"The Winter of Our Discontent"

Elmo Roper

HOW CULTURALLY ACTIVE
ARE AMERICANS?

Elmo Roper (1900–   ) was born in Hebron, Nebraska. He attended the
University of Minnesota and the University of Edinburgh, and holds four
honorary degrees. His distinguished record during World War II included
service with the Office of Facts and Figures and the Office of Strategic Services. From 1935 to 1950 he was research director for the Fortune Survey
of Public Service. The famed marketing consultant has taught at Columbia
and serves as editor-at-large for the *Saturday Review*. His books include
You and Your Leaders (1958).

IN AN ERA when culture is being promoted with all the
enthusiasm once reserved for breakfast cereal and we are
being reminded daily that ignorance is obsolete, how
"cultural" are Americans? Where does learning rank in our range of interests?

The answers to some questions recently asked of a cross-section of adult
Americans shed some light on our intellectual and cultural involvement. To
begin with, respondents were offered a list of subjects and asked to name
those in which they had "a good deal of interest." The results appear below:

Religion	49%
Sports	47
Music	46
Politics and government	40
International affairs	37
Cooking	36
Home decoration	35
History	22
Science	20
Literature	19
Art	13
No opinion	7

Reprinted from *Saturday Review*, XLIX, May 14, 1966 by permission of the author.

Clearly, the egghead still has a long way to go before he replaces the baseball player as a national hero. Religion, sports, and music command the broadest appeal and top the list of interests. Politics and international affairs, interests that for various people have varying degrees of intellectual content, barely edge out the frankly down-to-earth concerns of home and kitchen. And at the very bottom lie the clearly intellectual and cultural subjects (with the exception of music, which may or may not reflect as deep a cultural interest), each mentioned by less than a quarter of the people interviewed: history by 22 percent, science by 20 percent, literature 19 percent, with art trailing off at 13 percent.

The next question inquired how often people read books that they felt would "advance their knowledge or education in some way." Twenty-two percent replied "frequently," 29 percent said they did so "occasionally," and 46 percent said "rarely" or "never." Another question found that 35 percent had less than twenty-five books in the home, and another 35 percent between twenty-five and 100, with only 27 percent owning more than 100 books (3 percent didn't know). Other questions also were asked about newspaper and magazine reading, and educational achievement.

Who, then, are the culturally and intellectually involved? Needless to say, the various indices do not all work in the same direction. While the heavy book *readers* are apt to be found among the young (20–34), the heaviest book *ownership* comes at a later age (35–55). Interest in international affairs goes up with age; interest in science is higher with youth. Among the intellectually involved, traditional sex differences in interests are very much in evidence, with women leaning toward such subjects as art and literature, men toward science and politics.

But perhaps the most interesting difference is that women, particularly college-educated women, have *more* interests than men. On the list of interests, seven items were singled out as subjects of a "good deal of interest" by 50 percent or more of college women. Among college men, only three items elicited that degree of interest. Also, the low point of intellectual interest for college women is science, which nevertheless is called interesting by 24 percent. The cultural "low" of college men is art, which at 18 percent is comparable with their interest in the female realm of home decorating (16 percent) and cooking (10 percent).

To get a rough measure of the general level of cultural and intellectual activity in the population, a scale was developed on which each respondent was given a score. Respondents were given one point each for such activities as regular reading of two or more newspapers or "fairly regular" reading of any leading news magazine or magazines with intellectual content such as *Harper's,* the *New Yorker,* or *Saturday Review;* one point each for expressing a "good deal of interest" in politics and government, international affairs, art, history, science or literature; five points each for "frequent" reading of books to advance knowledge or having more than 100 books in the home; two points for attending college; five points for graduating; and five points for taking academic, business or professional courses since graduating from college—with a maximum possible score of thirty-five points.

Using this measure of what might be loosely described as the "level of cultural activity," respondents fell into four main groups. Fifty-one percent received scores of from zero to three, and might be described as the "culturally inert." Another 26 percent received scores of from four to nine, and might therefore be considered "fairly inactive" culturally. Thirteen percent received scores of from ten to fifteen, and might be described as "fairly active." Only 10 percent received scores over fifteen (out of a possible thirty-five), thereby gaining the description of "culturally active"—the term is relative!

What is the relationship between cultural activity and formal education? If you're culturally active, does it mean you've been to college? And if you've been to college, are you thereby culturally active?

The answer to the first question is, by and large, yes. Only 1 percent of grade school people and only 4 percent of the high school educated fell into the culturally active category, whereas 26 percent of those who had had some college and 62 percent of people with college degrees received culturally active scores (abetted, of course, by the credit given for college in their scores).

But the answer to the second question is another thing. Before everyone who's been to college starts resting on his cultural laurels, thinking of the great gap that separates him from the lowly people who make up the rest of the population, let him take a look at the ranking of interests by those with college backgrounds:

Has a good deal of interest in:

International affairs	60%
Politics and government	59
Music	56
Sports	53
Religion	49
Literature	39
History	37
Science	36
Home decoration	36
Cooking	31
Art	26

Political and international events replace religion, sports and music as the prime interests of the college educated. But pure cultural and intellectual interests still cluster, along with cooking and home décor, at the bottom of the list. Asked how often they read edifying books, 44 percent of college educated people answered "frequently"—which means that a majority read to learn infrequently after they leave the academic groves. Asked about book ownership (an easier test than book reading, and the books could be about anything), nearly one quarter (23 percent) of the college educated had less than fifty books in their homes, and just slightly over half (56 percent) owned more than 100 books.

All in all, it must be said that intellectual and cultural activity is still distinctly a minority taste. A college education is no guarantee of developed cultural or intellectual interests, although it certainly makes such interests more probable. In our national rush to get more and more people to college, it should perhaps be kept in mind that half the people who have gotten there show only minor intellectual after-effects. Regarding the other half who can be described as culturally and intellectually involved, the most important question is one that can not be answered by a survey. It is the depth and quality of that involvement.

Some years ago I wrote, "There is an urgent need—in fact a national survival need—for invigorating intellectual life, for upgrading the general regard for intellectual excellence. The United States must experience an intellectual renaissance or it will experience defeat. The time cannot be far off—if indeed it is not already here—when the *strength* of a nation, measured in terms of any kind of world competition, will depend less on the number of its bombs than on the number of its learned men."

The statement is equally valid today. Unquestionably, there have been changes in recent years in our attitude toward the intellectual life. But the changes have not gone far enough. There is no upsurge of intellectual interest in the young—except in the field of science. And too many people who consider themselves educated have really just gone through the motions. The question that should most concern our educators is not how far they can spread learning but how deep it goes.

STUDY QUESTIONS

1. Which of the subjects in Roper's list does he consider "cultural"? Are there any subjects you would add to the list?

2. Why does Roper make a distinction between book *owners* and book *readers*? How do you account for the fact that the heavy book readers are between the ages of 20 and 24?

3. Roper lists three magazines "with intellectual content": *Harper's,* the *New Yorker,* and the *Saturday Review.* Having examined a copy of each of these magazines, do you agree? Does *Playboy* have intellectual content?

4. Does Roper in any way suggest that his rating scale is not an accurate measure of what it is supposed to measure?

5. What conclusions does Roper draw from his survey? Can you suggest other conclusions?

Frank Lloyd Wright

TALIESIN

Frank Lloyd Wright (1869–1959) was born at Richland Center, Wisconsin. He has been called "the greatest of all architects" as a result of the nearly 500 structures he designed and saw completed between 1890 and 1959. He was educated by serving as chief assistant to famed Chicago architect, Louis H. Sullivan. Founder of the "Prairie School" of architecture, he was first successful in Europe, particularly in Germany, where his works were published in 1910. For six years he lived in Tokyo, the site of one of his most famous structures—The Imperial Hotel. Among his other works are New York's Guggenheim Museum and the Johnson and Son administration building and tower. His books include *Modern Architecture* (1931), *An Autobiography* and *The Disappearing City* (1932), *Architecture and Modern Life* (1937), *An Organic Architecture* (1939), *A Testament* (1957), and *The Natural House* (1959).

$\mathcal{T}$ALIESIN WAS the name of a Welsh poet, a druid-bard who sang to Wales the glories of fine art. Many legends cling to that beloved reverend name in Wales.

Richard Hovey's charming masque, "Taliesin," had just made me acquainted with his image of the historic bard. Since all my relatives had Welsh names for their places, why not Taliesin for mine? . . . Literally the Welsh word means "shining brow."

This hill on which Taliesin now stands as "brow" was one of my favorite places when as a boy looking for pasque flowers I went there in March sun while snow still streaked the hillsides. When you are on the low hill-crown you are out in mid-air as though swinging in a plane, the Valley and two others dropping away from you leaving the tree-tops standing below all about you. And "Romeo and Juliet" still stood in plain view over to the southeast. The Hillside Home School was just over the ridge.

As a boy I had learned to know the ground-plan of the region in every line and feature. For me now its elevation is the modeling of the hills, the weaving and the fabric that clings to them, the look of it all in tender green or covered with snow or in full glow of summer that bursts into the glorious blaze of autumn. I still feel myself as much a part of it as the trees and birds and bees are, and the red barns. Or as the animals are, for that matter.

When family-life in Oak Park that spring of 1909 conspired against the freedom to which I had come to feel every soul was entitled, I had no choice, would I keep my self-respect, but go out a voluntary exile into the uncharted and unknown. Deprived of legal protection, I got my back against the wall in this way. I meant to live if I could an unconventional life. I turned to this hill in the Valley as my Grandfather before me had turned to America—as a hope and haven. But I was forgetful, for the time being, of Grandfather's Isaiah. His smiting and punishment.

And architecture by now was quite mine. It had come to me by actual experience and meant something out of this ground we call America. Architecture was something in league with the stones of the field, in sympathy with "the flower that fadeth and the grass that withereth." It had something of the prayerful consideration for the lilies of the field that was my gentle grandmother's: something natural to the great change that was America herself.

It was unthinkable to me, at least unbearable, that any house should be put *on* that beloved hill.

I knew well that no house should ever be *on* a hill or *on* anything. It should be *of* the hill. Belonging to it. Hill and house should live together each the happier for the other. That was the way everything found round about was naturally managed except when man did something. When he added his mite he became imitative and ugly. Why? Was there no natural house? I felt I had proved there was. Now I wanted a *natural* house to live in myself. I scanned the hills of the region where the rock came cropping out in strata to suggest buildings. How quiet and strong the rock-ledge masses looked with the dark red cedars and white birches, there, above the green slopes. They were all part of the countenance of southern Wisconsin.

I wished to be part of my beloved southern Wisconsin, too. I did not want to put my small part of it out of countenance. Architecture, after all, I have learned—or before all, I should say—is no less a weaving and a fabric than the trees are. And as anyone might see, a beech tree is a beech tree. It isn't trying to be an oak. Nor is a pine trying to be a birch, although each makes the other more beautiful when seen together.

The world had had appropriate buildings before—why not appropriate buildings now, more so than ever before? There must be some kind of house that would belong to that hill, as trees and the ledges of rock did; as Grandfather and Mother had belonged to it in their sense of it all.

There must be a natural house, not natural as caves and log-cabins were natural, but native in spirit and the making, having itself all that architecture had meant whenever it was alive in times past. Nothing at all I had ever seen would do. This country had changed all that old building into something inappropriate. Grandfather and Grandmother were something splendid in themselves that I couldn't imagine living in any period-houses I had ever seen or the ugly ones around there. Yes, there was a house that hill might marry and live happily with ever after. I fully intended to find it. I even saw for myself what it might be like. And I began to build it as the brow of that hill.

It was still a very young faith that undertook to build that house. It was the same faith, though, that plants twigs for orchards, vineslips for vineyards, and small whips to become beneficent shade trees. And it planted them all about!

I saw the hill-crown back of the house as one mass of apple trees in bloom, perfume drifting down the Valley, later the boughs bending to the ground with red and white and yellow spheres that make the apple tree no less beautiful than the orange tree. I saw plum trees, fragrant drifts of snow-white in the spring, loaded in August with blue and red and yellow plums, scattering them over the ground at a shake of the hand. I saw the rows on rows of berry bushes, necklaces of pink and green gooseberries hanging to the under side of the green branches. I saw thickly pendent clusters of rubies like tassels in the dark leaves of the currant bushes. I remembered the rich odor of black currants and looked forward to them in quantity.

Black cherries? White cherries? Those too.

There were to be strawberry beds, white, scarlet and green over the covering of clean wheat-straw.

And I saw abundant asparagus in rows and a stretch of great sumptuous rhubarb that would always be enough. I saw the vineyard now on the south slope of the hill, opulent vines loaded with purple, green and yellow grapes. Boys and girls coming in with baskets filled to overflowing to set about the rooms, like flowers. Melons lying thick in the trailing green on the hill slope. Bees humming over all, storing up honey in the white rows of hives beside the chicken yard.

And the herd that I would have! The gentle Holsteins and a monarch of a bull—a sleek glittering decoration of the fields and meadows as they moved about, grazing. The sheep grazing too on the upland slopes and hills, the plaintive bleat of little white lambs in spring.

Those grunting sows to turn all waste into solid gold.

I saw the spirited, well-schooled horses, black horses and chestnut mares with glossy coats and splendid strides, being saddled and led to the mounting-block for rides about the place and along the country lanes I loved —the best of companionship alongside. I saw sturdy teams ploughing in the fields. There would be the changing colors of the slopes, from seeding time to harvest. I saw the scarlet comb of the rooster and his hundreds of hens—their white eggs and the ducks upon the pond. Geese, too, and swans floating upon the water in the shadow of the trees.

I looked forward to peacocks Javenese and white on the low roofs of the buildings or calling from the walls of the courts. And from the vegetable gardens I walked into a deep cavern in the hill—modern equivalent of the rootcellar of my grandfather. I saw its wide sand floor planted with celery, piled high with squash and turnips, potatoes, carrots, onions, parsnips. Cabbages wrapped in paper and hanging from the roof. Apples, pears and grapes stored in wooden crates walled the cellar from floor to roof. And cream! All the cream the boy had been denied. Thick—so lifting it in a spoon it would float like an egg on the fragrant morning cup of coffee or ride on the scarlet strawberries.

Yes, Taliesin should be a garden and a farm behind a real workshop and a good home.

I saw it all, and planted it all and laid the foundation of the herd, flocks, stable and fowl as I laid the foundation of the house.

All these items of livelihood came back—improved from boyhood.

And so began a "shining brow" for the hill, the hill rising unbroken above it to crown the exuberance of life in all these rural riches.

There was a stone quarry on another hill a mile away, where the yellow sand-limestone uncovered lay in strata like outcropping ledges in the façades of the hills. The look of it was what I wanted for such masses as would rise from these native slopes. The teams of neighboring farmers soon began hauling the stone over to the hill, doubling the teams to get it to the top. Long cords of this native stone, five hundred or more from first to last, got up there ready to hand, as Father Larson, the old Norse stone mason working in the quarry beyond, blasted and quarried it out in great flakes. The slabs of stone went down for pavements of terraces and courts. Stone was sent along the slopes into great walls. Stone stepped up like ledges on to the hill and flung long arms in any direction that brought the house to the ground. The ground! My Grandfather's ground. It was lovingly felt as intimate in all this.

Finally it was not so easy to tell where pavements and walls left off and ground began. Especially on the hill-crown, which became a low-walled garden above the surrounding courts, reached by stone steps walled into the slopes. A clump of fine oaks that grew on the hilltop stood untouched on one side above the court. A great curved stone-walled seat enclosed the space just beneath them, and stone pavement stepped down to a spring or fountain that welled up into a pool at the center of the circle. Each court had its fountain and the winding stream below had a great dam. A thick stone wall was thrown across it, to make a pond at the very foot of the hill and raise the water in the valley to within sight from Taliesin. The water below the falls thus made was sent by hydraulic ram up to a big stone reservoir built into the higher hill, just behind and above the hilltop garden, to come down again into the fountains and go on down to the vegetable gardens on the slopes below the house.

Taliesin, of course, was to be an architect's workshop, a dwelling as well, for young workers who would come to assist. And it was a farm cottage for the farm help. Around a rear court were to be farm buildings, for Taliesin was to be a complete living unit genuine in point of comfort and beauty, yes, from pig to proprietor. The place was to be self-sustaining if not self-sufficient, and with its domain of two hundred acres was to be shelter, food, clothes and even entertainment within itself. It had to be its own light-plant, fuelyard, transportation and water system.

Taliesin was to be recreation ground for my children and their children perhaps for many generations more. This modest human programme in terms of rural Wisconsin arranged itself around the hilltop in a series of four varied courts leading one into the other, the courts all together forming a sort of drive along the hillside flanked by low buildings on one side and by flower gardens against the stone walls that retained the hill-crown on the other.

The hill-crown was thus saved and the buildings became a brow for the hill itself. The strata of fundamental stone-work kept reaching around and on into the four courts, and made them. Then stone, stratified, went into the lower house walls and up from the ground itself into the broad chimneys. This native stone prepared the way for the lighter plastered construction of the upper wood-walls. Taliesin was to be an abstract combination of stone and wood as they naturally met in the aspect of the hills around about. And the lines of the hills were the lines of the roofs, the slopes of the hills their slopes, the plastered surfaces of the light wood-walls, set back into shade beneath broad eaves, were like the flat stretches of sand in the river below and the same in color, for that is where the material that covered them came from.

The finished wood outside was the color of gray tree-trunks in violet light.

The shingles of the roof surfaces were left to weather silver-gray like the tree branches spreading below them.

The chimneys of the great stone fireplaces rose heavily through all, wherever there was a gathering place within, and there were many such places. They showed great rock-faces over deep openings inside.

Outside they were strong, quiet, rectangular rock-masses bespeaking strength and comfort within.

Country masons laid all the stone with the stone-quarry for a pattern and the architect for a teacher. The masons learned to lay the walls in the long, thin, flat ledges natural to the quarry, natural edges out. As often as they laid a stone they would stand back to judge the effect. They were soon as interested as sculptors fashioning a statue; one might imagine they were as they stepped back, head cocked one side, to get the general effect. Having arrived at some conclusion they would step forward and shove the stone more to their liking, seeming never to tire of this discrimination. Many of them were artistic for the first time, and liked it. There were many masons from first to last, all good. Perhaps old Dad Signola, in his youth a Czech, was the best of them until Philip Volk came. Philip worked away five years at the place as it grew from year to year—for it will never be finished. And with not much inharmonious discrepancy, one may see each mason's individuality in his work at Taliesin to this day. I frequently recall the man as I see his work.

At that time, to get this mass of material to the hilltop meant organizing man and horse-power. Trucks came along years later. Main strength and awkwardness, directed by commanding intelligence, got the better of the law of gravitation by the ton as sand, stone, gravel and timber went up into appointed places. Ben Davis was commander of these forces at this time. Ben was a creative cusser. He had to be. To listen to Ben back of all this movement was to take off your hat to a virtuoso. Men have cussed between every word, but Ben split the words and artistically worked in an oath between every syllable. One day Ben with five of his men was moving a big rock that suddenly got away from its edge and fell over flat, catching Ben's big toe. I shuddered for that rock as, hobbling slowly back and forth around it, Ben hissed and glared at it, threatening, eyeing and cussing it. He rose to such heights, plunged to such depths of vengeance as I had never suspected, even in Ben. No Marseillaise nor any damnation in the mouth of a Mosaic prophet ever exceeded Ben at this high spot in his career as a cusser. William Blake says exuberance is beauty. It would be profane perhaps to say that Ben at this moment was sublime. But he was.

And in Spring Green (the names in the region are mostly simple like Black Earth, Blue Mounds, Cross Plains, Lone Rock, Silver Creek) I found a carpenter. William Weston was a natural carpenter. He was a carpenter such as architects like to stand and watch work. I never saw him make a false or unnecessary movement. His hammer, extra light with a handle fashioned by himself, flashed to the right spot every time like the rapier of an expert swordsman. He with his nimble intelligence and swift sure hand was a gift to any architect. That William stayed with and by Taliesin through trials and tribulations the better part of fourteen years. America turns up a good mechanic around in country places every so often. Billy was one of them.

Winter came. A bitter one. The roof was on, plastering done, windows in, men working now inside. Evenings the men grouped around the open fire-places, throwing cord-wood into them to keep warm as the cold wind came up through the floor boards. All came to work from surrounding towns and had to be fed and bedded down on the place somewhere during the week. Saturday nights they went home with money for the week's work in pocket, or its equivalent in groceries and fixings from the village. Their reactions were picturesque. There was Johnnie Vaughn who was, I guess, a genius. I got him because he had gone into some kind of concrete business with another Irishman for a partner, and failed. Johnnie said, "We didn't fail sooner because we didn't have more business." I overheard this lank genius, he was looking after the carpenters, nagging Billy Little, who had been foreman of several jobs in the city for me. Said Johnnie, "I built this place off a shingle." "Huh," said Billy, "that ain't nothin'. I built them places in Oak Park right off'd the air." No one ever got even a little over the rat-like perspicacity of that little Billy Little.

Workmen never have enough drawings or explanations no matter how many they get—but this is the sort of slander an architect needs to hear occasionally.

The workmen took the work as a sort of adventure. It was adventure. In every realm. Especially in the financial realm. I kept working all the while to make the money come. It did. And we kept on inside with plenty of clean soft wood that could be left alone pretty much in plain surfaces. The stone, too, strong and protective inside, spoke for itself in certain piers and walls.

Inside floors, like the outside floors, were stone-paved or if not were laid with wide, dark-streaked cypress boards. The plaster in the walls was mixed with raw sienna in the box, went onto the walls natural, drying out tawny gold. Outside, the plastered walls were the same but grayer with cement. But in the *constitution* of the whole, in the way the walls rose from the plan and spaces were roofed over, was the chief interest of the whole house. The whole was supremely natural. The rooms went up into the roof, tent-like, and were ribanded overhead with marking-strips of waxed, soft wood. The house was set so sun came through the openings into every room sometime during the day. Walls opened everywhere to views as the windows swung out above the treetops, the tops of red, white and black oaks and wild cherry trees festooned with wild grape-vines. In spring, the perfume of the blossoms came full through the windows, the birds singing there the while, from sunrise to sunset—all but the several white months of winter.

I wanted a home where icicles by invitation might beautify the eaves. So there were no gutters. And when the snow piled deep on the roofs and lay drifted in the courts, icicles came to hang staccato from the eaves. Prismatic crystal pendants sometimes six feet long, glittered between the landscape and the eyes inside. Taliesin in winter was a frosted palace roofed and walled with snow, hung with iridescent fringes, the plate-glass of the windows shone bright and warm through it all as the light of the huge fire-places lit them from the firesides within, and streams of wood-smoke from a dozen such places went straight up toward the stars.

The furnishings inside were simple and temperate. Thin tan-colored flax rugs covered the floors, later abandoned for the severer simplicity of the stone pavements and wide boards. Doors and windows were hung with modest, brown checkered fabrics. The furniture was home-made of the same wood as the trim, and mostly fitted into the trim. I got a compliment on this from old Dan Davis, a rich and "savin' " Welsh neighbor who saw we had made it ourselves. "Gosh-dang it, Frank," he said. "Ye're savin' too, ain't ye?" Although Mother Williams, another neighbor, who came to work for me, said "Savin'? He's nothin' of the sort. He could 'ave got it most as cheap ready-made from that Sears and Roebuck . . . I know."

A house of the North. The whole was low, wide and snug, a broad shelter seeking fellowship with its surroundings. A house that could open to the breezes of summer and become like an open camp if need be. With spring came music on the roofs, for there were few dead roof-spaces overhead, and the broad eaves so sheltered the windows that they were safely left open to the sweeping, soft air of the rain. Taliesin was grateful for care. Took what grooming it got with gratitude and repaid it all with interest.

Taliesin's order was such that when all was clean and in place its countenance beamed, wore a happy smile of well-being and welcome for all.

It was intensely human, I believe.

Although, thanks to "bigger and better publicity" among those who besieged it Saturdays and Sundays from near and far, came several characteristic ladies whose unusual enterprise got them as far as the upper half of the Dutch door, standing open to the living room. They couldn't see me. I was lying on a long walled-seat just inside. They poked in their heads and looked about with Oh's and Ah's. A pause. In the nasal twang of the more aggressive one, "I wonder . . . I wonder, now, if I'd like living in a regular home?"

The studio, lit by a bank of tall windows to the north, really was a group of four studies, one large, three small. And in their midst stood a stone fireproof vault for treasures. The plans, private papers, and such money as there was, took chances anywhere outside it. But the Taliesin library of Genroku embroidery and antique colored wood-block prints all stayed safely inside. As work and sojourn overseas continued, Chinese pottery and sculpture and Momoyama screens overflowed into the rooms where, in a few years, every single object used for decorative accent became an "antique" of rare quality.

If the eye rested on some ornament it could be sure of worthy entertainment. Hovering over these messengers to Taliesin from other civilizations and thousands of years ago, must have been spirits of peace and good-will. Their figures seemed to shed fraternal sense of kinship from their places in the stone or from the broad ledges where they rested.

Yes. It all actually happened as I have described it. It is all there now.

But the story of Taliesin, after all, is old: old as the human spirit. These ancient figures were traces of that spirit, left behind in the human procession as Time went on its way. They now came forward to rest and feel at home, that's all. So it seemed as you looked at them. But they were only the story within the story: ancient comment on the New.

The New lived for itself for their sake, as long ago they had lived, for its sake.

The storms of the north broke over the low-sweeping roofs that now sheltered a life in which hope purposefully lived at earnest work. The lightning in this region, always so crushing and severe, crashed (Isaiah) and Taliesin smiled. Taliesin was minding its own business, living up to its own obligations and to the past it could well understand. But the New, failing to recognize it as its own, still pursued and besieged, traduced and insulted it. Taliesin raged, wanted to talk back—and smiled. Taliesin was a "story" and therefore it and all in it had to run the gauntlet. But steadily it made its way through storm and stress, enduring all threats and slanderous curiosity for more than three years, and smiled—always. No one entering and feeling the repose of its spirit could ever believe in the storm of publicity that kept breaking outside because a kindred spirit—a woman—had taken refuge there for life.

STUDY QUESTIONS

1. Where did Taliesin get its name? Was it an appropriate name for Wright's new school?

2. What does Wright mean in his statement that a house should not be *on* a hill, but *of* a hill? What details in Wright's description of Taliesin indicate that his architects' workshop was indeed *of* the hill?

3. Did Wright permit his workmen to be "creative" as they labored on Taliesin?

4. What storms does Wright discuss in his last paragraph?

5. Is there a rhetorical principle behind Wright's use of sentence fragments and one-sentence fragments?

Ashley Montagu

FRANK LLOYD WRIGHT

Ashley Montagu (1905–   ) was born in England and became a United
States citizen in 1940. An anthropologist and social biologist, he was educated at the Universities of London and Florence, and received his Ph.D.
from Columbia University in 1937. He has taught at New York University,
Rutgers-The State University, and the New School for Social Research.
Since 1930 he has served as a legal expert on scientific problems related to
race and, in 1949, helped draft the UNESCO statement on race. Among his
books are *Coming into Being Among Australian Aborigines* (1937), *Man's
Most Dangerous Myth: The Fallacy of Race* (1942), *The Natural Superiority of Women* (1953), *Life Before Birth* (1964), *The Idea of Race* (1965),
and *Man and His First Two Million Years: A Brief Introduction to Anthropology* (1969).

THE LIFE of Frank Lloyd Wright as an architect could well
serve as the point of departure for a discussion of what is
both right and what is wrong with Americans. I do not
say "with American judgment" or "American critical taste," for much more
is involved than that. Wright, like the land of which he was a product, was
full of promises, potential talents which by their very prodigality endan-
gered their possessor. Talents require discipline, and the greater the talents,
the greater the discipline required. What is talent? It is involvement. But
involvement is not enough. What is necessary for substantive achievement is
disciplined involvement, the devotion to the critical and systematic, the
skillful organization of one's potentialities. Essentially this means the
sharpening of one's wits on the whetstone of all the best that has been said,
written, and done in the field of one's major interest. Genius can afford to
take shortcuts. Frank Lloyd Wright not only considered himself to be a genius, but also imperiously demanded of others that they be in fealty bound
to his own valuation of himself—a valuation to which most Americans

Reprinted by permission of G. P. Putnam's Sons from *The American Way of Life* by
Ashley Montagu; © 1967 by Ashley Montagu.

readily acceded. Americans like their geniuses to be flamboyant, especially when they are homespun, as Frank Lloyd Wright was, the "Prairie Genius," a gross national product, if ever there was one.

But Frank Lloyd Wright was no genius. What was he then?

He was a huckster who had somehow blundered into architecture, a vainglorious man of overweening arrogance, effrontery, hardness, and insensitivity; a snake-oil salesman who talked convincingly of organic architecture but who, when it came to putting the talk into practice, committed the most atrocious blunders. I suppose the supreme early example of Wright's idea of organic form is the Tree House in a Chicago suburb. Here Wright built the house around the tree. I forget whether the tree stands in the hall or in the living room—it doesn't matter which. What does matter is that the house is a monument of ugliness and at the same time a monument to the gullibility of mankind and the impracticability of a plausible theory.

Nevertheless, Americans went on taking Wright at his own valuation for more than two generations. Was not Wright a genius, the greatest of American architects? Was he not always unconscionably late, and with never so much as an apology? Were not his houses the most talked about in America?

One of the most endearing qualities of Americans is their willingness to try almost everything. Those who could afford the luxury were willing to try the conjurations of Wright and pay for the experiment he called a house. The houses were not entirely wanting in magical qualities, but they were for the most part unlivable. The overhanging eaves shut out the light, making the bleak interiors even more dingy than they already were, a dinginess which was further emphasized by Wright's penchant for the darkest woods, with which the rooms were frequently paneled. As Henry Hope Reed, Jr., recently wrote, "Many of his houses, even in sunny Pasadena, are so dark that you need a miner's lamp to find your way about them. And, alas, the houses designed for 'the prairie' are always to be found in second-class suburbs where 'the far-reaching vistas' consist of views of the neighbors."

Wright built houses for cave dwellers, troglodytes, it would almost seem as a practical joke practiced by the High Priest of Ugliness and Contempt for Humanity.

Being a short man, Wright designed his rooms with very low ceilings. This barbarity was made to appear as a very great innovation. It was Wright "lowering the room on the American household." What in fact "the Isadora Duncan of American architecture" was actually doing was to play an egomaniacal joke on the American public. He would show them what organic architecture was, and if he were unable to add a cubit to his own stature, he would bring them down to his own dimensions. And so he produced elaborate versions of the cave and perpetrated what can be described only as the abysmal errors. "Organic architecture," forsooth!

The last of Wright's organic follies is among the worst of all his uglinesses, the Guggenheim Museum in New York. This has been appropriately dubbed a huge spiral of contempt for its contents. As anyone who has visited the museum knows, it is scarcely possible to hang a picture properly on its leaning walls, and what is worse, it is hardly possible to view a picture comfortably. It was Wright's final testament to his contempt for humanity.

The tragedy of Wright was that he was denied the discipline his fellow Americans might have given him through their criticism of his work, a criticism which might have prevented the development of that corrosive arrogance and self-blindness which made Frank Lloyd Wright the colossal failure he was.

STUDY QUESTIONS

1. If Montagu's thesis is stated in his first sentence, does his essay demonstrate the validity of that thesis?

2. How does Montagu define *talent?* What does he mean by *involvement?*

3. In what way is Wright a "flamboyant" personality?

4. Montagu's criticism of Wright is severe. Is this criticism aimed at Wright himself or at Wright's work? What evidence does Montagu provide for his judgment of the Tree House? What other evidence could he have provided?

5. Who does Montagu blame for Wright's "colossal failure" as an architect?

"... BENJAMIN WILL SURVIVE...." An Interview with Charles Webb, author of The Graduate

Charles Webb (1939–   ) was born in San Francisco, California, and grew up in Pasadena, where he now lives. He attended Williams College. *The Graduate,* his first novel, was published in 1964, but not until the film version was released in 1967, did the critical world turn its attention to Webb's book. He and his wife, Eve, have two sons. His second novel, *Love,*

Reprinted with permission of the authors.

Roger, was published in 1969 to high critical acclaim. This was followed by
Thoughts of a Young Stockbroker (1969).

F. A. Macklin (1937–   ) was born in Philadelphia. He received both
his B.A. (1960) and M.A. (1963) from Villanova University. An assistant
professor of English at the University of Dayton, he is also editor of *Film
Heritage* and film critic for the Dayton *Journal Herald.* His film criticism
has been published in *Nation, New Leader, Commonweal, America, Film
Quarterly, Film Comment,* and *College English.*

Interviewer: F. A. Macklin.

INTERVIEWER: J. D. Salinger is supposed to have refused to sell *The
Catcher in the Rye* to the movies because "Holden wouldn't like it."
How does Benjamin now feel about the sale of his story?

WEBB: I think Benjamin will survive the sweat-shirt ads, Peace
Corps ads, and the other side effects that the movie has had upon
him. As an individual, as originally conceived, his first concerns
were with his relationships to the people immediately around him.
This is not something that would change with accidental popular
success, or whatever else might befall him.

INTERVIEWER: One often hears the statement that Dustin Hoffman *is*
Benjamin. Does he fit with your view of the character?

WEBB: As the author, I don't feel that any single definition of the
character of Benjamin could possibly be definitive. The one ren-
dered by Dustin Hoffman was honestly and genuinely portrayed,
and these are the reasons it succeeded to the extent that it did.
This doesn't mean that someone else couldn't also have played the
part in a convincing and moving manner.

INTERVIEWER: Jacob Brackman, in a long piece in *The New Yorker,*
asked "Has Benjamin . . . checked out psychedelics, heavy sex, solitude, S.D.S., mysticism, and so on?" He says that many viewers assume Ben has. Has he?

WEBB: As far as the contemporary scene is concerned, which is
something, in the novel especially, with which Benjamin is not concerned, (psychedelics, etc., which you mentioned) this is something
in our environment which is constantly changing. There are other
things which don't change, such as relationships between parents
and children, males and females, and it was to these more classical
elements of fiction that I, as the author, addressed myself in writing the novel.

INTERVIEWER: Is Benjamin a product of Eisenhower America, Kennedy America, or revolution America?

WEBB: Benjamin is a product of America, as are Kennedy, Eisenhower.

INTERVIEWER: One of the major questions about the film is Ben's motivation. In one of the funniest scenes in the book Ben tells his father about having slept with whores. The scene suggests that Ben does have a vital sexual appetite. There is a sexual motivation that is dropped from the film. Pauline Kael once scoffed at *Fantastic Voyage's* being only through the upper part of a man's body. It seems to me that the quick shots of Mrs. Robinson's discombobulated breasts equal this for safe boldness. Were you satisfied with the film's handling of Ben's "affair" with Mrs. Robinson?

WEBB: Regardless of how bold Hollywood may be, compared to earlier days, there are certain aspects of human behavior, sexual and otherwise, which do not translate from literature into film. One of these is the quality of human relationships.

INTERVIEWER: What is the motivation for Ben and Elaine's relationship?

WEBB: The motivation of Ben's and Elaine's relationship was a combination of things, including love, physical attraction and a desire, subconscious, to upset things.

INTERVIEWER: Stanley Kauffmann, in *The New Republic,* accuses you of using a trite device in allowing Ben to find out about the wedding in a note on a door. It seems to me that the device though obvious is easily possible. Do you feel that the film improves upon this?

WEBB: Stanley Kauffmann would perhaps best be left alone.

INTERVIEWER: Did the film do anything that you felt was an improvement on the book?

WEBB: No.

INTERVIEWER: In a letter to *The New Republic* you accused the film of failing to take a moral stance. You seemed to base your argument on the fact that in the film Benjamin does not reach Elaine until *after* the marriage ceremony while in the book he does arrive in time to prevent it. Why is this change crucial, and how does it invalidate the story's morality as you conceived it?

WEBB: There is a range of values, which can be called either human or moral, which, although under some skirmishing attacks at this time, have endured from the beginning of recorded history and which assumedly will continue to do so. Formalized arrangements between individuals is one of these. Benjamin, in the book, although unconsciously, recognized this fact of human nature. In the film version he was ignorant of it, therefore less intelligent and less sympathetic (perhaps more mod, however).

INTERVIEWER: I know that a few viewers of the film have wept because of the annihilation of ritual when Benjamin invades the church, while the majority laugh with glee. What is your response to the two reactions?

WEBB: The reason Ben goes in after Elaine in a Church is because it is there he happens to find her. If he found her in a department store, he would go in after her there (at that juncture of the story). The particular building in which she is contained at that moment is not relevant to his purposes.

INTERVIEWER: Both Kauffmann and Hollis Alpert (*Saturday Review*) have accused you of equating morality with marriage licences. In your mind, is it the vows that are supreme?

WEBB: In my mind, the vows are irrelevant.

INTERVIEWER: Isn't annulment possible?

WEBB: I'm not sure I understand what the basic issue is here, as regarding the possibility of annulment, etc. There are larger issues, and perhaps these others could best be solved by qualified lawyers.

INTERVIEWER: Why doesn't the fact that Ben arrives before sexual consummation of the marriage compensate for the loss of the formalized arrangement?

WEBB: Sex is only peripherally connected to the moral issues. Therefore, Carl's, and Ben's, or anyone's, sexual relationship to Elaine is not of central importance.

INTERVIEWER: I agree that the ending of the film is vacillation as you stated in your letter to *NR,* or at best it's badly done ambiguity, but I am surprised to see that you seem to see Ben as heroic and effective. Is this the way you view him?

WEBB: In his own way, in the attainment, one way or another, of what he wants, I would say that Ben is both heroic and effective.

INTERVIEWER: You consider the book's conclusion to be optimistic rather than ironic?

WEBB: Yes.

INTERVIEWER: Why is Ben so noncommittal to Elaine's questioning "Benjamin?" Why does he merely answer a dull "What" to her appeal?

WEBB: He has a plan.

INTERVIEWER: Mike Nichols (the director) and you seem to differ decisively about the film's ending. He has said that at the end Ben and Elaine are destined to a future that is similar to their parents. Your ending seems much more affirmative.

WEBB: I think Mr. Nichols' comment that Ben and Elaine are destined to a future that is similar to their parents is not a well thought-out one.

INTERVIEWER: Nichols is unable to clarify his ending, if what he has said publicly is true—and it may not be. Most viewers (Kauffmann and Hollis Alpert, *SR,* included) see the ending as uplift. Many don't even realize the ceremony has taken place. Do you see the film's ending as uplift?

WEBB: The ending means that Benjamin has, in his own way, achieved one of his goals. In his own way, I would hope, this would indicate, he will now go on to achieve more of them.

INTERVIEWER: Can you give me some background on how the making of the film came about?

WEBB: The making of the film came about by the producer finding the book on a book-stand and buying its rights from me.

INTERVIEWER: What control, if any, did you have over the film?

WEBB: The amount of control I had over the end result is open to interpretation.

INTERVIEWER: Did you have any preferences for the director or actors?

WEBB: I was pleased with the choice of director and the choice of actors and actresses.

INTERVIEWER: If you had it to do all over again, would you?

WEBB: Yes.

INTERVIEWER: What are your plans? Do you have any film plans?

WEBB: Right now I am going ahead with the sale of a novelette, and of a novel I wrote last summer, to Hollywood. I have been somewhat fearful of going ahead with these things, but from *The Graduate* experience feel I know enough of the ropes by now not to be overwhelmed, coerced into writing screenplays, or in other ways having time drawn away from my writing.

INTERVIEWER: I have heard that you have a new novel *Loves Roger.*

WEBB: The title of the book is *Love, Roger,* and the book is due to be published by Houghton Mifflin in the Spring of 1969.

INTERVIEWER: If Mr. Nichols wanted to direct it and Mr. Turman to produce it what would be your reaction?

WEBB: I would encourage it.

INTERVIEWER: What's the novel about?

WEBB: The story is about a young travel agent who lives in Boston. He meets a girl who is up from the South looking for a job, and she, and a third girl, a nursing student from Wisconsin who gives up school and comes to Boston, make up the three characters of the book.

INTERVIEWER: What's the theme?

WEBB: The theme is more or less one of the main character being in a position in which it seems as though he should be choosing between the two girls. However, he doesn't seem to choose. Instead, they all go along and in the end move into a house in the suburbs.

INTERVIEWER: What about the leading character?

WEBB: He is a middle-class, non-revolutionary character, likable (I hope), who aspires to be happy and stable in his life. He is naive, but naive on purpose, because he sees its benefits.

INTERVIEWER: Would you prefer that your audience dismissed the film of *The Graduate,* responded to book and film as the same work, or tried to keep them separate?

WEBB: Try to keep them separate.

INTERVIEWER: *Film Heritage* has a feature in which it asks writers two questions about Hollywood and the artist. In summation, perhaps you can answer them. 1) Has Hollywood treated your work justly? 2) Can the serious writer's work survive in Hollywood?

WEBB: I'm not sure I know the answer. My own work was treated as justly, I think, by Hollywood, as it is possible for an author's work to be treated. However, there are losses, as well as gains, in translating a novel into a movie, so that I suppose the only way of judging it would be to add up all the losses, balance them against the gains, and see where things stood. In my case, I think they balance out fairly evenly, so that, in the end, I wouldn't feel any more justified in making a sweeping denunciation of the industry than I would in saying it is the salvation of authors.

STUDY QUESTIONS

1. What are the "more classical elements of fiction" to which Webb says he addressed himself in writing *The Graduate?*

2. Often, Webb seems to be side-stepping Macklin's questions. Is he? Why, then, are his answers phrased as they are?

3. Why does Webb feel that the film version of his novel failed to take a moral stance? Do you agree?

4. Webb says that Ben is both "heroic and effective." How would Webb define *heroic?* How is this related to Webb's agreeing that the film's ending is "uplift"?

5. Webb says that the hero of his second novel is "a middle-class, nonrevolutionary character." He also says that Ben and Elaine had a "subconscious" desire "to upset things." Does Webb imply, then, that Ben and Elaine are revolutionary characters?

Stanley Kauffmann

CUM LAUDE

Stanley Kauffmann (1916–   ) was born in New York City. He has been an actor, a director, the film critic for the *New Republic*, and drama critic for the New York *Times*. While on the *Times* staff, he and Broadway producer David Merrick engaged in their now-famous feud. Kauffmann is presently associate literary editor for the *New Republic*. He is the author of seven novels, more than 40 plays, most of them one-acters, and books of film criticism. His books include *Hidden Hero* (1949), *The Tightrope* (1952), *Man of the World* (1956), *If It Be Love* (1960), and *A World on Film* (1966). In 1964 he received a Ford Foundation Traveling Fellowship and was named an honorary fellow of Morse College, Yale University.

HAPPY NEWS. Mike Nichols' second film, *The Graduate,* proves that he is a genuine film director—one to be admired and concerned about. It also marks the screen debut, in the title role, of Dustin Hoffman, a young actor already known in the theatre as an exceptional talent, who here increases his reputation. Also, after many months of prattle about the "new" American film (mostly occasioned by the overrated *Bonnie and Clyde*), *The Graduate* gives some substance to the contention that American films are coming of age—of our age.

The screenplay, based on a novel by Charles Webb, was written by Calder Willingham and Buck Henry. The latter, like Nichols, is an experienced satiric performer. (Henry appears in this picture as a hotel clerk.) The dialogue is sharp, hip without rupturing itself in the effort, often moving, and frequently funny except for a few obtrusive gag lines. The story is about a young cop-out who—for well-dramatized reasons—cops at least partially in again.

Ben is a bright college graduate who returns to his wealthy parents' Hollywood home and flops—on his bed, on the rubber raft in the pool. Politely and dispassionately, he declines the options thrust at him by barbecue-pit society. The bored wife of his father's law partner seduces him. Ben is increasingly uncomfortable in the continuing affair, for moral reasons of an unpuritanical kind. (The bedroom scene in which Ben tries to get her to *talk* to him is a jewel.) The woman's daughter comes home from college, and against the mother's wishes, Ben takes her out. He falls in love with the girl —which is predictable but entirely credible. He is blackmailed into telling her about his affair with her mother and, in revulsion, the girl flees—back to Berkeley. Ben follows, hangs about the campus, almost gets her to marry him, loses her (through her father's interference), pursues her, and finally gets her. For once, a happy ending makes *us* feel happy.

To dispose at once of the tedious subject of frankness, I note that some of the language and bedroom details push that frontier (in American films) considerably ahead, but it is all so appropriate that it never has the slightest smack of daring, let alone opportunism. What is truly daring, and therefore refreshing, is the film's moral stance. Its acceptance of the fact that a young man might have an affair with a woman and still marry her daughter (a situation not exactly unheard of in America although not previously seen in American films) is part of the film's fundamental insistence: that life, today, in our world, is not worth living unless one can *prove* it day-by-day, by values that ring true day-by-day. Moral attitudes, far from relaxing, are getting stricter and stricter, and many of the shoddy moralistic acceptances that dictated mindless actions for decades are now being fiercely questioned. Ben is neither a laggard nor a lecher; he is, in the healthiest sense, a moralist— he wants to know the value of what he is doing. He does not rush into the affair with the mother out of any social rote of "scoring" any more than he avoids the daughter—because he has slept with her mother—out of any social rote of taboo. (In fact, although he is male and eventually succumbs, he sees the older woman's advances as a syndrome of a suspect society.) And the sexual dynamics of the story propels Ben past the sexual sphere; it forces him to assess and locate himself in *every* aspect.

Sheerly in terms of moral revolution, all this will seem pretty commonplace to readers of contemporary American fiction. But we are dealing here with an art form that, because of its inescapable broad-based appeal, follows well behind the front lines of moral exploration. In America it follows less closely than in some other countries, not because American audiences are necessarily less sophisticated than others (although they *are* less sophisticated than, say, Swedish audiences) but because the great expense of American production encourages a producer to cast the widest net possible. None of this is an apology for the film medium, it is a fact of the film's existence; one might as sensibly apologize for painting because it cannot be seen simultaneously by millions the way a film can. Thus the arrival of *The Graduate* can be viewed two ways. First, it is an index of moral change in a substantial segment of the American public, at least of an awakening of some doubts about past acceptances. Second, it is irrelevant that these changes are arriving in film a decade or two decades or a half century after the other arts, because their statement in film makes them intrinsically new and unique. If arts have textural differences and are not simply different envelopes for the same contents, then the *way* in which *The Graduate* affects us makes it quite a different work from the original novel (which I have not read) and from all the dozens of novels of moral disruption and exploration in recent years. Recently an Italian literary critic and teacher deplored to me the adulation of young people for films, saying that the "messages" they get from Bergman and Antonioni and Godard were stated by the novel and even the drama thirty or forty years ago. I tried (unsuccessfully) to point out that this is not really true: that if art as art has any validity at all, then the film's peculiar sensory avenues were giving those "old" insights a being they could not otherwise have.

This brings us to the central artist of this enterprise, Mike Nichols. In his first picture *Who's Afraid of Virginia Woolf?,* Nichols was shackled by a famous play and by the two powerhouse stars of our time; but considering these handicaps, he did a creditable job, particularly with his actors. In *The Graduate,* uninhibited by the need to reproduce a Broadway hit and with freedom to select his cast, he was moved fully into film. He is perceptive, imaginative, witty; he has a shrewd eye, both for beauty and for visual comment; he knows how to compose and to juxtapose; he has an innate sense of the manifold ways in which film can be better than *he* is and therefore how good he can be *through* it—including the powers of expansion and ellipsis.

From the very first moment, Nichols sets the key. We see Ben's face, large and absolutely alone. The camera pulls back, we see that he is in an airliner and a voice tells us that it is approaching Los Angeles; but Ben has been set for us as *alone*. We follow him through the air terminal, and he seems just as completely, even comfortably isolated in the crowd as he does later, in a scuba suit at the bottom of his family's swimming-pool, when he is huddling contentedly in an underwater corner while his twenty-first birthday party is being bulled along by his father up above.

Nichols understands sound. The device of overlapping is somewhat overused (beginning the dialogue of the next scene under the end of the present scene), but in general this effect adds to the dissolution of clock time, creating a more subjective time. Nichols' use of non-verbal sound (something like Antonioni's) does a good deal to fix subliminally the cultural locus. For instance, a jet plane swooshes overhead—unremarked—as the married woman first invites Ben into her house.

In *Virginia Woolf* I thought I saw some influence of Kurosawa; I think so again here, particularly in such sequences as Ben's welcome-home party where the camera keeps close to Ben, panning with him as he weaves through the crowd, moving to another face only when Ben encounters it, as if Ben's attention controlled the camera's. As with Kurosawa, the effect is balletic; it seeks out quintessential rhythms in commonplace actions.

On the negative side, I disliked Nichols' recurrent affection for the splatter of headlights and sunspots on his lens; and his hang-up with a slightly heavy Godardian irony through objects. (The camera holds on a third-rate painting of a clown after the mistress walks out of the shot. When the girl leaves Ben in front of the monkey cage at the San Francisco zoo, the camera, too luckily, catches the sign on the cage: Do Not Tease.) And a couple of times Nichols puts his camera in places that merely make us aware of his cleverness in putting it there: inside the scuba helmet, inside an empty hotel-room closet looking past the hangers.

But the influences I have cited (there are others) only show that Nichols is alive, hungry, properly ambitious; the defects only show that he is not yet entirely sure of himself. Together, these matters show him still feeling his way toward a whole style of his own. What is important is his extraordinary basic talent: humane, deft, exuberant. And I want to make much of his ability to direct actors, a factor generally overlooked in appraising film directors. (Some famous directors—Hitchcock, for example—can do nothing with actors. They get what the actor can supply on his own. Sometimes—again like Hitchcock—these directors are not even aware of bad performances.) He has helped Anne Bancroft to a quiet, strong portrayal of the mistress, bitter and pitiful. With acuteness he has cast Elizabeth Wilson, a sensitive comedienne, as Ben's mother. From the very pretty Katharine Ross, Ben's girl, Nichols' has got a performance of sweetness, dignity, and a compassion that is simply engulfing. Only William Daniels, as Ben's father, made me a bit uneasy. His WASP caricature (he did a younger version in *Two for the Road*) is already becoming a staple item.

In the leading role, Nichols had the sense and the courage to cast Dustin Hoffman, unknown (to the screen) and unhandsome. Hoffman's face in itself is a proof of change in American films; it is hard to imagine him in leading roles a decade ago. How unimportant, how *interesting* this quickly becomes, because Hoffman is one of the best actors of his generation, subtle, vital, and accurate. Certainly he is the best American film comedian since Jack Lemmon, and, as theatregoers know, he has a much wider range than Lemmon. (For instance, he was fine as a crabby, fortyish, 19th-century Russian clerk in Ronald Ribman's play *Journey of the Fifth Horse*.)

With tact and lovely understanding, Nichols and Hoffman and Miss Ross —all three—show us how this boy and girl fall into a new kind of love: a love based on recognition of identical loneliness on their side of a generational gap, a gap which—never mind how sillily it is often exploited in poli-

tics and pop culture—irrefutably exists. When her father is, understand-
ably, enraged at the news of his wife's affair with his prospective son-in-law
and hustles the girl off into another marriage, Ben's almost insane refusal to
let her go is his refusal to let go of the one reality he has found in a world that
otherwise exists behind a pane of glass. The cinema metaphors of the chase
after the girl—the endless driving, the jumping in and out of his sports car,
even his eventual running out of gas—have perhaps too much Keaton
about them; they make the film rise too close to the surface of mere physical-
ity; but at least the urgency never flags. At the wedding, when he finds it—
and of course it is in an ultra-modern church—there is a dubious hint of
crucifixion as Ben flings his outspread arms against the (literal) pane of
glass that separates him from life (the girl); but this is redeemed a minute
later when, with the girl, he grabs a large cross, swings it savagely to stave
off pursuers, then jams it through the handles of the front doors to lock the
crowd in behind them.

The pair jump on to a passing bus (she in her wedding dress still) and sit
in the back. The aged, uncomprehending passengers turn and stare at them.
(One last reminder!—of Lester's old-folks chorus in *The Knack*.) Ben and
his girl sit next to each other, breathing hard, not even laughing, just happy.
Nothing is solved—none of the things that bother Ben—by the fact of
their being together; but, for him, nothing would be worth solving without
her. We know that and she knows that, and all of us feel very, very good. The
chase and the last-minute rescue (just after the ceremony is finished) are
contrivances, but they are contrivances tending toward truth, not falsity,
which may be one definition of good art.

Paul Simon has written rock songs for the film, sung by Simon and Garfunkel, and as in many rock songs, these lyrics deal easily with such matters
as God, *Angst,* the "sound of silence," and social revision. But they *are* typical of the musical environment in which this boy and girl live.

Some elements of slickness and shininess in this wide-screen, color film
are disturbing. But despite them, despite the evident influences and defects,
the picture bears the imprint of a man, a whole man, warts and all: which is a
very different imprint from that of many of Nichols' highly praised, cagy,
compromised American contemporaries. *All* the talents involved in *The
Graduate* make it soar brightly above its shortcomings and, for reasons
given, make it a milestone in American film history. Milestones do not guarantee that everything after them will be better, still they are ineradicable.

Study Questions

1. According to Kauffmann, what is daring and refreshing about the "moral
    stance" of "The Graduate"? Why does he feel that the screen is necessarily "well

behind" American fiction in its exploration of contemporary morality? How does he dispose of such criticism of the film?

2. What does Kauffmann feel Ben and Elaine's love is based on? Does he conclude that Ben and Elaine solve their problems? How does he explain his acceptance of the film's contrived ending?

3. A critic has used the word *mania* in discussing Ben. Does Kauffmann use any word with similar connotations?

4. What minor deficiencies does Kauffmann find in "The Graduate"?

5. Why does Kauffmann feel that the musical score is appropriate?

Stephen Farber and Estelle Changas

THE GRADUATE

Stephen Farber (1943–   ) was born in Cleveland, Ohio. He received his B.A. from Amherst College, and M.A.'s in English and Theater Arts from, respectively, the University of California at Berkeley and UCLA. He is currently Los Angeles editor of *Film Quarterly*, and has contributed articles on the film to *Sight and Sound*, the *Hudson Review*, and *Film Quarterly*.

Estelle Changas (1939–   ) was born in Detroit, Michigan. She received a B.A. in English from UCLA in 1962, and later attended graduate school at the University of California at Berkeley. After teaching high school English for two years, she was accepted into the Graduate Division of the Motion Picture Department at UCLA, where she completed her M.A. Miss Changas has served as a consultant for "An Oral History of the Motion Picture in America," a project sponsored by the American Film Institute and the National Endowment for the Humanities.

©1968 by The Regents of the University of California. Reprinted from *Film Quarterly*, Vol. 21, No. 3, pp. 37–41, by permission of The Regents.

Director: Mike Nichols. Producer: Lawrence Turman. Screenplay by Calder Willingham & Buck Henry, from the novel by Charles Webb. Songs: Simon & Garfunkel. Photography: Robertsurtees. Embassy.

$\mathcal{M}$IKE NICHOLS'S name is so magical today that even if *The
Graduate* had been the worst movie of the year, people
would be buzzing reverently about it. As it is, *The Graduate* is only the most cleverly fashionable and confused movie of the year—
and the responses, from critics and customers alike, have been ecstatic. We
expected a lot—we're young, and so is Nichols; in addition to youth, he has
money, talent, intelligence, irreverence. And after lots of quickie exploitation films about teenyboppers and acidheads, *The Graduate* might have
been the first movie about today's youth to tell it like it is. But Nichols has
too much at stake to risk involving us. He's adored because he's hip and safe
at the same time; his audiences know that he won't go too far.

The Graduate opens promisingly enough. Ben, a successful young Eastern college graduate, is returning home to Los Angeles, and Nichols immediately and effectively conveys his isolation by focusing exclusively on
Dustin Hoffman's apprehensive face moving through the crowded LA air-
port. Nichols has said that he chose the thirty-year-old Hoffman (a talented
comedian—to get that out of the way) to play his callow young hero because he had a face that suggested suffering. Hoffman himself thought there
was something strange about the choice; he felt he wasn't suited to the part,
which he described as "a young, conventional, squarejawed *Time* Magazine
Man of the Year type." Hoffman was right of course. We soon learn that
Ben, for all of his credentials and in spite of his vulnerable face, is clean-cut
and stupid. He's supposed to be a champion college debater, but he can
hardly form a sentence. In the first scenes he's thrown into his rich parents'
cocktail and poolside parties; it's easy enough to caricature suburban phoni-
ness, and we see quickly—Nichols provides a slick, superficial summary of
anti-bourgeois satire of the last decade—everything that's wrong with LA
society. But what does Ben see? He gapes a lot, but he never looks more than
bewildered by what's going on. He certainly can't articulate any sort of protest. All he knows is that he wants his future to be "well . . . different. . . ." He really sweats to get that word out, but he doesn't seem capable of going further. When he's troubled, he stares into his bedroom aquarium.

Of course we're supposed to like Ben because he's victimized by all of
those nasty, aging country clubbers. In the face of their boozing and their
twaddle, he has a chunky innocence that is to endear him to us. Nothing is
going on in his head, but because he's "mixed up," as he says at one point,

and abused by his parents, audiences cluck over him and rush to give him credit for understanding anxieties that are actually beyond his grasp.

Nichols does use a few fine Simon and Garfunkel songs (written long before the film was conceived) to pump poetic and intellectual content into *The Graduate*. Because the songs, especially "The Sounds of Silence," are so concise, lyrical, eloquent, we're tempted to believe that the film contains their insights and that Ben understands them. We're supposed to assume that Ben shares Paul Simon's perceptions of "people talking without speaking, people hearing without listening" in a world whose "words of the prophet are written on the subway walls," but in truth Ben couldn't *begin* putting the world in that kind of order. He's only a beer-drinking *Time* magazine type, as Hoffman recognized, rather harmlessly stupid and awkward, but tricked up with a suffering face and an *Angst* ridden song intent on persuading us that he's an alienated generational hero. And audiences eager to believe that all young people are sensitive and alienated and that all old people are sell-outs or monsters gratefully permit Hoffman's mannerisms and Paul Simon's poetry to convince them of a depth in Ben that the part, as written, simply does not contain.

The film's best scenes are the early ones in which Ben is seduced by the wife of his father's partner (superbly played by Anne Bancroft—her performance is reason enough to see the film). Bancroft, a young man's deliciously provocative sexual fantasy come to life, makes us aware that there *is* something to be said for women over thirty. When she's on, Ben might just as well roll over and play dead. Bancroft is engagingly wicked as Mrs. Robinson; she is at once supremely confident of her sexual power and mercilessly casual in the face of Ben's adolescent fear of her. Alone with him in her house, she takes calm delight in exposing her legs, while he ejaculates moral misgivings. Her sophistication enables her to see through his repeated protests: "You *want* me to seduce you, is that what you're trying to tell me, Benjamin?" she chants in poker-faced style. And finally, having trapped him in her daughter's bedroom, she remains utterly cool, while her daring flirtatious assault, comically caught by rapid cuts from bare bosom to Ben's anguished face, leaves him helplessly gasping, "Jesus Christ, Mrs. Robinson!"

Unfortunately, this is about the only scene which allows us to see that Ben is sexually attracted to Mrs. Robinson. Most of the time Nichols insists that Mrs. Robinson is repulsive because she is sexual and Benjamin lovable because he is not. Sheer boredom, Ben confesses, is the only thing which brings him to her time after time. And later he explains that bedding down with Mrs. Robinson meant nothing; it was "just another thing that happened to me . . . just like shaking hands." Apparently we are to believe, as Stanley Kauffmann has written, that Ben "sees the older woman's advances as a syndrome of a suspect society," and that he deserves congratulations for his indifference; what seems an astonishing blindness to Mrs. Robinson's very real sexiness is to be taken as a moral victory.

Ben's voice of morality, though, is rather unpleasantly self-righteous: "Do you think I'm proud that I spend my time with a broken-down alcoholic?" The scene in which he tries to liven up their evenings by getting Mrs. Robinson to *talk* to him has been much praised, and it *is* an interesting scene, though not for the reasons given, but because it presents Mrs. Robinson with more complexity than usual. When, in the middle of their abortive conversation, she orders Ben not to take out her daughter, the only reason he can guess for the command is that she thinks he isn't good enough for Elaine, and he announces angrily that he considers this liaison "sick and perverted." Bancroft's face, marvelously expressive of deeply rooted social and personal discontents, makes clear to us that this is *not* Mrs. Robinson's reason, that her reasons are much more intense and tortured than Ben suspects—mostly, presumably, an envy of youth and a fear of being cast off for her daughter—and deserve his sympathy, not his moralistic outrage. Ben is too insensitive to see that when she seems to acknowledge that she thinks her daughter too good for him, it's only out of desperation and confusion; she has feelings more intricate and disturbed than she knows how to explain to him. His rejection of her at this moment may look moral, but given the depth and the anguish of her emotional experience, it's a pretty ugly, unfeeling response. Mrs. Robinson's answer to Ben's plea that she talk to him—"I don't think we have much to say to each other"—proves to be quite accurate, but it doesn't expose her shallowness, as Nichols seems to have intended, it exposes *Ben's*. She has so much more self-awareness than he, and so many more real problems, why *should* she talk to him? Anne Bancroft is really too interesting for Nichols' sentimentalities about the generational gap, so he treats her characterization with no respect; after this scene, he turns her into a hideous witch, an evil Furie maniacally insistent on keeping Ben and her daughter apart. This goes along with the current urge to see the generational conflict as a coloring-book morality play—the young in white, the old in black—but it's a cheap dramatic trick.

What really wins the young audience to Ben is his compulsive pursuit of Mrs. Robinson's daughter Elaine in the second half of the film. His single-minded dedication to securing the girl he pines after may be the oldest staple of movie romance, but it is also manna to today's Love Generation. Elaine, though, is a problem. She's gorgeous, all right, she's earnest, and she smiles nicely, but what Ben sees in her beyond her lovely face is kept a secret from us. She does seem to be as clean-cut and stupid as he is. But since she wears her hair long and uncombed and goes to Berkeley (another put-on, much like Hoffman's suffering face), we're to assume that she's an extraordinary catch. Doesn't the fact that she dates and almost marries a smooth, starched medical student confirm the opposite? Ben, incidentally, doesn't even admit her physical attractiveness; his excuse for wanting her so desperately is that at last he has found someone he can talk to. What two such uninteresting people could talk about is a real stumper; and Nichols must have thought so too, for he bars us from one of their few conversations, placing them behind the windshield of Ben's convertible. Perhaps if Nichols were a more experienced film director, he could have convinced us of the vitality of Ben's and Elaine's love with some pungent, seductive visuals; but he relies only on modish out-of-focus shots of flowers and foliage (shots that looked a lot prettier in *Two for the Road* anyway).

All that does express their love is an old-fashioned Hollywood Kiss. On their first date, after treating her quite wretchedly, Ben tries to get her to stop crying and kisses her. And that does it. She forgets her humiliation and smiles. It's love at first sight, just like in the movies, but because the actors look casual and sensitive and alienated, audiences think their instant jello of a romance is "real." A little later Elaine learns of Ben's affair with her mother and flees back to Berkeley; he follows her there, and she comes to his room at night to ask why. But first she asks him to kiss her once more, and when he does, she's satisfied; her doubts are erased, and she's ready to marry him. It's all very reminiscent of Betty Grable cheerleader movies. And it's interesting that there seems to be no real sexual attraction between Ben and Elaine. Even their two or three kisses are awfully restrained. After receiving her second kiss, which looks about as exciting as a late-night cup of hot chocolate, Elaine darts quickly out of Ben's door. The movie is rather offensively prudish in splitting sex and love, implying that sexual relationships are sick and perverted, but that in a healthful Young Love relationship— why, sex is the furthest thing from the kids' minds. In this respect the film fits nicely with the flower talk about love, which for all of the bubbles and incense and the boast of promiscuity, is equally insipid, passionless, ultimately quite as sexless.

How bizarre it is that the vacuous Elaine, who has been so easily conned into marrying the fraternity's ace make-out king, can cause such a cataclysmic change in Ben. He throws off his lethargy, chases after her and breaks up her wedding at the last minute, bellowing an anguished "Elaine" as he beats against the glass that separates him from the congregation. A minute later, when Ben punches Elaine's father in the stomach, when he beats off the suburbanites with a giant cross and locks the door with it, the audience cheers vigorously—and to give Nichols his due, it's a pleasing, outrageous image. But it's much too glib to turn Ben suddenly into a rebel hero—this same Ben who's spent most of the film staring blankly into his aquarium and lounging by his pool, transformed by a kiss from a sweet little coed into a fighter for his generation. The motivation may be phony, but we can all laugh at how the old folks get theirs in the end.

The Graduate, like Nichols' film of *Virginia Woolf,* has been applauded for its boldness—never before in an American movie, it is said, could a hero have slept with a woman and married her daughter. The premise *is* arresting, but it's interesting how Nichols blunts it, makes it as easy as possible for his audiences to accept the outrageous. By minimizing Ben's participation in the affair with Mrs. Robinson, by suggesting that it's boring and unpleasant to him, and then by leaving sex out of the relationship with Elaine altogether, the film scampers away from a situation that would be truly challenging and compelling—a young man with strong sexual desire for mother and daughter. Ben doesn't have any sexual desires, apparently, and his unwilling involvement in the affair with Mrs. Robinson lets us off too comfortably. And at a time of much irrelevant nudity and bedroom talk in movies, this is one film that's entirely too fastidious; the absence of sex in *The Graduate* is a real failure (as it was in *The Family Way*) because the film is, to a large extent, *about* sexuality. But the urgency of Ben's triangular predicament is lost because we don't know much about what goes on in the bedroom, or even in Ben's fantasies. The incestuous longings that lie beneath the surface of the relationships are too uneasily sketched to carry much force. Any development of the oedipal rivalry between mother and daughter is also skimped. This hostility must be behind Mrs. Robinson's command that Ben not see Elaine, and if Elaine is human, she would have certain feelings of jealousy toward her mother. By making her outrage at Ben's affair *purely moral,* by ignoring its psychological content, the film misses an opportunity to explore its potentially explosive situation with depth and humanity—just as it cheated earlier by defining Ben's response to Mrs. Robinson in purely moral terms. Nichols titillates us with an intrigue that we haven't seen before in a movie, but he never gets close to feelings that would upset us. He knows how to startle, but he also knows how to please.

The movie as a whole is a Youth-grooving movie for old people. Nichols' young people have senile virtues—they're clean, innocent, upright, and cute too. Tired rich audiences can relax and say, "So *that's* what this youthful rebellion is all about; the kids want just what you and I want, Daddy—a happy marriage, a nice home, and they're really so well-behaved." Nichols doesn't risk showing young people who are doing truly daring, irreverent things, or even young people intelligent enough to seriously challenge the way old people live. All that ennobles Ben, after four years of college, is his virginity. He and Elaine are very bland, and that suits the old folks just fine; bankers and dowagers know that it's "in" to celebrate the young, and in *The Graduate* they can join the celebration with a minimum of fret or identification. The film is actually an insult to the young who aren't so goody-goody —young people who have complicated conflicts of loyalty and affection and who aren't able to make such a decisive moral rejection before they marry the most beautiful sweetheart of Sigma Chi.

Yet young people are falling for the film along with the old people, because it satisfies their most infantile fantasies of alienation and purity in a hostile world, their most simplistic notions of the generational gap, and their mushiest daydreams about the saving power of love. The movie swings on their side, though from a safe, rather patronizing position, and bleats that even when the middle-aged degenerates are cruelest, all you need is a closed-mouth kiss.

As for Nichols' film sense, he does seem to be learning. He still holds shots much too long or dresses them up much too self-consciously—as in the scuba-diving episode, a good idea ruined by clumsy direction. His images are mostly clichéd—not just blurs of flowers and sun-rippled water and car headlights reflecting on his lens, but even monkeys in the San Francisco zoo. He's good when you feel he's enjoying an unpretentiously silly, charming comic touch for its own sake, and he shows a nice eye for good natured satiric detail (he's hardly a caustic talent)—Mrs. Robinson watching *The Newlywed Game* on TV, a daffy, myopic lady organist at Elaine's wedding. And perhaps it's not fair to give the impression that the film fails because of expediency and calculated compromise; it may be that Nichols actually did not know what he was doing. He has stated recently, in an interview, that Ben and Elaine are not to be envied at film's conclusion, and that Ben will end up exactly like his parents—which suggests attempts at a more harshly sardonic point of view than the film manages to convey. Why do people cheer so exuberantly and walk out so happily if the film means to criticize Ben? Have they all missed the point? Whatever Nichols' intentions, *The Graduate* never really seems to be attacking the young people; all that can be said is that it celebrates them with a strange lack of conviction, which may once have been meant as savage irony, but comes across only as particularly hollow and ineffective film-making. Along with his handling of actors, Nichols' only real success in the movie is with the same sort of light-hearted, inconsequential farce routines he's provided for Neil Simon's comedies on Broadway; there's no point in encouraging him to believe that he's the seriocomic prophet of the plastic generation. Maybe Nichols does have the talent to do something more important—so far he has the energy and the ambition—but we're not going to find out as long as an evasive gimmicky hoax like *The Graduate* is trumpeted as a milestone in American film history.

STUDY QUESTIONS

1. Why do Farber and Changas call Benjamin *shallow?* What scene forces them to conclude that Mrs. Robinson is a more sensitive human being than Ben is?

2. Why do they feel it significant that Nichols has not allowed the movie-goer to hear the conversation in Ben's convertible?

3. Farber and Changas feel that the Benjamin–Mrs. Robinson–Elaine triangle is a "truly challenging and compelling" situation but that Nichols fails to grapple with it. How and why has he failed?

4. In their last sentence, the reviewers call "The Graduate" "an evasive gimmicky hoax." Why *evasive? Gimmicky? Hoax?*

5. Why do Farber and Changas feel that the musical score is inappropriate?

Charles Webb

LETTER TO STANLEY KAUFFMANN*

December 26, 1967

Dear Mr. Kauffmann,

In the event that you should read my novel, *The Graduate,* I would appreciate hearing your views of it.

Sincerely,
Charles Webb

* After Stanley Kauffmann's first review of "The Graduate" appeared in the *New Republic,* Webb wrote him this letter. Although the letter was not printed, Kauffmann's second review indirectly acknowledges it. The letter appears here with Webb's permission.

Stanley Kauffmann

SECOND LOOK

⅁OESN'T the film split in half? This is the recurrent question in a number of letters about *The Graduate*—although almost all correspondents start by saying they enjoyed it! I have now seen it again and have read the novel by Charles Webb on which it is based, and some further comment seems in order.

I like what I liked in the film even more, but now, having read the original, I can see a paradox about its shortcomings. (Many of which were noted in my review.) Besides the fact that a great deal of Webb's good dialogue is used in the screenplay, the structure of the first two-thirds of his book—until Benjamin goes to Berkeley—is more or less the structure of the film. The longest scene in the picture—the one in which Benjamin tries to get his mistress to talk to him—is taken almost intact from the book. But Mike Nichols and his screenwriters rightly sensed that the last third of the book bogged down in a series of discussions, that Webb's device for Benjamin's finding the place of Elaine's wedding was not only mechanical but visually sterile, and that in general this last third had to be both compressed and heightened. In reaction to the novel's weaknesses, they devised a conclusion that has weaknesses of its own. But there is a vast difference between weakness and compromise.

Benjamin does *not* change, in my view, from the hero of a serious comedy about a frustrated youth to the hero of a glossy romance; he changes *as Benjamin*. It is the difference between the women in his life that changes him. Being the person he is, he could not have been assured with Mrs. Robinson any more than he could have been ridiculous and uncommanding with Elaine. We can actually see the change happen—the scene with Elaine at the hamburger joint where he puts up the top of the car, closes the windows, and talks. *Talks*—for the first time in the film. Those who insist that Mrs. Robinson's Benjamin should be the same as Elaine's Benjamin are denying the effect of love—particularly its effect on Benjamin, to whom it is not only joy but escape from the nullity of his affair and the impending nullity of himself.

There is even a cinematic hint early in the picture of the change that is to come. Our first glimpse of Mrs. Robinson's nudity is a reflection in the glass covering her daughter's portrait.

In character and in moral focus the film does not split, but there is a fundamental weakness in the novel which the film tries, not quite successfully, to escape. The pivot of action shifts, after the story goes to Berkeley, from Benjamin to Elaine. From then on, he knows what he wants; it is she who has to work through an internal crisis. It was Nichols' job to dramatize this crisis without abandoning his protagonist, to show the girl adjusting to the shocking fact of Benjamin's affair with her mother, and to show it with, so to speak, only a series of visits by her to the picture. To make it worse, the environment—of the conventional campus romantic comedy—works against the seriousness of the material. The library, the quad, the college corridor have to be *overcome,* in a sense. Nichols never lets up his pressure on what he feels the film is about, but the obliqueness of the action and the associative drawbacks of the locale never quite cease to be difficulties. And, as I noted, the final chase—though well done—does get thin.

But I think that, with some viewers, Nichols also suffers from his virtues. He has played to his strength, which is comedy; for, with all its touching moments and its essential seriousness, this is a very funny picture. A comedy about a young man and his father's partner's wife immediately seems adventurous; a comedy about a young man and a girl automatically gets shoved into a pigeonhole. This latter derogation seems to me unjust. We have only to remember (and to me it is unforgettable) that what is separating these young lovers is not a broken date or a trivial quarrel but a deep taboo in our society. For me, the end proof of the picture's genuine depth is the climax in the church, with Dustin Hoffman (even more moving the second time I saw him) screaming the girl's name from behind the glass wall. A light romance? That is a naked, last cry to the girl to free herself of the meaningless taboo, to join him in trying to find some possible new truth.

Yes, there are weaknesses. Yes, there are some really egregious gags. ("Are you looking for an affair?" the hotel clerk asks the confused Benjamin in the lobby.) But in cinematic skill, in intent, in sheer connection with us, *The Graduate* is, if I may repeat it, a milestone in American film history.

STUDY QUESTIONS

1.   In his second look at "The Graduate," Kauffmann focuses his attention on the second half of the film. What change occurs in Benjamin as a result of his discarding Mrs. Robinson for Elaine?

2. Why does Kauffmann feel that the conversation in the convertible is very important? How does his interpretation of this scene differ from that of Farber and Changas?

3. While Kauffmann admits that the film has some very funny moments, he is reluctant to label it as comedy. Where does he find "proof of the film's genuine depth"?

4. Does he, on second look, find new weaknesses in the film?

Charles Webb and Stanley Kauffmann

CORRESPONDENCE: "THE GRADUATE"

Sirs:

As the author of the novel, *The Graduate,* it has been extremely rewarding and gratifying to me to have had a film made of the book, and have the film so well received. Up till now I've made no criticisms of the film, either public or private. I would like to make one now, however, partially in response to the film itself and partially in response to two reviews of the film which Stanley Kauffmann wrote for *The New Republic.*

In a December 23 review he emphasizes the film's "moral stance." After considering the matter with care, I would have to say that my one greatest objection to the film is that it fails to take a moral stance.

In a February 10 review of the film, Mr. Kauffmann makes the point that the ending is proof of the picture's genuine depth. However, it is in the ending that the moral vacillation on the part of the film makers is, to me, most obvious. In the book the hero arrives at the church in time to rescue the girl before she's married. In the movie the hero arrives at the church after the vows have been spoken and drags her off anyway.

Benjamin Braddock, the hero, is a highly moral person as he is portrayed in the book. In the early portions he evinces a cynicism and defeatism which are clearly a reflection of the society he finds himself in. In the second half of the book he overcomes these feelings of self-defeat, or at least begins to. As a moral person he does not disrespect the institution of marriage. In the book the strength of the climax is that his moral attitudes make it necessary for him to reach the girl before she becomes the wife of somebody else, which he does. In the film version it makes no difference whether he gets there in time or not. As such, there is little difference between his relationship to Mrs. Robinson and his relationship to Elaine, both of them being essentially immoral.

> Charles Webb
> So. Pasadena, Calif.

In reply . . .
My first reaction to this letter was that it was written by Elaine May. But it comes from the same address, with the same signature, as an earlier letter from Mr. Webb after my first review, asking me to read his novel. I did so, and that was part of the reason for my second review.

Some authors are desecrated by film adaptation; some are lucky and don't always know it. In my second article I said that I thought Mike Nichols and his writers had sensed the novel's weaknesses and had tried to compensate for them. One such weakness was Mr. Webb's device by which Benjamin learns the place of Elaine's wedding, enabling him to get there in time to stop the ceremony. Nichols evidently felt the device was pat, the timing much too opportune, and the avoidance of difficulty (for the lovers) inconsistent with such moral confrontation as the film attempts. Nichols' solution is imperfect, but at least it avoids the destructive cliché of having Benjamin get there Just in Time. Equally important, Benjamin's desperation and Elaine's compassion are both heightened by the fact that the ceremony is over. And it is their feelings—not the question of the ceremony as such— that I said give that last scene its depth.

I still don't understand how the author of this novel, even though possibly upset at having been brushed off in all the furor about the film, can equate morality with marriage-licenses so absolutely. "There is little difference between his relationship to Mrs. Robinson and his relationship to Elaine, both of them being essentially immoral." . . . No, really, *is* it Elaine May?

> Stanley Kauffmann

STUDY QUESTIONS

1. According to Webb, how does Benjamin change in the second half of the novel?

2. What is Benjamin's attitude towards the institution of marriage?

3. Why does Webb think that, in the film version of his novel, Elaine is "essentially immoral"?

4. Why does Kauffmann insist that the marriage ceremony, as such, is irrelevant?

5. Is he just in his accusation that Webb equates morality with marriage-licenses?

Marya Mannes

THE CONQUEST OF TRIGGER MORTIS

Marya Mannes (1904–   ) was born in New York City. She holds an honorary L.H.D. from Hood College, Maryland. From 1942 to 1945 she was an intelligence analyst for the United States government. Her television appearances, university lecture tours, and numerous periodical articles have made her a familiar figure to the American public. She has published *Message from a Stranger*, a novel (1948), *More in Anger* (1958), *Subverse*, satiric verse (1959), *The New York I Know* (1961), *But Will It Sell?* (1964), and *They*, a novel (1968).

THE RULING was passed in 1970, over the total opposition of the TV and radio networks and after ten years of controversy, six investigations, 483 juvenile murders, and the complete reorganization of the Federal Communications Commission. What finally pushed it through was the discovery of *trigger mortis* in a number of American children born in widely separated areas. In this malformation the index finger is permanently hooked, forcing partial contraction of the whole hand in the position required for grasping a revolver. "The gun," said a distinguished anthropologist, "has become an extension of the American arm."

This mutation had been suspected some time before by others, who had found it worthy of note that in 1959, for instance, American toy manufacturers had sold more than $60 million worth of guns and revolvers and that on any given day on television between one and ten o'clock there were more than fifteen programs devoted to violence, and that in each of these programs a gun was fired at least once and usually several times. The only difference between the programs was that in some the shooting was done out of doors and often from horses and that in others it was done in hotel rooms, bars, or apartments. The first category was called Western and was considered a wholesome fight between good men and bad men in healthy country; the second was called Crime and Detective and was considered salubrious in its repeated implication that "crime does not pay," although the women and the interiors shown were usually expensive and the criminal's life, though short, a rich one.

Although this wholesale preoccupation with killing by gun coincided for many years with the highest rate of juvenile crime ever known in this country, and with open access to firearms for all who desired them, television and radio violence was considered by most experts of minimal importance as a contributory cause of youthful killing. Psychiatrists, social workers, program directors, advertisers, and sponsors had a handy set of arguments to prove their point. These (with translation appended) were the most popular:

Delinquency is a complex problem. No single factor is responsible. (Don't let's stick our necks out. Don't let's act. Don't let's lose money.)

It's all a matter of the home. (Blame the parents. Blame the neighborhood. Blame poverty.)

Crime and adventure programs are a necessary outlet for natural childhood aggressions. (Keep the little bastards quiet while Mummy fixes supper.)

We don't really know what influences children. (Let's wait till they kill somebody.)

Only disturbed or abnormal children are affected by what they see on programs. (And they are a minority. Let their psychiatrists worry about them.)

Everybody was very pleased with these conclusions, particularly the broadcasters, who could continue presenting thirty shootings a day secure in those sections of their old printed Code, which stated: ". . . such subjects as violence and sex shall be presented without undue emphasis and only as required by plot development or character delineation"; and "Television shall exercise care in . . . avoiding material which is excessively violent or would create morbid suspense, or other undesirable reactions in children." These same officials continued also to exercise care in not letting their own children look at the programs of violence which they broadcast.

So for years, and in spite of sporadic cries of alarm and protest from parents and a number of plain citizens, there were always enough experts to assure the public that crime and violence had nothing to do with crime and violence, and that gunplay was entertainment. Psychiatrists continued to say things like this about young killers: "The hostility, festering perhaps from the time he had been trained to the toilet, screamed for release," and educational groups came out periodically with reports on delinquency in which a suggested solution would be "to orient norm-violating individuals in the population towards a law-abiding lower-class way of life."

Dialogues like the following were frequent in Congressional investigations. This one occurred in a hearing of the Senate sub-committee on Juvenile Delinquency in 1954:

SENATOR: "In your opinion, what is the effect of these Western movies on children?"
EXPERT: "No one knows anything about it."
SENATOR: "Well, of course, you know that little children 6, 7, 8 years old now have belts with guns. Do you think that is due to the fact that they are seeing these Western movies and seeing all this shooting?"
EXPERT: "Oh, undoubtedly."

In the early 1950s, psychiatrist Fredric Wertham, from whose *The Circle of Guilt* the above was quoted, began a relentless campaign against what he called, in another book, *The Seduction of the Innocent*. Concentrating at first on horror and crime comics, the doctor moved inevitably into other fields of mass communication and provided impressive evidence along the way that although their gigantic dosage of violence could not be the sole factor in child criminality, it could certainly be considered a major one.

In attacking the slogan "It's all up to the home," he wrote: "Of course the home has a lot to do with it. But it is wrong to accuse the home as a cause in the usual abstract way, for the home is inseparable from other social circumstances to which it is itself vulnerable. . . . A hundred years ago the home could guard the children's safety; but with the new technological advances, the modern parent cannot possibly carry this responsibility. We need traffic regulations, school buses, school zones, and police to protect children from irresponsible drivers. Who will guard the child today from irresponsible adults who sell him incentives, blueprints, and weapons for delinquency?"

Wertham also countered the familiar claim that youthful violence was a result of wars by stating that it was not backed up by any scientific, concrete study and that neither the Second World War nor the Korean War explained the phenomenon: ". . . after the First World War the type of brutal violence currently committed on a large scale by the youngest children was almost unknown."

But Wertham was dismissed by many of his colleagues and much of the public as a man obsessed; too aggressively and intemperately committed to one cause—the rape of children's minds by mass communications—to be seriously considered. And the broadcasters and crime-comic publishers, first needled and exasperated by him, soon were able to view him with calm detachment as a crackpot. Thirty murders a day continued on the screen.

Then, early in 1959, the Nuffield Foundation in England put out a thick book called *Television and the Child,* by Hilde T. Himmelweit, A. N. Oppenheim, and Pamela Vince. For four years they examined thousands of children in five cities and of every class and background, and to this they joined a survey of American programming and viewing. They did not confine themselves to programming specifically for children, since it had long been obvious in England, as it was here, that children usually watched adult programs in preference. In more than four hundred pages of meticulous research, scientific detachment, and careful reasoning, they came to certain conclusions—the basis for a weight of further evidence that led, ten years later, to government intervention into broadcasting practices. Here are a few of their findings about the twenty percent of programs seen by children in their peak viewing hours that are devoted to aggression and violence:

"At the center of preoccupation with violence is the gun. Everyone has a gun ready for immediate use—even the barbers and storekeepers, who are not cowboys. People in Westerns take guns for granted. . . . Finally, while guns are used mostly for killing, they are also let off for fun. Nevertheless, guns spell power, they make people listen, and force them to do what is wanted.

"It is said that these programmes have two main desirable effects: they teach the lesson that crime does not pay; and they provide a harmless outlet through fantasy for the child's hostile feelings. We shall take issue with both statements. . . . The lesson as taught in these programmes is entirely negative (it is best not to offend against the law). . . . To present such a one-sided view, repeated week after week, is contrary to the recognized educational principle that a moral lesson, to be effective, must teach what should be done as well as what should not be done.

"More serious is the fact that . . . the child may equally well learn other, less desirable lessons from these programmes; that to shoot, bully, and cheat is allowed, provided one is on the right side of the law; and that relationships among people are built not on loyalty and affection but on fear and domination. . . ."

As for being a "harmless outlet for aggressive feelings," the authors— quoting the testimony of Dr. Eleanor E. Maccoby of Harvard that this discharge in fantasy alters nothing in the child's real life and so has no lasting values—write that when aggressive feelings exist, "They are not as a rule discharged on viewing crime and violence." "We cite three sets of data . . . [which] show that aggressive feelings are just as likely to be aroused as to be lessened through viewing these programmes—indeed, this seems more often to be the case." And, quoting Dr. Maccoby again, ". . . the very children who are presumably using the movie as an outlet for their aggressive feelings are the ones who carry away the aggressive content in their memories, for how long we do not know."

Miss Himmelweit and her colleagues sum up as follows: "It is suggested that crime and violence programmes increase tension and anxiety, increase maladjustment and delinquent behaviour, teach children techniques of crime, blunt their sensitivity to suffering and, related to this, suggest to them that conflict is best solved by aggression.

"Our findings and those of Maccoby suggest, then, that these programmes do not initiate aggressive, maladjusted, or delinquent behaviour, but may aid its expression. They may not affect a stable child, but they may evoke a response in the 5–10 percent of all children who are disturbed or at least emotionally labile, 'a group to be reckoned with by all the responsible people in the field of mass communications.' "

"We find . . . ," says the Nuffield Report, closing this chapter, "evidence that [these programs] may retard children's awareness of the serious consequences of violence in real life and may teach a greater acceptance of aggression as the normal, manly solution of conflict. . . . Just as a nation improves public hygiene when the evidence *suggests, without necessarily proving it* [my italics], that harm may otherwise result, so, we think there is need of remedial action here."

The Nuffield Report authors had obviously fallen into the error of blaming the industry instead of the child. For in most "acceptable" studies of television and its influence, wrote Wertham, "the assumption seems to be that when anything goes wrong the child must be morbid but the entertainment normal. Why not assume . . . that our children are normal, that they like adventure and imagination, that they can be stimulated to excitement, but that maybe something is wrong with what they are looking at? Why assume that they need death and destruction . . . ?"

Voices, voices, voices. "Beefs," "squawks," the broadcasters called these surges of protest year after year. And they would point with pride to the one children's program out of ten that was educational, the one out of twenty that had no shooting.

But their biggest defense became, in the end, their undoing. They had assured themselves that by removing the physical effects of violence, the violence was stripped of its harm. They showed no blood, no close-ups of agony, no open wounds, no last convulsions of a riddled body. Men were shot, they clapped their hands to their stomachs and either fell forwards or backwards as the camera panned away and returned to the gun. And while the broadcasters felt this a noble concession to the sensibilities of young viewers ("Brutality or physical agony," says the NBC Code, "is not presented in detail nor indicated by offensive sound or visual effects"), they were in actuality presenting, day after day, two great immoralities: that shooting is clean—and easy. To pull a trigger requires neither strength nor skill nor courage: it is the bullet that kills. And to kill with a gun is quick and painless. Hero or criminal, both were cowards who answered questions by pulling triggers. This was the daily lesson for sixty million children for twenty years.

Until, of course, the people finally rose. Some cool legal heads first managed to draft legislation banning the sale of pornographic and sensational printed material without in any way curbing individual liberty or preventing the sale of *Lady Chatterley's Lover* or Aristophanes. And then came the famous FCC ruling Bylaw A 41-632. In effect, this gave the FCC, by then reorganized into a body of able and dedicated communications experts who functioned in areas of human values as well as in electronics, the power to revoke the license of any broadcaster showing fictionalized killing, whether by gun or knife or bludgeon, without also displaying the natural consequences to the person killed. The bill as originally drawn was a forthright ban on all fictionalized killing except by direct bodily means, without weapons: killing had to involve strength, skill, and direct physical involvement. But after long wrangling, the later version was adopted as being less tainted by censorship and more practicable. For if a program showing a killing had to show a head blown to bits at close range, or blood gushing from mouth and nose, or a jagged stomach wound—all natural results of shooting—the sponsor would not sell many goods. It was therefore far easier to cut out guns entirely.

Far easier, that is, for everyone but the writers. After the law was put into effect, there was mass unemployment among the television writers in Hollywood and New York. They had relied so long on their collaborator, the gun, that they were incapable of writing a plot without it. As Wertham quoted an experienced TV crime writer: "You have to work backwards. You're given a violent situation and you have to work within that framework." Start with the murder and then fit in the people. And suddenly the poor writers had to think up situations where people and ideas provided the excitement instead of a Colt 45. It was a period of anguish none of them will forget.

But for every ten writers who became alcoholics or joined insurance firms, one began to tap resources he had never used and to write well and truly for the first time. And after a hiatus of incredible sterility, when frantic producers threw in anything innocuous, however old and poor, to fill up the time formerly used by crime plays and Westerns, television slowly began to get better and better, more inventive both in the uses of realism and fantasy.

A new generation of American children grew up with no appetite for guns and no illusions about the fun of painless killing. Instead they learned judo or, through compulsory strenuous exercises then conducted daily by their schools, became a race of confident acrobats, able to show their prowess in feats of skill, daring, and endurance without knifing, stomping, or shooting anyone.

Disarmament—at least of the young—was finally a fact.

STUDY QUESTIONS

1. Define *trigger mortis*. What is *rigor mortis?*

2. What arguments were used to counteract the charge that television had contributed to the rising juvenile crime rate? How effective are Miss Mannes' parenthetical remarks in answering these arguments?

3. Why was Frederic Wertham's campaign dismissed by his colleagues and the public?

4. In self-defense, what modifications did the networks make?

5. In general, what is the tone of Miss Mannes' essay? Is it sarcastic? Satirical? Is the essay humorous?

Russell Lynes

WHAT REVOLUTION IN MEN'S CLOTHES?

Russell Lynes (1910–   ) was born in Barrington, Massachusetts. He received a B.A. from Yale University in 1932 and holds an honorary A.F.D. from Union College, Schenectady, New York. Lynes is an associate fellow of Berkeley College, Yale University, and has been one of *Harper's* contributing editors since 1967. His books include *Highbrow, Lowbrow, Middlebrow* (1949), *Snobs* (1950), *Guests* (1951), *Tastemakers* (1954), *A Surfeit of Honey* (1957), *Cadwallader* (1959), *The Domesticated Americans* (1963), and *Confessions of a Dilettante* (1966).

ONE CAN HARDLY pick up a magazine or a newspaper without seeing a reference to the revolution in men's clothes.
I have been collecting material for several years on this
so-called revolution, and the more I collect, the less like a revolution it
seems to be. What I read is scarcely reinforced by what I see on the streets or
among my contemporaries and my children's contemporaries or in men's
shops. There seems to be a moderate shift in the nature of the way men
dress, most men, that is, and the rate of change seems about the standard
rate that has prevailed since the beginning of the Industrial Revolution a
century and a half ago. Lapels change their width; the length of jackets goes
up and down; waistcoats come and go; buttons move an inch in one direction
or another; collars turn from high to low and back to high; hat brims expand
and contract; neckties are wide and gaudy or narrow and bleak. But I can't
see that there has been a revolution in clothes of any real consequence since
the French Revolution, when fops were not only heedless but became head-
less. The only real revolutionary I can think of in my time was Raymond
Duncan, who long survived his more famous sister, the dancer Isadora Duncan; he went about in homespun, skirted garments and wore a rope garland
around his head to restrain his long, gray hair. He did it out of some sort of
conviction that modern men's clothes make no sense, and who can argue
with that?

Something interesting, if not revolutionary, has obviously been going on,
and I think it is worth considering why the changes are surprising enough to
be thought of as a revolution.

The most obvious thing that has happened to male attire was rather sur-
prisingly summed up for me by a narcotics-squad detective testifying before
a New York County grand jury of which I was a member. Speaking of some
individuals he had under surveillance on the street, he said, "One of them
was an *apparently male* Puerto Rican . . ."

"Apparently male," indeed. There has, of course, been a great deal of
comment in the last few years about how male fashions and female fashions
are meeting at a center point where their inhabitants become indistinguish-
able. Like many people I am frequently misled by the long slim legs in tight
pants, box jackets, and medium-long hair into thinking that what I am looking at (especially from behind) is not what I am looking at at all. But to say
that this is a change in male fashion is to get the matter back-end to. It is a
radical change in female fashion and a slight shift in what is considered ton-
sorially acceptable for men. Very long hair on men is still cause for sharp
comment in many quarters, but moderately long hair is increasingly acceptable even to the conservative members of the community . . . any community. Very soon the American Civil Liberties Union, which has expended

a good deal of energy on defending boys who have been thrown out of (or kept out of) high school because their hair is too long to suit the school principal, will be able to return to their more proper functions of defending more urgent causes.

What has caused the confusion between the sexes is the female affectation of male styles and not the other way around. Teen-age boys, for example, are not trying to look like Barbra Streisand, with their hair longish and down over one eye; Barbra (she wants everyone to know her as just Barbra) is trying to look like a teen-age boy, and the effect has been theatrically successful. She has made what is essentially a rather homely face into something remarkably attractive.

There has been a good deal of unnecessary and unjustified comment by the slowly vanishing crew-haircut crew about the sissy fashion of long hair. Actually, long tresses on men seems to be a socio-political rather than a sexual manifestation. There are sissies with long hair, I have no doubt, but homosexuals seem to incline more to tidy little bangs than to locks falling down over the backs of their necks. By and large, it seems to be true that homosexuals want to be conspicuous to each other but inconspicuous to the community in general. They have their own set of tonsorial signals which should not be confused with what is generally accepted as male fashions. The long haircut, incidentally, is working a hardship on some factions of the barbering business. A *Wall Street Journal* reporter several months ago quoted a barber in New York whose shop is near Columbia University as saying, "This used to be a growing business. Now it's not. Long hair did it." And another barber in Manchester, Connecticut, says he specialized in the "nothin' haircut . . . nothin' off the top, nothin' off the sides, nothin' off the back." It is preferred by what he calls "Beatle types." Historically, of course, there is no connotation of sissiness in long hair for men. Davy Crockett and Buffalo Bill wore their hair long, but today's hair styles among the young are tending rather more toward styles popular with men at the height of the Italian Renaissance than anything that has come along since.

The feminization of male fashions has been criticized within the male clothing industry. George H. Richman, who is president of a major men's clothes manufacturing business that also has retail outlets, got himself in wrong with some of his colleagues by publicly deploring "creeping feminization in the men's and particularly the boys' wear in this country." To this the vice-president in charge of merchandizing for Hart Schaffner & Marx replied, "There's only an infinitesimal percentage of buyers and producers who take fashions to such an extreme you might charge a feminine trend." A guest columnist in *The Arizona Republic* of Phoenix expressed the opinion that a reputation for effeminate attire in high school can follow a boy through life; though the effeminate attire he describes ("long curled hair

. . . extremely pointed shoes, and pants that are revealingly tight . . .")
has perfectly good, indeed excellent, historic precedent as the most mascu-
line of clothes.

What he is really talking about is not effeminacy but the revolt of the
young against their parents' generation, which is another subject, another
aspect of fashion, indeed. It can be argued that the elaborateness of dress,
the concern with fancy details in shoes and scarves and shirts and jackets, is
man trying to reclaim from women his right to plumage which he gave up at
the time of the Industrial Revolution, when he wished to divorce himself
from the frippery which was associated in the public mind with the old aris-
tocracy. The Industrial Revolution man, as Quentin Bell [1] has pointed out,
dressed in black like the chimneys of his factories, and his object of "conspicuous consumption" (Bell elaborates on Veblen) became his wife, whom
he dressed in acres of silks and satins ornamented with miles of ruffles and
bows. It took him more than a century to get sick of his smoke- (or soot-)
colored garments, but he's no less a man for being bored with them. If some
of the young are revolting to (and against) their parents and grandparents, it
is because they have chosen to take a giant step in a corner of human male
behavior where tiny steps have been the accepted practice.

There is a good deal of speculation in the press about what has caused the
change in men's fashions, who are the leaders who set the styles, if, of
course, there is any great change.

The change is mostly among the young, and the source of their inspiration
is said to be pop singers. John Crosby, writing in *The Observer* (London)
quoted David Mlinaric, a designer and "one of the best-dressed young men
in London," as saying, "The pop singers have the panache of the movie stars
in the 'thirties. The pop singers and designers and film stars dress adven-
turously—and others have followed them."

Carnaby Street, in the West End in London, as every teen-ager who
knows anything knows, is the Mecca of the "mod" fashions which became so
popular that nearly every department store in America which caters to the
young opened special shops for them. Though the fad has already declined
somewhat, it was from there that the inspiration came for the "fancy floral-
print cotton shirts," the "hip-hugging trousers with low belt lines," the jackets that were long and nipped in at the waist, the bell-bottom trousers, the
high-heeled boots and gorgeous cuff links. In London, however, Carnaby
Street is looked down upon with some disdain by the young men like Mlinaric who are the most conscientiously elegant and self-consciously fashionable young men in England, as producing rather shoddy wares of inferior
materials and design. These young men, mostly in one way or another associated with the arts and therefore free of the confining conventions of the
business world, regard themselves as dandies; their concern with what is in

[1] *On Human Finery*, A. A. Wyn, 1949.

general socially acceptable is, if it exists at all, contemptuous. The scorn of dandyism for middle-class notions of suitability is far more like the beatnik scorn for middle-class morality, objectives, and conventions than either the dandy or the beatnik would be likely to recognize or, if he recognized it, admit.

But Carnaby Street and dandyism (some more accurately call it foppishness) are symptoms and not causes. The causes are in the changing social structure, in the nature of a society so affluent that it has the leisure to consume several wardrobes, on the one hand, and a society bored with itself (as England seems to be) on the other. It reflects as well changes in a society in which manual labor is continually giving way to automation and in which professionalism is increasingly in demand in every aspect of the economy. Clothes have always been a means of typecasting, a means of class identification, professional identification, regional identification, and even intellectual identification. The function of clothes in this respect has not changed; but the rules of the game have changed somewhat and will continue to change.

Let us leave the young aside for a moment, though we cannot ignore them in considering what has happened to the looks of their elders. Essentially, American men are extremely conservative in their dress and they change their habits slowly. What is suitable for the banker today and what was suitable forty years ago can be almost superimposed on each other. Like the military uniform, the bank uniform has given up the high, stiff collar; otherwise it remains, except for changes in details of lapels, width of trouser bottoms, and length of jacket almost precisely what it was in 1910.

In a catalogue of "Men's Nobby Clothes, made to measure" for the spring and summer of 1905, Magnus Brothers of Chicago shows page after page of suits which only the most meticulously up-to-date man would hesitate to wear to the office today. The double-breasted suits are three-button instead of two and the straight jackets are four-button instead of two or three, but the lapels are just about in today's fashion, so are the cuffless trousers. The dinner jackets have shawl collars, not notched lapels; short boxed topcoats are *au fait* for spring. The principal differences are in the width of hat brims, the length of overcoats, and the prices of everything. The suits cost from $10 to $20 (with "Rain-proof Overcoat, Fancy Vest, or Silk Umbrella FREE"); a Tuxedo Suit cost $30 to $40 and a Full Dress Suit (tailcoat) from $30 to $45. Clothes advertised by Hart Schaffner & Marx a couple of years later are a little more dashing and a little closer to what is being revived by Carnaby Street today as "Edwardian," than those offered by Magnus Brothers. The jackets are a little longer and some of them have piping on the lapels and down the front.

Most men dress most of the time to be inconspicuous, to draw as little attention to themselves as possible. No one, for example, notices a professor in tweeds, but a professor on campus in a dark business suit, white shirt with French cuffs, and a stickpin in his tie might be taken for a member of the board of trustees or of the upper echelons of the college administration. A man in tweeds in a New York business office is probably from the "creative" department of an advertising firm. Men's uniforms, in other words, vary only slightly and within a narrow range depending on how and where they work. The president of a Chicago or New York bank would be as much out of place in a tweed jacket and slacks as a man in a dinner jacket who turned up to read the gas meter. There are, to be sure, regional differences in what are considered suitable uniforms: California, for instance, and especially the southern part of the state, is a law unto itself; the light (even white) wide-brimmed hat is conventional for businessmen in the Southwest, and in Dallas men can reasonably wear tweed jackets to their offices; in Florida it is often difficult to tell the native real-estate man from the migrant vacationer in his winter plumage.

Obviously it is in the off-day or leisure or sports clothes that the greatest revolution has taken place, but it is not a new revolution at all. The trend to male "separates" (trousers and jackets that don't match) started (or I should say restarted; jackets and trousers of different materials were common in the last century) about twenty-five years ago in earnest; but just last year the number of sports coats that were sold increased from 12.5 million in 1965 to about 13.4 million. The number of suits, on the other hand, went down from 22.4 million in 1965 to about 21 million in 1966. More surprising, however, is the fact that, according to the *New York Times,* "More suits were made in 1953 than in 1966, even though the number of males in the country grew sharply during this thirteen-year period." Still more surprising, to me, and I would think to those who believe the American man to be increasingly clothes-conscious, is a statement by the clothing industry that "male apparel has been receiving a smaller share of the total consumer disposable income" than it did two decades ago.

It is quite possible, of course, that this diminishing percentage of income spent on clothes is attributable to the increased spending on equipment for leisure—for skis and outboards, for camping trailers and golf clubs and fishing tackle. Costumes for leisure are far less expensive for the average man than the clothes he needs for his office and for the formal aspects of his leisure. There is an interesting sidelight, however, on leisure clothes that is worth mentioning. Many men are inclined to wear as their leisure clothes the working uniform of other men. The businessman, for instance, wears blue jeans, the uniform of the farm or cowhand; the farmer, when he gets dressed up for his leisure, wears the uniform of the office worker, a business suit. (World War I uniforms, at the moment anyway, are dear to the hearts of teenagers who buy them, or copies of them, in Army and Navy stores.)

It is also in leisure clothes that the peacock in many men reveals itself, but even so, the efforts of the clothing industry to make men gorgeous has never quite succeeded. Do you remember in the mid-1950s when there was an attempt to get men into bright dinner jackets? Where are they now? An advertisement for a "tangerine double-breasted blazer" in *The New York Times Magazine* this February said, "Who says a tasteful outfit must be dull? And if you can't quite summon up the ego for Tangerine, how about Canary, Sky, or Skipper?" It does, as the ad implies, still take a great deal of summoning up of the ego for most men to wear flashing colors.

High style for mature men, like high style for the dashing young, comes to America from Europe as it has since the founding of the Republic, and before, and as it does for women. The influence of Italian tailors, so evident a few years ago (remember the silk suitings?) seems to have given way to the influence of Paris and London on those men whose closets bulge with thirty suits and fifty pairs of shoes. Pierre Cardin of Paris, whose reputation is based on *haute couture* for women, but who now runs a business that makes five times as much on men's clothes as on women's, is a current mentor of the fashionable (as opposed to the foppish) male, though much of what he advocates is greatly modified for the American scene. The jackets are long and tightly fitted, the waistcoats are high, and often have lapels, trousers are narrow and without cuffs, shirt collars spread wide (but are not long), and neckties are also wide but, compared with Carnaby Street fashions, they are rather subdued. Cardin's English counterpart, also a dressmaker, is Hardy Amies of Savile Row.

Their fashions are likely, however, to penetrate the general American market in greatly modified ways and very slowly. The primary influence on men's fashions comes, as it has not come in the past, from the young. It does not come from those young who are hopefully outrageous, from the black-leather jacket and surfing young or from the beats; it comes from the amused and urbane young who, without being foppish, have decided that there is more to dressing than putting on a shirt and a suit and a tie that nobody will notice and that their elders can certainly not complain about. What is evolving is not a revolution in men's clothes; it is an echoing of the past overlaid with a kind of humor and a sense of fun. Lord Chesterfield is quoted by Quentin Bell as saying, "The difference . . . between a man of sense and a fop is that the fop values himself upon his dress; and the man of sense laughs at it, at the same time that he knows he must not neglect it."

There are inevitably a great many people of my generation who think the young are going to hell in a basket because their hair is long, their shirts frilled, their trousers tight, their neckties loud as brass bands, and inevitably they will try to harness them, discourage them, lay down the law . . . keep them out of school, indeed. One is reminded of the "sumptuary laws" that have been enacted by almost every civilization at sometime or other to quell elaborateness of dress on grounds of extravagance, immorality, and the breaking down of social distinctions. As Mr. Bell says, ". . . the history of sumptuary laws is a history of dead letters."

STUDY QUESTIONS

1. Russell Lynes seems to feel that "modern men's clothes make no sense." What does he mean by *no sense?* Do you agree?

2. According to Lynes, what has caused the confusion—of styles— between the sexes? How does Barbra Streisand demonstrate his point? Can you suggest other examples?

3. Lynes calls long hair on men "a socio-political rather than a sexual mani-festation." What socio-political issues does he then discuss?

4. What is *typecasting?* How are clothes a means of typecasting? How is the matter of typecasting with clothes connected to Lynes' statement that "most men dress most of the time to be inconspicuous"?

5. What is a *fop,* as defined by Lord Chesterfield? As defined by a diction-ary? Why might "a man of sense" laugh at his dress?

Tom Wolfe

THE MARVELOUS MOUTH

Tom Wolfe (1931–   ) was born in Richmond, Virginia. He received his B.A. from Washington and Lee (1951) and his Ph.D. from Yale (1957). He has been a reporter for the Springfield, Mass. *Union,* the Washington *Post,* and the *New York Herald-Tribune.* His essays were published in 1965 under the wildly improbable but singularly appropriate title of *The Kandy-Kolored Tangerine-Flake Streamline Baby.* His most recent books are *The Electric Kool-Aid Acid Test* and *The Pump House Gang* (1968). A talented artist, his works have been exhibited in a one-man show.

ONE THING that stuck in my mind, for some reason, was the
way that Cassius Clay and his brother, Rudy, and their
high-school pal, Tuddie King, and Frankie Tucker, the
singer who was opening in Brooklyn, and Cassius' pride of "foxes," Sophia,
Burton, Dottie, Frenchie, Barbara and the others, and Richie Pittman and
"Lou" Little, the football player, and everybody else up there in Cassius'
suite on the forty-second floor of the Americana Hotel kept telling time by
looking out the panorama window and down at the clock on top of the Paramount Building on Times Square. Everybody had a watch. Cassius, for example, is practically a watch fancier. But, every time, somebody would look
out the panorama window, across the City Lights scene you get from up high
in the Americana and down to the lit-up clock on that whacky Twenties-
modern polyhedron on top of the Paramount Building.

One minute Cassius would be out in the middle of the floor reenacting his
"High Noon" encounter with Sonny Liston in a Las Vegas casino. He has a
whole act about it, beginning with a pantomime of him shoving open the
swinging doors and standing there bowlegged, like a beer delivery man.
Then he plays the part of the crowd falling back and whispering, "It's Cassius Clay, Cassius Clay, Cassius Clay, Cassius Clay." Then he plays the part
of an effete Las Vegas hipster at the bar with his back turned, suddenly
freezing in mid-drink, as the hush falls over the joint, and sliding his eyes
around to see the duel. Then he plays the part of Cassius Clay stalking
across the floor with his finger pointed at Sonny Liston and saying, "You big
ugly bear," "You big ugly bear," about eighteen times, "I ain't gonna fight
you on no September thirtieth, I'm gonna fight you right now. Right here.
You too ugly to run loose, you big ugly bear. You so ugly, when you cry, the
tears run down the back of your head. You so ugly, you have to sneak up on
the mirror so it won't run off the wall," and so on, up to the point where
Liston says, "Come over here and sit on my knee, little boy, and I'll give you
your orange juice," and where Cassius pulls back his right and three guys
hold him back and keep him from throwing it at Liston, "And I'm hollering,
'Lemme go,' and I'm telling them out the side of my mouth, You better *not*
lemme go.'" All this time Frankie Tucker, the singer, is contorted across
one of the Americana's neo-Louis XIV chairs, breaking up and exclaiming,
"That's my man!"

The next minute Cassius is fooling around with Rudy's phonograph-and-
speaker set and having some fun with the foxes. The foxes are seated around
the room at ornamental intervals, all ya-ya length silk sheaths, long legs
and slithery knees. Cassius takes one of Rudy's cool jazz records or an
Aretha Franklin or something like that off the phonograph and puts on one
of the 45-r.p.m. rock-and-roll records that the singers keep sending to him
at the hotel.

"Those are Rudy's records, I don't *dig* that mess. I'm just a boy from Louisville"—he turns his eyes up at the foxes—"I dig rock and roll. Isn't that right?"

All the girls are hip, and therefore cool jazz fans currently, so most of them think the whole thing over for a few seconds before saying, "That's right."

Cassius puts a 45-r.p.m. on and says, "This old boy's an alley singer, nobody ever heard of him, he sings about beans and bread and all that old mess."

Cassius starts laughing at that and looking out over the city lights, out the panorama window. The girls aren't sure whether he is laughing with or at the alley singer.

Cassius scans the foxes and says, "This is *my* crowd. They don't dig that other mess, either."

The girls don't say anything.

"Is that your kinda music? I know it's *hers*," he says, looking at Francine, who is sitting pretty still. "She's about to fall over."

And may be at this point somebody says, "What time is it?" And Rudy or somebody looks out the panorama window to the clock on the Paramount Building and says, "Ten minutes to ten."

Cassius had just come from the Columbia Records studio, across from the hotel at Seventh Avenue and 52nd, where he was making an album, *I Am the Greatest,* a long pastiche of poems and skits composed wholly in terms of his impending fight with Sonny Liston. The incessant rehearsing of his lines for two weeks, most of them lines he had sprung at random at press conferences and so forth over a period of a year and a half, had made Cassius aware, as probably nothing else, of the showman's role he was filling. And made him tempted by it.

After cutting up a little for Frankie Tucker and the foxes and everybody —showing them how he could *act,* really—he went over to one side of the living room and sat in a gangster-modern swivel chair and propped his feet up on the panorama-window ledge and talked a while. Everybody else was talking away in the background. Somebody had put the cool jazz back on and some husky girl with one of those augmented-sevenths voices was singing "Moon Over Miami."

"What's that club Leslie Uggams was at?" Cassius asked.

"The Metropole."

"The Metropole, that's right. That's one of the big ones out there, ain't it?"

His designation of the Metropole Café as "a big one" is an interesting thing in itself, but the key phrase is "out there." To Cassius, New York and the hot spots and the cool life are out there beyond his and Rudy's and Tuddie's suite at the Americana and beyond his frame of reference. Cassius does not come to New York as the hip celebrity, although it would be easy enough, but as a phenomenon. He treats Broadway as though these were still the days when the choirboys at Lindy's would spot a man in a white Palm Beach-brand suit heading up from 49th Street and say, "Here comes Winchell," or "Here comes Hellinger," or even the way Carl Van Vechten's Scarlet Creeper treated 125th Street in the days of the evening promenade. Cassius likes to get out amongst them.

About 10:15 P.M. he motioned to Sophia and started leaving the suite. All five girls got up and followed. The procession was spectacular even for Seventh Avenue on a crowded night with the chocolate-drink stands open. Cassius, six feet three, two hundred pounds, was wearing a black-and-white checked jacket, white tab-collared shirt and black tie, light gray Continental trousers, black pointed-toe Italian shoes, and walking with a very cocky walk. The girls were walking one or two steps behind, all five of them, dressed in slayingly high couture. There were high heels and garden-party hats. Down at the corner, at 52nd Street, right at the foot of the hotel, Cassius stopped, looked all around and began loosening up his shoulders, the way prizefighters do. This, I found out, is Cassius' signal, an unconscious signal, that he is now available for crowd collecting. He got none on that corner, but halfway down to 51st Street people started saying, "That's Cassius Clay, Cassius Clay, Cassius Clay, Cassius Clay," the way he had mimicked it back in the hotel. Cassius might have gotten his crowd at 51st Street —he was looking cocky and the girls were right behind him in a phalanx, looking gorgeous—but he headed on across the street, when the light changed, over to where two fellows he knew were standing a quarter of the way down the block.

"Here he comes. Whatta you say, champ?"

"Right, man. Hey," said Cassius, referring the girls to the taller and older of the two men, "I want you all to meet one of the greatest singers in New York." A pause there. "What is your name, man, I meet so many people here."

"Hi, Pinocchio," said one of the foxes, and the man smiled.

"Pinocchio," said Cassius. Then he said, "You see all these queens are with me?" He made a sweeping motion with his hand. The girls were around him on the sidewalk. "All these foxes."

"That's sump'n else, man."

Cassius could have gotten his crowd easily on the sidewalk outside the Metropole. When it's warm, there is always a mob out there looking in through the front doorway at the band strung out along the bandstand, which is really more of a shelf. If there is a rock-and-roll band, there will always be some Jersey teen-agers outside twisting their ilia to it. That night there was more of a Dixieland or jump band on, although Lionel Hampton was to come on later, and Cassius entered, by coincidence, while an old tune called "High Society" was playing. All the foxes filed in, a step or so behind. The Metropole Café has not seen many better entrances. Cassius looked gloriously bored.

The Metropole is probably the perfect place for a folk hero to show up at in New York. It is kind of a crossroads, or ideal type, of all the hot spots and live joints in the country. I can tell you two things about it that will help you understand what the Metropole is like, if you have never been there. First, the color motif is submarine green and Prussian blue, all reflected in huge wall-to-wall mirrors. If the stand-up beer crowd gets so thick you can't see over them to the bandstand, you can always watch through the mirror. Second, the place attracts high-livers of a sort that was there that night. I particularly remember one young guy, standing there at the bar in the submarine-green and Prussian-blue light with sunglasses on. He had on a roll-collar shirt, a silvery tie, a pale-gray suit of the Continental cut and pointed black shoes. He had a kingsize cigarette pasted on his lower lip, and when the band played "The Saints," he broke into a terribly "in" and hip grin, which brought the cigarette up horizontal. He clapped his hands and hammered his right heel in time to the drums and kept his eyes on the trumpet player the whole time. The thing is, kids don't even do that at Williams College anymore, but they do it at the Metropole.

This same kid came over to ask Cassius for his autograph at one point. He thought "The Saints" was hip, but he must not have thought autograph-hunting was very hip. He wanted an autograph, however. He handed Cassius a piece of paper for his autograph and said, "It's not for me, it's for a buddy of mine, he wants it." This did not score heavily with Cassius.

"Where's your pen?" he said.

"I don't have a pen," the kid said. "It's for a friend of mine."

"You ain't got no pen, man," said Cassius.

About a minute later the kid came back with a pen, and Cassius signed the piece of paper, and the kid said, "Thank you, Cassius, you're a gentleman." He said it very seriously. "It's for a buddy of mine. You're a real gentleman."

That was the tone of things that night in the Metropole. Everything was just a little off, the way Cassius saw it.

From the moment he walked into the doorway of the Metropole, people were trying to prod him into the act.

"You *really* think you can beat Sonny Liston, man?"

"Liston must fall in eight."

"You *really* mean that?"

"If he gives me any jive, he goes in five," Cassius said, but in a terribly matter-of-fact, recitative voice, all the while walking on ahead, with the foxes moseying in behind him, also gloriously bored.

His presence spread over the Metropole immediately. As I said, it is the perfect place for folk heroes, for there is no one in there who is not willing to be impressed. The management, a lot of guys in tuxedos with the kind of Hollywood black ties that tuck under the collars and are adorned with little pearl stickpins and such devices—the management was rushing up. A guy at the bar, well-dressed, came up behind Cassius and touched him lightly at about the level of the sixth rib and went back to the bar and told his girl, "That's Cassius Clay. I just touched him, no kidding."

They sat all the foxes down in a booth at about the middle of the Metropole Café and gave Cassius a chair by himself right next to them. Lionel Hampton came up with the huge smile he has and shook Cassius' hand and made a fuss over him without any jive about when Liston must fall. Cassius liked that. But then the crowd came around for autographs, and they wanted him to go into his act. It was a hell of a noisy place.

But the crowd at the Metropole hit several wrong notes. One was hit by a white man about fifty-five, obviously a Southerner from the way he talked, who came up to Clay from behind—people were gaggled around from all sides—and stuck the blank side of a Pennsylvania Railroad receipt, the kind you get when you buy your ticket on the train, in his face and said in a voice you could mulch the hollyhocks with:

"Here you are, boy, put your name right there."

It was more or less the same voice Mississippians use on a hot day when the colored messenger boy has come into the living room and is standing around nervously. "Go ahead, boy, sit down. Sit in that seat right there."

Cassius took the Pennsylvania Railroad receipt without looking up at the man, and held it for about ten seconds, just staring at it.

Then he said in a slightly accusing voice, "Where's your pen?"

"I don't have a pen, boy. Some of these people around here got a pen. Just put your name right there."

Cassius still didn't look up. He just said, "Man, there's one thing you gotta learn. You don't *ever* come around and ask a man for an autograph if you ain't got no pen."

The man retreated and more people pressed in.

Cassius treats the fact of color—but not race—casually. Sometimes, when he is into his act, he will look at somebody and say, "You know, man, you lucky, you seen me here in living color." One time, I remember, a CBS news crew was filming an interview with him in the Columbia Records Studio A, at 799 Seventh Avenue, when the cameraman said to the interviewer, who was moving in on Cassius with the microphone: "Hey, Jack, you're throwing too much shadow on Cassius. He's dark enough already."

All the white intellectuals in the room cringed. Cassius just laughed. In point of fact, he is not very dark at all.

But he does not go for any of the old presumptions, such as, "Put your name right there, boy."

Another wrong note was hit when a middle-aged couple came up. They were white. The woman struck you as a kind of Arkansas Blanche Dubois. They looked like they wanted autographs at first. They did in a way. They were both loaded. She had an incredible drunk smile that spread out soft and gooey like a can of Sherwin-Williams paint covering the world. She handed Cassius a piece of paper and a pencil and wanted him to write down both his name *and* her name. He had just about done that when she put her hand out very slowly to caress his cheek.

"Can I touch you?" she said. "I just want to touch you."

Cassius pulled his head back.

"Naw," he said. "My girl friends might get jealous."

He didn't call them foxes to her. He said it in a nice way. After she left, though, he let her have it. It was the only time I ever heard him say anything contemptuously of anyone.

"Can I *touch* you, can I *touch* you," he said. He could mimic her white Southern accent in a fairly devastating way.

"Naw, you can't touch me," he said, just as if he were answering her face to face. "Nobody can touch me."

As a matter of fact, Cassius is good at mimicking a variety of white Southern accents. He doesn't do it often, but when he does it, it has an extra wallop because he has a pronounced Negro accent of his own, which he makes no attempt to polish. He only turns it on heavier from time to time for comic effect. Once I heard him mimic both himself, a Louisville Negro, and newspapermen, Louisville whites, in one act.

I had asked him if the cocky act he was putting on all over the country, and in England for that matter, surprised the people who knew him back home. What I was getting at was whether he had been a cocky kid in Louisville back in the days before anybody ever heard of him. He changed the direction slightly.

"They believe anything you tell 'em about me back in Louisville. Newspapermen used to come around and I'd give 'em predictions and they'd say, 'What is this boy doing?'

"I had a fight with Lamar Clark, I believe it was, and I said [*Clay mimicking Clay, heavy, high-flown, bombastic Negro accent*]: 'Lamar will fall in two.' I knocked him out in two, and they said [*Clay mimicking drawling Kentucky Southern accent*]: 'Suht'n'ly dee-ud.' " (Certainly did.)

"I said, 'Miteff will fall in six.'

"They said, 'Suht'n'ly dee-ud.'

"I said, 'Warren will fall in four.'

"They said, 'Suht'n'ly dee-ud.' "

Clay had a lot better look on his face when people came by to admire what he had become rather than the funny act he puts on.

One young Negro, sharp-looking, as they say, in Continental clothes with a wonderful pair of Latin-American sunglasses, the kind that are narrow like the mask the Phantom wears in the comic strip, came by and didn't ask Cassius when Liston would fall. He shot an admiring, knowing look at the foxes, and said, "Who are all these girls, man?"

"Oh, they just the foxes," said Cassius.

"Man, I like your choice of foxes, I'm telling you," the kid said.

This tickled Cassius and he leaned over and told it to Sophia.

The kid, meantime, went around to the other side of the booth. He had a glorified version of how Cassius was living. He believed Cassius as he leaned over to the girls when the waiter came around and said, "You get anything you want. I own this place. I own all of New York." (Sophia gave him a derisive laugh for that.)

The kid leaned over to one of the girls and said: "Are you all his personal property?"

"What are you talking about, boy. What do you mean, his *personal property?*"

"You know, *his,*" said the kid. He was getting embarrassed, but he still had traces of a knowing look salivating around the edges.

"Why do we have to be his personal property?"

"Well, like, I mean, you know," said the kid. His mouth had disintegrated completely into an embarrassed grin by now, but his eyes were still darting around, as if to say, "Why don't they level with me. I'm a hip guy."

Cassius also liked it when a Negro he had met a couple of nights before, an older guy, came around and didn't ask when Liston would fall.

"I saw a crowd on the sidewalk out there, and I might have *known* you'd be inside," he told Cassius. "What's going on?"

"Oh, I'm just sitting here with the foxes," said Cassius.

"You sure are," the fellow said.

A young white kid with a crew cut said, "Are you afraid of Liston?"

Cassius said mechanically, "That big ugly bear? If I was worried I'd be out training and I'm out partying."

Cassius had a tall, pink drink. It was nothing but Hawaiian Punch, right out of the can.

"How you gonna beat him?"

"I'll beat that bear in eight rounds. I'm strong and I'm beautiful and I'll beat that bear in eight rounds."

"You promise?" said the kid. He said it very seriously and shook Cassius' hand, as though he were getting ready to go outside and drop off a couple of grand with his Weehawken bookmaker. He apparently squeezed pretty hard. This fellow being a fighter and all, a guy ought to shake hands like a man with him.

Cassius pulled his hand away suddenly and wrung it. "Don't ever squeeze a fighter's hand, man. That hand's worth about three hundred thousand dollars," he said, making a fist. "You don't have to shake hands, you doing good just to lay eyes on me."

The kid edged off with his buddy and he was saying, "He said, 'Don't ever squeeze a fighter's hand.' "

By now Cassius was looking slightly worse than gloriously bored.

"If they don't stop worrying me," he said, "I'm gonna get up and walk out of here."

Sophia leaned over and told me, "He doesn't mean that. He loves it."

Of all the girls, Sophia seemed to be closest to him. She found him amusing. She liked him.

"You know, he's really a normal boy," she told me. She threw her head to one side as if to dismiss Cassius' big front. "Oh, he's got a big mouth. But aside from that, he's a real normal boy."

The foxes were beginning to stare a little morosely into their Gin Fizzes and Brandy Alexanders and Sidecars, and even the stream of autograph seekers was slowing down. It was damned crowded and you could hardly hear yourself talk. Every now and then the drummer would go into one of those crazy sky-rocketing solos suitable for the Metropole, and the trumpet player would take the microphone and say, "That's what Cassius Clay is going to do to Sonny Liston's head!" and Cassius would holler, "Right!" but it was heavy weather. By this time Richie Pittman had dropped in, and Cassius motioned to him. They got up and went out "for some air." At the doorway there was a crowd on the sidewalk looking in at the bandstand, as always. They made a fuss over Cassius, but he just loosened his shoulders a little and made a few wisecracks. He and Richie started walking up toward the Americana.

It was after midnight, and at the foot of the hotel, where this paseo-style sidewalk pans out almost like a patio, there was a crowd gathered around. Cassius didn't miss that. They were watching three street musicians, colored boys, one with a makeshift bass—a washtub turned upside down with a cord coming up out of the bottom, forming a single string; a drum—a large tin-can bottom with spoons as sticks; and one guy dancing. They were playing "Pennies from Heaven," a pretty good number for three guys getting ready to pass the hat. Cassius just walked up to the edge of the crowd and stood there. One person noticed him, then another, and pretty soon the old "That's Cassius Clay, Cassius Clay, Cassius Clay" business started. Cassius' spirits were rising. "Pennies from Heaven" stopped, and the three colored boys looked a little nonplussed for a moment. The show was being stolen. Somebody had said something about "Sonny Liston," only this time Cassius had the 150-watt eyes turned on, and he was saying, "The only thing I'm worried about is, I don't want Sonny Liston trying to crash *my* victory party the way I crashed his. I'm gonna tell him right before the fight starts so he won't forget it, 'Sonny,' I'm gonna tell him, 'Sonny Liston, I don't want you trying to crash my victory party tonight, you hear that? I want you to hear that now, 'cause you ain't gonna be *able* to hear anything eight rounds from now.' And if he gives me any jive when I tell him that, if he gives me any jive, he must fall in five."

A soldier, a crank-sided kid who looked like he must have gone through the battered-child syndrome at about age four, came up to take the role of Cassius' chief debater. Cassius likes that when he faces a street crowd. He'll hold a press conference for anybody, even a soldier on leave on Seventh Avenue.

"Where you gonna go after Sonny Liston whips you?" the kid said. "I got some travel folders right here."

"Boy," said Cassius, "you talk about traveling. I want you to go to that fight, 'cause you gonna see the launching of a human satellite. Sonny Liston."

The crowd was laughing and carrying on.

"I got some travel folders," the kid said. "You better look 'em over. I can get you a mask, too."

"You gonna bet against me?" said Cassius.

"Every cent I can get my hands on," said the kid.

"Man," said Cassius, "you better save your money, 'cause there's gonna be a total eclipse of the Sonny."

Cassius was standing there looking like a million dollars, and Richie was standing by, sort of riding shotgun. By this time, the crowd was so big, it was spilling off the sidewalk into 52nd Street. All sorts of incredible people were moving up close, including sclerotic old men with big-lunch ties who edged in with jag-legged walks. A cop was out in the street going crazy, trying to prod everybody back on the sidewalk. A squad car drove up, and the cop on the street put on a real tough tone, "All right, goddamn it," he said to an old sclerotic creeper with a big-lunch tie, "get up on the sidewalk."

Cassius looked around at me as if to say, "See, man? That's only what I predicted"—which is to say, "When I walk down the street, the crowds, they have to call the police."

The autograph business had started now, and people were pushing in with paper and pens, but Cassius wheeled around toward the three colored boys, the musicians, and said, "Autographs are one dollar tonight. Everyone puts one dollar in there" (the musicians had a corduroy-ribbed box out in front of the tub) "gets the autograph of Cassius Clay, the world's strongest fighter, the world's most beautiful fighter, the onliest fighter who predicts when they will fall."

The colored boys took the cue and started up with "Pennies from Heaven" again. The kid who danced was doing the merengue by himself. The kid on the bass was flailing away like a madman. All the while Cassius was orating on the corner.

"Come on, man, don't put no fifty cents in there, get that old dollar bill outa there. Think at all you're getting free here, the music's so fine and here you got Cassius Clay right here in front of you in living color, the next heavyweight champion of the world, the man who's gon' put old man Liston in orbit."

The dollar bills started piling up in the box, and the solo merengue kid was dervishing around wilder still, and Cassius wouldn't let up.

"Yeah, they down there right now getting that Medicare ready for that old man, and if I hit him in the mouth he's gonna need Denticare. That poor ol' man' he's so ugly, his wife drives him to the gym every morning 'fore the sun comes up, so nobody'll have to look at him 'round home. Come on, man, put yo' money in that box, people pay good money to hear this—"

The bass man was pounding away, and Cassius turned to me and said, behind his hand, "Man, you know one thing? If I get whipped, they gonna run me outa the country. You know that?"

Then he threw his head back and his arms out, as if he were falling backward. "Can you see me flat out on my back like this?"

The colored kids were playing "Pennies from Heaven," and Cassius Clay had his head thrown back and his arms out, laughing, and looking straight up at the top of the Americana Hotel.

STUDY QUESTIONS

1. Why does Wolfe begin so abruptly?

2. Wolfe begins three consecutive paragraphs with "Cassius" and a verb in the present tense. What does he accomplish by this rhetorical parallelism?

3. Is there any evidence that Clay does not take himself seriously, that he is amused by his public image? Can you tell Wolfe's attitude toward Clay?

4. Sophie says Clay has a *big* mouth; Wolfe calls it *marvelous*. What does each mean?

5. What is the point of Wolfe's final paragraph?

Joseph Wood Krutch

MUST WRITERS HATE THE UNIVERSE?

Joseph Wood Krutch (1893–   ) was born in Knoxville, Tennessee. He received his B.A. (1915) from the University of Tennessee and his M.A. (1916) and Ph.D. (1932) from Columbia University. He has taught English, journalism, and drama at Columbia; lectured at the New School for Social Research; served as drama critic for the *Nation;* and acted as president of the New York Drama Critics Circle. Krutch now lives in Tucson, Arizona, and is a trustee of the Arizona-Sonora Desert Museum. He has edited the works of William Congreve, Eugene O'Neill, Marcel Proust, and Thomas Gray; and written critical studies of Restoration comedy, and of Samuel Johnson, Edgar Allan Poe, and Henry David Thoreau. Other books include *The Modern Temper* (1929), *The Desert Year* (1952), *The Measure of Man* (1954), *Grand Canyon* (1958), and the revised *Baja California, and the Geography of Hope* (1969).

$\mathcal{T}$HERE ARE not many nations so indefatigably given to honoring men of letters that a cabinet minister would preside over a ceremony in which the principal speaker eulogized a *poet maudit* upon whose newly erected monument was inscribed the poet's own clarion call to his fellows: "We have set out as pilgrims whose destination is perdition . . . across streets, across countries, and across reason itself." Simultaneously, and in accordance with a French custom which always reminds me of the monkish habit of digging up old bones to make way for new ones, the name of a street was changed from that of a forgotten worthy to Rue Guillaume Apollinaire.

The cabinet minister involved was André Malraux; the sculptor of the

From *And Even If You Do: Essays on Man, Manners, and Machines* by Joseph Wood Krutch. Appeared originally in *Saturday Review* 50: 19–21, 47 (May 6, 1967). Reprinted by permission of William Morrow and Company, Inc. Copyright © 1967 by Joseph Wood Krutch.

The translation of Baudelaire by Robert Lowell is reprinted with permission of Farrar, Straus & Giroux, Inc., from *Imitations* by Robert Lowell. Copyright © 1958, 1959, 1960, 1961 by Robert Lowell.

monument was Picasso; the honored poet, Guillaume Apollinaire, was that champion of, successively, Cubism, Dada, and Surrealism, among whose own best known works are the volume of poems called *Hard Liquor (Alcools)*, the novel *The Assassinated Poet,* and the play *The Breasts of Tiresias*. One of his more notable pronouncements was the prediction that the dominant influence upon the twentieth century might well be that of the Marquis de Sade—a prophecy which, incidentally, seems in the course of being fulfilled.

Even if we had in this country a Minister of Arts, we cannot quite imagine him officially honoring a poet who urged painters as well as men of letters to set out resolutely on a road leading to that pit of hell, the descent into which —so an elder poet said—is easier than the road back again. No, one can't imagine an American Minister of Culture doing that. In fact, the proponents of government support to the arts are most likely to fear that we would be, officially at least, oppressively pure, genteel, and middlebrow.

But if we are not yet quite up to the French in this respect, there is no doubt that the avant-garde, even when perverse and sadistic, is no longer without honor even in rather surprising quarters, and that mass-circulation magazines give frequent and extensive treatment to movies, plays, novels, and poems which in one way or another—extravagant concern with usually abnormal sexuality, violence, cruelty, or at least the nihilism of the absurd—seem to be headed along the road which Apollinaire bid them take.

In March 1966, Cyril Connolly, a leading English critic, was commissioned by the ultrarespectable *Sunday Times* of London to make a list of the hundred literary works which best presented various aspects of modernism in intellectual literature. He headed his list with that same Guillaume Apollinaire whom the French Minister of Culture was so eager to honor, and though it is true that his list does include certain works which are neither beatnik, sadistic, existential, nor sexually perverse, at least a half—and perhaps two-thirds—of them might, I think, be classified as guideposts to perdition.

Among them—and remember these are not offered merely as striking works of literature but as typical of the modern spirit—are *Nadja (Nothing)* by the surrealist André Breton; *Journey to the End of the Night* by the pro-Nazi and violently anti-Semitic Céline; *The Immoralist* by Gide; *Là Bas* by Huysmans; *Cruel Stories* by Villiers de L'Isle-Adam; *Les Illuminations* by Rimbaud; and many others more or less in the same spirit of world-weariness, world-hatred, or perverse indulgence. And he finds the quintessence of modernity in Baudelaire as translated by Robert Lowell:

> Only when we drink poison are we
> well—

> We want, this fire so burns our brain
>   tissue,
> To drown in the abyss—heaven or hell.
> Who cares? Through the unknown
>   we'll find the new.

Readers curious enough to consult the full text with Connolly's own comments on individual works will find that he calls Baudelaire's poetry "a beam of light glowing for posterity," even though, it would seem, the poet himself declares that he does not care whether it points the way to a heaven or a hell. Connolly also states that Breton, one of his heroes, proposed to "wring the neck of literature" and quotes with apparent approval the following sentence, of which it is said "nothing more surrealist has ever been written": "Beautiful as the chance encounter on a dissecting table of an umbrella and a sewing machine."

Commenting on the list and Connolly's explanatory notes, *Time* (which certainly does not appeal to merely minority interests) remarks that though the list will seem perverse to many, it is, nevertheless, "an achievement in taste and learning."

I do not believe that more than a very small fraction of *Time*'s readers really share the convictions or admire the enterprises of such writers. Yet they are obviously much interested in them and they are timid about expressing any doubts. When they give deserved praise to, say, Tennessee Williams for his theatrical skill, they are half afraid of not taking seriously enough the implications of his extraordinary notions concerning sexual abnormality and are half convinced that their own normality needs to be apologized for. If a whole school of novelists (now a bit démodé) defines its conception of the good life as driving a stolen automobile at 90 miles an hour after a revivifying shot of heroin, almost nobody says merely, "Pooh," or, "Don't be silly."

Those of us who read such highbrow (or is it middlebrow?) weeklies as *The Nation* or *The New Leader* have come to expect a curious contrast between the front and the back of the book. Though the opening pages are full of schemes for improving the condition of this or that, the section devoted to the arts is occupied frequently by reviews of books, movies, paintings, and musical compositions which are bitterly cynical, pessimistic, and, by old-fashioned standards, obscene. This seems to reflect truly a similar contrast between the tastes and preoccupations of two different groups of "intellectuals." Most of them are either do-gooders on the one hand or, on the other, ready to entertain at least the possibility that the road to perdition is the wise one to take. If you are not a potential member of the Peace Corps, you are almost certainly a devotee of the absurd. You want either to rescue the underdeveloped countries or to explore once more the meaninglessness of the universe or the depravity of some version of the *dolce vita*. When *Time,* as it recently did, puts Sartre and Genet on its "best reading list" for a single week, neither of these writers can be said to be, by now, attractive to only a few.

Do I exaggerate either the violence, perversity, or nihilism of most of the most discussed modern writers or the tendency of even the mass magazines to select their works as the best or, sometimes, as only the most newsworthy books?

Let us look at a few excerpts from two or three publications which illustrate what I am driving at. Look first at a review in *The New Leader.* It concerned James Baldwin's so-called novel, *Another Country,* and it was written by the magazine's staff critic Stanley Edgar Hyman, who, though far from approving of the book, described it as follows:

> The protagonist of *Another Country,* a young Negro jazz drummer named Rufus Scott, kills himself on page 88, and the rest of the book is taken up with the adventures and misadventures, mostly sexual, of the half-dozen people who had been close to him. Of the important characters, only Rufus and his sister Ida are Negro, but almost everything in the book that is powerful and convincing deals with Negro consciousness.
>
> That consciousness, as the novel shows it, seethes with bitterness and race hate. "Let the liberal white bastards squirm" is Rufus's most charitable feeling towards Vivaldo, his best friend; his less charitable feeling is a passionate desire for the extinction of the white race by nuclear bombs. Ida is even fiercer. She regularly affirms, in language not quotable in this family magazine, the total sexual inadequacy of whites, as well as their moral sickness and physical repulsiveness. . . . The other Negroes in the book share this bitterness and hatred without exception. A big Negro pimp who lives by beating up and robbing the white customers of his Negro whore clearly does it out of principle; before robbing Vivaldo he stares at him "with a calm steady hatred, as remote and unanswerable as madness." The Silenski boys are beaten up by Negro boys unknown to them out of simple racial hostility and Richard, their father, automatically comments: "Little black bastards." Rufus's father, seeing his son's mangled corpse, remarks only: "They don't leave a man much, do they?" A musician who had been Rufus's friend, finding Ida out with a white man, calls her "black white man's whore" and threatens to mutilate her genitals twice, once for himself and once for Rufus.

Though *The New Leader*'s critic was by no means favorably impressed, the jacket of *Another Country* is able to cite the even better known and academically very respectable critic Mark Shorer, who called *Another Country* "powerful." Is that the adjective he would have chosen if this almost insane outburst of racism had been the work of some Southern Ku Klux Klanner— as it might easily be made to seem by reading "white" where Baldwin says "black" and "black" where he says "white"? Why is black racism "powerful," white disgusting?

Now for a movie, as admiringly described in *Time:*

The *Naked Prey* spills more beauty, blood, and savagery upon the screen than any African adventure drama since *Trader Horn.* Squeamish viewers will head for home in the first twenty minutes or so, when producer-director-star Cornell Wilde swiftly dooms three last century white hunters and a file of blacks, attacked and captured by a horde of warriors from a tribe they have insulted. One victim is basted with clay and turned over a spit, another is staked out as a victim of a cobra.

The only survivor is Wilde. In a primitive sporting gesture, the natives free the courageous white man without clothes, weapons, or water—and with ten stalwart young spearsmen poised to track him down. Hunted now, the hunter begins to run, and *Prey* gathers fierce momentum as a classic, single-minded epic of survival with no time out for faint-hearted blondes or false heroines.

It used to be said that the theater was often more searching, more bitter, and more "adult" than the movies ever dared to be. Today it can hardly keep up with them but it tries, as witnessed by this account of the latest play by a man widely regarded as Britain's leading playwright:

A Bond Honoured, British playwright John Osborne's adaptation of an atrocious horror show by seventeenth-century Spaniard Lope de Vega, has a hero who commits rape, murder, treason, multiple incest, and matricide, and blinds his father—after which he is crucified in precise imitation of Christ. London's critics cast one look at the tasteless mayhem at the Old Vic and held their noses. Whereupon Osborne, thirty-six, flipped his Angry Aging Man's lid, firing off telegrams to the London papers. Osborne declared an end to his "gentleman's agreement to ignore puny theater critics as bourgeois conventions. After ten years it is now war, open and frontal war, that will be as public as I and other men of earned reputations have the considerable power to make it."

The account is again from *Time* but its pooh-poohing of this masterpiece got an angry reply from Kenneth Tynan, the drama critic who was for a time the regular reviewer for *The New Yorker:*

Of the twelve newspaper critics, at least four held their breath. Herald Hobson in the *Sunday Times* said of Osborne: "He is not only our most important dramatist; he is also our chief prophet." According to Randall Bryden of the *Observer,* "The effect of *A Bond Honoured* in performance is marvelously theatrical." Allen Brien of the *Sunday Telegraph* thought it "a serious, ambitious, and valuable play which matures in the memory and fertilizes the imagination," while for Milton Shulman in the *Evening Standard* it was "a stunning parable with a magnificent theatrical impact."

Having glanced at a conspicuous American novel, a conspicuous movie, and a conspicuous play, let's look now at two serious American critics, taking first Leslie Fiedler. His well known contention is that the best American fiction from *Huckleberry Finn* to Hemingway and Faulkner is always concerned with a repressed homosexuality. In his most recent book he comes up with the following opinions:

> [On the death of Ernest Hemingway] . . . One quarry was left him only, the single beast worthy of him; himself. And he took his shotgun in hand, probably renewing his lapsed allegiance to death and silence. With a single shot he redeemed his best work from his worst, his art from himself.
> [Of President Kennedy and the arts] . . . John F. Kennedy, as Louis XV, seemed up to the moment of his assassination the true symbol of cultural blight; not only our first sexually viable President in a century, after a depressing series of uncle, grandfather, and grandmother figures, but the very embodiment of middlebrow culture climbing.

I have been leaning heavily on *Time* because it seems to me to be the publication which best gauges the interests, if not necessarily the opinions, of the largest number of literate Americans. But for a second critic—and, incidentally, an excellent example of the schizophrenia of the liberal weeklies—I will choose an essay by Susan Sontag, the most "in" of contemporary "far-out" critics. It was, paradoxically, published in *The Nation,* which has been for long the very paradigm of do-goodism. The article takes off from a discussion of Jack Smith's film *Flaming Creatures,* which is described thus:

> A couple of women and a much larger number of men . . . frolic about, pose, posture, and dance with one another; enact various scenes of voluptuousness, sexual frenzy, romantic love, and vampirism . . . to the accompaniment of a sound track which includes . . . the chorale of flutish shrieks and screams which accompany the group rape of a bosomy woman, rape happily converting itself into an orgy. . . . shots of masturbation and oral sensuality. . . . *Flaming Creatures* is outrageous and it intends to be. But it is a beautiful film ·. . . a triumphant example of an esthetic vision of the world and such a vision is perhaps always, at its core, epicene.

Just why an esthetic vision of the world is perhaps always, at its core, homosexual is not explained and suggests the same reply which Chesterton made to the estheticism of the Nineties. The art of those who professed it, so they claimed, was morally neutral, but, said Chesterton, if it really were neutral it would often find itself dealing sympathetically with respectability, virtue, piety, and conventional behavior. The fact that it never did treat any of these things in even a neutral manner was sufficient proof that the art of its practitioners was not morally neutral but actually—to come back to Apollinaire again—an invitation to take the road to perdition.

If Miss Sontag does not explain why an esthetic vision must be epicene, she does undertake to explain why modern art must be "outrageous": "Art is always the sphere of freedom. In those difficult works of art we now call avant-garde, the artist consciously exercises his freedom." This argument is obviously parallel with that favorite of the Sartrian existentialists, namely, the contentions that: 1) the unmotivated act is the only positive assertion of freedom; and 2) the best unmotivated act is one of arbitrary cruelty. Why this should be so I have never understood, nor do I understand why the freedom of the artist can be demonstrated only by the outrageous. In the atmosphere of the present moment, the boldest position a creative or critical writer could take would be one championing not only morality but gentility and bourgeois respectability. Even the article which I am writing at this moment will probably be more contemptuously or even vituperatively dismissed than it would be if I were defending sadism, homosexuality, and nihilism.

Look at how "square" and "fuddy-duddy" the American Telephone & Telegraph Company can be, as demonstrated by recent full-page advertisements which answer the question posed in headline type: WHAT CAN YOU DO ABOUT OBSCENE, HARASSING, OR THREATENING TELEPHONE CALLS? Doesn't AT&T know that one of the simplest beginner's techniques for achieving existential freedom in a splendidly unmotivated act is to make an obscene telephone call? From that one can easily work up to the various vandalism so popular with teen-agers and, finally, to unmotivated murder. What can so triumphantly demonstrate an existential freedom as torturing and killing for kicks? Didn't Apollinaire himself say that de Sade was the freest man who ever lived?

What, precisely, is the road—or are the roads—which have led to the state of mind illustrated by the quotations in this article? I do not think that any analysis ending in a satisfactory answer to that question has ever been made. Someone with the stomach for it might undertake a study as nearly classic as Mario Praz's *The Romantic Agony,* which traces so brilliantly the origin and destination of 1890 decadence to which modernism is more closely parallel than is usually admitted, and of which it is, perhaps, only another phase. Cyril Connolly has this to say:

[It] began as a revolt against the bourgeois in France, the Victorians in England, the Puritanism and materialism of America. The modern spirit was a combination of certain intellectual qualities inherited from the Enlightenment: lucidity, irony, skepticism, intellectual curiosity, combined with the impassioned intensity and enhanced sensibility of the Romantic, their rebellion and sense of technical experiment, their awareness of living in a tragic age.

All that is true enough and familiar enough but it doesn't go far enough. It does not explain why the most obvious and unique characteristics of the current avant-garde are not any of the characteristics of the Enlightenment or of any romanticism except that commonly called decadent. How, for instance, do lucidity, irony, skepticism, or even intellectual curiosity become preludes to "the century of de Sade"? How did an assault on Victorian complacency and hypocrisy end by practicing a sort of unmotivated vandalism? In London a recent city-wide series of "happenings" in which forty "artists" from ten nations took part was publicized as a reminder that "society will ignore the manifestations of destruction in art at its peril." Perhaps, as we say, the publicist had something there. Were certain members of the public justified when they objected to the performance of Juan Hidalgo, the representative from Spain, whose specialty, it seems, is cutting off the heads of chickens and flinging them at the audience?

I suppose that anyone who undertook to trace the development of modernism would have to begin by asking whether or not there is a single dominating characteristic of this latest development, any one which, at least by its frequent emphasis, seems to distinguish contemporary modernism from the movement out of which it is said to have grown. True, this modernism does indeed seem to be compounded of many simplicities and not all who represent it include all of them in their mixtures. Thus one distinguishing characteristic is the tendency to elevate raw sexual experience to a position of supreme importance so that the Quest for the Holy Grail becomes a quest for the perfect orgasm. Other characteristics are homosexuality, nihilism, and that impulse to self-destruction typified in the cult of drugs. Still another is that taste for violence which, as in the case of Baldwin, becomes unmistakably sadistic. If I had to answer the question, "What is most fundamental?" I should be inclined to say "the taste for violence." The belief that violence is the only appropriate response to an absurd world is the one element most often present in any individual's special version of the moment's avant-gardism.

Psychiatrists often say that suicide is frequently motivated by the desire for revenge against some person who, so the self-destroyer likes to believe, will be made to suffer. And psychiatrists are inclined to call this motive irrational. But in modern literature and modern criticism it is sometimes accepted as the ultimate rationality—as in these two examples:

In Friedrich Dürrenmatt's much discussed play *The Visit,* the principal character explains her conduct by saying, "The world made a whore of me, so I am turning the world into a brothel"; and in *The Nation* the reviewer of a novel calls the self-destruction of its hero "an alcoholic strike against humanity." In common-sense terms all such retaliations and revenges come under the head of biting off one's nose to spite one's face. But that seems to be what some modernists advocate.

Seldom, if ever before, has any of the arts been so dominated by an all-inclusive hatred. Once the writer hated individual "bad men." Then he began to hate instead the society which was supposed to be responsible for the creation of bad men. Now his hatred is directed not at individuals or their societies but at the universe in which bad men and bad societies are merely expressions of the fundamental evil of the universe itself.

It was once hoped that the iconoclasts who flourished during the early years of our century would clear the ground for higher ideals and truer values. Somewhat later it was argued that existentialism, having demonstrated that the universe was in itself morally and intellectually meaningless, now left man free to construct meanings and morals for himself and in his own image. What that has come down to, the Baldwins, the Burroughses, and the Jack Smiths have demonstrated in our language; the Apollinaires and the Genets, in theirs.

There is, of course, always the literature of social protest to which one may turn if one has had enough of sadism and the absurd. But sometimes the reviewers sound as though they were getting the same sort of sadistic kick in a less open way. Here, for example, is the way in which a recent novel is praised in (of all places) *Vogue:*

> *The Fixer,* a brilliant new novel by Bernard Malamud, is harrowing. It is a dreadful story that cuts and lacerates without relief; it is a drama of ferocious injustice and then more injustice.

If anything except unrelieved violence in one form or another is "escapism"; if human nature, the world, and even the universe itself are what so many esteemed artists declare them to be, then what can anyone reasonable choose to do except escape in either life or literature—if he can? Perhaps that is why 18,000 people recently crowded a London exhibit devoted to memorabilia concerning the creator of Peter Rabbit.

STUDY QUESTIONS

1. Does Krutch answer the question he poses in the title?

2. According to G. K. Chesterton, as paraphrased by Krutch, the advocates of art-for-art's-sake professed the moral neutrality of art. How did Chesterton disprove the validity of their statement? Does Krutch accept Chesterton's proof as valid? How might Chesterton define *neutral?*

3. What does Krutch feel is the most fundamental characteristic of "modernism"?

4. Does the selectivity of Krutch's examples help him prove his point? Is this an honest approach? A neutral approach?

5. Krutch says that the contemporary arts are "dominated by an all-
    inclusive hatred." How does flower-children culture and its art refute
    Krutch's conclusions?

Saul Bellow

MIND OVER CHATTER

Saul Bellow (1915–   ) was born in Quebec, Canada, the son of emi-
grant Russian parents. He attended the University of Chicago, received his
B.A. from Northwestern University in 1937, and was awarded an honorary
Litt.D. by Northwestern in 1962 and Bard College in 1963. Bellow now
teaches at the University of Chicago. His novels include *Dangling Man*
(1944), *Victim* (1947), *The Adventures of Augie March* (1953), *Seize the
Day* (1956), *Henderson the Rain King* (1959), and *Herzog* (1964). Both
Augie March and *Herzog* were awarded National Book Awards. *Mosby's
Memoirs,* a collection of short stories, was published in 1968. Bellow's
other honors include awards from the Ford and Guggenheim Foundations
and the Prix International de Littérature.

THE FACT THAT there are so many weak, poor, and boring
stories and novels written and published in America has
been ascribed by our rebels to the horrible squareness of
our institutions, the idiocy of power, the debasement of sexual instincts, and
the failure of writers to be alienated enough. The poems and novels of these
same rebellious spirits, and their theoretical statements, are grimy and
gritty and very boring too, besides being nonsensical, and it is evident by
now that polymorphous sexuality and vehement declarations of alienation
are not going to produce great works of art either.

There is nothing left for us novelists to do but think. For unless we think,
unless we make a clearer estimate of our condition, we will continue to write
kid stuff, to fail in our function, we will lack serious interests and become
truly irrelevant. Here the critics must share the blame, for they too have
failed to describe the situation. Literature has for several generations been

its own source, its own province, has lived upon its own traditions, and accepted a romantic separation or estrangement from the common world. This estrangement, though it produced some masterpieces, has by now enfeebled the novel.

The separatism of writers is accompanied by the more or less conscious acceptance of a theory of modern civilization. This theory says in effect that modern mass society is frightful, brutal, hostile to whatever is pure in the human spirit, a wasteland and a horror. To its ugliness, its bureaucratic regimes, its thefts, its lies, its wars, and its unparalleled cruelties, the artist can never be reconciled. This is one of the traditions on which contemporary literature has lived uncritically. But it is the task of artists and critics in their own day to look with their own eyes. Perhaps they will see evils even worse than those they have taken for granted, but they will at least be seeing for themselves. They will not, they can not, permit themselves, generation after generation, to hold views they have not individually examined. By refusing to look at civilization with our own eyes we lose the right to call ourselves artists; we have accepted what we ourselves condemn—received opinion, professionalism, snobbery and the formation of a caste. And unfortunately the postures of this caste, postures of liberation and independence and creativity, are attractive to poor souls dreaming everywhere of a fuller, freer life.

The writer is admired, the writer is envied. But what has he to say for himself? Why, he says, just as writers have said for more than a century, that he is cut off from the life of his own society, that he is despised by its overlords who are cynical about intellectuals and have nothing but contempt for the artist, and that he is without a true public, estranged. He dreams of ages when the poet or the painter expressed a perfect unit of time and place, had real acceptance, and enjoyed a vital harmony with his surroundings—he dreams of a golden age. In fact, without the golden age, there is no wasteland.

Well, this is no age of gold. It is only what it is. Can we do no more than complain about it? We writers have better choices. We can either shut up because the times are too bad, or continue writing because we have an instinct for it, a talent to develop, which even in these disfigured times we cannot suppress. Isolated professionalism is death. Without the common world the novelist is nothing but a curiosity and will find himself in a glass case along some dull museum corridor of the future.

Mechanization and bureaucracy are permanently with us. We cannot pretend the technological revolution has not occurred. We are its beneficiaries; we may also become its slaves. The first necessity, therefore, is to fight for justice and equality. The artist, along with everyone else, must fight for his life, for his freedom. This is not to advise the novelist to rush immediately into the political sphere. But to begin with he must begin to use his intelligence, long unused. If he is to reject politics, he must understand what he is rejecting. He must begin to think, and to think not merely of his own narrower interests and needs, but of the common world he has for so long failed to see. If he thinks his alienation has much significance, he is wrong. It is nine-tenths cant. If he thinks his rebellion significant, he is wrong again because the world is far more revolutionary in being simply what it is. In their attempts to imitate power, *Realpolitik,*[1] by violence or vehemence, writers simply make themselves foolish. The "romantic criminal" or desperado cannot get within miles of the significant human truth. It is with this truth that the writer must be concerned.

STUDY QUESTIONS

1. Bellow's essay was a speech delivered at the presentation of the 1965 National Book Awards. How might the occasion have influenced both the form and content of "Mind over Chatter"?

2. On what points do Krutch and Bellow agree? Disagree?

3. According to Bellow, what has been the result of the novelist's and critic's estrangement from the common world?

4. With what task does Bellow charge the contemporary writer? What choices does he suggest are open to the writer?

5. What does Bellow mean by "the significant human truth"?

[1] Literally, realistic politics; the politics of violence.

INDEX OF AUTHORS
AND TITLES